PRAISE FOR *Killing the Cranes*

"Ed Girardet has accumulated more experience in Afghanistan than almost anyone else in the press corps, and the result is a truly remarkable book about a completely misunderstood country. *Killing the Cranes* may well be the most gripping and thorough account ever written about our numerous missteps and lost opportunities—it reads like a great novel but informs like the best kind of magazine journalism. Both his writing and reporting are absolutely superb."

—SEBASTIAN JUNGER, best-selling author of *War* and other books

"Edward Girardet puts all of his thirty years' experience to use in this vivid, enlightening, humane, yet alarming book. Few other observers have had the determination to cover Afghan events from before the Soviet invasion to the preparations for American withdrawal. Girardet describes that whole saga, points out why and whether things could have gone differently, and explains the realistic prospects ahead. This is a life's-work testimony in the best sense."

—JAMES FALLOWS, author of *Blind into Baghdad* and
Postcards from Tomorrow Square

"Edward Girardet has a unique story to tell. . . . He has been a consistent and keen observer of political events. He has come to know all the major characters. . . . His is a very personal tale as well as being one of great historical importance."

—AHMED RASHID, author of *Taliban, Jihad,* and *Descent into Chaos*

"After reading *Killing the Cranes*, I felt like I had spent three decades in Afghanistan at Girardet's side. This is the most thorough and knowledgeable book on Afghanistan I have come across, and his conclusions about what has gone wrong and what can be done about it are unassailable."

—HOWARD DEAN, former chair of the Democratic National Committee

"Drawing on more than three decades of personal travels to Afghanistan, Edward Girardet offers a ruminating set of reflections on the history of the region and its diverse groups. He captures the dynamism, the pride, and the potential of the people living in Afghanistan. He also examines the limitations of military interventions and the possibilities for policies more deeply connected to rural communities. Girardet's book is a must-read for anyone seeking a deeper understanding of contemporary Afghanistan."

—JEREMI SURI, author of *Liberty's Surest Guardian:
American Nation Building from Washington to Obama*

"Edward Girardet's knowledge of Afghanistan, both its many problems and its many attractions, is profound. He writes with great authority and grace, and his love for the country comes through on every page of this fascinating, important, and thoughtful book."

—PETER BERGEN, author of *The Longest War:*
The Enduring Conflict between America and Al-Qaeda

"For most of us, until September 12, 2001, the country of Afghanistan was a cipher—mysterious, remote, most often forgotten. For Ed Girardet, however, a seasoned foreign correspondent who has roamed and reported from its cities, its valleys, and its mountaintops for more than thirty years, the country is a familiar place of specific places and people.

So when Afghanistan exploded into our consciousness, Girardet had already been there, witnessing the country's resistance to the Soviets, and following it over the decades since, from the civil war of the nineties that laid the ground for the rise of the Taliban, to today, where it is once again mired in a fight with foreign powers. Now he has produced a seminal work of reporting and history, putting Afghanistan's experience of foreign armies—the Soviet Army, the American Army, not to mention the British Army of the nineteenth century—into immediate context, illustrating the many pitfalls ahead for the United States and its NATO allies. The former Soviet airmen now working in Kabul after their country's defeat have plenty to say about the current western strategy, as do those who know the country well through their work with NGOs, foreign aid, and diplomacy, not to mention the many Afghans whose names may be unrecognizable but whose fate is being closely tied to our own. You can hear the echoes in these pages of past efforts by foreign armies to subdue the country. In the process, Girardet provides a vivid feel for this majestic and widely misunderstood country.

Part travelogue, part memoir, part political analysis, Girardet has produced a fine work of reportage, moving from the bird's-eye view to the view from the back of a jeep rumbling over the dusty mountain roads, to the lairs of warlords and the larger-than-life figures whose fight for—and against—their country has been entangled with the United States' 'war on terrorism.' *Killing the Cranes* provides unparalleled insights into the immense challenges presented by the war in Afghanistan, and the reasons, Girardet predicts, for a denouement that is likely to resemble those of other failed engagements by foreign powers."

—MARK SCHAPIRO, senior correspondent,
Center for Investigative Reporting, and author of *Exposed*

KILLING THE CRANES

KILLING THE CRANES

A Reporter's Journey Through
Three Decades of War in Afghanistan

Edward Girardet

CHELSEA GREEN PUBLISHING
WHITE RIVER JUNCTION, VERMONT

Project Manager: Patricia Stone
Developmental Editor: Joni Praded
Copy Editor: Laura Jorstad
Proofreader: Eric Raetz
Indexer: Peggy Holloway
Designer: Peter Holm,
          Sterling Hill Productions

Printed in the United States of America
First printing July, 2011
10 9 8 7 6 5 4 3 2 1   11 12 13 14 15

Chelsea Green is committed to preserving ancient forests and
natural resources. We elected to print this title on 30% postconsumer recycled paper, processed chlorine-free. As a result,
we have saved:

25 Trees (40' tall and 6-8" diameter)
10 Million BTUs of Total Energy
2,491 Pounds of Greenhouse Gases
712 Gallons of Wastewater
11,235 Pounds of Solid Waste

Chelsea Green made this paper choice because our printer,
Thomson-Shore, Inc., is a member of Green Press Initiative,
a nonprofit program dedicated to supporting authors, publishers, and suppliers in their efforts to reduce their use of fiber
obtained from endangered forests.

For more information, visit www.greenpressinitiative.org

Environmental impact estimates were made using the Environmental Defense
Paper Calculator. For more information visit: www.edf.org/papercalculator

Our Commitment to Green Publishing
Chelsea Green sees publishing as a tool for cultural change and ecological stewardship. We
strive to align our book manufacturing practices with our editorial mission and to reduce the
impact of our business enterprise in the environment. We print our books and catalogs on
chlorine-free recycled paper, using vegetable-based inks whenever possible. This book may
cost slightly more because we use recycled paper, and we hope you'll agree that it's worth it.
Chelsea Green is a member of the Green Press Initiative (www.greenpressinitiative.org), a
nonprofit coalition of publishers, manufacturers, and authors working to protect the world's
endangered forests and conserve natural resources. *Killing the Cranes* was printed on Natures
Natural, a 30-percent postconsumer recycled paper supplied by Thomson-Shore.

Library of Congress Cataloging-in-Publication Data
Girardet, Edward.
  Killing the cranes : a reporter's journey through three decades of war in Afghanistan / Edward
Girardet.
    p. cm.
  Includes index.
  ISBN 978-1-60358-342-8
  1. Afghanistan--History--Soviet occupation, 1979-1989. 2. Afghan War, 2001- 3. Afghani-
stan--History--1989-2001. 4. Afghanistan--History, Military--20th century. I. Title.
  DS371.2.G56 2011
  958.104--dc22

                                        2011014661

Chelsea Green Publishing Company
Post Office Box 428
White River Junction, VT 05001
(802) 295-6300
www.chelseagreen.com

To Lori, Elisa, and Alexander

Things When You Need Them

Where are the shields
When arrows descend in showers?
Where are the feathers
And wings when I want to fly?
My friends live far away.
Where's the homing pigeon?
Where can I find the messenger,
The morning breeze from home?

—Khalilullah Khalili, twentieth-century Afghan poet
  (translated by Masood Khalili and Whitney Azoy)

CONTENTS

KILLING THE CRANES

It was late March 2004. One of those dry and not-too-cold nights in Kabul when the heavens are clear and brilliant with stars. I had just spent the evening with Masood Khalili at the house built by his father, the late-twentieth-century Afghan poet Khalilullah Khalili, on the western outskirts of the capital. The younger Khalili had been with northern resistance leader Ahmed Shah Massoud when he was assassinated by two al Qaeda suicide bombers on September 9, 2001. He was still finding it difficult to concentrate for long periods, having sustained severe injuries with over two hundred pieces of shrapnel in his body. Khalili was now Afghanistan's ambassador to India.

We talked about what was happening to Afghanistan after so many years of war and where the international community was leading the country. For Khalili, with so many human beings killed since popular revolt first broke out in the summer of 1978, so much of his homeland destroyed, Afghanistan had become a nation traumatized. If Afghans wished to emerge intact, they had to undertake a long and difficult spiritual recovery. Above all, he argued, they had to assume their own responsibilities. Afghans were in denial about who and what they had become.

As we strolled through the garden to the front gate of the walled compound, Khalili took my arm and looked up into the night sky. "For me, the end of March has always been the time when you cannot hear your voice for the sound of the migrating cranes," he said. Khalili was referring to Siberian cranes, large white birds with dark red masks and flutelike honking, that every spring have flown northward from the southern wetlands of Afghanistan and Iran to the Russian Arctic and western Siberia.

After gazing silently upward, Khalili turned wearily to me. "You know, I have not heard a single crane since being here." He paused and then shook his head. "Have we even killed all the cranes?"

ACKNOWLEDGMENTS

Over the past 30-odd years, I have had the privilege to work with innumerable friends and colleagues, who, like me, share a fascination with Afghanistan. Many told me that they were disturbed by the distorted information about this troubled country and felt that, given my extensive experience that started with my first reporting trip in October 1979, I would be able to provide a first-hand historic perspective. Their encouragement and help were invaluable. I would like to thank them all, but in particular Don Larrimore, who successfully harassed me into finishing the book, and then spent endless hours questioning and verifying historical facts to ensure utmost accuracy. Don was hoping that this would be the definitive book about Afghanistan, but we both realized that to achieve this I would have to write two or three more volumes. And besides, there is nothing definitive about Afghanistan.

My cherished wife, Lori, though frenetically busy with her own United Nations humanitarian work and raising two children, generously spent days ruthlessly chopping out entire pages from a too-long and -detailed text, thereby making it more accessible to general readers. A simple thanks cannot express the deep gratitude I feel for her commitment to my work and our family.

I would also like to thank Emily Pantalone and Mark Rafferty, my two interns from Tufts University. It was a joy to work with such committed and enthusiastic, but above all knowledgeable, young researchers. Bill Dowell brought his wry wit and copyediting skills to the manuscript, and for this I am grateful. My dear friends Nikki Meith and Peter Hulm selflessly hosted me in their Swiss mountain retreat so that I could write undisturbed, all the while drinking countless cups of tea, just as I had done while reporting Afghanistan's wars.

Others who have helped with suggestions and insight include—in no particular order—Ahmed Rashid, Jon Randal, Emmanuel Tronc, Nora Niland, Charles Norchi, Michael Keating, Tim Weaver, Tom Woods, Mohammed Shuaib, Peter Jouvenal, Gordon Adam, Whitney Azoy, Masood Khalili, Zuki, Jean-Michel Monod, Rauli Virtanen, Donatella

Lorch, Amaury Coste, Sebastian Turbot, Jono Walter, Nick Mills, Mort Rosenblum—plus numerous others.

I would also like to thank my erstwhile editor David Anable and *The Christian Science Monitor* for having persevered in their belief that Afghanistan needed to be reported in a consistent and durable manner. This tradition continues with a new generation of Monitor correspondents providing some of the best and most critical international coverage of the current situation. I would also like to thank Jeff Carmel, formerly my desk editor with the Monitor, for his constant interest in Afghanistan and innumerable suggestions. There are also various young Afghan journalists with whom I have talked and who provided some very candid views about the international presence and what they believe the future of their country should be.

Finally, I would like to pay homage to the countless individuals I have interviewed over the past decades. Some lost their lives to Afghanistan's ongoing tragedy. Many have unwittingly helped develop my current perspective. There were a lot of anecdotes and incidents, both amusing and tragic, that should have been incorporated, but how does one sum up so many diverse experiences?

My final thanks go to my wife, Lori, daughter, Elisa, and son, Alexander. There were times, I am sure, when you wondered whether this book would ever get finished. This is for you.

PROLOGUE

It was a warm Thursday afternoon on August 5, 2010, in a remote wood-land of the Hindu Kush mountains when a band of men with full beards and ankle-length white gowns appeared out of nowhere. Brandishing Kalashnikovs, they walked up to a team of mostly foreign aid volunteers who had just picnicked near their Land Rovers following a medical mission in Afghanistan's northeastern Nuristan province. The eight men and three women had been bringing eye care, dental treatment, and other forms of medical relief to an isolated highland valley. For two weeks, unarmed and unprotected, they had trekked with packhorses from village to village offering medical assistance to some fifty thousand subsistence farmers and shepherds living in this rugged high-mountain region.

The gunmen forced the workers—six Americans, three Afghans, a German, and a Briton—to sit on the ground. They ransacked the vehicles and demanded that everyone empty their pockets. Then they lined them up against a craggy rock face and executed them, one by one. Only the Afghan driver was spared. He had pleaded for his life by reciting verses of the Koran and screaming: "I am Muslim. Don't kill me!"

The bullet-riddled bodies of the medical team were found the next day, and news of their assassination traveled swiftly. Theories abounded as to who murdered them and why. The Taliban and Hezb-e-Islami, both insurgent groups fighting the Western Coalition forces in Afghanistan, each claimed responsibility. Yet as with so many such attacks against civilians, the perpetrators were never found and never brought to justice.

Two of the executed Americans, Tom Little and Dan Terry, were long-standing members of the International Assistance Mission, a Christian non-governmental organization (or NGO) that has been working in Afghanistan since 1966. "Dr. Tom," as he was known, was a low-key sixty-two-year-old optometrist from Delmar, New York, who had been working with his wife, Libby, in Afghanistan since the late 1970s. They had first started out helping wayward hippies stranded in Kabul. Running a series of eye clinics, they had remained throughout the Soviet-Afghan war and during the Battle for Kabul of the mid-1990s until the Taliban drove them out. The Littles came straight back after the collapse of the Talib regime.

Dan was a cheerful and dogged aid worker with a dry sense of humor who first visited the country in 1971. During the latter days of the Taliban, when they were destroying villages and killing civilians in central and northern Afghanistan, Dan had mounted a humanitarian relief effort in midwinter to bring food across the front lines.

Both were my friends.

For those familiar with Afghanistan, the killing of the IAM team underscored the brutal reality that much of this mountain and desert country at the cusp of Central Asia and the Indian subcontinent had become a perilous, no-go zone. Whereas parts of the country, including Nuristan and the neighboring province of Badakshan where the murders took place, had been considered relatively safe for aid workers, the Afghan traditions of hospitality and protection of guests had finally and irretrievably been shattered. Decades of conflict, competing worldviews, and outside interests had turned Afghanistan into a land where neither the Western-backed Kabul government nor the insurgents are in control—and basic humanity seems to have vanished.

For me, the deaths of Dr. Tom and Dan marked the end of an era. They were "old Afghan hands" who, like me, had first ventured into Afghanistan in the 1970s and found themselves inexplicably drawn to this utterly romantic country of cultural contrasts and staggering topographic beauty, but also human tragedy. They kept returning despite being threatened, and despite the personal risk their work entailed. Although both were indeed Christians, they were not missionaries. They were in Afghanistan because of their own convictions and because they simply wanted to help a beleaguered people.

By the time of the IAM murders, the outlook for the future of Afghanistan was already bleak. One senior United Nations official in Kabul with years of Afghan experience was blunt: "It's become an absolute disaster." While NATO by early 2011 had largely accepted that there could be no military solution, Western governments were still placing too much emphasis—and funding—on their generals for leadership rather than investing in more imaginative out-of-the-box initiatives and longer-term civilian-led approaches, including talking with the insurgents.

The US-led invasion in October 2001, which was in response to the events of 9/11, helped oust the Taliban but has contributed little to overall security. The American intervention has moved from a limited "war on terrorism" coupled with other agendas, notably counternarcotics, to a full-fledged counterinsurgency. The presence of over 150,000 troops from the United States, Britain, and forty-six other countries as part of the NATO-led International Security Assistance Force (ISAF) has led to a situation many Afghans find comparable to the Soviet-Afghan war—a large occupying force, a weak central government, and endless skirmishes and attacks that kill innocent civilians and incite new recruits to the fundamentalist ranks. For a growing number of Afghans and foreign analysts, the Western military presence has proved a failure, with lost opportunities littering the trail of international intervention since the collapse of the Talib regime. Even the killing, by the Americans, of Saudi terrorist Osama Bin Laden in May 2011 was unlikely to bring about much change.

Not unlike their Red Army counterparts during the 1980s, the Americans and their military allies are increasingly perceived by ordinary Afghans as an unwelcome foreign occupation force. Their behavior and lack of cultural awareness often emerge as affronts to Afghan customs and their sense of independence. NATO forces also have been involved in bombing and other military assaults that have inflicted severe civilian casualties. While such incidents may be regarded officially as unfortunate "collateral damage," Afghans consider them a blatant disregard for human life. This is disheartening for those among the Western troops who genuinely regard their role as one of helping maintain peace and bringing socioeconomic development to a desperately impoverished land.

The growing resentment of Afghans toward the Western presence is not because Afghans necessarily prefer the Taliban and other insurgents, but because they have always resented outsiders, particularly those who insist on imposing themselves. Even more disconcerting, many Afghans no longer differentiate between soldiers and aid workers. Western policies have largely undermined the recovery process by usurping the traditional humanitarian role through the deployment of military Provincial Reconstruction Teams (PRTs) and the deployment of foreign mercenaries and private contractors with little or no understanding of the country. Afghans also legitimately question the purpose of the United

States spending one hundred million dollars a day on its military effort given that such funds might be far better spent on recovery itself. If US troops were to pull out tomorrow, what would they have left behind? The Soviets spent nearly a decade fighting their war in Afghanistan. Little tangible remains of their past involvement today.

NATO forces have now occupied Afghanistan longer than the Soviets. In a war with objectives difficult, if not impossible, to define, Western military casualties have been swelling steadily since 2004, when the Taliban began to reemerge as a formidable force. By mid 2011, over twenty-five hundred American, British, French, German, Canadian, Italian, and other soldiers had been killed. More than half the injuries and deaths were not the result of direct combat. The insurgents have been inflicting increasing casualties by roadside bombs, booby traps, and other improvised explosive devices (or IEDs). In contrast, over eighteen thousand Afghans had lost their lives in less than a decade, at least half of them civilian. A further forty thousand, both military and civilian, have been wounded. While NATO analysts argue that current Afghan casualties are "modest" compared with the 1.5 million believed to have died during the Soviet-Afghan war, others point out that the current conflict could have been avoided had the West adopted a more realistic approach to Afghanistan during the early 2000s and not been obsessed by terrorism, narcotics, and other distracting factors—notably the war in Iraq.

The reality is that overall security, particularly in the countryside, is worsening. Former mujahideen whom I knew in the 1980s and '90s, and who had contacts with the insurgents, apologized for not being able to take me into parts of eastern Afghanistan. "We cannot guarantee your safety," they told me. Even friends whom I know are involved with the insurgents, but still respect traditional Afghan hospitality, are reluctant to take me through their zones of control. Traveling has become a highly hazardous undertaking. I had felt far safer trekking clandestinely through the mountains during the Soviet era than today.

But Afghanistan's problems are not just a lack of security. Too much money, combined with expectations too high and unrealistic, has been thrown at Afghanistan, propping up an ineffectual and corrupt regime. The overall economy is highly artificial and largely dependent on international development aid, military expenditure, and narcotics trafficking. In addition to the foreign aid contractors, the bulk of the revenue has gone to a small but powerful privileged elite of Afghans, notably senior government officials, warlords, and businesspeople with the right connections. In 2010, Transparency International ranked Afghanistan as the world's most corrupt country, with graft permeating all levels of the administration, including President Hamid Karzai's own family, who have benefited overwhelmingly from the recovery process.

Certainly, there are areas where significant progress has been made. These include education, health, freedom of the media, and some highly imaginative employment initiatives based on local entrepreneurship. Impressively, the number of boys and girls attending school has leapt by over 500 percent to seven million—although seven million more still have no access to education. However, militant threats since 2007 against female pupils and teachers have been forcing the closures of hundreds of schools. And while the number of health care facilities has improved dramatically, many rural populations still lack access to even the most rudimentary medical services.

This is not surprising. Although rural Afghanistan has nearly 80 percent of the population, it has been seriously neglected in the recovery process, leading Afghans to wonder who is benefiting from the huge amounts of aid they keep hearing about. The bulk of international funding has remained focused on Kabul and other urban centers. Too much emphasis has been placed on quick fixes that do not necessarily improve the lives of ordinary Afghans, but that play well back in Washington, London, and Bonn.

Although billions of dollars in aid and military support are being given to Afghanistan by the United States and other Western countries, it remains difficult to comprehend the strategy behind either the war or the recovery plan. There appears to be no long-term vision nor any real sustainable commitment beyond the NATO "endgame" of 2014, the deadline set to pull out troops in order to satisfy increasingly dissatisfied electorates back home. Many Afghans, including government ministers, are hedging their bets, making as much money as they can from the system before the game is up. Property purchases by Afghans in Dubai, Abu Dhabi, and elsewhere have shot up since mid-2005. Visa applications in 2011 to leave Afghanistan are the highest since the Soviet-Afghan war.

This panic and profiteering before yet another deluge in Afghan history is familiar to me. As a young foreign correspondent based in Paris, I made my first reporting trip to Afghanistan in October 1979, three months prior to the Soviet invasion. My few weeks in Peshawar, in what was then Pakistan's Northwest Frontier Province (or NWFP, though in 2010 the Islamabad government changed the name to Khyber Pakhtunkhwa), where Afghanistan's new resistance groups were establishing their exile bases, led me to believe that I was witnessing the emergence of a conflict—or a series of conflicts as it later turned out—with profound global implications.

Little did I imagine in 1979, however, that this initial Afghan war would evolve into yet more wars, each distinct, involving a plethora of international players, notably the Soviet Union, United States, Britain, Pakistan, India, China, Iran, Saudi Arabia, and NATO. Nor could I have thought that by 2010 the international community would be mired in a conflict that threatened to become a new Vietnam, not only for the United States but also for NATO.

From 1979 onward, I remained based in Paris but operated out of Peshawar, which had become the principal humanitarian center for refugees and for providing clandestine cross-border relief to Afghanistan. For Western journalists unable to cover the war from the Soviet side— visas were virtually impossible to get—the city became our jumping-off point for reporting inside the country. I covered Afghanistan on a regular basis, visiting the region at least two or three times a year, sometimes for several months. Throughout the Soviet occupation, Peshawar was a tantalizing mix of Casablanca, Shanghai, and Paris spiced up with real or perceived dangers. For many of us, particularly those working in war situations around the world, the Pakistani frontier city became addictive.

Working in Afghanistan was like being a character in Rudyard Kipling's *The Man Who Would Be King*. Journeying hundreds of miles by foot, horse, vehicle, and camel, I was handed from one mujahed group to another based on personal contacts and traditional handwritten letters of recommendation. I also trekked with humanitarian caravans operated by the "French doctors" (Médecins sans Frontières and other French medical groups were the first international aid bodies to operate clandestinely inside Afghanistan) and other voluntary relief organizations working among destitute civilian populations across the border. Most of these trips were "illegal" (from the Soviet point of view) and took me through some of the world's most arduous but also spectacular terrain involving daily sixteen-hour slogs over sixteen-thousand-foot-high snow-covered mountain passes and across scorching, rocky deserts.

When not in Pakistan or Afghanistan, I reported humanitarian and conflict situations in such places as Angola, Somalia, Sudan, Mozambique, and Sri Lanka. In steamy jungles and arid deserts, I gained a deep insight into how guerrilla wars are fought and understood that many were proxy conflicts with each superpower supporting its respective side, thus becoming indirect extensions of the Cold War. During the 1980s, the United States and Soviet Union were both supporting rival factions in Somalia and Ethiopia in the Horn of Africa, both conflicts in which Afghanistan served as a benchmark.

While reporting the Afghan wars, I quickly grasped that every valley, district, province, and region was distinct, with its own peculiar characteristics. One could not assume that what one witnessed in one part of the country was the same as another. It was difficult to talk about "typical" Afghans. All tribal, clan, and ethnic groups were different, so I made a point of traveling with diverse guerrilla factions throughout the southern, eastern, and northern parts of the country. These ranged from turbaned Baluch fighters operating among the desert Chagai Hills in Helmand province to the south to enthusiastic but largely incompetent Pushtun nationalists in the thickly forested Safed Koh range of Nangrahar in the east to long-haired, battle-hardened Tajik mujahideen in the mighty Hindu Kush to the north. I preferred the Tajiks, who seemed better organized, but I also met and traveled with exceptional commanders among the Pushtuns and Hazaras. I also encountered some of the leading figures, such as Ahmed Shah Massoud, Gulbuddin Hekmatyar, and Osama bin Laden.

My numerous journeys throughout Afghanistan provided a firsthand understanding of the way Afghanistan's broad mosaic of resistance fronts operated. It is clear that the Taliban and other insurgents who emerged during the post-2001 period have embraced these same tactics. In fact, many of today's fighters were trained with American support and earned their combat spurs during the Soviet-Afghan war. By 2009, numerous insurgents were even calling themselves "mujahideen" in an effort to recall the legitimacy of the anti-communist resistance movement. Often, while examining how the Americans, British, and other NATO forces are fighting this latest Afghan conflict, I am reminded of the uncanny resemblance to the anti-Soviet jihad. Coalition efforts to hunt down the guerrillas by "clearing" areas only to find that the insurgents slip back in again once they have left hark back to similar efforts by the Red Army. The advantage of traveling on foot, the only form of transportation available to me for most of my journeys (in some areas, I was able to travel by vehicle), was that I was in daily contact with ordinary Afghans. I met villagers, peasant farmers, guerrillas, teachers, doctors, civil servants, and engineers as well as urban refugees fleeing Soviet-occupied cities. As part of traditional Afghan hospitality, particularly in Pushtun areas that twenty years later became the killing zones for NATO forces, I spent many hours discussing the fighting while drinking tea in makeshift *chaikhane* (teahouses) along caravan routes or on carpets laid out under mulberry trees. Such constant mingling is the only way to understand this country.

In comparison, the bulk of Western coverage of the post-2001 insurgency has involved a stream of journalists "embedded" with the Coalition forces. Many American and European reporters never have the chance to see the "real" Afghanistan by living and working among Afghans themselves. Such NATO-linked reporting may provide largely sympathetic insights into the lives and fighting capabilities of Western troops emblazoned with Hollywood labels such as "Task Force Mountain Warriors." Frustratingly, however, this has also led to often one-sided, if not misleading, stories that fail to capture the realities of Afghan civilians caught up in the fighting. Such reporting cannot really gauge the effectiveness of the guerrillas or how they operate.

For a nation traditionally dominated by Pushtuns but riddled with ethnic and tribal division, it was both the Soviet-Afghan war and Islam that helped bring Afghans together as a people. I was always impressed by the sight of Afghans from contrasting parts of the country who had never met before, but who readily knelt together in the direction of Mecca to pray on a mountaintop, the bank of a river, or the roof of a house. Then they would rise, wrap their *patous* (blankets) over their shoulders, and head off in different directions to continue their struggle against the outside infidels. This unity of cause is a factor that cannot be ignored in the current NATO counterinsurgency.

Understanding the lessons of the past is critical for the Western intervention to have any long-lasting positive impact on Afghanistan. Yet experience has convinced me that whether out of political expedience, arrogance, or plain ignorance, too many Western policy makers continually fail to examine the history of this defiant country. They refuse to learn the lessons from the previous two hundred years, starting with the rise of strategic rivalry between the British and Russian empires in Central Asia followed by the disastrous First Anglo-Afghan War of 1842. All of this was part of the "Great Game," as British writer Rudyard Kipling dubbed Britain's involvement with Afghanistan in its confrontation with tzarist Russia during the nineteenth century. This same game is still being played today, but with a cast of new players.

One cannot help but be overwhelmed by Afghanistan's past. While Paleolithic humans probably lived in what is now northern Afghanistan fifty thousand years ago, the country has provided a backdrop to two of the world's great religions, Gandhara Buddhism and Islam. Historically, Afghanistan has repelled, absorbed, or simply let pass through all those who have invaded, rampaged, or marched across its borders. As many as twenty-five ruling dynasties have swept through Afghanistan over the past three millennia. Alexander the Great, Cyrus the Great, Genghis Khan, Tamerlane, and Babur all had preceded the Russians in attempting to gain a foothold in Afghanistan, mostly with disastrous results. Few if any of these invaders stayed—albeit some left behind traces of their passage. Some blue-eyed, fair-haired Nuristanis claim descent from Alexander's soldiers, while the Mongolian-featured Hazaras (*hazara* means "one thousand") suggest ancestry among the hordes of Genghis Khan, who is reputed to have left behind detachments of troops "one thousand strong" to protect the far-flung southern outposts of his empire.

Throughout much of the nineteenth and early twentieth centuries, British military strategists considered Afghanistan a buffer zone against tzarist Russia's forward thrust, with various isolated Afghan fortresses such as Herat, Kandahar, and Ghazni serving as the "key" to India. They also perceived insurgent Afghan tribes, who often led raids deep into

India, as a threat. As part of the "Great Game," Britain sought to prevent invasion through intrigue, sorties by intelligence officers, diplomacy, bribery, assassination, and direct military intervention. The Russians did the same. The two sides confronted each other with often missionary zeal—at one point coming close to outright war over a small village near the Oxus—but also through the deployment of sometimes flamboyant and gentlemanly adventurers, who, dressing like Afghans and speaking the language, would disappear into the interior for months if not years on end. More than a few lost their lives along the way.

While some of these gung-ho intelligence officers had a close understanding of what to do—or not to do—in Afghanistan, the British government clearly did not. British armies twice invaded Kabul within the space of forty years in a bid to control unruly tribesmen and to shore up the western approaches to India. The first British invasion ended in a spectacular defeat in 1842 involving the near annihilation of a sixteen-thousand-strong military expeditionary force; the second proved a fruitless intervention. In the end, the British managed to impose in 1893 a unilateral demarcation between Afghanistan and India known as the Durand Line, which today still constitutes the de facto Afghan-Pakistani border. (It has yet to be recognized by the Kabul government.) But the British never controlled Afghanistan.

While Britain fought a third (but short) war in 1919, most colonial strategists had realized by then that there was no point in trying to seek military solutions in this rugged, mountainous country. This was a lesson the Soviets failed to heed in December 1979. It is also one that the US-led Coalition forces have ignored more than two decades later. Perhaps the West should have invested more astutely in a few flamboyant and adventurous agents willing to embed themselves into the Afghan heartland rather than relying on satellite links, remote-controlled drones, or heavily armed sorties, which provide little insight into the soul of this hard and insolent land.

When the United States started bombing in October 2001, in retaliation for 9/11, the Bush administration refused to acknowledge that Afghanistan could not be treated simply as part of a jingoistic propaganda show of black versus white, good versus evil. As part of its "war on terror," the administration initially invaded Afghanistan to root out al Qaeda for their suspected role in the attacks on American soil. But it seemed unaware that it was reentering a civil war that the United States had largely abandoned shortly after the Soviets withdrew from Afghanistan in 1989. The diverse conflicts that followed had left an indelible and painful stain on the country and its people. It wasn't long before the Americans were treated with suspicion over their motives. For many Afghans, the post-9/11 war was simply another episode in a country whose people were tired of invasions, betrayal, and international grandstanding.

At the same time, it was hard to fathom the full intent of renewed American military interest in Afghanistan. Al Qaeda operatives could be more easily ousted through good intelligence than bombings. Were there justifiable strategic or economic interests, such as mineral resources, that needed to be defended? Had the West determined that peace in Afghanistan is the key to regional security with regard to Central Asia, the Gulf, Pakistan, Iran, India, and China? Could the world afford to ignore Afghanistan?

Whatever the reasons, history has shown repeatedly that there are no military solutions in Afghanistan. The Great Game of the nineteenth and twentieth centuries has become the Great Pretend Game of the twenty-first. It is a pretense to believe that military intervention, even with responsibility now being shunted onto the Afghan security forces, can bring about peace after more than three decades of war. There is broad skepticism that the West will be able to train a capable security force of army and police by 2014, as NATO has promised. Nor is simply pouring in more aid going to make a difference. The Taliban and other insurgents are not succeeding out of military prowess, or because they are popular, but rather because the vast bulk of the international community has failed to understand how to deal with Afghans in an effective and pragmatic way.

Nor does the West understand the nature of the Taliban and their insurgent allies, including ongoing support by elements of Pakistani's military Interservices Intelligence Agency (or ISI). While groups close to Mullah Omar, the spiritual leader of the Islamic movement, may regard themselves as Taliban, the current anti-Western insurgency is really a loose formation of guerrilla fronts, all with their own motivation. These include groups such as "neo-Taliban," the Haqqani Network, Hezb-e-Islami,

Pakistani Taliban, angry local tribesmen, and various so-called foreign Taliban sympathetic to al Qaeda or its affiliates. Even such an influential figure as Mullah Abdul Qayuum Zakir, a former Guantanamo detainee who by 2010 was believed to be the day-to-day head of the Taliban, can only speak for the Helmand and Kandahar region and a few other scattered allies. Nevertheless, Western media reports repeatedly refer to the Taliban as a homogeneous movement even though no single faction can claim to speak for the insurgency as a whole.

Ultimately, what will determine the credibility of the Western-backed recovery effort—and the government it supports—is not whether the Taliban is vanquished militarily but whether justice is ever rendered in Afghanistan. Justice remains a primordial issue for ordinary Afghans traumatized by so many years of war and abused by so many still in positions of power and influence. The communists were not the only ones to commit crimes against humanity. From the mujahideen in the 1980s to the Americans and Taliban today, human rights abuses and crimes against humanity continue to be carried out with impunity.

Building a just nation is not simply an imperative of the West. It is an obligation for Afghans themselves. Weaving a united country out of the twisted patchwork of self-interest, corruption, and greed that Afghanistan has become will not be easy. However, it is only when those who have regularly acted with impunity are brought to justice, including the perpetuators of the IAM medical team's executions, that Afghanistan can consider itself on the road to recovery.

The journey of Tom and Dan through the decades of war in Afghanistan ended in their deaths in the mountains of Badakshan bordering Nuristan. My journey continues, but it is increasingly marked by a sense of despair at the senseless loss of dedicated aid workers, Afghan civilians, and young Western soldiers. The ongoing insistence of the West that somehow a combination of military force with sufficient international recovery support over the next few years will provide the solution appears far-fetched. Occupying Afghanistan with foreign soldiers has never been and never will be the solution. Nor will simply throwing more money at the problem, particularly if it continues to involve wasteful (if not corrupt) foreign contractors with no real interest in the country.

In the end, as Masood Khalili maintains, it will be up to Afghans themselves to find their way. We cannot do it for them. But this may take another three decades, if not longer. The international community needs to make the effort to look beyond the short term with initiatives that respond to real Afghan needs, not those of the West. This includes bringing pressure on regional players such as Pakistan and Iran to halt their conniving, which only subverts Afghanistan's efforts at establishing renewed stability. If not, we will only entrench even further the current inability of Afghans to find peace among themselves.

—EDWARD GIRARDET
May 2011

CHAPTER ONE

Tracking the Lion, Part One

It was early September 2001 when we pulled into the parched, dust-blown settlement of Khoja Bahauddin in northern Afghanistan. The desert heat permeated the cabin of the Toyota. I was in desperate need of a cup of tea. I had been traveling since dawn with my translator and friend Mohammed Shuaib, and our driver, a stoic Afghan named Farid. His badly dilapidated four-wheel drive was a testament to years of nego-tiating war-shattered roads.

My body ached from the jolting trip and I was impatient to get out. Farid turned to us with a self-satisfied grin, amazed that we had made it this far. "We're here," he announced. I opened the car door and was hit by an intense blast of heat, like an abruptly opened oven. Khoja, as I had expected, was the epitome of bleakness.

Once a desolate *caravanserai* for nomads and traders, Khoja lay dry and inhospitable. It had carved itself a niche on the northern edge of a series of semi-arid hills gradually rising to the south to merge with the snowcapped mountains of the Hindu Kush. The town consisted of little more than scattered supply depots and concrete or mud-walled housing compounds. Whenever a truck jolted along its roughly graded streets, billows of fine dust rose to temporarily obscure buildings, people, and animals alike. Mingling with the dust was a stifling odor of decay, a sickly-sweet mix of burning rubbish and camel dung.

Thankfully, not all of Khoja was stark desolation. Clinging to the edge of a low, barren plateau, the town looked down onto a vast flood-plain of wheat fields and fruit orchards, lushly watered by irrigation canals fed by the Oxus River—in Persian, Amu Darya. It is thanks to this broad, fast-moving mass of water constituting Afghanistan's north-eastern frontier with Tajikistan that these sprawling, arid lands are able to bloom. The former Soviet republic has been steadily draining away more than its fair share of the river to irrigate hundreds of thousands of acres of thirsty cotton. A legacy of the Russian empire, this is a crop that makes no sense in the region because of the exorbitant amounts of water it uses. Competition for water can expect to become a source of future conflict between the two countries.

Khoja was now the site of the bustling rear base of one of the world's best-known twentieth-century guerrilla strategists, Massoud. Often referred to as the Tito, General Giap, or Che Guevera of Afghanistan, the charismatic Massoud had been waging wars for nearly two and a half decades: first against various left-wing or communist regimes in Kabul; then against the Soviet Red Army during its nearly decade-long occupation in the 1980s. These battles were followed by fighting against rival armed factions of former mujahideen embroiled in a brutal civil conflict following the 1992 collapse of the Moscow-backed government run by the People's Democratic Party of Afghanistan (PDPA). Then came his struggle for survival as the country's last commander of any significance against the Taliban.

Now, eight and a half years since the Taliban first emerged, Massoud's United Front forces were struggling to hold their own. The Pakistani ISI, a key supporter of the Taliban, had dubbed the United Front "the Northern Alliance" in a bid to promote regional division between the tribal Pushtuns to the south and the ethnic Tajiks and Uzbeks to the north. The Pakistani propaganda ploy succeeded, with much of the Western media referring to Massoud's resistance coalition as the Northern Alliance.

By 2001, the Taliban, which had first pushed Massoud's mainly Tajik forces out of Kabul in late September 1996, controlled as much as 80 percent of the country. Apart from Afghanistan's largest province, Badakshan—which borders Tajikistan to the north and China and Pakistan to the west—the only areas to remain under Massoud's control were his traditional stronghold in the Panjshir Valley north of Kabul and parts of Kapisa and Takhar.

The Taliban were a rapidly spreading host of radical "Islamic scholars," many of whom could not even read, but who had emerged militarily as a new fighting force in 1994. As a movement, however, elements of the Taliban had existed already in the 1980s during the Soviet-Afghan war. The Taliban were mainly dominated by the tall, black-turbaned

Kandaharis under their spiritual leader, Mullah Mohammed Omar. With the eager backing of Pushtun (or Pathan) tribes and clans from the southern and eastern provinces, plus various enclaves in the north, the Taliban wished to reestablish historic Pushtun control over the entire country. They also benefited from significant support among their tribal brethren in the frontier agencies of neighboring Pakistan.

Initially, the Taliban had drawn widespread backing among Afghanistan's war-fatigued civilians, fed up with the lawlessness of local warlords, bickering mujahideen, and armed bandits. The new movement was further sponsored by Afghanistan's—and Pakistan's—versatile transport cartels based in the Baluchistan provincial capital of Quetta, which, in war or peace, always found ways of shipping goods—Russian refrigerators, Japanese car parts, Indian cloth, Chinese pots and pans, secondhand clothing from the United States—by truck or horse caravan across the country. But they had grown tired of paying incessant "road tolls" at makeshift checkpoints set up by anyone with a gun. The Taliban imposed a harshly enforced rule of law by amputating the limbs of brigands and unceremoniously shooting or hanging local chiefs who resisted. They now boasted that, on payment of a single road tax in their areas of control, a transporter could drive a truckload of gold across Afghanistan without fear.

The largely ignorant Taliban were increasingly manipulated by Pakistan's ISI, which saw in them the best way to finally overthrow the unbowing Massoud and set up its own Pushtun-dominated and politically compliant government in Kabul. The Pakistanis had never managed to achieve this through factions they had previously supported, notably Gulbuddin Hekmatyar's Hezb-e-Islami resistance group. The ISI had never liked Massoud because he threatened to undermine their backing of Pushtun Islamic extremists to achieve their own regional objectives. Even during the height of the Soviet-Afghan war, when both Massoud and other "inside" commanders, many of them non-Pushtuns, proved themselves as the most effective among the guerrilla leaders, the Pakistanis preferred their own cohorts.

The Taliban derived major support from Arab fundamentalists, including influential Saudi Arabians, seeking to promote a purist and highly intolerant form of Islam that had little to do with traditional

Afghan culture. One of these "purists" was Osama bin Laden, whose rapidly growing al Qaeda (the Base) organization was now operating freely in Afghanistan. In return for Land Cruisers, satellite phones, weapons, and hard cash, the Taliban allowed the Arabi, as these wealthy outsiders were known, to set up their own training camps hidden among the rocky outcrops and dry riverbeds of eastern Afghanistan. These encampments attracted volunteer Islamists from as far away as Indonesia, Canada, the United States, and Europe—including respectable-looking students from Manchester; bank clerks from Jakarta; or already battle-hardened fighters from Chechnya, Bosnia, and Algeria. All were eager to hone their practical combat and terrorism skills while attending short-term field courses, sometimes during their vacations. Nearly forty thousand foreign Islamists are believed to have fought in Afghanistan since they first became involved in the country's jihads during the early 1980s. Some later used this experience to fight in the 2011 uprisings against the dictatorial regimes of North Africa.

In 2001, Afghanistan was caught up in a punishing drought that was dragging on into its fourth year. The effects of the drought were dramatically evident in Khoja. The only hints of green were the occasional pistachio trees, remnants of once thick copses cut down by villagers and lumber traffickers for firewood and timber. As I walked through the town's streets, I recognized a small handful of offices of international aid agencies by the logo-adorned flags flapping in the hot wind from rooftop poles. The aid workers were based in Khoja to provide aid to the thousands of refugees—recently displaced by nearby fighting—who were now living in tented camps on the outskirts of the town.

Hot, and filthy with dirt and sweat, Shuaib and I strolled into the entrance of a single-story, L-shaped bungalow. The compound was surrounded by a large wall with broken brick and bags of cement piled by the gate. A small bed of roses had been laid out in the middle. A withered old gardener with a deformed hand and a severe limp from a land-mine injury was planting red geraniums at the far end. This was the United Front's Foreign Ministry guesthouse, where journalists and other visitors stayed.

A second, far grander pavilion with spacious terraces and Greco-Roman columns of the sort one sees in the suburbs of Dubai or Kuwait

City dominated a connecting compound. This was the VIP lodge, which served as Massoud's intelligence headquarters and the venue for high-level gatherings. Standing where the plateau dropped several hundred feet down onto the floodplain, the villa sported a magnificent view of deliciously green hedgerowed cultivations spreading northward toward a distant backdrop of low, dull brown mountains on the Tajikistan side of the border. A clutch of Toyota Land Cruisers with curtained or smoked-glass windows and high radio antennae were parked out in front. At least a dozen United Front fighters with *pakuls* (woolen Nuristani caps), khaki army fatigue jackets and trousers, black leather boots, and heavily loaded ammunition vests loitered around. All were armed with the latest version AK-74 Kalashnikovs. Two or three shouldered RPGs, with rounds of grenades bristling from their belts. In the back of one of the vehicles, a mounted anti-aircraft gun pointed menacingly at the sky.

"Looks like a commanders' meeting," said Shuaib. "Maybe Massoud is here," he added hopefully.

A good friend from the 1980s in Afghanistan, "Engineer" Shuaib was a congenial and balding former resistance activist, now in his early forties. A devout Muslim and politically moderate, he had fled to the United States as a refugee following threats by both the ISI and funda-mentalist Afghan factions, mainly because of his affiliation with Western journalists.

During the early days of the Red Army occupation, Shuaib had accompanied American and European reporters into Afghanistan as a press officer for Jamiat-e-Islami (Islamic Society), one of the seven main resistance parties based in the Pakistani Northwest Frontier town of Peshawar. Later, he began working directly with a small group of experienced journalists such as British BBC cameraman Peter Jouvenal, American Bill Branigin of *The Washington Post*, and Frenchman Patrick de Saint-Exupéry of *Le Figaro*. We had all made repeated trips to the Afghan interior with him and treasured his resourcefulness in helping us track down our stories.

Shouldering our backpacks, Shuaib and I stepped into the guesthouse office. There Assim Suhail, a young man in his late twenties wearing neatly pressed blue jeans and a dark blazer, sat diligently working at a desktop computer. A black Thuraya satellite phone, the Rolls-Royce of mobile phones, lay charging next to it. During the 1980s, Afghan resistance members wore cheap, pyjamalike cotton *shalwar-kamiz* and were lucky to have a secondhand typewriter or a limited-range walkie-talkie. Most communications at the time were in the form of notes hand-carried by messengers traveling by foot or on horseback into Afghanistan.

Assim looked up expectantly. *"A Salaam Aleikum,"* he said, gesturing for us to sit down in the huge, plastic-leather sofas that took up most of the room. "I trust you had a good journey." We introduced ourselves and shook hands. Assim, it turned out, was the guesthouse manager as well as an intelligence officer with the Foreign Ministry.

"Of course I know who you are and that you were coming. Welcome to Khoja Bahauddin," he declared, sheepishly reaching over to switch off his computer. I suspected that he had been playing a computer game. As with all electrical appliances in a country debilitated by years of war, the computer only worked when the diesel generator was running. I could hear it coughing like a congested lawn mower from somewhere behind the building.

Shuaib quickly explained our mission as Assim called for tea before sitting back to study our letters of recommendation. Not unlike nineteenth-century Europe, personal introductions in Afghanistan, often briefly scribbled on scraps of paper, were still crucial. I was on assignment for *National Geographic* magazine, and a note from the editor on his letterhead was the extent of our security clearance. Satisfied, Assim smiled and leaned back in his chair.

"Unfortunately, Commander Massoud is not here," he explained. His careful English was learned in a Peshawar high school while living in Pakistani exile with his family. Like many Afghans, he was an avid listener to the BBC World Service, whose pronunciation he tried to emulate. He clearly had a career ahead of him in the diplomatic corps— that is, if Massoud's troops won the war. "We've been waiting for him for several days. But the wind and dust are too strong. The helicopters have not been able to land. *Inshallah*, if God wills, maybe tomorrow. Or the day after." The United Front leader was either in the Panjshir or somewhere on the front lines near Taloqan, maybe even Tajikistan, Assim suggested.

I nodded, resigning myself to the prospect of a long, uncertain wait. Up till now, our trip across the north had proceeded with few hitches, but delay was to be expected in Afghanistan. As anyone who has worked in this country knows only too well, it is impossible to stick to a timetable, particularly in the more hazardous rural parts where much depends on happenstance. I had gotten used to landslides knocking out roads, early snowfall closing mountain passes, flash floods swelling river crossings, low clouds canceling flights, or previously passable areas blocked by fighting. I often found myself waiting for days, and sometimes weeks, to interview a commander or to catch a flight to another part of the country. Over the years, I had seen many a carefully planned schedule of timestretched diplomats or television producers crumble, turning normally collected individuals into distraught, crazed, even sobbing wrecks.

The front lines lay barely thirty miles to the southwest of Khoja. It was unclear whether Massoud still had the weapons and the ammunition to launch a sustained counteroffensive by the onset of winter. It was also uncertain whether this hardy engineering-student-turned-commander had the stamina to galvanize his people for a last series of pitched battles against the spreading swath of Pushtun jihadists.

It was not for lack of sound military strategy that the United Front proved unable to repel the Taliban. Indeed, Massoud was renowned for his strategic prowess. But the Taliban had cleverly learned—with the help of the ISI—that the way to win the war was by buying off opposition commanders rather than by relying on their own military guile. With wealthy Arab and other Middle Eastern backers, money was no problem. Some of Massoud's key allies had defected to the Taliban or had melted off to the Gulf countries, their wallets stuffed with payoffs. In Kabul, aid workers and journalists were already talking about Massoud making a tactical withdrawal to the other side of the Oxus and continuing his struggle from Tajikistan, ironically with help from his former enemies, the Russians and Indians who had supported the communist Kabul regime of the 1970s and '80s. The prospects for an end to the war seemed even more remote.

In short, Massoud's future looked as bleak as Khoja itself. I had followed Massoud's trajectory from unknown guerrilla fighter to his current status as Afghanistan's last major resistance leader. He was a complex man, and I had often questioned his actions. But I never doubted his devotion and commitment to his concept of a free Afghanistan. As with so many Afghans, he seemed tired of the fighting. What he wanted more than anything else, he often told me, was the chance to start rebuilding the country with peace and stability.

My principal purpose in visiting Khoja was to explore with Massoud the impact of so many long years of conflict and economic neglect on Afghanistan and its people, from the first time popular armed revolt broke out against the communist-backed regime in Kabul in July 1978 to what appeared to be the latest, increasingly futile attempt to wrestle back control from the Taliban. I had not spoken with the "Lion of Panjshir" since the mid-1990s and I was anxious to probe precisely why this exceptional guerrilla leader had pursued the cause of an independent, moderately Islamist Afghanistan with such persistence over so many years. What was it that could keep a man going even when the best of odds appeared insurmountable? I was particularly interested in exploring what Massoud thought he had done right—and wrong—as a resistance commander against the Soviets and also when he was part of the Afghan government during the mid-1990s, a highly controversial period.

But I did have a timetable to adhere to. I had to be back in Europe by September 13, my wife's birthday. "The wrath of the Taliban will be nothing compared with what my wife will do to me if I don't get back in time," I said in jest to Assim, who gave me a puzzled look, not quite understanding my joke. My plan was to head back to my home in Geneva for a week or two and then return to Afghanistan toward the end of September, this time covering the situation from the Talib side using an official visa granted to me by their embassy in Islamabad. At the time, only three countries—Pakistan, Saudi Arabia, and the United Arab Emirates—had recognized the Taliban. But instead, I settled into Khoja and waited for Massoud.

The United Front commander was clearly interested in making his views known and had sent a message saying he was eager for our interview. From our back-and-forth communications by radio and by satellite telephone, Massoud seemed to know that time was running out to set the record straight.

Since the earliest of my reporting days in Afghanistan, I had met up with "the Commander," as he was known by his men, at different times and places. I had always maintained a polite, but professional, relationship with Massoud. He was the resistance fighter and I was the journalist. During the 1980s, I had accompanied him through high-mountain gorges as he prepared yet another assault against a Red Army convoy or an Afghan communist government fort. Once we sat hunkered in a hidden mountain cave around a hissing pressure lamp with Soviet MiGs pounding the narrow side valleys nearby, and chatted about the future over tea and stale *nan*, the local unleavened bread. That's when he told me that he would like nothing better than to leave "these damn mountains" once the war came to an end.

As I waited for Massoud, it occurred to me that this man, who had been fighting for more than a quarter century, simply wished to chat with me as an old acquaintance about the world at large—as we had done on previous occasions—and about what life might be like in an Afghanistan no longer at war. While Massoud could discuss military strategy for hours, he was passionate about Persian poetry and existential debate, and would often ask rhetorical questions such as the purpose of life. Massoud often undertook these impromptu meetings late at night or in the early hours of the morning, as if he needed to talk and our presence served this purpose. Once, he brought along his son, Ahmed. Wearing a gold-laced waistcoat and gray *shalwar* trousers, the boy watched his father attentively. No more than four or five, he was perfectly aware of the respect that his father had imbued among his men. The boy was obviously very proud of this.

On another occasion when I was shooting a television documentary with French filmmaker Christophe de Ponfilly in Kabul during the height of the civil war in 1993, I stayed at one of Massoud's safe houses in the northern residential area of Wazir Akbar Khan. We were awakened abruptly at two in the morning by the Commander's sudden appearance at the door with a retinue of aides and bodyguards. We emerged bleary-eyed from our sleeping bags, and for the next two hours listened as he carefully and very deliberately outlined his plans for defending the city. Every so often, he leaned over to play a piece in an ongoing game of chess with one of his officers.

"The important thing is for the people of Kabul not to suffer," he insisted, echoing a concern for civilians that he regularly expressed in our conversations. "They have suffered enough. If we have to save lives by leaving the city, then we'll do so." A mile or so away, in the direction of Shar-e-Now near the Ministry of Interior, a flurry of rockets began crashing down methodically, one every minute or so. No one took notice. Massoud continued talking while playing his game, a match he never seemed to complete, but always picked up again at some later stage in a different location.

Then, just as suddenly as the Afghan commander had come, Massoud rose swiftly to his feet, his men scrambling with their Kalashnikovs, boots scraping and sliding on the tiled floor. He bade us farewell with a powerful handshake and a broad grin.

"*A bientôt.* See you soon," he said softly in French. He then strode off into the night as the first rose-tinted slivers of dawn daubed the horizon.

It was not difficult to understand the reverence in which many Afghans held Massoud. Nor to understand why so many others hated him. As much as Massoud was seen as a national hero for many, he was bitterly criticized by others for having indulged in excessive use of force, even human rights abuses, against his rivals, resulting in unnecessary civilian casualties during the Battle for Kabul from 1992 to 1996. One critic, a Pushtun writer, called him the Jonas Savimbi of Afghanistan, referring to the highly ambitious and intolerant UNITA rebel leader I had met covering the war in Angola, who was supported by the South Africans and Americans during the 1980s and '90s against the communist Luanda government. Another, an Italian aid consultant with many years' experience in the country, went as far as to describe Massoud as a war criminal.

There was much talk, too, about the corruption and arrogance of the people who surrounded him, the so-called Panjshiri Mafia. These included Massoud's former United Front intelligence chief Marshal Fahim, a murky figure linked to human rights abuses and narcotics trafficking, yet who later managed to become vice president in the Western-backed Karzai government in Kabul.

Such allegations were deeply hurtful to Massoud, who always liked to be seen as promoting the protection and safety of civilians as paramount. But as he himself had already admitted on several occasions, he had committed more than his fair share of blunders; looking back, there were many things he would have done differently.

I hoped that our conversation would also provide insight into why the West had missed so many opportunities during the Soviet-Afghan war as well as during the Talib period by sidelining effective commanders such as himself in the north, Abdul Haq in the east, and Ismail Khan in the west. During the 1980s, the United States had allowed the Pakistanis to dictate the direction of their support for the mujahideen. With Washington under Reagan intent on undermining the Soviets in Afghanistan, the Central Intelligence Agency and other American spy organizations relied overwhelmingly on the ISI for their information, which the Pakistanis manipulated accordingly. This policy proved disastrous, as the bulk of US aid ultimately went to the fundamentalist Islamic groups who scarcely hid their hatred and contempt for infidel Westerners and who later formed the basis for the current anti-NATO insurgency. Later, during the 1990s, the United States chose to ignore the rising influence of Arab extremists, such as al Qaeda, inside Talib-controlled parts of Afghanistan. Many of these earlier mistakes have dogged the West's involvement ever since. I was eager for Massoud's views and wondered if I would come any closer to understanding this enigmatic figure. But first, the United Front commander had to return to Khoja.

The young Foreign Ministry official had an aide take Shuaib and me to a room that we were to share with a visiting Afghan doctor working with one of the Western relief agencies. He was somewhere on the other side of town dealing with new refugee arrivals from the front-line battle zones. More drought victims were also flocking in. Two or three other Afghans, whom I knew from my earlier years reporting the war, were staying at the guesthouse. So, too, were nine foreigners, primarily journalists.

We threw down our packs. The shower was not working but there was a large black plastic barrel, compliments of the United Nations High Commissioner for Refugees (UNHCR), filled with cool water. It felt good to wash and put on clean clothes. We strolled over to the courtyard where chairs had been set up in a semicircle to wait for dinner. A young man immediately rushed out with a large thermos of steaming green tea, which we sipped while watching a fiery red sun setting amid the dust-filled evening haze.

One by one, the journalists came out of their rooms. A Russian from the Prague-based US station Radio Liberty, an Uzbek from the Institute for War and Peace Reporting in London, and two French freelance reporters. Some had already been here for days and had just returned from trips to the refugee camps or the front lines. In addition, there were three women, an American, a Swiss, and an Afghan, from the Feminist Majority in the United States on a fact-finding trip looking into the status of women in Afghanistan. Fahim Dashty, a talented young Afghan reporter, was another guest. Two Arab journalists, Karim Touzani and Kassim Bakkali, were also present. All had come to see Massoud.

I was surprised to see the Arabs. The two men, who wore jeans and T-shirts, did not join us for dinner. Instead, they sorted through equipment on the veranda just outside their room. Adjacent to my own quarters, it was crammed with the usual bulky packs of a television team. One normally did not find Arabs covering the United Front side of the story. They tended to report more from the Talib areas. Furthermore, given the large number of volunteers from the Middle East and North Africa fighting alongside the Islamists, many Massoud supporters regarded the Arabi with suspicion, even hatred. However, new Middle East satellite news organizations, notably Al Jazeera, were beginning to cover conflict stories normally reserved for weightier international broadcasters, such as the BBC and CNN, and I assumed the Arab journalists were part of a similar new venture.

Curious, I walked up to them and shook hands, introducing myself, first in English, then in French, as an American journalist. I asked them where they were from.

"Morocco," replied the older one in French, but added that they lived in Belgium. He was a severe, intense-looking man in his mid- or late thirties with a tightly rounded face, short hair, and wire-rimmed glasses. He reminded me of the North African intellectuals one sometimes finds hanging out in the cafés of Paris or Brussels. "We're doing a TV report," he volunteered before returning to his sorting. The other Arab, a burly younger man with the broad face of a boxer, glanced at me briefly. He said nothing. When I asked them which network, the severe one shrugged. "A Middle East one," he said. He nodded to his colleague and they both withdrew to their room, closing the door behind them.

Within a day of our arrival, heavy sand clouds began to envelop the mountains to the west, one of the effects of Afghanistan's dust-bowl drought, but also a normal seasonal occurrence when the summer gusts known as hundred-day winds can blow for days, even weeks on end. With the sand reducing visibility to less than five hundred yards, the helicopters could not operate, and Massoud could not fly in. We repeatedly asked where he was, but for security reasons no one would say. Assim, in a conspiratorial tone, hinted that the Commander might be on the front line. Or, then again, in Dushanbe, where Massoud's wife and children lived, to arrange for more ammunition and supplies for the much-awaited counteroffensive. He begged us to be patient.

"The dust will settle soon," he said. When I suggested that Shuaib and I take off to do some reporting, perhaps even go to the front line, he pointed out that Massoud might come by vehicle. "You should not go far," he warned.

Frustrated, I turned to Mohammed Kamaludin, a heavyset Afghan engineer from the Panjshir and an old acquaintance from Peshawar.

"How long will this continue?" I asked.

"It could last another day," Kamaludin said, but then added philosophically, "It could also drag on much longer." He had previously worked as a logistics coordinator for the Swedish Committee for Afghanistan (SCA), one of the first international organizations to provide clandestine cross-border development aid during the Soviet-Afghan war. He was now head of Massoud's reconstruction team and had come to Khoja in search of funding for a sheaf of irrigation and hydroelectric projects. The Afghan engineer had exalted plans for supplying towns, even Kabul, with hydroelectric power as part of a series of grids fed into by local villages with their own river-generated supply stations. But for this, he needed Massoud's support.

"Everyone is obsessed with the war, but we must rebuild in those areas where there is no fighting," he explained, showing me his project proposals splayed out on Assim's office sofa. "If we do nothing now, there will be nothing left."

Kamaludin had a point. Shuaib and I had indeed seen a number of road and bridge projects on our way to Khoja carried out by the British relief agency AfghanAid and the UN's World Food Program (WFP) as part of their food-for-work initiatives. Yet numerous roads, irrigation canals, and other essential infrastructure were derelict for lack of maintenance.

Frustrated, Shuaib and I debated what to do. There was no question that we would wait it out in Khoja, at least for a few more days. But we had to do something. I was keen to visit other parts, perhaps even one of the camps where Massoud had incarcerated his prisoners of war. The nearest one at Shah Ab held mainly Taliban, but also Arabs and other foreign nationals. There were rumors that some Pakistani officers, including an air force pilot, were being held. The Islamabad government vigorously denied any form of military involvement on behalf of the Taliban, claiming that any Pakistani nationals fighting in the war were volunteers or retired military personnel. I wanted to confirm this for myself. But these locations were all five or six hours away by road. I could not risk missing Massoud should he suddenly show up, as he was apt to leave again just as quickly.

For nearly a week we waited. The only times we ventured out were to visit the bazaar or to talk with refugees, many of whom were camped out in a series of fields on the eastern side of town. Each morning, Shuaib and I would scrutinize the dust clouds, just in case the wind lapsed long enough to allow the helicopters to fly in. Massoud still had a force of about a dozen helicopters shuttling back and forth among the front lines, Khoja, the Panjshir, and Tajikistan. Occasionally, we saw Russian-made Mi-8 helicopters cruising in low over the hills, but these were only local sorties or flights returning from the Panjshir to the south where visibility was better. No helicopters were coming in from Dushanbe.

To bide our time, I chatted with the other journalists and the American women's group. I also tried conversing with the taciturn Arabs whenever I saw them. But they kept to themselves. They left the compound every morning, their vehicle loaded with equipment, apparently to shoot footage in and around Khoja. When I asked the severe one how the filming was going, his responses were always unenthusiastic.

"Good, I suppose," he said glumly. Neither appeared particularly energetic about their work.

I assumed that they were dejected about the endless wait for Massoud. Once, they made a trip to the Shah Ab POW camp, returning late in the evening. When I saw them the next day standing outside their room, I wandered over, inviting them to join us for tea. The older one declined politely. "*Merci*, you're very kind, but we have things to do."

When I asked him what he had seen at the camp, he proved more forthcoming.

"We talked with some of the Taliban," he said.

"Really?" I said, amazed. "What about Pakistanis?"

"Yes, there were some." Then he smiled apologetically. "I am sorry. We must go. We have work." They both disappeared back into their room.

Later, I stopped by Assim's office to ask about them. He gave me a quizzical look. "Do you know them?" he asked.

"No, I'm just wondering who they are. Any idea which television network they work for?"

Assim reached into a desk drawer, pulling out a photocopied document. It was a letter of recommendation—in English—from a London-based organization, the Islamic Observation Centre, signed by its director Yasser Al-Siri. It vouched for the two men, Karim Touzani and Kassim Bakkali, as journalists for Arabic News International. I had never heard of the agency.

"They wish to interview Massoud," Assim said, gesturing to another page with a typed list of questions. "In fact, they've been trying for weeks to get an interview. They were in the Panjshir before. I have told them to wait until Massoud comes. They're only Arabs, not very important. The Commander will decide. He is very busy."

By now it was clear that the dust was not going to settle. We would have to catch up with Massoud at a later date. We had only a few days left on our schedule before I would need to head back to Islamabad and then Europe. Most of the other journalists in Khoja were anxious to leave, either to return home or to get on with assignments elsewhere. Reluctantly, Shuaib and I decided to pull out. We planned to accompany the Feminist Majority women to Faizabad, traveling in two vehicles in case one broke down. They wanted to meet with President Burhanuddin Rabbani, the United Front head of the constantly diminishing rump state of Afghanistan still recognized by most of the international community.

It was now September 6. While waiting to leave the next morning, I saw the older Moroccan emerge from his ablutions in the bathhouse, a towel carefully draped over his head to protect himself from the sand. I walked over to say good-bye.

"Will you try and go?" I asked. "This dust could persist for days."

He shook his head. "No, we'll wait for Massoud."

On our way back to catch the UN flight, our car broke down on a lone mountain road. Shuaib and I crammed ourselves into the vehicle of the Feminist Majority team, who had doubled back when they failed to see our cloud of dust behind them. Two days later, we were back in Islamabad.

The next morning well before dawn—on September 10—I stood waiting outside our guesthouse for the taxi to take us to the airport for the British Airways flight to London. As usual, I had my pocket shortwave radio with me. I tuned in to the BBC to catch the news. There had been an assassination attempt in Khoja Bahauddin against Massoud the day before—on September 9—by two Arab suicide bombers posing as journalists. They were reported to have packed explosives on their bodies as well as in a camera. One of them triggered the device as Massoud settled down to do an interview. The Arabs were believed to have died immediately, as had several Afghans in the room. Later, we learned that one had been killed in the explosion, while the other, wounded, was shot dead when he tried to escape. One report had Massoud dead; another had him still alive but severely injured. The United Front commander, the BBC said, had been flown to Dushanbe for emergency medical treatment.

On the return flight to Europe, I pondered the few details available. Massoud's security was atrocious when it came to the media. Both he and his entourage still cultivated the naive notion that journalists could never possibly be part of the threat but rather were there to report the story. It occurred to me that had we stayed on, both Shuaib and I might have been killed, or at least badly injured. Massoud had a habit of inviting any friends or visitors present to sit in on his interviews.

I arrived back in Geneva on the morning of September 11. Once at my house in Cessy, a small village on the French side of the border with Switzerland, I climbed exhausted upstairs to catch up with some sleep before calling contacts for an update on Massoud's condition. Several hours later, as I was still slumbering from jet lag, my wife, Lori, called me from downstairs.

"You'd better come and see this. You can't believe what's happening. Planes are smashing into the World Trade Center in New York," she said. She had just returned from the United Nations, where she worked, after several friends and family in the States had telephoned to tell her that America was under attack. She had rushed to pick up our seven-year-old daughter Elisa from school and then had rushed back to the house to turn on the television.

As I sat numbly watching the unfolding of events in the United States, six hours behind European time, I realized that the timing of the attempt against Massoud's life could not have been a coincidence. The names of Osama bin Laden and al Qaeda kept cropping up as the possible architects of the Trade Center assaults. While a few commentators mentioned Afghanistan as bin Laden's operational haven, no one referred to Massoud. Yet there had to be some connection with what was happening in New York. Evidently, al Qaeda had agreed to assassinate Afghanistan's last principal opposition leader to help the Taliban secure, once and for all, the rest of the country. At the same time, Massoud's death guaranteed Afghanistan as a safe haven for al Qaeda operatives seeking to conduct terror missions elsewhere in the world.

Four days later, on September 15, came the official announcement. Massoud was dead. The United Front commander had died of his wounds within half an hour of the Khoja explosion. In order to gain time to appoint a successor, Massoud's aides had deliberately delayed the confirmation of his demise. They did not want the Taliban or al Qaeda to take advantage by launching another offensive at a moment when the alliance lacked leadership.

Assim, the young Foreign Ministry official, had been killed alongside his commander. Among the wounded were other acquaintances and friends: Masood Khalili, the Afghan ambassador to Delhi and an old friend from the early 1980s, and Fahim Dashty, the Afghan journalist. Severely injured, both had been flown by helicopter with Massoud's body to Tajikistan for immediate surgery.

The Lion was laid to rest at a hero's funeral in his home valley of the Panjshir attended by thousands of followers. Many wailed as they jostled around the coffin to throw flowers or to touch it. It was heartrending to watch on television his son Ahmed, now eleven years old, the same boy I had seen back in 1994 in Kabul, standing visibly in the forefront and looking very much like his father. Some were already heralding him as a future leader for Afghanistan.

Massoud's death marked the end of an extraordinary epoch of hope and defiance. For me, it closed a chapter in my own life. It was also a historic turning point. I realized that the murder of the "Lion of Panjshir," and the subsequent terrorist attack on the United States, were intrinsically entwined.

In many ways, my notion of Afghanistan had been a romanticized one. It had been based on grassroots heroes even more intriguing than Simón Bolívar, Che Guevera, or the Hollywood version of Rob Roy MacGregor. I was also able to experience a determined popular resistance movement operating astride two centuries in some of the world's most staggeringly beautiful landscapes. Every trip to Afghanistan was a step into another world, another time that was real adventure. It was a place of constant challenge from which one would emerge, one hoped, with an inspiring story of simple humanity.

Every journalist or aid worker I know who encountered Massoud was struck by this extraordinary individual. He had a powerful but also accommodating presence. There were few like him. You knew that you were dealing with someone who was already part of history. Even Russians who had fought and hated the Lion during the Soviet-Afghan war, when they tried to crush him, considered him a more-than-worthy adversary. Curiously, almost all his foreign critics had never actually met him. And yet, looking back, there is no knowing how Massoud would have fared had he survived—and persevered in the new game that emerged following the events of 9/11. Another question is whether he, as an ethnic Tajik, could ever have been able to unite Afghanistan. For some, Massoud would never have proved acceptable to the Pushtun south. Nor would Pakistan or Iran have tolerated such an independent-minded leader whose vision stretched well beyond regional borders, embracing a mix of ideals represented by Kennedy, de Gaulle, and Ho Chi Minh—all men he admired.

But all this collapsed with Massoud's assassination and, less than two months later, the murder by the Taliban of Afghanistan's only other widely revered resistance figure capable of anything resembling nation-wide leadership, Pushtun commander Abdul Haq.

Suddenly there was a whole new slew of players, demons, and outside interests with little to do with the true needs of the Afghan people to whom I had grown so attached. Afghanistan's reality at the turn of the twenty-first century, however, was far harsher. One that had no room for romanticism, heroes, or inspiring stories of hope. Even more tragic, few people on the outside knew or cared enough about this country's tangled history to realize that both of these devastating attacks—Massoud's assassination and the events of 9/11—could have been avoided had only the lessons of Afghanistan's recent conflicts been heeded.

CHAPTER TWO

A Coward in Afghanistan

Three months before the Soviet invasion of Afghanistan, I was a restless young journalist in Paris, aching for a good story. Paris in mid-September 1979 was still in a good mood. The French, who had abandoned their capital in August to the tourists, were still basking in the glow of their summer vacations. For me, however, it was time to explore new horizons. As much as I savored this city of light with its cafés and street theater of style, where even the early-morning rushing of water in the gutters as North African cleaners plunged and swept with their brooms inspired new life, I felt I could not stay. I wanted something different.

Part of this urge had been spurred by my final years at Clifton College, a liberal British "public" or high school in the west of England. Over the past century and a half, Clifton had produced its fair share of adventurers, among them British explorer Francis Younghusband. His travels in Tibet had inspired an oddball band of Old Cliftonians, who had ventured out to Africa and Asia during the nineteenth and early twentieth centuries, some of them never to return. All I could think about was that it was time to do the same.

I wanted to become a writer and envisaged my future as one long journey overcoming daunting challenges. Now living in Paris, all I had achieved thus far was a trip to India, undertaken in my gap year between school and university. On leaving Nottingham University, I had rushed straight to France in my Deux Chevaux, a swaying high-wheeled Citroën car that French president Charles de Gaulle had once referred to as an "umbrella on wheels." My dream was to become a foreign correspondent, a war reporter perhaps. I got a job with United Press International.

Paris at the time was a perfect base for foreign correspondents. Most of the key photo agencies—Sygma, Magnum, Sipa, and Gamma—maintained bureaus, as did major newspapers and broadcasters. Most of the international journalists covered wars and humanitarian crises rather than just French politics, and I wanted to do the same. Sipping kirs or pastis and downing *fine de claire* oysters at La Coupole or the Terminus Nord brasseries, the French photographers—all wearing their requisite silk scarves—recounted their exploits, usually invoking food and women. They spoke with a fashionably rough argot, or slang, that made war coverage brutally romantic. They ate well and always had a tale about liberating a bottle of fine Bordeaux at a shot-up hotel in Central Africa or eating exquisite fish at a corner restaurant in San Salvador.

Desperate to join this elite group, I applied for a nine-month Journalists in Europe fellowship at the Centre pour la Formation Professionelle des Journalistes (CFPJ), the French journalism school in Paris. I had no idea what this was, but, several weeks later, I received a phone call. Could I stop by for an interview? I immediately headed over, but was forced to wait for more than an hour. I was on the point of leaving when the director— a frenetic, white-haired man in his midsixties—bounded into the room.

"Ah, Mr. Girardet, I'm so sorry. My name is Philippe Viannay. Please come with me," he beamed. He led me upstairs and opened the door of a long, narrow room. Inside, I found a dozen distinguished-looking men and women, all in their sixties and seventies, sitting behind a broad table.

Viannay went down the line to introduce me. Their names read like a *Who's Who* of World War II resistance figures. Jean Marin, head of Agence France Presse and a former member of the French *maquis*, or partisans. Hubert Beuve Mery, founder of *Le Monde*. Klaus von Bismarck, head of the Goethe Foundation and a member of the small but determined German opposition to Hitler. Gerald Mansell, head of the BBC's external services and ex-British-liaison to de Gaulle and the Free French, and Claire Richey, another resistance member. Viannay himself had been editor in his early twenties of *Defense de la France*, a resistance newspaper, which they distributed along the Champs-Élysées by chucking copies out of a black Citroën under the noses of the Nazis.

I was accepted for the fellowship. During the months that followed, I spent hours discussing the concept of resistance and foreign occupation with Viannay, a theme that fascinated me. It was one that I was to explore more closely while covering Afghanistan and other wars.

A year later on that warm September morning in 1979, I found myself strolling down the Rue Saint-Honoré with William Dowell, a friend from *Time* magazine. A tall, normally gentle American, Dowell had one of those deeply resonant broadcast voices that could be mercilessly blunt. We had met several years earlier while covering a demonstration against the Franco regime at the Spanish embassy. With the CRS, the French riot police, resolutely firing gas canisters against equally determined demonstrators, we had retreated to a nearby café for a coffee.

Dowell had been in Vietnam, first as a soldier, then a reporter. He eventually returned to the United States via Europe to work with National Public Radio in Washington, but soon headed back to Paris. One of his goals, he declared, was to travel to Afghanistan, which he had visited briefly. Not only did he wish to see the Hindu Kush once again, but he wanted to explore the country that British writer Robert Byron had referred to so succinctly in 1933 as "at last, Asia without an inferiority complex."

"I also need a change," I gloomily told Dowell. I was thinking about Ethiopia or Southeast Asia, or maybe even trying to base myself in North Africa or Beirut. What I was really looking for was my own Spanish Civil War or Vietnam to cover. As with many who had reported Indochina, Dowell had been affected darkly by the experience—but it also left him strangely nostalgic. Journalists and aid workers often find themselves longing for the adrenaline rushes and passions of their past wars, conveniently forgetting the harsh realities.

Dowell pondered my dilemma. "There're too many journalists who already know Southeast Asia. Why not go to Afghanistan? There's a small war brewing there. You'll get some good reporting experience." Besides, he noted, what was happening there could one day have an impact on the West. "Even the most obscure conflicts have a nasty habit of coming back to haunt us, particularly if you ignore them. It would be good if you could get in at the beginning."

Fighting had broken out in Afghanistan several months after the communist takeover in the so-called Saur (April) Revolution of 1978. The Soviet Union was providing hands-on support to the new Marxist-Leninist regime of the People's Democratic Party of Afghanistan (PDPA). Traditionally, newspaper editors had always regarded Afghanistan as a page filler, an incident, a distant bus crash perhaps, or a minor avalanche, to fill a paragraph or two. No one cared about the story itself. And few had any idea even where the country was. I vaguely knew Afghanistan, having crossed it at the beginning of the 1970s on my way overland to India.

The thought of returning to this extraordinary country initially brought back memories of this first trip as a student. I could recall trundling across the spectacular desert expanses of southern Afghanistan in a wildly painted bus packed with turbaned Afghan farmers and merchants. I remembered long soft shafts of evening sun bathing the snow-covered summits of the Hindu Kush, the westernmost stretch of the Himalayas. Above all, I remained enthralled by that wonderful sense of Afghan pride and hospitality, which Byron had observed so well.

I started proposing a series of "on spec" assignments with various newspapers and magazines. One was the *International Herald Tribune.* Another was the Canadian Broadcasting Corporation (CBC), which had a bureau in Paris. It commissioned me to produce a radio documentary on the Pathans, the British name for the Pushtuns, the fiercely independent and oft-romanticized Semitic people whose clans and tribes straddle both sides of the Pakistani-Afghan border.

Reading up on the region, I devoured *The Pathans* by Olaf Caroe, the last British governor of the Northwest Frontier Province, and a well-worn copy of James Spain's *The Way of the Pathans* loaned to me by Arthur Higbee, my former bureau chief at UPI—who had roamed Pakistan during his early days as a foreign correspondent. "They sound like the sort of people you might enjoy. Determined, independent, and incapable of being controlled," he remarked wryly as he handed me the book. Within ten days, I had completed my plans. The cheapest airfare was via New Delhi. From there, I would make my way to Pakistan and then Kabul.

However, I first needed to obtain an Afghan visa. The Afghan embassy, then run by the Khalq (Masses) faction of the communist PDPA government, was situated in a late-nineteenth-century town house in the haute bourgeois sixteenth arrondissement. I phoned about a tourist permit and was asked to stop by with my passport plus two photographs. I decided not to tell them that I was a journalist. A French photographer, recently back from Kabul, had warned me that it might take weeks to obtain press clearance.

I was issued—to my surprise—a month-long tourist visa. A consular official in his late twenties, dressed in a gleaming Boulevard suit, solemnly handed back my passport. He threw in several tourist brochures extolling the virtues of Afghanistan as a cultural paradise. A portrait of President Mohammed Hafizullah Amin was already prominently displayed behind his desk. Only days earlier on September 14, 1979, he had grabbed power after ruthlessly murdering his predecessor Nur Mohammed Taraki. The young man mildly inquired where I hoped to go.

"Oh, Kabul, of course," I ventured. "And then Bamiyan to see the Buddhas. Maybe Kandahar," I added with confidence. "And, if I have time, Herat." I was pushing my tourist identity for what it was worth.

The official shrugged. I wondered if he had ever traveled in his own country. Judging by his excellent French and stylish Mediterranean looks, he had probably lived abroad most of his life. He offered no hint that Afghanistan was caught up in an expanding civil war that had shattered any illusion of a thriving tourist industry. "*Je vous souhaite un bon voyage*," he finally said, shaking my hand. There was no one else waiting when I left the building.

I bade farewell to Paris, equipped with new notebooks, roller pens, a small Uher tape recorder, a box of tapes, two cameras, and several books—plus my backpack and sleeping bag. My most important piece of equipment was a pair of honey-colored Timberland boots. These became my most trusted footwear whenever I trekked across the mountains and deserts of Afghanistan. They were no protection against land mines, but dried quickly after traversing streams and rivers, and conveniently served as a pillow at night. The soles were worn down whenever I returned. But the boots were worth it. Only once did they fail me, when a nail wore through. Not the sort of thing you wanted in the middle of a war zone, when your life depends on walking. I complained to Timberland, and the company immediately replaced the boots for free.

Once in Delhi, I realized how much I had missed those balmy Indian odors, a combination of airport fuel, *bidi* cigarettes, garbage, and humidity. I caught an early-morning flight to Amritsar in the Punjab and the next day left by bus for the Indian-Pakistani frontier. Sweating under the weight of my bags, I trudged across the border guarded by the tallest Indian and Pakistani soldiers I had ever seen. Both nations deliberately dispatched their loftiest men to this critical crossing point. Every day, at sundown, they strutted in a roosterlike marching routine to slam their respective gates shut and impress the hell out of everyone as they stood cheering and waving flags from the two sides of the demarcation line.

On the Pakistani side, I picked up a visa issued by a cheerful immigration officer who seemed to interpret my departure from India as a victory. "Welcome, welcome," he exclaimed, nodding his head in a roundabout manner. "You are happy? You are very happy." I resolutely agreed, hurrying off to board a bus to Lahore, once the "Pearl" of the British Raj, and then another to Islamabad—a five-hour ride in all.

Pakistan's sprawling new capital, Islamabad—the "City of Islam"— was designed by Greek architects at the end of the 1950s. The government had situated it in the cooler, northern reaches of the country at the foot of the Margalla Hills leading up to the Himalayan Hindu Raj range. The idea was to replace hot and sticky Karachi, the former administrative center on the Indian Ocean, with a city worthy of its name. It was hoped also that Pakistani civil servants would work more efficiently.

On my first trip in early 1970, Islamabad was little more than a massive construction site with a few scattered and barely finished buildings. To provide an open landscape of forests, parks, and avenues, huge stretches of saplings had been planted amid the former villages and river-carved ravines. Now, nearly a decade later, the city had grown decisively, with more residential areas, shopping plazas, and offices being added every year.

Islamabad lies ten miles from the former British garrison town of Rawalpindi, headquarters of the Pakistani army, where the country's official—and covert—Afghan policy was planned from the early 1970s onward. It was from here, too, that the ISI, the powerful military intelligence agency, and the United States collaborated with the mujahideen during the 1980s. Later, "Pindi" served as the ISI's center of operations in support of the Afghan Taliban right up to their ousting by the US-backed United Front in late 2001. With Pakistan's penchant for military dictatorship, Pindi stands as a constant reminder for the civilian politicians in Islamabad as to who is really in charge.

For several days, I made the rounds of the embassies, most of them grouped in huge leafy compounds. I was trying to find out what was happening in Afghanistan and to collect contacts, particularly for my radio documentary on the Pathans. Some of the diplomatic missions—the Canadian, Australian, and Swiss—served both Pakistan and Afghanistan. Traditionally, too, Kabul was an attractive R&R destination, a day's journey by road for many foreigners and their families based in Islamabad, especially during the hot summer months before the relief of the monsoon rains. So there was usually a flow of reliable information brought back by travelers.

But now, with the emerging war, Kabul was off limits. Most international organizations had wound down their Afghan operations. The Americans had refused to name a replacement for their ambassador, Adolphe Dubs, who was killed in February 1979 during a hostage-taking at the once-resplendent Kabul Hotel (now The Serena) in the heart of the city.

In Islamabad, most foreigners could offer little tangible information about the cross-border situation. Much was based on rumor or unsubstantiated reports. And no one seemed at all apprised about these supposed mujahideen, or Islamic warriors, everyone was talking about. No one really knew who was organizing them. What was known was that ordinary Afghans, primarily conservative farmers and villagers, did not like the socialist policies, such as land reform or education for girls, being enforced on them by the new PDPA regime. The communists were also arresting or killing people, particularly Islamists, who were opposing them.

Ever since the communists had taken power during the Saur Revolution, people had begun rising up. Insurgents were attacking government targets, making the roads and countryside increasingly unsafe. Thousands of refugees were pouring across the border into Pakistan, bringing with them stories of fighting and repression by communist militants. These influxes were beginning to result in a steady rise of international aid workers based out of the frontier cities of Peshawar and Quetta to cope with what was rapidly becoming a humanitarian problem of disastrous proportions. Still, Afghanistan did not figure highly in the regional concerns of most Western governments.

I was warmly welcomed at the Canadian High Commission. After all, I was representing *Concern*, a well-respected CBC program. "Perhaps you could stop by and see us when you return," noted the high commissioner. No surprise that the diplomats were hoping to rely on us, the itinerant journalists, to let them know what was going on.

I was staying at the Holiday Inn—where most journalists, aid workers, and diplomats hung out—and bumped into David Lay, a BBC Middle East expert. Lay spoke in a careful, studied manner and told me that he, too, was producing a radio documentary on the Pathans. With both of us on limited budgets, we agreed to team up, sharing travel costs and interviews. I was very much the novice in this partnership, but Lay seemed to appreciate my company, and we got on well. Michael Fathers, a Reuters correspondent, agreed to take us down by car to Peshawar, a three-hour journey along the old Grand Trunk (GT) Road, which used to link the Khyber Pass on the far-flung northwestern frontier with the British Raj's eastern cities of Lahore, Delhi, and (finally) Calcutta. For the small handful of foreign correspondents based in Islamabad, and increasingly those reporting the subcontinent out of Delhi, a regular road trip to Peshawar had become a prerequisite part of their coverage.

Peshawar at the end of the 1970s still represented a pleasant backwater. The capital of Pakistan's Pathan-dominated Northwest Frontier Province (or NWFP) its bustling Khyber Bazaar in the Old Town was probably little different from when Rudyard Kipling frequented the region less than a century earlier. His books and poems about the dangers of those daring, or foolish, enough to confront Afghanistan's hostile tribes seem just as pertinent now as they did then. There were still the same smoke-filled *chaikhane*, ancient wood-latticed buildings and hidden courtyards, most of them sadly crumbling, and chaotic alleyways jammed with shops and stalls selling food, spices, hardware, textiles, shotguns, carpets, and gold.

The Old Town was dominated by the Bala Hisar, an early-nineteenth-century Sikh fort. However, this was off limits to twentieth-century visitors because of its use by the Pakistani army. The military still regarded ancient forts as state secrets. The fact that many of these monuments were thoroughly documented in museum-archived photographs and drawings, and even reproduced in books found in the bazaars, did not seem to matter.

Most foreigners lived in the city's quiet, tree-lined cantonment. To roam around, one took a *tonga*—a two-wheeled, horse-drawn cart—or a motor-scooter *tuk-tuk*. As the Afghan crisis persisted over the next two decades, Peshawar's population would triple to 1.5 million with refugees, foreign aid workers, Islamic fundamentalists, and Pakistanis all attracted by its exploding economy.

But now, prior to the Soviet invasion, the cantonment retained a peaceful colonial look. St. John's, the neo-Gothic Anglican church, could have been in Norfolk or Dorset, while the public garden, just up the road from the Victorian cricket pavilion, was still referred to by older-generation Pakistanis as "Company Park," harking back to the days of the East India or "John" Company. The former British administrative and residential complexes, now inhabited by senior Pakistani army officers, civil servants, and established frontier families, boasted well-watered rose beds and even the odd red-painted English postal box. As with military compounds throughout the country, every officers' mess, barracks, and hospital was meticulously lined with lime-washed stones.

I called on the secretary of the Peshawar Club, once one of the Raj's most regaled institutions and now a run-down version of its former splendor. The secretary, I was told, could provide an interesting historical perspective on the Pathans since the end of the colonial era. Humidity-stained black-and-white photographs lined the corridors, depicting formally attired huntsmen and ladies with expectant hounds at their feet. The club still boasted wood-paneled dining and reception rooms as well as lawn tennis and open-air squash courts. There was a well-endowed library, but hardly a book had been withdrawn since the final days of Partition in 1947, when British India split into India and Pakistan. I explained the purpose of my visit. Dressed in white *shalwars*, a tweed jacket, and brown leather sandals, the secretary listened thoughtfully, then waved his hand to a waiting servant. "*Du chai*," he ordered in Pushto. Two teas.

He settled back in his wicker chair, studying me closely. "You have come for a membership?" he suggested, almost hopefully.

"Actually, I am only here for a few days to do some research."

"Ah, but you are welcome to join." Then, with theatrical aplomb, he announced, "We can provide you with free membership." He seemed determined that I become a member. *Why not?* I thought. The secretary slid over an official-looking form. The words DRINKING PERMIT were emblazoned across the top in poorly printed letters. As I picked up my pen, I noticed that it requested to know the "Name of Drunkard," "Father's Name of Drunkard," "Nationality of Drunkard," and "Religion of Drunkard." It appeared that I had the right—as a Christian "drunkard"—to purchase alcohol in Pakistan. In hushed tones, the secretary explained that the club used to make its revenue on liquor sales. Now, with prohibition under the Islamic military dictatorship of General Zia ul-Haq, everything had to be done discreetly. Hence my free membership—that is, as long as I did not plan to drink. The club would use my permit to buy whiskey and beer for resale to its members, including leading citizens of the Peshawar establishment. From then on, whenever I returned to Peshawar, I rejoined the club—not to exercise my right as a Christian drunkard, but primarily to play squash.

Together with Fathers, Lay and I had taken rooms at nearby Dean's Hotel, which was to become my Peshawar haunt whenever I returned during the early 1980s. Dean's was a throwback to the past. Although the food was awful, the rooms, which had once served as bachelor quarters for British officials, were spacious—with a lounge, dressing area, and bathroom. They had good working space and long, English-style bathtubs.

Lay and I traveled around Peshawar and parts of the NWFP to interview officials, academics, merchants, and other local residents. Among them was Khan Abdul Gaffar Khan, the "Frontier Gandhi" who had sought to create a Pathan state by peaceful means, but who would end up dying under military house arrest in 1988. We also met with foreign aid workers and longtime expatriates who knew the country well, and made the inevitable trip to Darra Adam Khel, an artisanal gun-manufacturing village in a tribal area. This dated back to the end of the nineteenth century, when the British considered it better for the Pathans to make their own weapons. Not only would this dissuade them from stealing from the British frontier troops, but the quality of weaponry produced would be inferior. The guns were constructed with poor metal and plagued by constant misfiring. During the 1980s, visits to Darra became de rigueur for any visiting Western journalist or VIP because the gunsmiths would make working replicas of virtually any kind of weapon you wanted, ranging from bullet-firing pens to Kalashnikovs. Even film stars such as Kirk Douglas and Sylvester Stallone traveled to Darra on brief visits to the region. It enabled them to boast that they had dared venture into the forbidden tribal zone near the Afghan border.

In those days, the government still guaranteed a degree of security in the tribal belt, an autonomous and largely mountainous border region running from north to south through the NWFP. Totaling some 10,400 square miles, the NWFP consisted of seven Federally Administered Tribal Agencies (FATA). Six are separated from neighboring Afghanistan, which has its own tribal belt, by the 1893 Durand Line drawn by Sir Mortimer Durand to unilaterally demarcate the British Empire's westernmost borders. This boundary has remained a bone of contention ever since and is still not recognized by the Kabul government. The accepted agreement in the tribal agencies was that outsiders were safe as long as they stayed within a yard on each side of the road.

A trip to Peshawar was never complete without an interview with the political agent for the Khyber, one of the best-informed individuals regarding the ways of the Pathan. With Pathans (or Pushtuns, as they are more commonly known in Afghanistan) operating on both sides of the border, this was a good way of obtaining a broader understanding into the functioning of these tribal groups. The institution of the political agent, or PA, was one of the British Raj's most exceptional legacies. The PA represented the government in its relations with the tribal agencies. Empowered to intervene in disputes and to enforce policy, the PAs were supported by armed local militia—the Frontier Scouts, whose officers were mainly Punjabi from the regular army.

"They're a tricky, devious lot, these tribal people," explained Shakhil Durrani, the Khyber PA at the time. "They are not to be trusted. It's the same with those on the Afghan side. They're all the same people." He pointed to the names of previous British and Pakistani PAs painted in gold on a framed board in his office. "Some of my predecessors met a sticky end at the hands of these tribesmen." According to Durrani, some were murdered, others shot while riding through the mountains. Some, too, were assaulted by tribesmen because they believed the government was providing preferential treatment to another tribe or clan.

"To deal with the Pathans one needs to maintain a sense of balance and fairness," he maintained firmly. "Without this, you'll have no respect." Durrani noted that he could offer protection for visitors in tribal territory, but only if escorted by his own scouts. "What happens in the mountains and hills beyond is out of our hands." Of course, said Durrani—very much a renaissance man with a deep interest in the protection of snow leopards and the Kalash, a non-Muslim minority—a tribe could always offer its own protection. Based on Pushtunwali, the Law of the Pathan, they would be responsible for your safety. If anything happened, it would be regarded as an affront to their pride. "But I am not sure that is an advisable risk," he said with a smile. I was well aware of the many reports of ordinary civilians, including foreigners, being kidnapped— even killed—in retribution for perceived wrongs until appropriate blood money or other forms of compensation were paid.

In Pakistan, the authorities cannot simply intervene when the Law of the Pathan is being upheld. People who have committed crimes— murder, for example—in "settled areas" often disappear into the tribal belt. Similarly, tribal inhabitants do what they like on their side, but must then answer to their own codes. A British officer during the latter days of the Raj described watching helplessly as a father stepped up to execute his own daughter for adultery in order to redeem family honor. The incident happened just inside the tribal zone but within yards of a settled area. To have taken action, the officer knew, would have risked provoking tribal revolt. The girl was slain as she ran toward him, her arms held out, desperately struggling to reach government territory.

As I explored the NWFP, Fathers was busy organizing a meeting with the mujahideen. We would be introduced to the leader of one of the main guerrilla groups now establishing their offices-in-exile on the Pakistani side. We agreed that they should come straight to my quarters at the far side of Dean's, where we could meet more discreetly. We wanted to avoid the pair of Pakistani plainclothes policemen, who, equipped with a motor scooter for hot pursuit, lounged in the shade of a large cotton tree outside reception.

Shortly after breakfast, there was a knock on the door. I opened to find a dozen Pushtuns with beards and turbans looking as if they had just stepped out of the Old Testament. One of them, a slight man in his thirties with a wispy beard and black headdress, sauntered over. "*A*

Salaam Aleikum, may peace be with you. We are the Afghan resistance!"
he announced with no uncertain arrogance and in perfect English. I
shook his hand. It was like grasping a limpid necktie in my palm. He
gave a wan, silky smile and then greeted Fathers and Lay. "I am Engineer
Gulbuddin," he declared.

I offered him a seat, the largest of the armchairs, which he accepted
with a lofty nod. He gestured to his men to sit and launched into a care-
fully enunciated speech. "These are my mujahideen. We are fighting for
Islam. We are fighting the Khalqis [the communist "Masses" faction] in
Kabul. They are trying to take over our homeland, our lives, our families.
We shall fight until we have taken our country back."

One could not help but be impressed. With their turbans, beards, and
hawk-nosed faces, these Afghans looked utterly wild, yet dignified. At
the time, I still had little idea about the nature of Afghanistan's conflict,
but it soon became apparent that these men were deadly serious about
overthrowing the communist regime. I ordered a round of green tea and
biscuits for all.

The haughty guerrilla leader was Gulbuddin Hekmatyar, who ran his
own Hezb-e-Islami (Islamic party) faction and who is still a key player
in Afghanistan. An Islamic extremist, Gulbuddin rapidly developed into
one of the most nefarious and hated of the resistance politicians. Little
did I imagine that this man, who was so evidently in charge of the men
now crammed like subdued schoolchildren onto the couch and armchairs
sipping their tea, would one day be responsible for the brutal deaths of
thousands of Afghan political rivals and critics, including some of the
country's most revered intellectuals. Heavily backed by the Americans,
Hekmatyar also murdered close friends and colleagues of mine. Finally,
he would threaten to kill me for reporting his abuses against ordinary
Afghans.

We talked for two hours. It was difficult to know what to take seriously. Only later did I learn that Gulbuddin had started out as a communist before becoming an insurgent and a leading CIA asset. He carefully
created the impression that he was the insurgency's main figure. Yet most
diplomats insisted that, as far as they could tell, there was no coordinated resistance. With his refined, murmuring tone, Gulbuddin claimed
to have thousands of guerrillas under arms. They were the ones, he

said, who were behind the assaults now being reported against police stations, party offices, teachers, schools and administrative buildings, even road construction and agricultural supply depots located in rural towns. His fighters were increasingly disrupting road traffic by firing on trucks and buses. "We're striking the communists wherever they are," he proclaimed with disdain. "With the support of the Afghan people, we will throw these Khalqis back into the laps of their Soviet masters. And then Afghanistan will be truly Muslim again."

Prior to its invasion, Moscow was already deploying several thousand military and civilian advisers in support of the regime. Many were closely involved with counterinsurgency operations, including punitive assaults against villagers supporting the mujahideen. Soviet pilots, too, were deployed in air strikes against towns such as Herat, where there had been anti-communist uprisings.

Hekmatyar nodded in anticipation when asked where his mujahideen were obtaining their weapons. He made no mention of the Pakistanis, who were already heavily backing him. Of course, many have their own guns. They use them for hunting or, he added with a slight grin, to deal with disputes. "It's a way of life in Afghanistan. But their guns are old. We're now capturing new ones. Many joining the jihad have deserted the army or the police. They have brought their weapons with them."

All this sounded plausible. I was now beginning to worry about heading up to Kabul. Hekmatyar's boasts about mujahed attacks were particularly disconcerting. This information confirmed diplomatic reports about roads being closed for days at a time—with trapped vehicles hit by crossfire, wounding and killing travelers. In one incident, gunmen had fired on an overland "magic bus" from London on the hippie trail to India, killing a Swiss, an Australian, and a Canadian tourist. Trucks, buses, and cars had begun driving in convoy accompanied by armored vehicles.

I began to reassess my plan to travel by public transport from Peshawar to Kabul. The journey alone would make a good story, but the romanticism of front-line reporting was no longer so appealing. All those tales of fierce tribesmen picking off British soldiers in rocky defiles during the three Anglo-Afghan wars of the nineteenth and early twentieth centuries did little to reassure me. It was difficult to determine how dangerous it really was. Should I go by plane? I immediately dismissed this latter option as the ultimate cop-out.

In a last-ditch attempt to talk myself out of the journey, I stopped by the "international" bus terminal in Peshawar. Secretly, I was hoping that the roads would be closed. Instead, a bored ticket clerk barely looked up. The bus for Kabul, he announced, left promptly at 4:30 AM. After a brief stop in Jalalabad, it would continue on to the Afghan capital. The whole journey would take eight hours.

Have there been any problems along the road, I inquired casually.

"Problems? Sometimes we have a breakdown. But we've good buses," the clerk assured me.

"No, I mean, have there been any problems with mujahideen?" I asked. "Bandits?" I added hastily, using the pejorative term for the Afghan resistance just in case he was a left-wing sympathizer, as were quite a few Pakistanis.

"No. No problems. Everything is safe in Afghanistan. We have good buses."

"What about going in convoy?"

"Oh, there're always cars on the road. No problem. You want a ticket?"

Resigned, I slapped my rupees—the equivalent of eight dollars— onto the counter.

"Inside seat or window seat?" the ticket clerk asked.

"Inside," I said. I had no intention of being a target for a well-positioned guerrilla marksman. Hardly eating my dinner, I went to bed early. But I couldn't sleep.

Up well before 3 AM, I sipped my tea in the deserted restaurant pondering my foolhardiness. I wandered over to the terminal. It was crowded with people loading bags onto buses and minivans. To my surprise, the Kabul bus was already full, mainly with hopeful migrants from Sri Lanka heading to Europe intent on sneaking into Britain. The bus driver glanced at my ticket and moved to shove a young Tamil clutching a green canvas bag away from a front window seat.

"No, no, that's all right. Mine is an inside seat. In the middle," I insisted.

The driver studied me curiously, bewildered by my lack of understanding of what constitutes a good seat. The Sri Lankans all smiled and greeted me. "It is good we travel together," said my neighbor, a student from Jaffna. Then, as if we were on the Bristol-to-Paddington train, he asked: "Are you going to London?"

We pulled out of Peshawar as the sun rose. The bus climbed the GT Road up the Khyber Pass until we reached Landikotal, a dusty town famous for smuggling. There, several frontier scouts in dark gray *shalwars* and armed with World War I Enfields boarded the bus, apparently more for the ride than to protect us. Half an hour later, we reached the border post at Torkham, recognizable by its World War II concrete tank traps and massive stone tower flying the green-and-white Pakistani flag. On the Afghan side, apart from some buildings and a slew of container trucks waiting to be processed, there was little except a desultory stone valley edging westward across a dry mountain landscape.

It took about two hours to clear customs. A few other vehicles were heading toward Jalalabad, but to my dismay there was no convoy, and certainly no armored vehicles. I climbed back on the bus, gingerly taking my middle seat. I felt more comfortable when we reached the Jalalabad plains, with irrigated fields and fruit orchards punctuated by mud-and-stone villages. Farmers were tilling the land with bullocks and the odd tractor, while children bathed in the canals by the side of the road. Women in bright-colored dresses but also light blue chadors, or full-length Afghan burqas, pulled water from nearby wells.

I scrutinized the land for signs of violence. We passed a burned-out vehicle. But this could have been the result of a road accident. Occasionally, I noticed tanks and armored personnel carriers (APCs) with uniformed *askari* standing or sitting next to them. It was a similar scene to what I would see thirty years later along the same road, only the tanks and carriers would then belong to a Western-backed government. The land was relatively flat, with the spectacular Hindu Kush rising to the north and the forested, snowcapped Safed Koh range glistening in the sun to the south. This did not look like ambush country. However, every few minutes I found myself wondering whether gunmen were lurking behind the mudstone walls to nip off the odd bus passenger or truck driver.

Looking at the distant fingerlike side valleys leading down from the mountains, I debated whether this was where the fighting was taking place. The Islamabad diplomats had mentioned armed groups descending from Safed Koh to make hit-and-run attacks. From the road, it was too hard to tell whether any of the villages had suffered war damage. At one point, we drove through a series of orange and olive plantations that constituted a large-scale agricultural project established by the Soviets during the 1960s. The objective was to turn hundreds of thousands of desert acres into viable farmland, but the Soviets chose the wrong types of oranges and olives. The oranges were sour, and not a single marketable olive was ever produced.

As we drew closer to Jalalabad, I saw more armored vehicles positioned by the side of the road. Several jeeps with what seemed like Russian or Eastern European advisers, some of them women, drove out from the farm gates. It was only when we passed the airport with its barbed wire and observation posts that there was any sign of serious military activity. Two Mi-8 helicopters surged in across the road at treetop level. The main entrance was guarded by tanks and soldiers. Once in the city, founded in the fifth century as a Gandhara Buddhist center, the bus stopped for lunch. I strolled over to a fruit stall to buy some white grapes. I sat down outside a *chaikhana*, where I ordered a tea and slowly ate my fruit. The grapes were delicious, sweet and succulent.

"*Russki?*" a grinning tea boy asked as he swept the plastic tablecloth with a filthy cloth. I immediately glanced around to see whether anyone had heard him calling me a Russian. I shook my head emphatically. "*Niet. Amerikanietz,*" and then felt like an idiot for having responded in Russian. I was now convinced that I was being watched. The reality, of course, was that no one cared who I was. The Afghans were far more interested in making money out of passing travelers than assassinating them. I looked over to the bus. The Sri Lankans all waved boisterously. "How are you?" they shouted. I wondered whether they had any inkling as to what was going on in Afghanistan. I also wondered whether I did.

Once back in the bus, my Sri Lankan friends kept offering me their window seats. Equally persistent, I thanked them for their kindness. "I really don't like the sun," I lied. However, the more we climbed toward the craggy defiles of Silk Gorge toward Kabul, the more I was convinced that I had made the right decision. The narrowing road was becoming too tight for comfort. Was that a figure peering from among the boulders assessing the worthiness of our bus as a target? I could not help reminding myself that this was the region where, 130 years earlier, in the mountains and ravines near Jagdalak, Afghan tribesmen had annihilated almost an entire British expeditionary force of forty-five hundred soldiers and twelve thousand camp followers attempting to retreat from Kabul in January 1842. Only a few dozen British prisoners and their families, who straggled back months later—and a wounded surgeon, Dr. William Brydon, the sole immediate survivor—avoided being shot or hacked to death.

I would have been even less happy had I known then that only a few years later, during the mid-1980s, this stretch was to become a prime attack zone for mujahideen to harass Soviet convoys. With the roaring Kabul River on one side and steep cliffs on the other, they would hide among the rocks to fire rockets first at the lead truck, then the last, making it impossible for the other vehicles to move forward or backward. The gambit offered little cover to the hapless drivers and troops to escape the murderous fire from above.

It was early evening when we pulled into Kabul. No attacks. No roadblocks. Not even a stray bullet. The capital itself was calm. Little had changed from when I first came here nearly a decade earlier. The bazaars were full and the streets chaotic with traffic. The only thing that appeared different was the lack of tourists. The hotels and dope restaurants were empty. The sole backpackers were an Italian couple with a baby living out of a VW bus. They were still hanging on to stock up on Afghan Black, reputedly the best hash around, before returning overland to Milan. The young man had no idea why everyone had left. The fact that the country was collapsing into civil war had escaped him. Almost with pride, he told me that he had not listened to a radio or read a newspaper in more than a year. I suggested that he take his girlfriend and child and leave.

I left him by the side of his van, pensively filling his chillum. Less than a week later, I saw their vehicle still parked by the side of one of the empty tourist hotels on the other side of the Kabul River.

In Chicken Street, the main thoroughfare for antiques and carpets in Shar-e-Now, the merchants complained of poor business. "Most of the foreigners have gone. The rest are leaving," moaned one vendor. The

Intercontinental Hotel was similarly empty. The Soviet and Eastern European advisers could not afford its bars or restaurants, as they charged US dollars. A Western-style band was solemnly playing to an empty nightclub, while several waiters in red uniforms stood by idly. The musicians were playing a song called "Is Anyone Out There?"

Kabul during the final days prior to the Soviet occupation exuded an eerie atmosphere of normality. For two weeks, I wandered around the capital, talking with people in the bazaars or chatting with students in side-street cafés and restaurants. Most young people were smartly dressed in jeans, short skirts, and chic leather jackets. Some wore scarves discreetly over their heads, but I was struck by their openness—men and women sitting together chatting and laughing. Their music, too, was a mix of Iranian, Afghan, and Western pop.

While one saw numerous women wearing light blue burqas, they were primarily from rural areas. Much of Kabul's middle class was fashionably clothed as if they were in downtown Istanbul or the Shah's Tehran. Some of the women were strikingly beautiful. In one café frequented by students, I settled down to take notes and eat fresh yogurt. "Brown Sugar" by the Rolling Stones blared out from a stereo tape deck. Two men and a woman in their early twenties chatted over Coca-Cola at a nearby table. The young woman, dark with piercing eyes, smiled at me encouragingly. Nothing would ever happen, of course. A relationship with a woman in Afghanistan was not a casual affair.

I ventured into the tourist office, but quickly retreated when the director began asking whether I had registered with the Ministry of Information. He clearly did not believe that I was a tourist. There were few visiting foreigners. Armed militiamen, paid government supporters as well *askari*, patrolled the streets or manned roadblocks. It was all very casual. The only real sign of security was a curfew. Apart from the patrols, the streets were empty by 8 PM. Occasionally, I would see Soviet jeeps with uniformed or plainclothes advisers, but they kept a low profile.

There were also Eastern Europeans—mainly Poles, Hungarians, Bulgarians, and Czechoslovaks—working in development aid. Many were staying at the downtown Kabul Hotel. One Pole, who made no effort to conceal his dislike of Russians or East Germans, specifically told me, in German, to stay away from what they called the GDR (East

German) "scum." "They're all police. They do the same here as in Berlin. They train the Afghan secret police. They're SS. Gestapo. We don't trust them. So why should you?"

At Shor Bazaar near the Friday Mosque, I met Ahmad (a shoe salesman) and his son, Raiz. The father made an overland buying trip once a year to Italy and Germany. They were concerned about the communist government. It was becoming increasingly difficult to travel abroad, they said; people were being arrested and disappearing. The more fortunate families were those who knew that their relatives were being held in Pul-e-Charkhi prison, the latest in prison architecture. Vast and intimidating, the towers and walls of this notorious East German–built edifice were clearly visible from the Jalalabad road on the eastern outskirts. Reports were emerging of suspected anti-government activists being executed within its high barriers. Others had been hauled off to secret police detention centers, where they were tortured. Resistance *shabnamah*, or night letters, were making the rounds—slipped under doors informing Kabulis of these and other developments, including the expanding armed opposition to the communist regime.

My Afghan friends invited me for dinner at their home in the Kabul district of Karte Parwan. Some twenty family members, including women and children, were waiting when I arrived. They had brought out their finest. The dining room table, overflowing with chinaware and cutlery, was set with plastic flowers. I was given the seat of honor. The meal was a feast: plates piled high with rice *pulao*, braised chicken, eggplant and yogurt, grilled beef and mutton, apples, and grapes. As we settled down to eat, the father stepped ceremoniously over to a frosted-glass buffet. It was effusively decorated with framed pictures of meadows from the Swiss Alps, the Kurfürstendam in Berlin, and the canals of Venice. He removed a small bottle of white wine, the sort you get on an airplane. "*Sie müssen trinken*," he announced in German, presenting the bottle to me. "You must drink."

The wine was well over a decade old. Without doubt, it had journeyed from Germany in the back of a truck undergoing dramatic temperature changes from baking desert heat to bitterly cold nights. I protested, saying that I did not need to drink. I wished to respect Muslim customs. But the family giggled, insisting. "You're a Christian from Europe, you must drink," said Raiz, as if all Europeans had to be Christians and consume alcohol. Looking up at this host of scrutinizing faces, I carefully poured the wine and drank. It was syrupy and sour. All I could do was smile, desperately countering each sip with spoonfuls of meat and rice.

While in Kabul, I met with remaining representatives of the international aid community. One, a Swiss agriculturalist, had been working in the Panjshir on a cattle project. The Swiss had opened a dairy outlet in the capital near the Iranian embassy where they sold fresh milk, new types of yogurt, and Swiss cheese. The aid worker said his government had just ordered him home. I also talked with various American and European embassy officials. They all warned of the deteriorating situation. The mujahideen were beginning to infiltrate the city. One young British woman walking at the golf course had been accosted by armed fighters. She only managed to save herself from being killed as a Russian by pleading that she was British and constantly repeating the words: "BBC, BBC." As with most Afghans, the insurgents all listened to the BBC, which they knew came from London, and let her go.

At the US embassy, the marines invited me to a film evening, their big social event of the week. They were friendly but bored and desperate for female company. "Bring any women journalists if they're any around," they shouted from behind their booth guarding the embassy entrance. "We've got beer, Heineken, and Colt 45." I clearly disappointed them when I turned up by myself. I asked how they kept themselves busy. "Oh, we go for runs inside the perimeter or up by the hill behind the military hospital. Apart from that, there's nothing much to do," the sergeant told me. "But we get to watch a movie once a week." They seemed oblivious to the fact that Afghanistan was edging closer to civil war.

It was time to return to Islamabad. I took the regular Pakistan International Airways (PIA) flight. I had considered traveling by bus again but wanted to see the country from the air. The plane, a Fokker F27 turboprop, faithfully followed the route of the bus. From my window, a cloudless day afforded a spectacular view of the Hindu Kush as well as the winding blackness of the asphalt road as it meandered eastward along the Kabul River toward Jalalabad, and onward to the Khyber.

Gazing down, I wondered how the troops of Alexander the Great or the British had ever managed to cross this desperate terrain. How had they kept themselves supplied while warding off marauding tribesmen? Clearly, the British expeditionary force of 1842 had failed miserably against the Afghans. How would the Kabul government and its Soviet advisers cope with this growing insurgency? It would take a massive force to assert even superficial control of the country. The mujahideen could be hiding anywhere. How on earth could an army, any army, track them down amid this tortured landscape of sprawling desert, barren hills, deep ravines, and countless valleys? It would prove a similar challenge for the US-led NATO forces more than a quarter century later. No expert in military matters, I decided that this is what perfect guerrilla country must look like.

Back at the Holiday Inn, there appeared to be more foreign correspondents than usual. "Afghanistan is finally becoming a story," announced Fathers, who, being based in Islamabad, had stopped by to get my impressions of Kabul. Several of us were discussing the latest developments in the coffee shop. I noted an elderly British gentleman at a table on the far side. It was Geoffrey Godsell, diplomatic editor of *The Christian Science Monitor* in Boston. I felt sorry that he should be eating alone and asked him to join us. He politely declined but seemed to appreciate the gesture. Over the next week I wrote my stories. We often chatted while swimming over lunchtime in the pool, where he steadily pursued a rigorous daily regime of laps. "The next time you come through Boston," he said, "please give me a call. Maybe you could do some writing for us."

Two weeks later, I was in New York. With my articles on Afghanistan having just come out in the *International Herald Tribune* coupled with a well-received CBC documentary, I was beginning to make a breakthrough with my foreign reporting. To mull things over, I decided to head up to Martha's Vineyard for the weekend. While waiting at the Boston bus station, I suddenly remembered Godsell. I gave him a ring.

"Where are you?" he asked. I said I was catching the next bus to Cape Cod.

"Can you come to the office? David Anable, the foreign editor, would like to see you. Is that possible?"

I quickly checked the timetable. "I'll catch a cab."

While at the *Monitor*, I briefed Anable on my Afghan trip. He had seen my *Herald Tribune* pieces and liked them. "Can you write something for

us, say, by Monday?" he asked. That Sunday morning, from the hallway
of a small bed-and-breakfast in Edgartown, I loudly dictated by phone my
Kabul story, much to the astonishment of a small handful of guests. Back
in France a week later, I received a call from Anable asking if I wished to
become their special foreign correspondent. Delighted, I agreed.

Toward mid-December, reports of increased Soviet military activity
in Afghanistan began emerging. I also received a long-distance telephone
call from my shoe friends in Kabul. The old man asked if I was returning.
"*Die Russen kommen*," he said. "The Russians are coming." I immediately
called the *Monitor* suggesting that I head out, but Anable was hesitant. I
was a new correspondent, and the paper could not risk such a costly trip
without firmer evidence of impending conflict.

By now, I was doing radio reporting for ABC News with an office at
its Paris bureau. I suggested the story to Pierre Salinger, who was then
bureau chief. But neither he nor Anable had received any solid information to confirm the Kabul reports. "Let's wait a bit," said Anable. Salinger
agreed. By December 24, 1979, more details emerged of large-scale Red
Army troop movements and stepped-up air traffic. On December 27,
the news broke. The Soviet Red Army had invaded Afghanistan. The
Afghan embassy issued me a visa in less than two days. Finally, I was
going to report the Soviet invasion of Afghanistan.

CHAPTER THREE

The Soviet Invasion: You Have Never Been to Afghanistan!

The Red Army invasion of Afghanistan was launched officially on December 27, 1979, with the overthrow and replacement of President Amin with Moscow's own malleable puppet, Babrak Karmal. Head of the Khalq (Masses) faction of the Communist Party known as the PDPA, the People's Democratic Party of Afghanistan, Amin was a brutish Pushtun who massacred thousands of opponents to his communist regime. Karmal, on the other hand, was an ethnic Tajik and head of the more intellectual Parcham (Banner) faction of the PDPA. The Soviets considered him pro-Moscow in outlook, and hence a stooge they could readily co-opt. When Karmal was himself replaced by Afghanistan's last communist leader, Mohammed Najibullah, in 1986, he left for Russian exile, where he died a decade later.

Major Soviet troop deployments, however, had already begun days before. The Soviets closed all civilian airspace and telecommunications, leaving Afghanistan cut off. As it later emerged, the first five thousand Soviet rapid-action troops began landing in heavy Antonov transport planes at Kabul airport two days before Christmas. Advance teams, however, had been flown in weeks earlier. Hemmed in by low mountains, their ridges powdered with snow, Kabul lay in a broad open kettle punctuated by irrigated vineyards among the surrounding hills and plains. Watching the planes dip in through the low clouds over the city, Kabulis mistakenly assumed that these were part of a general airlift bringing in more military advisers and equipment. Similar operations were taking place at Bagram air base to the north, Jalalabad to the east, Shindand to the southwest, and Kandahar to the south.

By the first evening of the invasion in Kabul, Soviet special forces, or Spetznaz, had blown up the main central communications building, cutting off the Afghan military command. They also overran the Ministry of Interior. At roughly the same time, an elite KGB counterterrorist hit team, the Spetsgruppa A, and a unit of special ops commandos stormed Darulaman Palace, a heavy Ottoman-style building ten miles south of the city and just down the road from the Soviet embassy. This was where Amin had taken refuge with his presidential staff and part of his family.

As with everything in Afghanistan, accounts of what happened in the early days of the Soviet invasion vary, often drastically. But all accounts agree that, almost to the very end, the Afghan president Hafizullah Amin, a large man with dark, bushy eyebrows and a heavyset face, had little understanding of what the Soviets had in store for him and the country.

Just two weeks prior to the invasion, the KGB tried to poison Amin through an infiltrated agent working as a cook. However, the Afghan president at the last minute switched his food and drink. Instead, his son-in-law ate the meal and fell violently ill. The KGB tried again to poison Amin, or possibly drug him, with the idea of kidnapping him and his family and removing them from the country. Amin was soon in a stupor and a Russian doctor, who appeared not to be part of the intrigue, was called. The medic put him on a drip as part of his efforts to revive him. Amin's bodyguards, however, would not let anyone else approach the president.

With two failed assassination plots behind them, the Soviets decided to use brute force to remove Amin from power. According to Oleg Balashov, a KGB Alpha commander who was wounded in the attack, only twenty-four Soviets took part in their assault against the three hundred palace guards and militia. Afghan sources suggest the Soviet force was far larger. They had to fight hard to enter the building. The Khalq party faithful put up bitter resistance and suffered high casualties in the process—two hundred dead according to the KGB version. The Afghan sources maintain that the Khalqis managed to stave off the attack for up to four hours, but Balashov claims that the operation took only forty-three minutes with a total loss of five Soviet dead. One version had a KGB attacker shoot Amin dead as he stood groggily by the bar, also killing one of Amin's young sons in the process. Another version has the president crouching behind the bar desperately trying to hide, then being killed by a grenade. For good measure, the Soviets reportedly shot other members of Amin's entourage to eliminate witnesses.

The Soviets announced Amin's overthrow and replacement on Radio Kabul on the evening of December 27. They broadcast a message by the new president pre-recorded in the southern Uzbek city of Termez. Karmal proclaimed that he had personally asked the Soviets to intervene on behalf of the Afghan people. Officially, the broadcast was designed to justify Moscow's invasion against "counter-revolutionary" elements, insinuating that the call for aid had come from the Afghans themselves and was not a unilateral decision by Moscow responding to its own interests. The fact that the Red Army had invaded several days prior to Karmal's broadcast and he was not even physically on Afghan soil when he made it was kept hidden from the Afghan people. It was only a week later that Karmal was brought into Afghanistan.

As these dramatic events unfolded in Kabul, farther north, columns of diesel-belching T-54 and T-64 tanks, heavy artillery, trucks, and fuel tankers of Field Marshal Sergei Leonidovich Sokolov's Fortieth Army, which had been massing for weeks along the USSR's southern frontier, started crossing the slow-moving waters of the Oxus on pontoon bridges into Afghanistan. Troop and supply trains rolled in from Termez, which served as the Red Army's main operations base, and across the wrought-iron Hairatan Bridge to the Afghan side. The dismal border town of Hairatan quickly became the main entry point for the bulk of Red Army soldiers deployed in Afghanistan. Nearly a decade later in February 1989, it was where the last Red Army soldier, General Boris Gromov, finally walked out of Afghanistan and across the bridge into the Soviet Union. Twenty years on in 2009, to mark the twentieth anniversary of the pull-out, a retired Gromov ominously warned that "no military solutions" are possible in Afghanistan and that the United States would suffer the same fate as the Red Army.

Eager to report firsthand the unfolding invasion, I caught the famed Pan Am round-the-world flight (002) as far as Karachi and from there the first available connection to Islamabad. All international flights were being diverted from overflying Afghanistan.

Despite the head start of my previous trip, I arrived irritatingly late. I immediately rushed to the Holiday Inn, where hundreds of journalists were already flocking on local flights or in cars to Peshawar, then by road to the Khyber Pass and the Afghan border, and on to Kabul. Others were heading from Moscow directly into Afghanistan. I immediately hired a car for Peshawar, where I found the town teeming with journalists, photographers, and camera teams, all trying to get to Kabul. Pondering my dilemma at Dean's Hotel, I studied a map. There had to be a better way. I decided to head down to Quetta, capital of Pakistan's Baluchistan province and only an hour's drive from the border to Kandahar, Afghanistan's second largest city. This would give me an unusual, if not unique, angle to the invasion story.

While paying my bill, I bumped into Thierry Boccon-Gibod, a robust bon vivant French photographer with a broad handlebar mustache. I knew Thierry vaguely from Paris—where he worked with Sipa, a photo agency. I convinced him to join me not only for his company but also to provide the *Monitor* with pictures. We grabbed the next flight to Quetta, the capital of Baluchistan in southwest Pakistan.

It was jarringly cold when we reached Quetta. We rode in from the airport in an open, horse-drawn *tonga*. A pall of smoke hung over the town, and there was the same strong smell of dust, burning charcoal, and petrol fumes that characterizes so many Indian subcontinent cities. A former colonial administrative center, Quetta was located in a broad, fertile valley hemmed in by dry, craggy mountains. Planes have to make a sharp, veering turn to land, causing passengers to close their eyes and pray. Irrigated fruit groves neatly lined with poplars surround the town before receding into the desert.

According to an American missionary working for years on Pakistani agricultural projects, Baluchistan could become the California of Pakistan; if only, he added, the military dictatorship were to develop proper irrigation in this arid, southwestern region—Pakistan's most neglected province—rather than spending billions every year on keeping itself in power. Baluch tribesmen seeking greater autonomy, or at least more attention, were regularly revolting against the Islamabad regime. By 2010, Baluchistan was hardly any closer to attaining this dream. Instead, Quetta had become a principal operating base for the Afghan Taliban headed by a *shura*, or council, representing different insurgent groups.

Thierry and I checked into the Lourdes Hotel, where we had to decide whether to sleep in a room warm but stifling with a smoking coal stove, or bitterly cold with fresh air. I had heard of people dying from asphyxiation from these ancient stoves, so we chose the latter. We crawled into our sleeping bags tucked inside the bed blankets. Of course, as a Frenchman, Thierry insisted on smoking his foul-smelling Gauloise cigarettes hunched up in his bed. I had worked long enough with French journalists to know better than to try to persuade one from forgoing his *cloppe*.

Quetta was already teeming with thousands of Afghan refugees. Many had fled Afghanistan prior to the invasion, but more were now crossing over in even greater numbers. Fueled by outlandish rumors, reports of entire villages being wiped out by nerve gas or mass executions had struck fear among ordinary Afghans. As in any conflict, rumor can prove even more destructive than war itself.

The refugees arrived with their pickups, buses, cars, bullock-drawn wagons, and even taxis—packed with suitcases, boxes, and chickens. Children bundled against the cold sat on top, curiously gazing at their new surroundings. For many, it was the first time they had seen a city. Others came by horse, camel, and donkey, some leading flocks of fat-tailed sheep. Destitute, many were already selling their animals. Their miserable tented camps were beginning to punctuate the outskirts of the town and the border areas.

The talk among Afghans and Pakistanis alike in the *chaikhane* was about the invasion. This was no surprise, as constant updates were being reported on the Dari and Pushtun services of the BBC and VOA. Political commentators endlessly debated the reasons the Soviets invaded Afghanistan.

Officially, the Kremlin claimed to have acted according to its treaty obligations with Kabul. On December 5, 1978, nearly eight months after the communists came to power, the USSR signed a "Treaty of Friendship, Good-neighborliness and Cooperation" with Afghanistan. According to the government line, the invasion (or "intervention," as Moscow preferred to call it) was a legitimate response to the subversion promoted by "imperialist external forces" and "terrorists." For the mujahideen, the Soviet invasion only hardened their resolve to resist both communism and unwanted foreigners.

Some analysts took a historic perspective. They reminded audiences of Russia's long-standing desire—dating back to Peter the Great in the early eighteenth century—for direct access to the warm waters of the Indian Ocean. Others spoke of Russia's fear of militant Islamic spill-over into the Soviet Union. The Soviets maintained vivid memories of the *basmachi* (bandit) wars in Central Asia, local and regional uprisings during the 1920s when Islamic militants and nationalists were brutally put down by the Bolsheviks.

In the end, there was probably no single motive, but rather a composite of geopolitical factors mixed with opportunism considered vital to Moscow's immediate and long-term interests.

Foremost was the need to prevent the PDPA regime from being toppled by the expanding mujahideen. The Soviets had spent more than half a century in direct competition with the Americans in Afghanistan as part of Cold War rivalry. Ever since the early 1950s, the two countries had been supporting Afghanistan with international development and military aid in a bid to strengthen their mutual positions in the region. The Soviets were not about to see these efforts undermined as Amin edged closer to the United States. But the Soviets probably misread Amin's actions. Amin, who had once worked for the American embassy as a translator, had no particular fondness for the United States but rather was engaged in the age-old Afghan game of playing off one outsider against the other. Furthermore, Amin was also reportedly engaged in wooing various insurgent tribal groups, some of them operating out of Pakistan. The rebels, he believed, might agree to accept him as leader in return for a watering down of his government's more radical reforms. This included the forced education of girls or mandatory land redistribution, which threatened to undermine traditional water and tenant rights. Nevertheless, the Soviets later conveniently labeled Amin as an "agent of American imperialism."

Even if the Kabul regime had fallen to the mujahideen, no truly independent Afghanistan could afford to act inimically toward its giant neighbor to the north. Moscow could have continued with its dominance through development aid and trade. Nevertheless, already worried by the collapse of the Shah's regime in Iran with a Khomeiny-led Islamic revival, the Kremlin was reluctant to have the same thing happen in Afghanistan. One radical Muslim regime on its border was enough.

Another motivating factor for the Soviet invasion was Afghanistan's strategic position. Complete control of this landlocked country—only a day's drive through Baluchistan to the Indian Ocean—would significantly augment the Soviet Union's leverage in South Asia, Africa, and the Middle East. It would significantly increase its access to the Gulf States, which contained 56 percent of the world's known oil reserves. An eventual base in the Pakistani warm-water port of Gwadar would furnish Moscow with a crucial anchor to complement its access to military base facilities in Ethiopia and Aden in South Yemen.

Most critical of all, the Soviet invasion eliminated Afghanistan as a traditional buffer between the USSR and what was once British India. With Moscow directly controlling Afghanistan, Pakistan suddenly found itself under pressure from two sides, India to the east, and Red Army troops to the west. The Soviets could now conduct cross-border subversion, such as the smuggling of arms to dissidents opposing Pakistan's dictator, Zia ul-Haq.

Pakistan's main foreign policy concern has always been India. The Indians maintained good relations with the Soviet Union, and the Pakistanis were concerned about a second front building on the Afghan border. They were also concerned that the Soviets would increase their support for Pushtun separatists who were clamoring for an independent Pashtunistan. The Pakistanis immediately stepped up their support for the mujahideen. By the mid-1990s, this resistance backing was translated into direct weapons and funding support by ISI, Saudi, and other Islamic interests for the Taliban.

But for the Soviets, Iran was even a greater threat. Like Pakistan, Tehran also began stepping up its support for the Afghan resistance, particularly those from the Shiite Hazara minority. Soon, the Khomeiny regime would radically heighten its anti-Soviet rhetoric.

With predictions heralding a general political destabilization throughout the region, I was eager to get into Afghanistan and find out what was really happening. According to local truck drivers, there was nothing preventing one from crossing into Afghanistan—the border post had been abandoned. The next morning, shortly after dawn, Thierry and I caught a local bus with only a handful of passengers to the frontier settlement of Spin Boldak to see for ourselves. As this was considered a "settled area," we did not need permits.

The Quetta-to-Kandahar highway, all asphalted, represented a vital trading route for both countries. With Karachi on the Indian Ocean serving as Afghanistan's free port, duty-free goods were shipped up to Quetta. On entering Afghanistan, much of this merchandise was turned around and smuggled back into Pakistan. Though supposedly clandestine, all this was done with the connivance of Pakistani officials. Everyone benefited from kickbacks. The same thing happened with the Peshawar-to-Jalalabad route. I was always bemused to behold tribesmen leading strings of bobbing camels, horses, and donkeys laden with air conditioners, tires, and refrigerators down narrow ravines or dry river-beds within sight of the Khyber Pass. Once in the settled areas, they sold their goods at rates far lower than those directly imported—and heavily taxed—into Pakistan.

Heading past the last Pakistani town of Chaman, we finally drew up at Spin Boldak, where Thierry and I presented our passports. The Islamabad government had ordered up additional troops to monitor the frontier. I chatted with the Punjabi officers, who were curious as to why two Westerners should wish to make their way into Afghanistan. I asked whether they had witnessed anything unusual.

"The Afghans have vanished like sands in a storm," announced a major with a thin black mustache in impeccable English. Well groomed in his khaki uniform, he looked the complete professional soldier. "There is no one there," he added, gesturing with his head to the Afghan side. The red, black, and green flag was clearly flying from a distant group of customs buildings, but I could see no one. We turned to leave. "May God be with you," the officer said, shaking my hand. "You are indeed brave people. You do know that these Russian chaps are in Afghanistan?"

I smiled at the archaic way he phrased his question. As journalists, I explained somewhat presumptuously, it was our job to report. He nodded gravely. "Very good, then you must come and have tea when you return."

Accompanied by two or three of the major's men, we trudged several hundred yards to a clutch of dusty yellow and white Afghan taxis waiting on the edge of no-man's-land. It was much warmer here than in Quetta, but I could see heavy rain clouds forming to the west. I negotiated with one of the drivers. He had just arrived from Kandahar with a carload of refugees and was delighted to have a return fare. The Soviets, he warned, were out by the airport. "Only the Khalqis are in the city," he explained, shaking his head. "We don't want these people in our country."

We both climbed in, with Thierry in the front to shoot photographs, and me in the back with my notebook, jerkily scribbling comments as we traveled. We drove the short stretch to the Afghan post. It was deserted apart from a few dogs rummaging around the rubbish heaps. We were half expecting to find at least a Red Army tank, but there was not a single Soviet. A bit farther on, we found a group of unshaven Afghan *askari* (soldiers). Part of the country's fifty-thousand-strong but heavily demoralized army, they lounged by the side of a road barrier with their assault rifles. A bored corporal glanced at our passports. He carefully studied mine upside down, making as if to read it by turning the pages from back to front in the Arabic manner. Then he smiled and waved us on. They did not seem the slightest bit concerned by the invasion, as if it had nothing to do with them.

There was little traffic along the fifty-mile highway, built by the Americans during the 1960s. In that period, the Soviets constructed the north-to-south roads, while the Americans focused on the east-to-west ones. Clearly, the direction chosen by the Soviets served the invasion better. The landscape was dry and barren, but became greener with irrigated farms the closer we got to Kandahar.

We stopped regularly to let Thierry photograph. Most of the refugees, the driver said, were traveling along backcountry tracks. Only occasionally were there cars or the odd bus carrying local travelers or unenthusiastic-looking Afghan conscripts. The Soviets were clearly not going to win a war if they had to rely on these troops.

On approaching the city, the only sign of the invasion was the heavy presence of helicopters and transport aircraft landing and taking off at the airport to the south of the highway. Tempting though it was to turn off to investigate this vortex of military activity, we decided to continue on to town and arrived just as twilight was setting in. It had been raining for several days, and the normally dusty provincial capital was a quagmire of mud. Everything appeared absurdly normal. Contradicting earlier reports of severe food shortages, we found the bazaar thriving, with turbaned merchants squatting behind abundantly piled stocks of vegetables and spices, loudly plying their trade.

In the crowded streets, cars and trucks jockeyed with horse-drawn *tongas*, aggravatingly honking their horns. Motor-scooter rickshaws, with colored plastic tassels attached to their windshields, zipped through the lanes—barely missing the dirt-caked street urchins selling cigarettes. Constantly pestering with groping hands and shrill voices, they beseeched passersby to buy—"*Cigaret? Cigaret?*" If refused, they cheekily demanded *baksheesh* or dollars. A blanket of blue haze hung languidly over a town that hardly seemed at war or at the brunt of a massive invasion.

We found a modern but empty hotel that had seen better days. Tourism had just begun to expand during the mid-1970s. Colorful posters on the walls depicted enticing scenes of the seventeen-hundred-year-old Buddhas at Bamiyan, the turquoise waters of Band-e-Amir, the Friday Mosque in Herat, and the Bala Hissar fort in Kabul. The owner, a friendly Pushtun, was excited at the prospect of visitors who were not Russian.

Over the past few months, he noted, the hotel had received small groups of tourists, either foolhardy or ignorant travelers making their way to Herat or the Afghan capital. In recent weeks, however, there had only been the occasional Westerner. When I asked about the invasion, he shook his head sadly. "This is not good for Afghanistan," he said. When Thierry and I ventured back out into the streets, the hotel owner anxiously warned us of the curfew. "You must not stay out too late. It can be dangerous."

By eight o'clock, half an hour before the government lockdown, the city was empty. Outside, the sonorous wailing of a mobile loudspeaker called on inhabitants to remain in their homes. With a stricter curfew than in Kabul (9 PM), Kandahar was considered to be far more insecure. It foreshadowed the immediate post-Talib period in 2003 and 2004, when the Americans remained holed up at the airport and most international aid agencies had curtailed the bulk of their activities for fear of attack. On our first night, however, the city remained eerily quiet. We heard only the muffled sounds from radio and television sets, the barking of dogs, and the grinding engine of a passing military vehicle.

For the next three days, Thierry and I wandered around Kandahar. There was just one other journalist there, and we exchanged notes standing amid the bustle and mud of the bazaar. "Really bizarre situation here," he said, equally astonished at the lack of a Soviet presence. "The place is not exactly crawling with the Red Army."

With Thierry, who moved among the shops and alleyways shooting photographs, I talked with shop vendors and artisans, but also a young engineering student sitting over a pot of tea in a smoky *chaikhana*. "The *Shouravi* don't come into town, but we know they're out there. Maybe they're afraid," he said with a cheeky smirk. As in other towns, the Soviets were confining themselves to the airports and the main bases. Instead, sulky *askari* were left to protect the main post office, government buildings, gas stations, banks, and other essential establishments. Armed hard-line militia wearing blazers or suit jackets with *shalwars* roamed the streets, stopping to check IDs or search for weapons.

During daylight hours, the only indications of military activity were the occasional army jeeps or APCs carrying armed soldiers and officers in Afghan uniform. Sometimes they were accompanied by men with European features in civilian clothes, probably the very Soviet advisers who had been laying the groundwork for the invasion over the past weeks and months. At night, it was a different story. Urban guerrillas controlled the rooftops and back alleys. They distributed *shabnamah*, night letters, a common form of communication later also used by the Taliban to send warnings to the local population not to collaborate with NATO forces.

I tried to piece together what had happened. "It was the most unusual coup," the Indian consul in Kandahar elaborated in a clipped, singsong voice. I had simply knocked on his door and was amazed that he invited me in to discuss the invasion. "There were no observers, no tanks, and no excitement. A very curious situation." Soviet aircraft had begun landing and taking off in only slightly larger numbers at the airport since Christmas, he explained, but that was nothing unusual. On New Year's Eve, however, the city erupted in protest. Gripped by panic, merchants abruptly shuttered their shops at nine in the morning, having just opened for the day. Huge crowds of men gathered in the streets and the main squares. Fantastic rumors spread of executions, rape, looting, and other atrocities by the communists.

"No one had actually seen the invaders," noted the Indian consul, "but this did not seem to matter. The people were clearly very angry. Very angry indeed."

At the central bus station, mob violence broke out. People screaming insults against the Soviet Union and the new Karmal regime rampaged through the streets attacking anything and anyone representing the communists. They overturned and burned army vehicles, smashed windows, ripped down propaganda signs, and tore the red Khalqi flag to shreds. Under the first PDPA government, the Khalqis had changed the Afghan flag to one more like that of a Soviet central republic. Amin had introduced a new version incorporating Afghanistan's traditional red, black, and green colors, but many of the older flags remained. Government troops appeared and shooting erupted. Unable to quell the rioting, the authorities called in the Afghan air force. They thundered in to strafe buildings and open spaces with rocket and cannon fire. According to witnesses, however, the aircraft appeared to try to disperse rather than kill the demonstrators. It later emerged that some Afghan pilots had refused to fire on their own people.

By the end of the afternoon, a dozen people had been killed. These included three unfortunate Soviet advisers from a nearby textile mill who had gone to the bazaar to do some New Year's shopping. They were dragged from their vehicle and lynched on the spot. The Soviets immediately evacuated all their families living at a UN residential complex. By late afternoon, large numbers of Afghan troops were patrolling the streets. Jeeps with loudspeakers appealed to the local population to remain calm. Once again, the Red Army troops stayed out of sight, a deliberate policy to enable the Afghan authorities to deal directly with the people.

The next day, on New Year's, the invasion proper of Kandahar began. "Then it was quite clear what was happening," the Indian consul continued. "And by God, it was a noisy affair." One transport plane after another droned in from the north, while just outside the airport perimeter, tanks and armored vehicles of the Sixty-sixth Motorized Division moved into position. The heavy air traffic, including the arrival of a fleet of Mi-24 helicopter gunships, continued for two days. The Soviets began running sorties almost immediately against guerrilla positions in the nearby mountains northeast of the city. The consul said he could hear the distant roar of fighter aircraft as they took off and then looped around the city before surging off to strike their targets.

Finally, armed with enough photographs and reporting, Thierry and I decided to head back to Quetta. We hired another taxi to the Pakistani border, but planned to stop off at the airport first. At the turnoff, we encountered a roadblock manned by *askari* and police. Two APCs were parked across the tarmac with spiked treads splayed out in front of them. A soldier armed with an AK-47 walked over.

"*Sarak band hast!*" he told us in Dari, dismissively waving for us to turn around. "The road is closed." Many soldiers were deployed in parts of the country well away from their home regions. A good portion of the *askari* in Kandahar were Dari speakers from northern or western Afghanistan. It was the same the other way around, with eastern Pushtuns positioned in towns like Mazar or Faizabad. This made it harder for them to desert.

Through the driver, who spoke some English, I insisted that we needed to catch the daily Bakhtar flight to Kabul. The soldiers and police briefly talked among themselves and then, with a shrug, lifted the spiked tread. Once at the terminal, we entered cautiously. No one challenged us. The building was packed with bewildered Afghan police, civilian airport personnel, and (finally) our first Red Army soldiers. Most of them conscripts, they stood or crouched in rows around their duffel bags and other gear. Dragging on their *papyrossi* cigarettes or playing cards, they looked up as we walked past. Behind them, mocking the absurd dilemma of a country now under military occupation, billboards continued to promote Afghanistan as a prime tourist destination. Equally enthusiastic posters were displayed for Ariana, the national airline, and Bakhtar, its domestic partner—both exhorting passersby to fly in comfort with "service and hospitality."

While Thierry wandered off to shoot pictures, I walked up to the Bakhtar counter, nonchalantly asking about the next flight to Kabul. The desk officer, a clean-cut young man wearing a suit, stared up at me in amazement. "There are no flights today," he said, shaking his head.

"Then what about tomorrow? First class if you're full," I could not help adding.

"No, there are no flights tomorrow." Then, leaning forward, he added: "You should not be here. You should leave. Now."

I acknowledged his concern with a slight nod, but continued roaming the terminal, hoping to obtain a more detailed glimpse of Soviet activity on the tarmac through the broad glass windows and doors. Five camouflaged Antonov transports were being unloaded by troops on the slipways. At one point, I even managed to step outside. Amazingly, no one stopped me. Over a thirty-minute period, I counted no fewer than a dozen Mi-8 and Mi-24 helicopter gunships with rocket pods and guns. They flew in low and then landed, rolling toward huge piles of supplies stacked along the aprons. Without cutting their engines, the crews waited as ground personnel loaded on new ammunition. Minutes later, the helicopters roared off toward the Khada Hills to the east or the Shah Maqsoud range to the west.

A friendly but anxious Afghan policeman stepped up to me. "It is much too dangerous for you to be here. You must leave," he begged. "Please. We do not want anything to happen to you. The KHAD may see you," he added, referring to the government's ruthless secret police. I thanked him for his concern and signaled Thierry. "We'd better go. I think we're pushing it," I whispered.

Slowly, we made our way out of the building. The taxi was still there, the driver talking in a low voice with three other men, all nervously smoking cigarettes. One hurried over to embrace us, warmly shaking our hands. He murmured a short prayer and placed his hand over his heart in greeting. We climbed back into the car and drove off to the highway before turning eastward in the direction of Pakistan. A pair of Soviet helicopter gunships roared across the road at several hundred feet and over irrigated farmlands before swinging off toward the desolate mountain ranges beyond. This was where growing numbers of mujahideen had begun establishing their bases, which would serve throughout the occupation as a launch area for hit-and-run assaults against the Soviets.

The irony with Kandahar Airfield, or KAF as the NATO forces called it more than two decades later, is that it was built by the Americans in the 1960s. Designed as a refueling stage for commercial flights linking Europe with India and the Far East, it was also intended to serve as a US military base should the United States and Soviet Union ever confront each other in armed conflict. By the time KAF International was ready, however, the first long-haul 747 jumbo jets had come onstream. There was no longer any need for the airport as a refueling stop. Instead, it provided the Red Army with a ready-made base when it invaded. By 2006, with US troops fighting their own war against the Taliban and their insurgent allies, KAF had been turned into a massive logistical headquarters for the Coalition's Regional Command South (operated by the Canadians). It also boasted the world's busiest military single runway airbase, with over five thousand takeoffs and landings every week.

By the time we returned to Spin Boldak, the Afghan authorities had reestablished themselves. We pulled up in front of the customs building, where a lone official in a dust-covered green uniform sat in front of a table outside his door. He frowned in astonishment when he glanced at our passports, letting out a stifled gurgle of dismay.

"Where is your entry permit?" he demanded, almost shouting.

"We don't have any. There was no one when we came in," I explained.

"This is not possible," he said, shaking his head. He scrutinized the documents even more closely, carefully turning the pages.

"There is no entry stamp," he said. "Where is the entry stamp?"

"There was no one here when we arrived," I insisted.

"That is not possible," he whispered.

Finally, he shook his head, clearly perplexed by this outrageous administrative gaffe. He looked quickly around and then surreptitiously slipped back our passports over the table. "Please go," he said quietly. "You have never been to Afghanistan."

I was delighted. I still had a valid visa.

As we drove out of Spin Boldak, I reflected on Afghanistan's varied and often inhospitable terrain and wondered how the Soviets thought they would prevail when so many foreigners before them had failed to achieve a stronghold in the country. Landlocked Afghanistan's northern plains reach into the steppes of Turkmenistan, Uzbekistan, and Tajikistan, while to the east the twenty-five-thousand-foot Hindu Kush mountains, known as the "Killer of Hindus," stretch westward before petering out into the foothills of Herat. To the south, the country's rough scrubland merges into the broad baking deserts of Baluchistan and, eventually, the Indian Ocean. Most of the country is uninhabited space, composed of semi-arid wastes or treacherous highlands with impassable ridges, gravel-strewn valleys, and deep gorges. Not the sort of land that lends itself to easy control by outside forces.

Nor were the Soviets likely to find a coherent people to control. Afghanistan is a linguistic, cultural, and geographic mosaic of highly diverse people—Pushtuns, Nuristanis, Tajiks, Uzbeks, Turkmen, Hazaras, and others—who, traditionally, never like being told what to do by foreigners. Nor do they like being ruled by one another. Every Afghan regards himself as "King amongst Kings," with the same right to have his views heeded as any other Afghan, beggar or monarch.

The Soviets, much like the Americans over twenty years later, engaged militarily in Afghanistan to impose an external form of government that ran inherently counter to Afghan traditions and beliefs. For local leaders, particularly tribal Pushtuns who have traditionally ruled Afghanistan and may still represent a majority (the last census was in 1978), their first allegiance has always been to their families, villages, and clans. Only secondarily do they identify with their valleys and regions before finally with Afghanistan itself. There was not then, nor is their now, any appetite in Afghanistan for strong central governments promoting a common vision of governance, whether it be communist or democratic.

Afghanistan, in short, is a country that was then and is now divided. Traditionally, the northern Uzbeks, Tajiks, and Turkmen have turned to Central Asia, as most can comprehend one another's languages and dialects. For their part, the Mongolian-featured Shiite Hazaras from the Central Highlands, historically the underdogs of Afghan society, have looked westward toward Iran for spiritual guidance, jobs, and (since the Soviet invasion) weapons and money. Most households will have a picture of the Iranian spiritual leader, Ayatollah Khomeiny, on the wall, while many still consider Iran as their best chance for migratory labor.

The primarily Tajik *Farsiwan* (Farsi speakers) of Herat have traditionally maintained close links with Iran for cross-border trade. The eastern or southern Pushtuns and the Baluch—another tribal group spread across Iran, Afghanistan, and Pakistan—have more affinity with Pakistan and the Indian subcontinent. Most of the trade for Kabul, Kandahar, and Jalalabad comes from Pakistan.

All this has made it patently difficult to encourage any form of lasting national unity. A few past rulers have managed to inspire a degree of nationhood, notably Ahmed Shah Durrani, the first of the Pushtun kings, who introduced the idea of a united Afghanistan in the mid-eighteenth century. Another king, Abdur Rahman Khan, further developed the vision of nation-building at the end of the nineteenth century by establishing firmer centralized rule. Even then, his control over the provinces remained precarious. For many Afghans, the regions are where the real power lies. Afghan politicians and warlords still prefer to be appointed provincial governors rather than ministers. Far from the capital, the provinces are where they successfully manage their fiefs and business ventures, be it narcotics, timber trafficking, land theft, or the large-scale theft of international aid and military funds.

Since the first heady days following the Soviet invasion, I have watched as first the Soviets—and now the West—attempted to impose a political and cultural future for Afghanistan that was not consistent with traditional Afghan culture and beliefs. Countless lives have been lost by those trying to impose themselves and their foreign ideas. The stony graves of many foreigners, from a nineteenth-century British soldier picked off by a Pushtun sniper to a Soviet pilot who preferred to shoot himself rather than risk capture, silently mark windswept passes or boulder-strewn hillsides.

Over the years, I encountered hundreds of Afghans who told poignant and sometimes gruesome stories of their encounters with "foreign invaders." Etched in my mind is the face of the gnarled old shepherd, whose voice trembled as he told the story of the night that red-starred helicopters suddenly emerged over the ridge to destroy his village. Equally vivid is the pride of the former mujahed who led me to the spot where he and his men had ambushed a Soviet patrol. Using his arm as a gun, he demonstrated how he fired point-blank at a wounded young Russian soldier who could only stare back at him with hatred and fear.

CHAPTER FOUR

Baluch Guerrillas, Learning · Curves, and Massacres

B y the time I got back to Peshawar, refugees were streaming across the sixteen-hundred-mile border in the thousands. Nationwide resistance did not happen overnight. Communist repression drove farmers, shopkeepers, teachers, civil servants, journalists, academics, army officers, religious leaders, tribal chiefs, and nomads into exile, but it was the invasion that transformed the exodus into a veritable deluge of humanity and eventually a "migratory genocide." This was a deliberate Soviet-backed strategy to rid the country of unwanted opposition elements by making conditions so intolerable that the country's estimated fourteen to fifteen million people could only accept the regime, leave the country, or die. As Sayed Abdullah, the Khalqi commander of Kabul's notorious Pul-e-Charkhi prison, announced in a party speech: "A million Afghans are all that should remain alive—a million communists. That's all we need."

My plan was to visit some of the hundreds of camps mushrooming in the desert and mountainous areas up and down Baluchistan and the NWFP and to report on the plight of the Afghan refugees. But what really excited me was the thought of undertaking my first clandestine trip with the mujahideen "inside"—the new expression used by journalists and aid workers for anything cross-border.

While in Quetta, a largely Pushtun city (*kwatta* means "fort" in Pushto), I had managed to contact two Baluch resistance representatives who were eager to take foreign journalists into Helmand. The province was best known for a broad strip of agricultural land watered by the Helmand River Valley Project, started by the Americans during the 1950s. The United States abandoned its support for the project's large-scale hydroelectric dam and network of irrigation canals when the communists took power in 1978. Somehow, though, even at the height of the Soviet-Afghan war it kept operating. Today it remains one of Afghanistan's most highly productive agricultural areas, boasting the world's largest opium poppy crop.

Even before the invasion, Baluch guerrillas had been launching raids against communist positions. When these stepped up following the events of December 1979, the Soviets started flying reprisal sorties with MiGs and helicopter gunships against suspected guerrilla targets. My Baluch contacts were working with several resistance parties. Nevertheless, they recommended that, once back in Peshawar, I should get in touch with Jamiat-e-Islami, which was already emerging as one of the major fundamentalist groups.

As with most of the exile political parties, Jamiat had established its headquarters in the Afghan colony on the northern side of the city. This consisted of a warren of concrete buildings, mud-and-stone compounds, inner courtyards, narrow alleys, and canals. Traditionally a residential and business district for Afghan merchants, it was now being taken over by refugees and mujahideen. Ensconced in Dean's Hotel, I caught a tuk-tuk to the Jamiat office. Four days later, a party representative stopped by to say that everything was ready. All I had to do was make my way back to Quetta, where further arrangements would be made to help me cross into Afghanistan.

But first, one of the Jamiat men took me to the Peshawar bazaar to purchase a beige *shalwar-kamiz*, brown leather sandals, and a *patou*—a woolen blanket to drape over my shoulders. The pièce de résistance was a twenty-foot-long strip of gray cloth, my turban. The guerrilla showed me how to wrap it around my head. "You now look like a mujahed," he said, stepping back. "But you must grow a beard." I swirled around like Peter O'Toole in *Lawrence of Arabia*, only to realize how ridiculous I must look. There was no way that I would pass as a surly Afghan with my blue eyes, blond curly hair, and clean-cut appearance. I never mastered the art of tying a turban. It kept unfurling whenever I walked.

Back at the hotel, I received a call from Judah Passau, an American photojournalist from Paris. A small man with black-rimmed glasses, he looked, acted, and sounded like Woody Allen. He was desperate to get into Afghanistan, but only for a few days. I told him about Baluchistan, even hinting that the trip could prove dangerous. I was feeling quite the veteran, and a bit smug (a hazardous sign—as I later learned—for anyone working in conflict zones). Judah had been a sapper in the Israeli army, so he did not seem overly concerned. In fact, his job was to remove land mines when his country's commander in chief, Ariel Sharon, traveled by jeep. Two other journalists, Kore Werpe from the Norwegian daily *Morgenbladet* and Rauli Virtanen of Finland's *Helsingin Sanomat*, also joined us. I sent them off to the bazaar for their local garb. When they returned, I noted with satisfaction that they looked even more absurd than me.

We caught the next flight to Quetta and headed to the mujahed office, a walled compound that doubled as sleeping quarters. It was owned by a Pakistani merchant who sympathized with the resistance. Many Pakistanis were helping their Afghan brethren in this way. Some were clan or family members, but others provided support as part of their Islamic charitable duty, known as *zakat*. About twenty turbaned fighters in their early twenties sat on the floor listening to the radio and drinking tea. To me, they looked saliently devious, but they all grinned and nodded when we entered, raising their right hands to their hearts in a concerted *"A Salaam Aleikum."*

It was hard to understand how the guerrillas had managed to galvanize a fighting body so quickly. According to Tariq, the mujahed liaison officer, his group had nearly a thousand men under arms, most of them fighting in southeastern Helmand with different parties. The truth was that I had little idea who these Baluch really were. I was aware that Baluchistan as a region straddled three countries—Afghanistan, Pakistan, and Iran—and that separatist factions had been confronting all three governments for decades. Some were overtly left-wing, others more nationalist. The Pakistani Baluch, who resented Islamabad's lack of investment in a province rich in natural resources—coal, natural gas, and possibly petroleum—had been stepping up their violence since the early 1970s with weapons and ammunition smuggled in from the Afghan side. For most of these groups, their goal was independence, or at least autonomy, and beyond that the unification of all Baluch regions into a single nation. But as with Pushtun nationalists seeking an independent Pushtunistan or the Kurds farther to the west in Iran, Iraq, and Turkey with their desire for an independent Kurdistan, none of their state rulers has any intention of allowing a united entity to emerge.

Many of the tribesmen now opposed to Kabul were involved in narcotics trafficking. Much of this trade was shifted across the desert at night by fast-moving pickup trucks into Pakistan and Iran. Helmand province was rapidly turning into a major opium-poppy-growing area. It was a trade that would continue throughout the Soviet-Afghan war and into the 1990s and 2000s. By the time the Americans intervened in 2001, Afghanistan was running a nearly three-billion-dollar-a-year drug-trafficking industry. By 2010, based on the average British street value of heroin with a 30 percent purity ratio, the total proceeds of annual Afghan heroin sales globally were more than $194 billion. This was the equivalent of the gross national product of countries such as Iran and Finland.

These frontier Baluch were born traffickers. They also dealt with highly prized falcons and other birds of prey, the majority protected by CITES, the Convention on International Trade in Endangered Species. The falcons were used for hunting by wealthy Arabs, who often paid as much as a hundred thousand dollars for a single bird. At one auction at the Pearl Continental Hotel in Peshawar during the early 1980s, the traffickers had taken over two entire floors. White gowned and red-turbaned Arabs with leather attaché cases stuffed with cash strolled the corridors in search of buys. Doors wide ajar, each room hosted up to a dozen birds—hawks, falcons, even eagles—perched blindfolded on stands. It was this contraband network that formed, and helped fund, Afghan Baluch resistance activities. This lucrative wildlife trafficking continues just as strongly today.

My principal concern, however, was to figure out how to get into Afghanistan embedded with the underground mujahideen. A lesson I was soon to learn was that Afghanistan is made up of myriad different tribal or ethnic groups and that no single valley, province, or region is representative of the country as a whole. As one Afghan told me, one needs to understand "a thousand" Afghanistans. I was at a loss as to which mujahed group would give me the best chance at writing an accurate story about the Afghan resistance.

An educated man in his midtwenties with a neatly trimmed mustache, my contact in Quetta, Tariq, had been a medical student at Kandahar

University prior to joining the resistance. Warning that it might take another two or three days to organize the trip, he later admitted that we were the first Western journalists he had ever met. In the meantime, I told him, we would visit the refugee camps, but regularly check the hotel for messages. With phones that never worked properly, handwritten notes sent by motor rickshaws were the only way to operate. Tariq nodded gravely. "That is good," he said. "Many of our people are suffering. You must see how they live."

A team of United Nations High Commissioner for Refugees (UNHCR) representatives staying at the hotel suggested that we visit the frontier area near the towns of Chaman and Pishin. Many new arrivals were coming across the border there, they said. We hired a van and clattered off on a crumbling road to Chaman, a four-hour journey across the mountains. In blinding snow, we reached the top of the 7,513-foot-high Khojak Kotal (pass) linking the nineteenth-century Qilla Abdullah Fort and Chaman, still fourteen miles to the west. One of two main passes linking Afghanistan with the Indian subcontinent—the other is the Khyber—the Khojak Kotal has long been a renowned smuggling route hotly contested by two rival Pushtun tribes, the Achakzai and the Noorzai.

Traversing the mountains, we caught sight of our first makeshift refugee settlements in the plain below. They were still in Pakistan and only a few miles from Spin Boldak. Their tents appeared like swarms of white butterflies clinging to the rocky wastes at the foot of western Pakistan's jagged Toba and Kakar mountain ranges. Chaman served as the initial arrival point for the hundreds of refugees slipping out of their country every night prior to the invasion. Now, with the fighting escalating against the Red Army, the refugees were pouring over the border in even greater concentrations.

The Pakistan government's regional refugee office was located in a colonial-style compound. Local aid workers were distributing blue and red quilts to anxiously waiting Afghan men. We introduced ourselves to the assistant commissioner, a former army officer delighted to have "representatives of the international press," as he put it, visit his zone. Standing in the snow, we sipped heavily sugared green tea from small glasses as he recounted recent events. "Many of the refugees come in their own trucks. But they come on unmarked trails. They have to bypass the Afghan border controls," he said. Sometimes, too, Soviet or Afghan aircraft overflew the border areas within sight of the Pakistani troops deployed nearby.

By the end of January 1980, official estimates put the number of Afghans seeking refuge in Pakistan at seven hundred thousand. But the Western embassies and aid agencies believed the real figure was fast approaching one million. As elsewhere in the country, where related ethnic and tribal groups lived on both sides of the frontier, some new arrivals initially found lodging among relatives. But more and more were now pitching their tents among the four main camps located in stubbled grazing lands a few miles out of town. With the recent heavy rains and snow, the normally parched plains had been turned into squelching, ankle-deep mud.

The enormity of the refugee problem had taken both the Pakistanis and the internationals by surprise. There was an acute shortage of tents, with the UNHCR trying to have them produced en masse in factories outside Karachi. Water had to be fetched from the town, and there were no sanitary facilities. People went to the toilet by trudging out into the fields, now marked by a lingering stench of feces. At least during the hot weather, the sun would burn away much of the detritus, but here it mixed in with the mud. The women, for reasons of modesty, only ventured out at dusk. In warmer areas, this brought the added problem of snakebites. As the evenings cooled, the snakes would seek the open trails where the stones were still warm from the sun.

The assistant commissioner shook his head in dismay. "All this is very bad for health. It brings the risk of disease," he said. "It will take time to build proper facilities. I have a feeling these people are here to stay for quite some time." Within a matter of years, many of these tented towns had become mud-and-stone settlements with thriving bazaars, schools, and clinics, but they remained refugee camps. Many inhabitants, who originally had fled their homes, farms, and businesses, had no means of livelihood other than their refugee rations.

At one hastily erected camp at Boghra, we met with a group of refugees from southern Kandahar who brought us cups of steaming tea. Despite near-freezing temperatures outside, their tent was surprisingly warm. Mohammed Zia, a white-bearded *malik* or clan leader, told us that he and his extended family, some sixty people, had reached Pakistan piled into a Bedford truck and a Soviet-made jeep. They had fled on the first night of the invasion.

There was not a girl or woman in sight. I had seen a few distant shapes wrapped in dark robes rush away as we approached. There were also hardly any young men. "They're fighting with the mujahideen in those mountains over there," the old man explained proudly, gesturing toward the Hada range some twenty miles to the west. "In Afghanistan, we gave the mujahideen food and shelter, whenever they came to our area," he added. "The Khalqis did not like this. They took young men for the army or for prison." I later met some of these young men who had been forcibly conscripted. They were deserters, press-ganged from distant parts of Afghanistan, who had managed to slip away at night to join the guerrillas.

The refugees said they had not seen any Soviet soldiers. "We left because the Khalqis came to take our land," said the *malik*, who as a traditional landlord ruled over some one thousand acres of fruit orchards and wheat fields. Members of his clan worked for him on a fifty–fifty crop-sharing basis, he told us. But when the communists arrived, they ordered the distribution of his properties. When I asked who had received the land, he sighed bitterly: "Khalq party members, peasants, favorites . . . "

"Were any of your people offered land?" I asked.

"Oh yes, but they refused," he declared with evident satisfaction. The man next to him nodded energetically. "I was offered land, but it's against Islam to steal from one man to give to another." Surprisingly, this was a refrain I would hear up and down the border in the months ahead. The refugees complained about other forms of "repression," notably Kabul's efforts to forcibly educate the girls. The Khalqis tried to set up a girl's school, one man remarked with disdain. "But no one went. They sent male teachers from Kabul. This is against Islam, too. We don't want our women to be educated. It's not good."

"Not even by female teachers?" I asked. "Surely girls deserve to be educated."

"No, not even by women," interjected the *malik*. "That is not their job. A woman has no face if she shows herself in public. These Khalqi women from the cities, they have no face." I gazed slowly around at the cluster of men, all middle-aged or older. "How many of you know how to read or write?" I queried. The men laughed. "Only our mullah knows," one of them said. "But he was arrested by the Khalqis. We don't know whether he is still alive."

A few days later, the other journalists and I were sitting at breakfast when Tariq walked in with Mansur, an obsequious man in his early thirties with a high-pitched voice. He was to be our interpreter and guide. Outside stood a dilapidated but sturdy gray Mercedes with a *D* for Deutschland sticker on the bumper. The driver lay back in the front seat, his eyes closed, listening to Iranian pop music.

"You go Afghanistan now," Tariq announced with evident pride.

Finally, my first clandestine trip. The route, Tariq explained, would take us to Dalbandin, halfway to the Iranian border. We would then branch off northward following a track into the Chagai Hills, which constituted the Pakistani-Afghan border. We would have to be careful, he said. Pakistani police and military patrolled the outback. What he did not say was that these patrols were deployed to counter smugglers, either to confiscate their goods or to demand bribes. People were sometimes killed in the armed skirmishes that erupted.

It was a long and hot drive through the desert. Thankfully, the road was tarred part of the way. A railway track for the once-a-week train from Quetta and telegraph lines with wooden poles ran alongside the road to the border town of Zahedan, some 370 miles to the west. Traffic was light, mainly local trucks but also brightly painted buses with jingling chains and multitoned klaxons. There were a few long-haul TIR trailer transports from Europe with British, German, and Turkish drivers. These overland transports would stop as the war in Afghanistan worsened. The Iranians, too, were tightening their controls, mainly to curb heroin trafficking.

To the south rose rocky *jebels* merging into a low range of craggy mountains that eventually opened up into the baking badlands that stretched down to the Indian Ocean. This was what the Soviets would have to traverse if they wanted access to a warm-water port. To the north, the land was flat, sandy, and barren—but occasionally punctuated with farms surrounded by irrigated fields, date palms, and orchards.

We halted at a roadside truck stop for tea, soft drinks, and a bite to eat. A jacked TIR truck with UK plates was parked off the road. Two lone British truckers sat dejected, half a dozen empty bottles of Fanta in front of them. Their rig had suffered a broken axle. They had been waiting for five days for their Karachi office to send up a relief vehicle to off-load the cargo. A hot wind was blowing from the north. Looking at the distant skyline, it seemed inconceivable that a war involving one of the world's superpowers was unfolding just beyond the frontier less than sixty miles away.

We reached Dalbandin toward nightfall. We skirted the town, passing through small adobe settlements before veering northward through a scattered fringe of irrigated farmlands and plunging back into a wasteland gradually rising into the Chagai Hills. That was where we were supposed to meet the guerrillas. Mansur scanned the darkness, incessantly arguing with the driver, who would veer off in one direction and then swerve back toward another. We were clearly lost.

"What are we looking for?" I finally asked Mansur.

"I am looking for the road, sir."

"Do you know where this might be?"

"Oh yes, sir, it is somewhere."

We stopped repeatedly to search the ground with our flashlights. The problem was trying to decipher which of the interlacing trails made by innumerable vehicles was the right one. Our headlights picked up a band of armed men frantically waving at us to stop. The driver began slowing down. I glanced at Mansur, who did not seem reassured. I suddenly realized they were most likely bandits. I bellowed to the driver not to stop. "Drive on!"

Still slowing down, he pointed at the men who now formed a line in front of us.

"No!" I shouted. "No stop. Drive! Fast! Mansur. Tell the driver no stop!"

"But these men are waving to us," he said.

All of us were now shouting. I grabbed the driver's shoulder. "You tell him that if he tries to stop, I'll kill him," I shouted at Mansur. The driver changed gear and we surged forward, hurtling past the gesticulating men. I noticed two pickup trucks parked slightly behind them. None looked broken down.

Eventually, we decided to stop until daylight in order to get our bearings. We slumbered in the car, but it was bitterly cold. As dawn broke, I could distinguish a series of low hills ahead. The driver started up the engine. Two hours later, now apparently in Afghanistan, we pulled into a large village. Three white but dusty Wagoneer four-by-fours, a favorite among the smugglers, were waiting. A throng of turbaned men, four or five shouldering Lee-Enfield rifles, surrounded our car. Several graybeards carried shotguns; one gnarled *baba* (old man) even sported a museum-piece *jezail*, a long-bore rifle that Afghan tribesmen used to deploy against the invading British. These hardly seemed the type of weapons likely to lead the fervent guerrilla fighters to victory against the Red Army.

The commander, a strapping man with a thick black beard, embraced us warmly. He led us to a large carpet laid out in front of a *kudik*, a traditional mud-and-stone dwelling with thatch. A *bacha*, a young servant boy, immediately appeared with green tea, *nan*, biscuits, and a large bowl with thick cream for dipping the bread. None of the thirty-odd Baluch standing around, all men, joined us. The commander smiled and beckoned for us to eat. He then signaled to Mansur. For the next few minutes the two of them spoke intently, sometimes gesturing to the north or to the west. Mansur finally turned to us.

"We leave Mercedes here and travel with mujahideen," he explained. Maybe, too, he suggested, they would take us on an operation. We nodded with solemn expectation. I could not deny that I was both excited and nervous at the prospect.

"Against the Soviets?" I asked.

Mansur translated back to the commander. He smiled. "Maybe the *Shouravi* or the Khalqis," he said. "Maybe both. They're all communist."

Both Judah and Kore wanted to know how long the whole trip would take. "You will be back in three or four days," Mansur assured.

"This is a promise?" queried Kore sternly, as if lecturing a group of schoolchildren. "I have a schedule. I need to be back in time."

Mansur questioned the commander. "Yes," he said, turning back to us. "He agrees."

"Good," said Kore, jotting down a point in his notebook as if this would determine all. "It has been agreed."

Refreshed, we climbed into the vehicles and headed deeper into Afghanistan. The rocky hills were sparsely vegetated with low brush. Sometimes the track followed a dry riverbed, sometimes open valleys and plains. Our three vehicles surged forward at throttling speed, throwing up suffocating clouds of dust. The guerrillas did not seem to care about being spotted by reconnaissance planes.

We passed through half a dozen villages. Each time, people flagged down the vehicles to talk to the commander. He would point at us and the old *babas* would nod thoughtfully, raising their hands in greeting followed by murmurings of *"A Salaam Aleikum."* It took us half a day to reach our first insurgent base in the Alehan Valley, thirty miles inside Afghanistan according to my map. Some two hundred tents were pitched along a parched riverbed with trucks, tractors, Wagoneers, and pickups parked among the boulders, or roaring in and out of camp churning up billows of dust. No effort had been made to conceal the base. Soviet aircraft would be able to easily destroy it through strafing and bombing if they located it.

Hajji Nur Mohammed Khan, the area commander and a highly respected *malik*, emerged from a *kudik* followed by a retinue of armed men. We embraced and he led us into the house, sharply barking an order. Within seconds, a *bacha* hurried out with a tray with small glasses jammed with sugar (never stirred but gradually diluted as new tea was poured), plates of raisins, and cream-lemon biscuits—while another carried two huge pump-action thermoses. The *malik* himself took a thermos and proceeded to carefully fill each of our glasses. "We are honored and happy to have you with us," he said through our interpreter. *"Inshallah*, you will witness our jihad against these communist infidels."

For the next hour, we discussed the war. A gray-bearded man in his fifties or sixties, Mohammed Khan said he and his people had fled to the mountains from Lashkar Gah during the summer of 1979, when the "anti-Islamic repression" by the communists had begun to make itself felt. As with many opposition Afghans, the Khalqi lack of respect for religion and traditional customs was a principal factor in their opposition to the government. "The Khalqis are without a god," he asserted angrily. "That is blasphemous. Every man must bow to Allah. There can be no exceptions."

Kore went through a carefully elaborated list of questions about tactics, equipment, and objectives. For his part, Judah wandered around shooting photographs. When I commented on how open the camp was and asked whether he did not fear assault by Soviet warplanes, Mohammed Khan shrugged. "They have never come before." Nor did he seem to care. "The Taraki government failed because it had no popular support. Amin also failed. So will Karmal and so will the Russians. It will be their Vietnam." An avid listener to the BBC and VOA, he was fully aware of the comparisons to Vietnam now being made back in Europe and North America. "Afghanistan will be a Russian graveyard," he added for emphasis.

All they needed, Mohammed Khan maintained, was guns. Much of what they possessed to ward off helicopter gunships and tanks was antiquated. Throughout the trip, I saw a disparate array of guns that would have made a collector's mouth water. One wizened old Baluch showed me a single-shot musket, beautifully inlaid with ivory, plus a tenderly polished clutch of homemade bullets and a black leather pouch for powder looking like the dried scrotum of an ox. "With more Kalashnikovs, anti-aircraft guns, and anti-tank guns," the commander declared, "we can defeat these Russians."

Over the next three days, we visited other camps. All seemed to have been defiantly pitched in the most exposed places. At each location, scores of fighters emerged to show their weapons and—above all—to be photographed. Despite the reputation of Afghan tribesmen as brilliant marksmen, I seriously began to question their ability when one commander insisted on demonstrating their shooting skills.

One by one, the mujahideen—chests impressively crossed by intricately latticed cartridge belts—fired three rounds with a captured AK-47 Kalashnikov. In those early days, it was rare to see a Kalashnikov. The target was a yellow piece of paper placed on top of a rock less than seventy-five yards away. Not a single bullet found its mark. Finally, swearing loudly, a stalwart former army officer stepped forward, picked up the weapon, and proceeded to level off successive shots, each hitting the target. Sighing, the commander admitted that training was a problem. Only a few guerrillas had received basic military training, and these were primarily deserters. "Many are from the towns and villages. They have never fired a gun," he said.

Another problem was the shortage of ammunition. No one had the luxury of practice. Bullets were too expensive. In the Pakistani border towns, a single AK-47 round cost $1.50 US—a fortune in these parts— while bullets for the highly accurate World War II Czech Mauser, the famous Brno Vz24 widely used in more recent conflicts around the world, went for a staggering $2.50 US each. A further complaint was that the men often sold captured weapons and ammunition in the bazaars to feed their families. "This means that we have to buy back the bullets that we previously captured," said one commander.

It was clear to us that modern weapons, ammunition, and training were not the only items at a premium. The guerrillas completely lacked any form of military strategy. Their basic approach was based on a gung-ho *Let's get the Russians* attitude. I saw no maps (few had any idea how to read mine), and there were virtually no means of communication other than hand-carried messages. Nor was there any sense of unit formation. No squads, platoons, or companies.

According to Mohammed Khan, who commanded three hundred fighters, when they decided to hit a target, they would call a meeting with other leaders. Over tea and *nan*, everyone loudly debated the oper-ation. When the objective was finally agreed on, the guerrillas would pile into the pickups, as many as twenty or thirty men to a vehicle. They made their way by night in loose columns toward their objectives, picking up more fighters who had walked in from the hills. One could only assume that if small groups of fighters from distant locations knew of the proposed attacks, then the government forces must have known as well.

It was doubtful whether some of the spectacular victories the muja-hideen claimed were real. While describing their attacks against army forts, barracks, convoys, government offices, and police stations, they asserted that some were Soviet. However, they tended not to differentiate between Afghan and Red Army forces. For them, anyone fighting with the enemy was regarded as *Shouravi*. As I quickly learned, Afghans have a vivid imagination when it comes to recounting events. Trucks quickly became tanks, while two or three APCs turned into huge tank columns. Often, when I would ask mujahideen to draw these "tanks" that they were attacking, the picture would look strangely like a jeep.

While such loose tactics might have worked well with the dispirited Afghan army during the pre-invasion days, it was questionable whether the resistance would find the same lackluster response from the Red Army. Not only were Afghan government units being taken over by Soviet officers, but recent reports were suggesting far closer Red Army–Afghan collaboration to boost efficiency and morale. Reports indicated that the Soviets were still refraining from major assaults except to protect road access or military installations, such as around Kabul and Kandahar. With the approach of spring, the Western embassies in Islamabad were expecting the Red Army to lash out with all its might against these ill-prepared mujahideen.

None of this seemed to thwart the enthusiasm of the guerrillas. Many spoke with extraordinary self-assurance of their ability to fight back. Typical was Mahmed, a twenty-three-year-old former political science student from Kabul University. He was a member of Jamiat, but insisted that his colleagues belonged to other parties such as Gulbuddin Hekmatyar's Hezb-e-Islami and the more moderate Mahaz-e melli-ye Islami (National Islamic Front) of the pro-king politician Sayed Ahmed Gailani. As we traveled deeper into the steppes of southern Afghanistan, he declared confidently: "All this area is in our hands. Thanks be to God, the Russians cannot touch us here." The particular region Mahmed was referring to lay on the outskirts of Lashkar Gah. We drove to the edge of the irrigated parts, close enough to see the lights of the town. We dared not proceed any closer.

Mahmed claimed that the parties worked closely together, particularly on the battlefield. But such assertions were not entirely convincing. While roaring through the desert in broad daylight or under the stars, we often encountered vehicles loaded with rifle-wielding fighters. The trucks would slow down and the groups would eyeball each other without uttering a word. Then they would tear off into the desert again, plumes of dust in their wake. When I asked Mahmed who they were, he replied evasively: "They are mujahideen . . . but they're not part of us."

It was time to return to base. The proposed attack never materialized. Only once did we see two Mi-8 helicopters moving across the horizon like silhouetted stick insects. And at one point, we approached a main road stretching like a thin ribbon across the plain north of the Chagai

Hills. Columns of vehicles, including buses, were moving in both directions. There was no way the guerrillas could have attacked the road without being perceived by the enemy. Thick, high-rising clouds of dust gave
away vehicles traversing these desert wastes.

Mohammed Khan proposed that we stay longer. I was tempted,
disappointed that we had not seen any action. Judah and Kore, however,
were anxious to head back. Judah was becoming increasingly paranoid
that these Muslim fighters might discover he was Israeli. While criticizing Moscow in viciously biblical terms, they bitterly lambasted Israel in
Islamic solidarity for its repression of Palestine. For Kore, truly Nordic
in his sense of procedure, it was a matter of sticking to his schedule. He
repeatedly demanded that the mujahideen honor their pledge of returning us to Quetta on schedule.

We began the eight-hour journey back to Dalbandin. To our astonishment, every village had prepared a lavish lunch. At the first, we alighted
enthusiastically to gorge on a spread of green tea and cooked meats—
mutton, beef, chicken—plus rice *pulao*, eggplant, potatoes, yogurt, fruit,
and honey. A few miles later, there was another meal. And then another.
And another. We had run into a gauntlet of Afghan hospitality. I had
already been long enough in Asia to know that we could not refuse. "We
can't eat anymore," cried Judah. "We've got to get out of this place." By
now, he was convinced that the mujahideen suspected his Israeli links.
"Whatever you do, don't even mention Israeli," he pleaded in a husky
whisper. For Kore, he was still insisting that they respect their word as
if the trip were part of a Swiss package tour. "You made a promise," he
lectured Tariq. Rauli and I tried to persuade them that they had to defer
to local custom and that Western norms did not apply in the deserts of
Afghanistan. By the fourth lunch, our two colleagues were refusing to
even step out of the vehicle. The Baluch were becoming visibly angry.

"Look, just take a few bites." I urged. "That's all. Sip some tea. But
show that you welcome their hospitality." I then added, "I really don't
think you've any choice."

Kore shook his head. "*These people made a promise,*" he enunciated
with loud precision. "*I have a schedule to be respected.*" As for Judah, he sat
resolutely clutching his camera bag. "I'm not going. We've got to get back
to Pakistan," he moaned. Finally, I signaled to Tariq and walked over

to the tribal elders. They were standing in a tight knot, arguing angrily among themselves.

"Look," I said to our guide. "Please tell these gentlemen that we all work for the BBC and that we have much news about their brave mujahideen fighting the Soviets." *BBC* was the only expression they would understand for describing the work of a journalist. "We want to tell the world about how the Khalqis are taking their land and their homes, forcing many, many Afghans to leave their country. But we need to get back to Pakistan. We need to send our reports to the BBC. That is why my friends are in a hurry. They do not wish to insult."

Tariq translated this back, embellishing grandly. The old men nodded gravely, emitting occasional "*ahhs*" and "*hamdillahs*" (praise be to Allah). The headman stepped up and embraced us, followed by the whole group. They walked over to the pickup and warmly shook hands with Judah and Kore, both of whom sat glumly in the back. Tariq came over to me smiling. "Let us go. We go Pakistan."

I was beginning to realize that to operate effectively in Afghanistan, I would have to quickly learn Afghan customs and demonstrate my willingness to honor and respect their traditions. In particular, I soon learned that taking the time to drink tea is imperative to establish trust and good relations with the Afghans.

On my return to Peshawar, the *Monitor* wanted more coverage of the rapidly growing refugee situation. I was now regularly visiting the vast tent cities spread out across the plain at the foot of the Khyber's Suleiman Hills. By the mid-1980s—at the height of the war—the Afghan refugee population in Peshawar would rise to more than two million, with a million more scattered throughout Pakistan.

I was intrigued by the seven tribal agencies located along the mountainous border areas of the Northwest Frontier. This was where many refugees headed as they made their way into Pakistan across the dozens of passes, from Chitral on the edge of the Himalayas down to Waziristan and Baluchistan in the south. Over the next decade, I took every opportunity to cross into the "no-go" areas. There was something intensely romantic about these tribesmen strolling through the bazaars, rifles slung over their shoulders, their eyes darting at you defiantly, or riding on horseback along back-hill trails and across fields of openly cultivated opium poppies. I found my boyhood imagination pricked by the sight of the solitary, Gunga Din stone pickets built by the British during the nineteenth century to contain these "truculent savages," as one colonial wrote. The forts now flew the green and white-crescent Pakistani flag but were still burdened with the same task of keeping order in a territory where only Pushtunwali reigned.

One day, while talking with the relief organizations, I heard reports of a widows' refugee camp in the mountainous tribal agency of Bajaur, just across from Kunar province in eastern Afghanistan. Apparently the women had fled in the spring of 1979, following a massacre of their menfolk by the Khalqis. This was under the regime of President Taraki and then prime minister Hafizullah Amin, and eight months prior to the Red Army invasion. Now, ten months later—together with Kore Werpe, Nicholas Proffitt of *Newsweek*, and Rauli Virtanen—I headed up to Bajaur to investigate.

When we arrived in the first week of February 1980, over thirty-five thousand refugees had already congregated among the agency's scattered valleys. It was a strikingly beautiful region with mud-and-stone villages enveloped by veils of wood or dung smoke from hearth fires. The late-afternoon sun bathed the terraced fields of corn, wheat, and opium poppies in a soft light.

We quickly found our widows, who had fled from the Afghan town of Kerala. Sharing accommodations with local villagers or living in spartan government dwellings and tents, we encountered destitute knots of dark-shawled women, dirt-caked children at their hems. We knew we were talking to widows, because they were the only women—now not much good to anyone from the tribal point of view—allowed to be seen by or talk with foreign males. Altogether they represented some four hundred families. Most had lost their husbands, sons, uncles, or brothers in a mass execution by the communists on April 20, 1979, of over one thousand men and boys.

It was an astonishing story. More men were killed in Kerala than the Lidice massacre in Czechoslovakia, where the Nazis slaughtered the entire male population during World War II, or My Lai in March 1968, when American troops deliberately killed Vietnamese civilians. According to the Afghanistan Justice Project, established in 2001 to document war crimes and crimes against humanity from 1978 through 2001, the Kerala massacre emerged as one of the most vicious human rights violations of the Afghan war.

Accompanied by several mujahideen and Pakistani officials, we walked from house to house, tent to tent, or met with small clusters of women in open fields, trying to piece together what had happened. Barely two hundred of the males had survived. A few had been out of town when the communists arrived. Others had escaped into the surrounding fields and hills.

Kerala lies only twelve miles northwest of an ancient mule track leading into Afghanistan through the Raghani Pass. At the base of the Hindu Kush, the town overlooks the Pech River, which forked into the Kunar as it flowed south through a broad, cultivated valley of fruit trees and wheat fields, and then eventually into the Kabul River. Two miles north of the Kunar capital of Asadabad or Chagaserai, where the PDPA maintained a major garrison, it consisted of mud-and-stone dwellings, a school, and a bustling bazaar with market stalls and repair shops. Many of its roughly five thousand residents in the late 1970s worked in the fields or chopped lumber in the cedar- and pine-forested mountains. By March 1979, most districts had been taken by the mujahideen. The government forces could penetrate other parts of the province, but only with armored columns.

That changed, though, on April 20, 1979, shortly after daybreak, when a slow-moving column of thirty tanks, APCs, and trucks rumbled up toward Kerala. Various townsfolk watched the approaching two-hundred-strong force—mainly *askaris*, but also police and members of the local Khalqi militia—cross the bridge over the Pech River. There were also some Soviet and Eastern bloc advisers. Most wore Afghan army uniforms—including a senior officer, a Slavic-looking man with dark blond hair and green eyes, who was known to local inhabitants as the "commandant."

There was nothing unusual about the force. Government troops often came into Kerala to buy supplies on their way north toward the upper reaches of the Kunar Valley. Despite increasing attacks by the mujahideen, the government still "controlled" the main road running alongside the river. In fact, the previous day, local guerrillas had attacked the Chagaserai garrison, but had been repulsed. Nevertheless, the rebels had inflicted casualties, forcing the besieged troops to request urgent military support from Kabul. The PDPA regime sent Jaggran Saddiq Alamyar and his 444 Commando Force, a unit of the Eleventh Afghan Army Division.

April 20 was the Muslim Sabbath, a day of peace and prayer. A tacit agreement existed between the two sides not to attack each other on Fridays. While numerous Khalqis were *kafirs*, or nonbelievers, the ordinary *askaris* were God-fearing. With many Keralans still at home, the soldiers encircled the town, tank barrels and heavy machine guns facing the center. Some of the soldiers hung back to guard the vehicles, while others deployed among the houses, banging on doors, calling for the men to come out.

"All the men were ordered to come to a *jirgha* to discuss the [insurgent] fighting in the area," explained Abdul Latif, a bearded Afghan traffic policeman from Kerala, who had deserted the government and now stood with a group of male survivors and widows outside the main Bajaur refugee office. "None of the men were armed. The women and children were herded into the mosque. There they could hear and see everything that was going on."

To illustrate his testimony, Latif hastily drew a map of Kerala on a piece of paper from my notebook. He showed the houses, the mosque, and the positions of the tanks and APCs. He also sketched the field by the edge of the Pech River near the bridge, where the men, including boys in their early and late teens, had been forced to gather. With the vast majority of Kerala's male population assembled, the officers began berating them for collaborating with the guerrillas. A principal interrogator was Alamyar, the 444 Commando commander and a close confidant of Prime Minister (soon to become president) Amin. Later Alamyar would manage to seek asylum in the Netherlands. With him were Bahramuddin, the 444th's operational commander (later killed in a mutiny in Jalalabad); and Jagran Gul Rang, another Eleventh Division officer, also believed to have died.

"The government soldiers were very annoyed about the mujahed attacks," remembered Khalil Ullah, a teacher wearing a stained black jacket over his gray *shalwar-kamiz*. "They knew very well that we had secretly been giving the mujahideen food, ammunition, shelter, and money." Another teacher, who had managed to slip away after sympathetic *askari* warned him that Khalqis planned to execute them, added: "They were particularly angry because the governor of Kunar had previously called on us to take up arms against the rebels, but we flatly refused."

The tanks blocked off the road overlooking the field, which was bordered by the river on one side and by piles of timber on the other. Soldiers stood in front of the houses near the mosque, cordoning off the town. Exhorted by their officers, the soldiers pointed their AK-47 assault rifles at the men, demanding that they shout pro-communist slogans. "They wanted them to cry 'Hooray for the regime!'" said Latif, who had helplessly watched the proceedings while standing back with some of the other security forces. "But instead, they all shouted *'Allah o Akbar'* [God is great]."

Further incensed, the Khalqi officers ordered the *askari* and police to line up the men. Prodding with their guns, the troops herded them together. An army officer stepped forward to take photographs. "They wanted to prove that the men of Kerala were supporters of the mujahideen and therefore had to die," explained Latif. He and several others described what happened in the final minutes, but I found the account of Nabi Madez Khan—a short, stocky schoolboy who had lost his father, uncle, and four cousins in the massacre—the most riveting and tragic. The men and women in the group nudged him gently to tell us his tale.

"I accompanied my father to the field for the meeting," said Nabi, now standing in front of the refugees, several carrying guns as permitted under tribal law. With his brown *pakul* perched on the back of his closely cropped hair, he looked younger than his eighteen years. "People were afraid and knew that something was going to happen. Some of the men and boys tried to join the women in the mosque, but they were turned back at gunpoint."

According to Nabi's and other testimony, a military helicopter suddenly emerged from beyond the river and hovered over the field, throwing up dust and bits of straw. The senior Soviet adviser, who was standing near Nabi, started conversing with the helicopter by field radio, clearly issuing orders. "I tried to ask the commandant if I could go, but he ignored me," said the boy. With no one paying attention to him, Nabi began edging toward the mosque, and then broke into a run, glancing back several times. Possibly because of his slight stature, no one tried to stop him.

Abruptly, the helicopter swung away. Orders were shouted and the townsmen were forced to crouch down, facing the tanks. Behind them, the soldiers stood with their AK-47s leveled. Several advisers, including the one Nabi had referred to as the commandant, placed themselves behind the soldiers. A few of the Kerala men began praying loudly. It was then that the shooting erupted.

Nabi was still running and had almost reached the mosque when he heard the firing. He glanced back. "The soldiers were firing their guns and men were falling to the ground. I could not see my father," he recalled. Not all the security forces were shooting. Some of the *askari* were horrified, even crying, at what was clearly turning into a slaughter. A few women quickly handed Nabi female garments as he slipped into the mosque. Several men had succeeded in entering the building and they, too, were trying to hide under head-to-foot chadors.

When the women realized what was happening, they started to scream, clasping their breasts and flailing their arms. By now, the bodies were falling where they had stood or on top of each other. According to Bibi Rakhara, a wizened woman who had lost her husband, four brothers, one son, and two nephews, they tried to run out to their menfolk. "We wanted to touch them, but the soldiers stopped us," she said, her face strained with emotion as she stood forlornly with her nine remaining children by her side. Many ran forward holding up copies of the Koran in their hands, pleading for the soldiers to stop shooting. But the guards pushed them back. When some sought to crawl forward to reach their men, some still alive, the soldiers warded them off by firing over their heads or kicking them back. Several soldiers and militiamen continued shooting into the melee, deliberately targeting victims who still moved.

Overall, the firing lasted no more than five minutes. A bulldozer appeared and began plowing the bodies into the ground, soft from recent furrowing. Some were still alive, crawling or lifting their hands. At the same time, both the officers and Soviet advisers began ordering their men to fan out through the town in search of remaining males. Some entered the mosque and tore off the burqas of those they suspected of being men or boys. Three or four men were discovered in this manner. They were taken, screaming, down to the field and shot.

One male survivor, now living with Pakistani relatives, told us he had been hiding in his house when the firing began. Gesturing to the other side of the ridge, he said: "I could hear the women screaming and realized what was happening, so I ran." Reaching the river, he hid among the willows along the graveled banks, waiting for nightfall. He then swam across the freezing waters, making his way into the mountains and to the Pakistani border. As for the policeman Latif, he was assumed to be a Khalqi, his loyalty unchallenged. Three days later, still in shock, he slipped out of town and made his way to Pakistan's Mohmand Agency.

Within hours of the massacre, groups of tearful, stunned women and children started to flee Kerala. Among them were men who had returned after the killings from woodcutting in the mountains. One particular group—fifteen men, thirty women, and twenty children—crossed the Kunar River by boat and then walked four days to Pakistan, hiding out in the forests and using a circuitous route to avoid government patrols. "It was a tragic sight," explained a Pakistani major as we walked through the refugee encampments in search of survivors to interview. "I watched all these wretched women and children gradually trickle over a period of days into Bajaur. They were all weeping."

Based on a list of names provided, 1,170 men and boys died in the Kerala massacre. They were buried in two mass graves. This was the first reported case of a large-scale reprisal by the communists since fighting had begun almost two years earlier. Until then, accounts had circulated about massacres and summary executions, but there had been no firm corroborative evidence based on detailed eyewitness accounts.

Twice, my colleagues and I tried to glimpse Kerala from the mountains overlooking the Kunar as we trekked with our mujahed guides toward the Raghani Pass. On each occasion, the Pakistanis prevented us from proceeding farther. The first time the Bajaur Scouts chased us, returning us at gunpoint to the valley. The second time, we made it almost as far as the frontier, only to be turned back by Pakistani army regulars. They stepped out of the forest in full combat gear, where they had been observing the Afghan side from posts dug along the ridges. The officer in charge was polite, but refused to let us approach the Durand Line. He did, however, invite us for tea.

My dispatch, which won a Sigma Delta Chi award for foreign reporting, ran in *The Christian Science Monitor* on February 11, 1980. Similar pieces written by my colleagues appeared in *Newsweek*, *Morgenbladet*, and *Helsingin Sanomat*. Accounts of the Kerala massacre were further reported extensively on the BBC, VOA, ABC News, and other broadcasters, but were firmly condemned as fabrications by Radio Kabul, Radio Moscow, as well as the official communist press elsewhere—including *L'Humanité*, the newspaper of the French Communist Party.

This was the first time that I felt my journalism had achieved something concrete. Naively perhaps, I figured that history would now remember Kerala much in the same manner as it remembered Lidice or My Lai. Unfortunately, the Kerala massacre quickly receded into oblivion. It had become yet another of the forgotten Third World massacres that blighted so many Cold War conflicts. When I finally succeeded in visiting Kerala in 1989, there were two mounds in the ground—one large, the other small, marking the mass graves. By 2004, when I again passed through the town, the people of Kerala had carefully enclosed them with mud-and-stone walls planted with roses and periwinkles. Yet there was no memorial plaque to remind passersby of the tragedy.

One of my close Afghan friends smiled sadly when I told him of my concerns that the men and boys of Kerala had died in vain. "So many people have died in Afghanistan with these wars. It is difficult to say that one person's tragedy is worse than another's. People will remember, maybe not the way you do in the West, but the way we Afghans always have . . . with songs, poems, and in our story."

Many years later, in late summer 2009, I was in Paris when my nephew called from Geneva. "The Dutch police are looking for you," he announced. "You've got to call this number." For a moment, I wondered whether I had forgotten an outstanding traffic ticket from the Netherlands. Intrigued, I called the number and found myself talking with Bertjan Tjeerde of the International Crimes Unit of the Dutch National Crime Squad. He wanted to interview me about Kerala.

His unit, he explained, was investigating war crimes committed by Dutch nationals or people residing within the Netherlands. They had already conducted penal investigations into torture by high-ranking Afghan KHAD officials of the communist regime currently living in Holland, a Dutch citizen linked to the arms trade in Liberia, and another Dutch national involved with chemical warfare in Iraq. More recently, they had received allegations concerning an individual currently living in the Netherlands who had been involved in the Kerala massacre.

Tjeerde and his unit had already spoken with a number of people involved with the massacre, including witnesses. He had come across my stories in *The Christian Science Monitor* and my first book, *Afghanistan: The Soviet War*. He asked if we could discuss the matter. "The people of Kunar have filed their complaints and are eager to cooperate," he explained. He then warned me that it was important for him to talk with as many people as possible who knew something about the massacre as "a long time has passed, not making things any easier."

I was pleased that even thirty years after the massacre, the long hand of justice could still bring the perpetrators to account. I believed that the people of Kerala deserved this dignity. I agreed to see him. Several weeks later, Tjeerde and a colleague flew down from Holland to meet me at my house outside Geneva. We talked for four hours. I began to understand the problems of undertaking such a detailed investigation after so many years. How does one confirm such allegations based on recalled testimony?

Tjeerde knew all the people cited in my *Monitor* story. I later returned to my notebook, which is part of a whole collection stored in a school trunk in my attic office, but found I could not provide Tjeerde with much more detail. The Dutch policeman was cautious in his explanations and would not name the Afghan individual concerned. But based on information received from other sources, notably the findings of the Afghanistan Justice Project, I figured that it had to be Jaggran Saddiq Alamyar of the 444 Commando Force, currently living in the Netherlands. As Tjeerde pointed out, there are no statutes of limitations in Holland. The problem was establishing sufficient hard evidence to prosecute him.

A month later, I found myself in Gdansk heading up a journalism workshop on pollution of the Baltic Sea. One of those taking part, a reporter of Afghan origin from Norway, mentioned that another former PDPA official responsible for Kerala was living as a refugee in Norway.

However, he noted, this man could no longer be prosecuted as the thirty-year statute of limitations had run out. Even though he was a perpetrator of this horrific crime, he was allowed to continue his life in exile.

In the summer of 2010, in a bill introduced by the former jihadist Abdul Rasoul Sayyaf, the Wolesi Jirgha (the lower house of Afghanistan's National Assembly) voted to grant immunity from prosecution to former fighters accused of war crimes. Presumably, too, this same law absolves those responsible for atrocities during the communist period.

Furthermore, there was the unresolved question of the United States and other Westerners being responsible for killing, torturing, or the "extraordinary rendition" of Afghans suspected of terrorist involvement or of being so-called unlawful combatants. The latter, a term invented by the George W. Bush administration, does not exist under international law—and in particular, the Geneva Conventions.

These are issues that will need to be dealt with if America's promotion of democracy, accountability, and transparency is to be taken seriously by ordinary Afghans. As acknowledged by the US military, at least three Afghans were allegedly murdered by American servicemen at Bagram air base north of Kabul during the early days of the intervention. Two of these cases were officially acknowledged by the US military as homicide. The families were never compensated; nor were those responsible charged. US and NATO troops have often abused Afghan civilians, including women and children, as part of raids, roadblocks, or convoys.

As many as one thousand Afghans, too, were incarcerated during 2002 and 2003 in what Human Rights Watch referred as a "climate of almost total impunity." Hundreds were sent to Guantanamo, Bagram, and other US detention centers, accused of being al Qaeda and held for years without charges or due process. Many were tortured. While some may have had Talib affiliations, which does not mean they were terrorists, others found themselves detained on flimsy accusations or as the result of highly questionable informer bounties—a thousand US dollars or more, a fortune for most Afghans. Some, too, were fingered without evidence by pro-government Afghan officials or ISI operatives as part of quotas to demonstrate "collaboration" with the US military, the CIA, or other intelligence agencies.

Such incarcerations have done far more to harm America's standing in Afghanistan and the region than anything else. Following the death at Guantanamo in early 2011 of Awal Gul, an Afghan held for nine years without charge or trial, his body was returned home, where five thousand people attended his funeral outside Jalalabad. According to the US authorities, Gul, who had apparently died of a heart attack, had been an admitted Talib recruiter and commander. He had also operated an al Qaeda guesthouse and had once met bin Laden, providing him with operational assistance on several occasions. Given that the Americans had themselves supported or otherwise collaborated with bin Laden, can these actions justify such internment? Where is the justice?

The Kerala massacre is only one of a host of crimes against Afghans that is likely to go unpunished. The only people who can now be charged with war crimes have to be living outside of Afghanistan and may then only be prosecuted if national laws permit. Impunity reigns in Afghanistan—yet without justice, the prospect for long-term reconciliation and recovery will never be fulfilled.

CHAPTER FIVE

You Can Rent an Afghan,
But Never Buy Him

Peshawar was the logistical gateway to Afghanistan for the Pakistanis, Americans, and other foreign interests supporting the mujahideen. It soon became my base for covering the Afghan resistance. I considered it imperative to attempt to understand the nature of these new guerrillas. Ever since my first meetings with the World War II resistance leaders who formed the board of the Journalists in Europe program, I had been intrigued by the concept of resistance. I read voraciously about the Maquis in occupied France and Tito's partisan war in Yugoslavia and found it fascinating to report firsthand how these "ragtag" Afghan resistance fighters—a favorite media descriptive—were faring against the Soviets.

For those of us covering the Red Army occupation, it was mind-boggling to note how little sustained media interest it drew outside of the immediate region or the Soviet Union, particularly given the potential consequences for the USSR and the world. By the summer of 1980, foreign coverage of the Afghan war had petered out. For much of the decade-long conflict, it was reported by no more than two dozen Western journalists at any time. Most were freelance, and all took repeated trips across the border. A small but determined group of cameramen and photographers, whose work keeps them on the front line, regularly risked their lives in the perpetual quest for good pictures. This was in stark contrast with the huge international reporting presence in Indochina over a decade earlier.

Some of those covering Afghanistan had come in search of a war, a new Vietnam on which to cut their teeth. Others were already experienced. The Islamabad- and Delhi-based correspondents of the BBC, VOA, Reuters, AP, and AFP monitored Afghan events as part of normal regional coverage. One of the most dogged was Kathy Gannon of the

Associated Press, who began reporting the war in 1986. Backed with
a wealth of comparative experience and insight, she was still covering
Afghanistan in 2010. Meanwhile, the Soviets and other Eastern Bloc
countries maintained foreign correspondents in Kabul, and visiting
reporters from the USSR embedded with Red Army units. Just as most
Western reporters today have no access to the insurgents, Soviet journalists were unable to cover the mujahed side. They would have been
considered the enemy.

Reporting with the Taliban and other insurgents today is widely
regarded as too dangerous. There are simply too many unreliable or
unknown factions. Although Al Jazeera and sometimes the BBC and
CNN have been able to penetrate the guerrillas using Pakistani or Afghan
reporters, few Western reporters have taken the risk. My own attempts
to travel with the insurgents through my own pro-Talib contacts proved
inadvisable. Sky TV managed to report with Kunar guerrillas in late
2010, while two or three others, such as David Rohde of *The New York
Times*, have witnessed the war from the Talib side—albeit reluctantly
after being kidnapped.

Ironically, some of the journalists who showed the most interest in
Massoud during his war with the Taliban more than a decade later were
Russian. A leading Moscow news show sent a team to the Panjshir in the
late 1990s to question the Lion about his favorite writer, historical figure,
food, and pop musician. When asked about his favorite film, Massoud
answered with a tolerant smile: "I don't have much chance to see films.
We haven't got any cinemas around here."

When I first went to Afghanistan, prior to the Soviet invasion,
resistance factions opposing the Kabul communist regime were already
setting up their exile headquarters in Peshawar and Quetta. A far
smaller number, primarily Hazaras, were doing the same in Iran—where
Ayatollah Khomeiny was funding a new Shiite alliance, the Shura, or the
"Tehran Eight." Within a month of the invasion, Peshawar had become
the operational headquarters for Afghanistan's twenty-odd opposition
parties.

At first, the Pakistanis welcomed everyone in the opposition, but
as the number of refugees swelled, they reduced their support to only
six—later seven—of the larger parties, which made control easier. They

faced an eclectic array of tendencies ranging from pro-Chinese Maoists to Pushtun National Socialists. Nearly all were Sunnis, Islam's largest branch. Through a combination of quiet persuasion, bribes, and threats, Islamabad obliged the remaining groups to amalgamate.

The Pakistanis hoped that reducing the number of groups, which became known as the "Peshawar Seven" or the Islamic Unity of Afghanistan Mujahideen, would encourage a common front against the Soviets. The alliance could also be used to promote Islamabad's own interests while instigating insurgency inside Afghanistan.

This was easier said than done. Growing corruption and bickering among the parties—which eventually split into two broad fronts, "moderate" and "fundamentalist"—alienated many Afghans. The united resistance that had been hoped for never emerged. Even when the politicians announced that they were operating together, it was little more than a sham. No resistance leader wished to weaken his position, or miss out on funding. The name of the game was money.

Depending on their financial resources, the resistance groups took over high-walled house compounds, back-alley offices, and even storefronts for their headquarters. While in Peshawar in October 1979, I had to make discreet telephone calls to arrange meetings and then slip out of my hotel to avoid the Pakistani secret police All this changed following the Soviet invasion. Within a week, most Afghan political groups had representatives sitting in hotel lobbies or posting press conference notices at the reception desk. Finding their headquarters was no longer a near-impossible task. One simply asked the cabdriver. During those early days, the popularity of the parties could by gauged by the number of Afghans thronging outside their gates. Everyone wanted something. They clutched signed chits for cash, weapons, or temporary accommodation. Whenever an adjutant opened one of the portals, the crowds would surge expectantly forward, thrusting their bits of paper.

Journalists based in Peshawar spent endless hours interviewing Afghan opposition leaders and the refugees. They soon learned that the great majority of the tens of thousands of Afghans who entered Pakistan every month during the first two years of the Soviet-Afghan war had little affinity with the Peshawar-based opposition parties. Few of the Afghan refugees cared about ideology, although several exile politicians were already known as traditional or spiritual leaders. One was Pir Sayed Ahmed Gailani, leader of the Qadiriyyah Sufi order in Afghanistan and founder of the moderate National Islamic Front of Afghanistan (NIFA). Another was Sibghatullah Mujaddedi of the Afghan National Liberation Front (ANLF), a widely respected Islamic scholar, who first fled the left-wing regime of Daoud Khan in 1973 for Danish exile.

The anonymity of the Afghan opposition leaders based in Peshawar began to change, however, when Radio Kabul began emphasizing their names in an effort to demonize them. The BBC, VOA, and Radio Tehran also began referring to the different groups and leaders in their broadcasts. Since even the poorest and most uneducated refugees listened to the radio, ordinary Afghans soon began to recognize the *Who's Who* of the exiled resistance figures and to align themselves with the varied factions.

The Peshawar Seven were well placed to mobilize grassroots registration. I sometimes traveled up to the frontier to watch party activists sign up new arrivals. The refugees often stood overwhelmed at the registration tables. Pointing to the space for political affiliation, the party supporters tried to create the impression that the Pakistanis would not provide them with food rations unless they scribbled their signatures (if they could write) or pressed their inked thumbs to paper (if they could not). The groups enlisted entire families and even villages in this manner. Unable to read, numerous refugees had little idea which group they had joined.

Soon after the Soviet invasion, diaspora Afghans—often dubious one-man operations, such as a former New York taxi driver who claimed to have close contacts with the main groups—swept into Peshawar from the United States and Europe, smelling opportunity. They claimed to represent the former king or various political groups, some of them fictitious. Desperate for new angles, journalists were ready to listen to anyone who spoke good English, regardless of credibility. Twenty years later, with the collapse of the Taliban, Kabul was similarly inundated by diaspora Afghans. Some were well meaning, intent on contributing to Afghanistan's recovery. Others, particularly when the aid dollars and euros began to roll in, were little more than scoundrels out for a fast buck.

Back in the 1980s, we had little idea of the influence that the CIA and other intelligence agencies in Washington were exerting over the covert scene alongside Pakistan's ISI. On July 3, 1979, President Jimmy Carter signed an executive order authorizing the CIA to conduct propaganda operations against the PDPA regime. US Defense Secretary (and former CIA director) Robert Gates maintained in his book *From the Shadows* that the United States had begun providing financial aid to the mujahideen six months prior to the invasion. It was one way of undermining the Afghan communists and their Soviet backers.

Western interest in media reports from Afghanistan reemerged during the Soviet-Afghan war only when the United States seriously upped the ante by supporting the mujahideen in what became known as Operation Cyclone. Well over three billion US dollars (some put the figure as high as eighteen billion) of military aid was supplied, including the Stinger anti-aircraft missile. Highly favorable coverage of how successful the United States was in helping the mujahideen was orchestrated by Washington. In one case, the CIA invited the publishers of *Newsweek* and *Time* for lunch. The next week embarrassingly similar stories lauding the US role appeared in the two magazines. There was similar pressure by NATO on the media, particularly those reporting with the military, to put a patriotic slant on their reports.

As the mujahideen became better funded, most of the Big Seven moved to more lavish quarters in University Town, a quiet tree-lined residential suburb. This is also where the bulk of the UN agencies and NGOs set up operations. The UNHCR, International Committee of the Red Cross (ICRC), International Rescue Committee (IRC), and other organizations all needed to cultivate close relations with the parties. The mainly French groups conducting cross-border relief—such as MSF (known also as Doctors Without Borders), Bureau International pour l'Afghanistan (BIA), and Aide Médicale International (AMI), but also Britain's AfghanAid and the Swedish Committee for Afghanistan (SCA)—needed to obtain agreements from the political leaders and to coordinate closely with the interior fronts in order to smuggle doctors, agricultural advisers, and aid convoys across the border.

Relief coordinators such as Anders Fange, the astute director of the Swedish Committee, and Juliette Fournot of MSF—an attractive dentist-turned-humanitarian who had been brought up in Afghanistan and whose nom de guerre was Jamila—learned to be politically savvy.

"We spent a lot of time drinking tea with the party leaders, but also meeting with commanders from different parts of the country. The safety of your operations depended on this," recalled Fange.

Fournot, whom I first met in Peshawar in 1980 when MSF was just starting, needed to know if certain mountain passes had been newly mined or whether a specific village was affiliated with the PDPA or a less friendly resistance faction. "It's a matter of keeping your finger on the pulse," she told me, her blond hair tucked inside her *pakul* as she checked horses in the MSF compound in Peshawar during the mid-1980s. "You need to talk to people, the [horse] drivers, the merchants, refugees . . . " Later during the war, this inside intelligence failed, resulting in one MSF doctor killed while his female colleague was brutally raped by rogue mujahideen.

Lack of cohesion is one reason the mujahed movement disintegrated so disastrously after the collapse of the PDPA regime in 1992. Uninhibited infighting and greed among the former jihadists eventually led to the military rise of the Taliban from 1994 onward. Even the Taliban began showing signs of imploding as different factions sought to propel their own interests. Some resented the continued dominance of reclusive Talib leader Mullah Omar and his Kandaharis, while others had begun quietly negotiating with Massoud. Had the Americans not intervened in late 2001, it is possible that the Taliban would have begun to collapse in a manner similar to the mujahideen. Some eastern Afghan Taliban (notably from Nangrahar and Paktia)—possibly as the result of Western pressure, but also tired of ISI manipulation—were beginning to go their own way, seeking new options with the outside world. A lack of unity has always dogged the Afghans. Even during the First Anglo-Afghan War of the mid-nineteenth century, it had always been possible to find someone ready to sell out. Hence the expression: "You can rent an Afghan; you can never buy him."

As one senior Pakistani Foreign Ministry official, reflecting on the mujahideen and later the Taliban over the past thirty years, put it to me at a 2008 United Nations meeting in New York: "The Afghans are perhaps the most unreliable people in the world . . . You may think you have them in your pocket, but they have taken your jacket."

Counterintuitively, the disunity among the mujahideen also proved to be a strength. The Red Army found it impossible to crush all the myriad fronts and factions, each with its distinct political and ideological agendas. By the time the Peshawar Seven had emerged as the main resistance focus, there were four so-called fundamentalist and three moderate parties. This did not mean that their followers could be similarly pigeonholed. Some of the more independent "commanders of the interior" linked to the fundamentalist parties were relatively modernist, such as Massoud, Abdul Haq, and Ismail Khan. Over the past decade, however, with both Massoud and Abdul Haq dead, Ismail Khan has become more rigid than the Taliban, who had captured and held him captive for three years in the late 1990s.

All four heads of the fundamentalist parties began their exile following the overthrow of King Zahir Shah in 1973, when the former president Mohammed Daoud began repressing conservative Islamists. A few went abroad to Egypt or Europe; others to neighboring Pakistan, Iran, and India. It was during this period that Islamabad began embracing its new "forward policy" for Afghanistan, notably to manipulate events on the other side of the border.

Fleeing Daoud, some fifty fundamentalists (a few leaders but mostly students) crossed into Pakistan, where Prime Minister Zulfikar Ali Bhutto took them under his wing. Between 1973 and 1977, Pakistan trained a reported five thousand dissidents in secret military camps. This was at a time when popular resistance had yet to emerge. The Pakistanis, however, realized that they could create the basis of an anti-Daoud insurgent force that would keep the Afghan government off balance. With the rise of the communists and the Soviet invasion, the ISI continued with this tradition by backing the mujahideen during the 1980s, but also other follow-up insurgent movements—notably Hekmatyar's forces during the early and mid-1990s, the Talib period, and now the anti-NATO war.

Many of these new fighters were Young Muslim dissidents. The movement was founded in 1964–65 by theologians at Kabul University, who had studied in the Middle East where they came under the influence of the militant Muslim Brotherhood, which was founded in 1928 by Hassan al-Bannah in the Egyptian port town of Ismailia. Vehemently anti-left-wing, Young Muslims not only clashed with the two PDPA factions, the Khalq (Masses) and Parchami (Banner), but accused Daoud of collaborating with the communists. In July 1975, Pakistani-backed dissidents attacked two police stations in the Panjshir. They occupied most of the valley for three days before being put to flight by government forces. Two of the young radicals were unlikely bedfellows: Gulbuddin Hekmatyar and Ahmed Shah Massoud.

Daoud immediately accused the Pakistanis of orchestrating the uprising, which Islamabad flatly denied. Several years later, former Bhutto officials privately admitted that they had been responsible for the weapons, financing, and timing of the incident. The abortive uprising gave the fundamentalist leaders their first taste of rebellion. During one late-night conversation in Kabul in 1993, Massoud mentioned that the experience had taught him "how not to launch an insurrection." Hekmatyar, on the other hand, arrogantly assured me that he was the one responsible for launching Afghanistan's struggle against the "infidels."

Among the most prominent of the fundamentalist parties was Jamiat-e-Islami, led by Burhanuddin Rabbani, a revered scholar. I often met with him during the 1980s and occasionally during the 1990s while he was president of the jihad government. When I saw him at his office in the Badakshan governor's residence in Faizabad shortly before Massoud's assassination, he was still president but at the head of a diminishing rump state. Prior to the Daoud period, Rabbani had enjoyed a significant student following. Since 1972, he served as chairman of Jamiat, Afghanistan's oldest Islamic political organization. After participating in the 1975 Panjshir uprising, Rabbani was forced to flee to Pakistan, where he began building an active resistance party. Jamiat, which was backed by Massoud, Ismail Khan, and other leading "commanders of the interior," quickly became one of the most effective guerrilla groups.

In 1983, Jamiat began drawing on Hekmatyar's own rank and file. As a primarily Tajik organization from the north, however, Jamiat never benefited from as much Pakistani or Western support as did Hekmatyar's Hezb. Rabbani later served as president of Afghanistan from 1992 to 1996 and then headed the United Front against the Taliban until the latter's collapse in the fall of 2001. In 2011, Rabbani remained influential as the head of the United National Front, the largest democratic bloc opposing the Karzai regime.

The second of the fundamentalist groups was the Hezb-e-Islami faction led by Maulawi Mohammed Younis Khales, a prominent Pushtun mullah with a glaring henna-dyed beard and piercing eyes. Khales, a staunch anti-communist, was the only resistance politician to have done any actual fighting. His faction had roped in some of Afghanistan's top-notch commanders—such as Abdul Haq; his brother, Hajji Qadir; and Maulawi Jalaluddin Haqqani, who emerged in the post-2001 anti-NATO war as a key insurgent. As with Hekmatyar's Hezb, Khales was heavily supported by the Americans during the 1980s. Within Peshawar, however, Khales was best known for having married a sixteen-year-old girl when he was already in his late sixties.

Following the collapse of the mujahideen, Khales became an ardent supporter of the Taliban. He was believed to have helped stage bin Laden's escape in 2001 from Tora Bora in the Safed Koh mountains. Ironically, Abdul Haq, a pro-American and the best known of his former commanders, was seeking to create a moderate alliance among the eastern provinces when the Taliban captured and executed him in November 2001. Khales reportedly died in July 2006, apparently at the age of eighty-seven. By 2010, numerous former Khales commanders and their successors were fully backing the insurgency against the Americans.

The third fundamentalist party was the Hezb-e-Islami faction led by Hekmatyar (or Gulbuddin—the two names are used interchangeably), often known as "the Big H" among the expatriate community. Many of his Afghan detractors, however, refer to him as the "Hyena" or "Jackal." Hekmatyar, who twice served as prime minister during the post-communist era, had done more to undermine the anti-communist Afghan resistance than any other. A former communist and possibly a KGB agent, he was regarded by some as a Soviet collaborator, leaking information on mujahed movements or indirectly favoring the Red Army by pulling out of guerrilla attacks at the last minute.

America's involvement with Hekmatyar during the 1980s and early 1990s was one of the most ignominious US policy decisions made in Afghanistan. Certainly the most manipulative of the Peshawar Seven, Hekmatyar's Hezb was massively backed by the ISI and, at the behest of Pakistan's Zia ul-Haq dictatorship, the Americans. It was Zia himself who persuaded Texas congressman Charlie Wilson and others supporting the mujahideen to focus on Pakistan's preferred resistance candidates, based on the regime's own interests rather than on the commanders who were doing the real fighting. Abandoned by the Pakistanis during the mid-1990s in favor of the Taliban, Hekmatyar fled to Iran. By early 2002, however, he was back—once again on the recipient list of ISI support for the insurgency.

In the spring of 2002, the CIA tried to kill Hekmatyar in an unsuccessful drone attack. A year later, Washington officially designated the Afghan extremist an "international terrorist" because he openly supported the Taliban, with pro-Hezb guerrillas increasingly attacking Western troops and Afghan civilians. Nevertheless, a certain blindness regarding Hekmatyar continues to influence the US approach. Various Hezbi, who have infiltrated themselves into the Karzai administration, have been knowingly backed by the Americans. Among the reasons for this are not only the often divergent interests and poor communication that exist within the US embassy itself (no fewer than five US ambassadors at the same time in 2009), but also the shocking lack of institutional memory regarding Afghanistan's past.

The fourth and smallest of the fundamentalist groups, the Ittchad-e-Islami (Islamic Union for the Liberation of Afghanistan), was a latecomer. Initially consisting of several factions, the party imploded within a matter of months in the early 1980s. Its remnants were taken over by Professor Abdul Rabi Rasoul Sayyaf, a fervent Wahhab (Wahhabism being an extremist form of Saudi-based Islam) who had been imprisoned by the communists in Kabul and who only came to Peshawar in 1980. He, too, was involved with the 1975 Panjshir uprising.

Working through his new Ittehad, Sayyaf used his Arab connections to obtain funding, primarily from private interests in Saudi Arabia. This impressed the ISI, which ensured that Ittehad was included among the recognized Peshawar parties. Sayyaf proceeded to support various Wahhabi groups and bring in Islamic volunteers from the Middle East and the Maghreb. His funds helped establish training bases just inside Afghanistan, notably Jagi, later used—and upgraded—by bin Laden for al Qaeda militants. By the late 1980s, Afghan and Arab guerrilla fronts under Sayyaf's patronage were operating in the eastern parts of the country. Sayyaf was also a significant recipient of US military aid.

In 1985, Sayyaf founded the Dawa'a-al-Jihad (Covert and Struggle), an Islamic university which allegedly functioned as a "pre-eminent school for terrorism." One of its attendees was Ramzi Ahmed Youssef, mastermind of the first World Trade Center bombing in 1993 and a plan, never activated, to blow up seven airliners in Hong Kong. Sayyaf was purported to have brought bin Laden back into the country following the Arab militant's expulsion from Sudan in 1996. During the Battle for Kabul in the 1990s, Sayyaf sided with Massoud against Gulbuddin and the Hazaras. According to Amnesty International and other human rights groups, his fighters were responsible for massacre, rape, and other forms of brutality against thousands of Shiite Hazaras in the western part of the capital.

Sayyaf cultivated an intense hatred for rival fundamentalists. He regarded the Taliban as a threat to his own position, a sentiment that persuaded him to operate with Massoud. In the end, he was the only senior-level Pushtun to be part of the United Front. Nevertheless, this did not prevent him from maintaining contacts with the Taliban. Some United Front sources bitterly assert that Sayyaf, fully aware of their mission, enabled the two Tunisian suicide bombers who killed Massoud to cross the lines from Talib-held areas into the Panjshir Valley in the summer of 2001. Currently living in Kabul, Sayyaf converted Ittehad into a political party, the Islamic Dawah Organization, in 2005, which is now part of the parliamentary opposition to the Karzai regime. He remains, however, one of the president's closest allies. He was also a major supporter of the 2009 blanket law that would pardon all crimes against humanity by former jihadists, including himself.

Since 2001, numerous Western policy makers have preferred to ignore the US role in building up Islamic extremists during the 1980s. The Americans have largely refused to acknowledge that their support for extremists, and later their abandonment of the country, are principal reasons why the West is now involved in the current war.

Unlike the fundamentalist parties, the more moderate and generally less effective of the Peshawar Seven only got moving from late 1978 onward. Many of their supporters, notably army officers, civil servants, and academics, were backers of the Zahir Shah and Daoud regimes. Some had initially rallied to the new PDPA government in the hope that the communists would implement promised reforms of democracy and modernization. It did not take long for them to be disappointed.

Foremost was Harakat-e-Inquilabi-e-Islami (the Islamic Movement), headed by a veteran Islamic scholar, Maulawi Mohammad Nabi Mohammadi. During the period leading up to the 1973 Daoud coup, he and a group of *ulema* (Islamic scholars well versed in legal jurisprudence) established a union of religious academics to counter left-wing propaganda, which they felt was undermining Islamic values. Elected to the Afghan parliament on an anti-Marxist platform in 1965, Mohammadi, a Pushtun, advocated Islam as a counterideology to communism.

When Khalqi PDPA leader Taraki came to power in April 1978, he placed Mohammadi and other *ulema* under police surveillance. The gloomy-eyed but eloquently spoken Mohammadi fled to Quetta, where he galvanized other *ulema* into promoting jihad by sending messages to supporters throughout Afghanistan. At the time, Harakat served as a coalition body for all parties intent on pursuing jihad, including Jamiat and Hezb. But these factions eventually went their own way and Harakat became a party in its own right, combining both secular and religious elements. Preferring the traditional Loya Jirgha (Grand Assembly) form of governance rather than the Western legislative system, Mohammadi attracted political backing among traditional mullahs and tribal chiefs as well as urban-based progressives and nationalists.

Nevertheless, Harakat began to suffer from Islamabad's and Washington's support of the fundamentalist groups. While Harakat had some good commanders, a sizable component broke off in 1983 to join the fundamentalists, primarily for logistical reasons. The moderate parties had fewer guns and dollars to distribute. Mohammadi was one of the jihadists invited in 1985 to the White House, where President Reagan described the visiting Afghans as "freedom fighters." When the Taliban came to power in 1996, Mohammadi maintained good relations with the movement (many of its leaders were his former students) but also with Massoud's United Front. Suffering from tuberculosis, he died at age eighty-two in April 2002 with full honors provided by the new Kabul government.

The second of the moderate parties, the National Islamic Front of Afghanistan (NIFA), was pro-monarchist. Headed by Pir Sayed Ahmed Gailani, a wealthy car salesman (he held the country's Peugeot car dealership concession) from the Surkh Rod area of eastern Afghanistan, NIFA was widely regarded as the most fashionable of the mujahed parties. One of its commanders, General Safi, looked more like a World War II British officer with his handlebar mustache and tilted *pakul* worn beret-style. Another was Colonel Rahim Wardak, Afghanistan's heavyset minister of defense since 2004. Both were trained in, and by, the United States and widely known as the "Gucci guerrillas." They knew how to look good on TV. How effective they were in the field was another matter. They reportedly had a number of excellent NIFA fronts that inflicted severe losses on the Soviets, but it was always hard to take their claims seriously.

At the same time, Gailani, who fled the communists in 1979, stood out as an influential figure within the resistance alliance. A quiet man, he preferred to wear Western suits and hardly bore the appearance of hereditary saint (as the title *Pir* indicated). He always looked uncomfortable wearing tribal robes and turban. Often traveling abroad, he advocated a democratic constitutional monarchy as the best solution for Afghanistan given its religious and ethnic diversity. While many Afghans would still support this today, a return of the monarchy seems remote, particularly with the death of former King Zahir Shah in 2007.

Since the collapse of the Taliban in 2001, Gailani became more of an éminence grise—largely eclipsed by his highly astute, cosmopolitan daughter, Fatima. Outspoken during the jihad period, and outspoken today, she has become a highly respected figure on the international scene—a fervent proponent of female rights and head of the Afghan Red Crescent Society, the Afghani arm of the affiliated Red Cross and Red Crescent societies around the world.

The third of the moderate Peshawar parties was Sibghatullah Mujaddedi's Afghan National Liberation Front (ANLF). A soft-spoken man, Mujaddedi considered himself a constitutional monarchist and even used the royal insignia for his party logo. As with Gailani, Mujaddedi never quite obtained the grassroots popularity that he would have liked. Well traveled, he was a graduate of Al-Azhar University in Cairo and a highly reputed Islamic scholar. After being imprisoned as a religious conservative, he left for self-imposed exile in the 1970s to become director of the Scandinavian Islamic Institute in Copenhagen.

When I first met him at his house along the Khyber Road in Peshawar in early 1980, Mujaddedi struck me as exceptionally modest, a man sensitive to the plight of his people. He warmed to me considerably following the accidental shooting to death of his son, Assiz. A bright student barely in his twenties, Assiz had often discussed the concepts of resistance with me. When I offered my condolences, Mujaddedi embraced me. "Thank you, young man, thank you. We shall lose many more before this war has finished," he declared to me solemnly.

Mujaddedi continues to cultivate an elder-statesman role. Elected president of the interim Islamic government of Afghanistan following the announcement in mid-1987 of the proposed withdrawal of Soviet troops, he served temporarily as the first head of the new Islamic State of Afghanistan when the mujahideen entered Kabul in 1992. Two months later, he transferred power to Rabbani as part of a previous agreement. With the outbreak of fighting among the different mujahed factions, he sought to intervene but to no avail.

Following years in political limbo, Mujaddedi served as chairman of the December 2003 Loya Jirgha, or Grand Assembly, to approve the country's new constitution. In an effort to appease the more than a hundred female delegates, he appointed a woman as one of his three deputies. When Malalai Joya, one of the women, vehemently criticized the former jihadists for their corruption and roles in destroying Afghanistan, Mujaddedi reportedly tried to switch off the microphone, provoking criticism that he was in bed with the warlords. More recently, Mujaddedi was elected leader of the Meshrano Jirgha, or 102-seat Upper House. He was also appointed chairman of the National Commission for Peace in Afghanistan for building a broad-based platform, including rapprochement with the insurgents.

Most Afghans were fully aware that the Peshawar Seven had profited handsomely from their positions. Without exception, all the politicians raked in small fortunes from the funds made available to them.

The Pakistanis issued their funds, refugee cards, and permits through the parties, and it was through them that Pakistani government and military officials made their underhanded deals to ensure that major portions of outside aid over the next decade passed into their private bank accounts. The corruption was tacitly accepted by the donor countries, whether the United States, Britain, Germany, or Saudi Arabia. As one US State Department official in Islamabad sighed: "It's the price we have to pay to keep the Pakistanis playing the game." For their part, the Pakistanis played it well and always to their advantage.

The rake-offs were massive: between 40 and 60 percent, sometimes even more, of the international humanitarian or military aid. Once the Pakistanis had taken their cut, and the Afghan politicians had taken theirs, the food relief found its way onto the open market. The ones to suffer were the ordinary Afghans.

When several colleagues and I began reporting this corruption for Britain's Independent Television Network and *The Christian Science Monitor* from 1986 onward, Congressman Wilson, who by now had helped appropriate at least six hundred million dollars a year in weapons and other support for the mujahideen, vehemently denied that "a single bag of American wheat" (or donated anorak, pair of boots, or gun) had gone missing. In a letter to the *Monitor*, he accused me of being an "anti-American, British socialist." I wrote back pointing out that I was not British. Nor did I consider myself to be anti-American or a socialist. I was simply reporting the situation. Wilson never replied.

Through pressure from my editors in Washington, I managed to obtain an interview with Larry Crandall, head of USAID (US Agency for International Development) for Afghanistan in Islamabad—but who also was reportedly involved with intelligence. Before I even sat down in his office (no offer of tea here), he warned me loudly that he would "fucking kill me" if I quoted a "single fucking word." I told him not to worry. I did not work for a British tabloid. Nor did my newspaper publish swear words. Scarcely hiding his intense loathing, he explained that he had been ordered to brief me, but that was as far as he was going. Much like Congressman Wilson, he proceeded to assure me that not a "single, fucking grain" of American wheat had gone missing. Nor were the Pakistanis or the Afghan resistance leaders corrupt. "Everyone's committed to this ship," he declared.

For the next half an hour, he continued to lambaste my reporting. "You have no idea what's going on," he growled. "What would you say if I told you that we've built six hundred schools inside Afghanistan?"

I told him that I would find that very hard to believe. "Well," he said, "I'm telling you, they exist."

I already knew about these supposed six hundred USAID schools. I had specifically traveled to Nangrahar and Kunar to look at some, but had found little more than incomplete brick walls or partially excavated ground. Or nothing at all. The Swedish Committee—which had been providing clandestine health, agricultural, and educational support since the early 1980s and had one of the most efficient monitoring systems of the international aid community—also maintained that most of USAID's claimed schools were bogus. "Some have been completed but they're empty because no one's paying teachers' salaries," director Anders Fange told me in 1989. If USAID has been paying for all these schools, he added, then the funds were not going where they were supposed to.

While the United States attempted to gain influence by combining the provision of substantial amounts of aid to the opposition and the expansion of their Peshawar consulate into a major listening post, other powers tried other means. For example, the Chinese simply drove from Islamabad once a week with bottles of whiskey for the supposedly teeto-taling mujahideen leaders. Other Western powers maintained low-key intelligence vantage points: a weekend bungalow (later rented by bin Laden) in Peshawar Cantonment for the UK embassy, and the Alliance Française cultural center in Saddar Bazaar for the French.

Certain aid groups, such as Mercy Fund (known as the "Murky Fund" because no one quite knew what it did), International Rescue Committee, AfghanAid, International Organization for Migration, and even some of the UN agencies occasionally served as fronts for the Western intelligence agencies. Most aid workers were legitimate, but a few remained vague about the true nature of their activities. The intelligence agencies were not directly involved in establishing the aid agencies, but they did their best to use them to keep in touch with the Afghans.

Some of my contacts, including several journalists and cross-border adventurers, were clearly collecting intelligence. It was hinted at in casual meetings or over drinks. By the mid-1980s, the American Club in University Town had become the main gathering place for the expatriate community and the prime location for intelligence operatives to obtain information.

Resistance representatives who spoke good English were more impres-sive to outsiders. The CIA clearly preferred Afghans with American accents, no matter how competent or incompetent. One of the former jihadists who lived in Peshawar and was favored by the Americans is the current president, Hamid Karzai. A suave, English-speaking Pushtun eager to please foreigners, he was head of public information for the ANLF, led by Sibghatullah Mujaddedi, when I first met him in the mid-1980s. Karzai liked to go to the Pearl Continental swimming pool, where he did laps and could meet Westerners socially.

His prestigious family connections in Kandahar certainly played a role in Washington choosing him to be their front man, but his command of English was equally important—while his charming, salon demeanor also helped. Conveniently, the Americans underplay the fact that Karzai briefly joined the Taliban in the early 1990s. In fact, many former mujahideen, fed up with the jihadists, turned to the Taliban as an alternative at some point in their careers. Karzai, however, became disenchanted, suspicious that the movement was being taken over by Arabs and Pakistanis—and returned to the Western fold.

Another former jihadist to emerge as a prominent figure in the post-2001 era was Abdullah Abdullah, a Panjshiri who served as foreign minister in the 2002 interim government and later ran against Karzai in the runoff 2009 presidential elections. A fluent English speaker, he was trained as a medical doctor in Kabul, where he cultivated contacts with the resistance. He eventually fled to Peshawar in 1985. After being assigned by the Swedish Committee to the Panjshir as an eye doctor, he soon become a close aide to Massoud. Clear, open, and forward in his thinking, he was precisely the type of man Massoud needed for handling his foreign relations. Constantly in Massoud's company, Abdullah spent most of his time on the satellite phone talking with journalists, foreign embassies, Western intelligence organizations, and international aid representatives.

Abdullah became spokesman for the United Front during the final days of the Talib regime. He adopted his second name in response to persistent requests for full attribution by journalists who did not realize that many Afghans only have one. "I kept telling them that my name was Abdullah, and I would repeat, Abdullah, Abdullah, so they made that my full name," he told me with amusement several years later in Kabul.

Other jihadists, such as former Kandahar governor Gul Agha Shirzai, have become warlords (and millionaires) through corruption, drug trafficking, and protection or extorsion rackets. Some, such as Jamiat's

Ismail Khan, have established their own fiefdoms. As the "Emir" of Herat following the collapse of the Taliban, he was appointed governor and later minister of water and energy in an effort to weaken his long-time hold over the western part of Afghanistan by obliging him to live in Kabul. For many, however, Khan remains the Emir.

Another ex-jihadist was "Marshal" Mohammed Qasim Fahim, a broad-faced man with a thick boxer's nose who joined Massoud's Panjshir resistance in the early 1980s. Fahim, with the collapse of the PDPA government in 1992, became head of KHAD (the Afghan secret police) as part of the jihadist government under Interim President Sibghatullah Mujaddedi. Karzai appointed him one of the country's two vice presidents in November 2009.

The most notorious perhaps is Rashid Dostum, a ruthless militia commander who changed sides repeatedly, murdered many, and is currently chief of staff to the commander of the Afghan National Army. The new police, including the secret police, are littered with former Eastern Europe–trained security professionals. Some, too, have been hired by US and British security companies, such as Blackwater (now Xe) and Dyncorp International.

Others have opted out completely, such as Mohammed Eshaq, whom I first met in the early 1980s when he was a magazine editor and head of information for Jamiat. He eventually became director of Afghan Radio and Television in the post-2001 government—but, increasingly disillusioned by the new Kabul regime, went into the IT business. Today Eshaq is highly critical of the way some of his fellow former jihadists have aligned themselves to the international community. "There are too many agendas which have nothing to do with Afghanistan," he said with a resigned shake of his head when I saw him at his Kabul office in the summer of 2009. "We had high hopes but many foreigners simply don't understand this country. They've spent a lot of money but with nothing much to show."

I spent much of my time in Peshawar in the early 1980s becoming better acquainted with the resistance moderates who, although as corrupt as the fundamentalist factions, would probably be the most palatable choice for a new government in Afghanistan. In February 1980, just weeks after the Soviet invasion, tribal, religious, and political chiefs began exploring the possibilities of a nationwide Loya Jirgha to establish a resistance government. The plan was to have Zahir Shah, the former king who had been living in Italian exile since 1973, as its figurehead leader. At the same time, those close to the royal family viewed this as an opportunity to bring the monarchy back.

To deepen my understanding of how these new resistance leaders, all now with armed retinues and flashy vehicles, were going to convene in the Loya Jirgha, I traveled to Islamabad to consult Afghan experts, in particular the well-known American ethnologist Louis Dupree. Both Louis and his wife, Nancy (another specialist later credited with reconstituting the Kabul Museum during the post-2001 period) knew most of the players personally and shared a wealth of knowledge about them with me. When National Public Radio asked me to do a radio interview with Dupree, a former US Marine, I had to plead with him to ease up on the expletives. It was impossible for me to edit them out, I explained. "Then leave them in. We're dealing with the fucking Soviets here," he barked.

Originally a tribal tradition with its roots in the Law of the Pathan, the Loya Jirgha has become a salient feature of Afghan society. It is convened only for special occasions, notably the election of a king, the adoption of a constitution, or to discuss a national emergency. Normally the delegates come from different walks of life, including respected tribal, religious, and regional leaders along with scholars, military commanders, business leaders, and politicians. Everyone has the right to speak, and frankness is expected.

The 2002 Emergency Loya Jirgha in Kabul, which was proposed by the Bonn accords and held under UN auspices with Zalmay Khalizad, the Afghan-born US envoy, made the mistake of involving the warlords in the process that led to the creation of Afghanistan's new constitution. The inclusion of the warlords immediately discredited the initiative in the eyes of many.

The first challenge of the proposed 1980 Loya Jirgha, however, was to determine who actually had the right to convene it. The more fundamentalist Pushtun groups, such as Hekmatyar's Hezb, vehemently opposed the gathering. So did the communists in Kabul. Both Daoud and the PDPA regime invoked their own respective Loya Jirghas. Daoud held his in 1977 to confirm his new constitution and government with himself as the president. The PDPA's National Fatherland Front called theirs in 1981 in a bid to create a nationwide base for public support. Neither had any legitimacy.

Convened in Peshawar, this first resistance-sponsored gathering, largely funded by the Saudis, brought together over a thousand tribal, nomad, religious, guerrilla, political, refugee, and diaspora personalities representing all of Afghanistan's provinces. While recognized as symbolic, all it could achieve was the basis for a provisional government-in-exile.

The hope among some was that this would enable Zahir Shah to return. While in Peshawar, I regularly bumped into Zahir Shah's representatives who were staying next to me at Dean's Hotel. The ex-king, they told me, was prepared to come, but only if invited by his people. This call was never allowed to happen. Pushing their own stooges, notably Hekmatyar, Khales, and Sayyaf, the Pakistanis succeeded in preventing the former monarch's return.

Within weeks of the Peshawar Loya Jirgha, efforts to create a government-in-exile were on the verge of collapse through constant bickering, with the bulk of the delegates going over to Gailani's NIFA. By April 1981, the alliance was formally dissolved. Two months later, the moderates announced the formation of their own Islamic Unity of Afghanistan Mujahideen. Several more attempted Loya Jirghas were held during the 1980s and '90s, but none was able to lead to a consensus.

Only the Loya Jirgha of 1993—organized during the Battle for Kabul by Massoud under the jihad presidency of Rabbani—made some political inroads. Tajiks, Massoud, and Rabbani had all succeeded in bringing in select tribal leaders and commanders from the southern Pushtun areas. But as we stood on the rocket-torn tarmac of Kabul airport, a diverse mix of Pushtuns disembarked. They were all stone-faced and glaring. Their looks personified hatred and suspicion.

Under the rules of a Loya Jirga, everyone has the right to speak for as long as they wish. The delegates made speeches for four days. At first, there was a degree of consensus that the war had to stop. Yet even then, it was apparent that an alternative to the former jihadists was in the offing, notably a new grassroots opposition: the Taliban. While not formally referred to as the Taliban, the southerners made it clear that the only option for Massoud and Rabbani was to join their Pushtun-dominated movement. This was something that northerners could not agree to.

In the absence of a unified Afghan resistance front, it was necessary to maintain contacts with all the varied groups. It did not take long for me to realize that no single group spoke for all Afghans. As a movement, the resistance consisted of a highly complex and diverse patchwork of several hundred fighting fronts. I realized that the only way to gain a comprehensive picture of operations within Afghanistan was by regularly stopping by different resistance party offices to glean details of their purported military operations. The representatives were always friendly, immediately calling for tea or soft drinks before launching into exaggerated stories regarding the exploits of their fighters. Most were terribly organized and touchingly naive about PR.

The parties did everything possible to promote their success on the front, as they needed to look good in the eyes of foreign donors to attract support. It was all part of the game. I would interview Afghans who had just arrived in Peshawar with carefully placed, nonleading questions about specific incidents. An alleged massacre or a bombing, perhaps. Or a major Soviet offensive, which had forced out even more refugees. It was the only way to piece together a picture of what was happening.

In one encounter during the early 1980s, I stopped by Hekmatyar's office with a visiting journalist from *The Dallas Morning News*. The Afghan politician proceeded to recount how his forces had destroyed an entire Soviet convoy. His aide, Hussein Mangal, known to us as "Black-eyed Mengele," was a thin Pushtun with dark, receding eyes. He handed me a piece of paper with neatly scribed words and figures.

"These are the losses of the *Shouravi*," Mangal grandly announced. Carefully annotated were the numbers of Red Army tanks, APCs, and trucks destroyed (over fifty) and soldiers killed (well over a hundred). If it had been true, this would have been a significant disaster for the Soviets. Months earlier, I would have been impressed. Now I simply shook my head. This was the third or fourth such claim in as many weeks. There was never ever any corroboration.

"Oh, for God's sake, Mangal, stop passing off this rubbish," I said. "I've heard nothing about this attack on the BBC or anywhere else. No one takes this stuff seriously." My American colleague looked on in horror. The Big H glared at me angrily, while Mangal wet his lips, slowly repeating the claims. "No, these figures are true. We are inflicting serious defeats against the Soviets," he insisted.

I quite liked Mangal, a graduate of the State University of New York at Fredonia. He took his job seriously and never allowed my dismissals to bother him. Mangal later emerged as one of the most influential of the Hezb leaders. In 2004, Karzai brought him in with two other key Hezb, Qazi Amin Waqad as minister of justice and Waheedulla Sabawoon, in a bid to strengthen his government's Pushtun composition.

We talked for another half an hour. As we climbed back into our taxi, my colleague turned to me nervously. "You gotta be nuts," he blurted. "I thought those guys were going to slit our throats." I assured him that Hekmatyar's people were too savvy for that. "They'll kill you when no one is looking," I replied half seriously.

Unfortunately, as I got to know Hezb better, it became clear that Hekmatyar, with close support of the ISI, was prepared to murder anyone who dared oppose him. These included resistance intellectuals and commanders—and journalists. America's unbridled support of Hekmatyar and other Peshawar-based extremists during the 1980s would prove to have perilous consequences. Despite endless opportunities to support moderate factions during the Soviet-Afghan war, the CIA—prompted by Pakistan—insisted on working closely with the most fanatical Islamic factions. This decision was fatal. It led to the destruction of Kabul, and provided the insurgency leadership that is now fighting NATO troops in Afghanistan. Simply put, it was the US backing of the Islamic extremists in the 1980s that helped produce the current military quagmire in Afghanistan.

CHAPTER SIX

Refugees, Tora Bora, and Fighting Veterinarians

B y early spring 1980, I found myself flying in and out of Pakistan to cover both the war and the resulting humanitarian crisis. The refugee population had swollen to three million, with white-tented camps donated by the UNHCR and the Red Cross springing up throughout the tribal agencies and in Baluchistan. A further two million Afghans, primarily Hazaras, crossed over into Iran. The wealthier, more urban Afghans fled to Western countries. Over the next six months, I traveled to Somalia, Ethiopia, Thailand, Hong Kong, Sri Lanka—and even French Guyana, Florida, and California—visiting refugee populations and gaining an ever clearer grasp of how this great migration drained away educated citizens that a developing nation like Afghanistan could not afford to lose.

Some of these returned to their homeland during the post-2001 period. Among the best-known returnees was the US ambassador to Kabul, Zalmay Khalizad. An ethnic Pushtun from Mazar-e-Sharif in the north, he first traveled to the States as an exchange student in his late teens. He later served with the Reagan and Bush administrations before working as a consultant for the US oil consortium UNOCAL on the proposed 890-mile Trans-Afghanistan Pipeline intended to link Turkmenistan with Pakistan. Khalizad had been involved in planning the overthrow of the Taliban and was Bush's special envoy before being appointed ambassador in 2003. While he was widely regarded by Afghans as a local boy done good, non-Pushtuns perceived him as favoring US and Pakistani policies, and as the real power behind the presidential palace in Kabul.

Another was Abdul Jabar Sabet, the long-haired and wild-looking former head of the VOA Pashto service in Washington. A former

Hekmatyar aide, this hard-line Pushtun became legal adviser to the minister of interior before being appointed attorney general by President Karzai in 2006 with US and British support. Many Afghans found it hard to understand why Westerners would back Sabet, who was accused of corruption and finally removed from power in 2008 after it became clear that he had his own political aspirations and planned to challenge the president in the next election.

I still found time in 1980 for several trips back to Peshawar, and my assignments now regularly included clandestine forays inside Afghanistan. Together with our mujahed guides, colleagues and I slipped into closed tribal areas for quick "in and out" sorties along the Pakistani-Afghan border. I was frequently arrested, but that was all part of the "game." As one Pakistani army officer so eloquently put it to me: "If you slip up, you get caught; if not, then bully for you." For the Pakistanis, it was important not to be perceived by the Soviets to be encouraging foreign aid workers and journalists to enter Afghanistan illegally.

Traveling through the border regions is highly dangerous today, but back in those earlier days I never felt nervous about roaming the tribal zones. Even in 2005, I was able to visit Khyber Agency without too much concern. By 2008, however, the Pakistani army was fighting a major war against local Taliban and al Qaeda elements, including foreign fighters from countries such as Yemen, Chechnya, and Libya. Much of this took place in the NWFP, including Swat, a traditional tourist area. Such World War II–style full-scale operations were almost unthinkable in the 1980s and '90s. Yet they involved tanks, mortars, rockets, helicopter gunships, and fighter aircraft.

From 2004 on, the United States stepped up its offensive in the tribal areas along the Pakistani-Afghan border region with predator drones, unmanned aircraft that carry intelligence-gathering cameras and sensors and carry out missile strikes. The Bush administration considered these drones one of America's most effective weapons in its "war on terrorism." Despite vehement protests by the Pakistanis about this infringement of sovereignty, *The Washington Post* reported in October 2008 that a secret deal had been reached between Washington and Islamabad to allow the overflights to continue. The use of drones was further endorsed, and later expanded, by President Obama.

The American leadership firmly believes that predators have helped decapitate much of the al Qaeda and Talib leadership, particularly in South and North Waziristan. One US embassy official in Kabul gleefully pointed out that local Talib leaders were becoming so unnerved by the attacks that they had begun fleeing their mountainous hideouts in the NWFP to Quetta and Karachi, a trend that prompted Washington to consider widening their scope to include Baluchistan.

Back in the 1980s, however, journeying through the tribal areas was like stepping back into the nineteenth or early twentieth century in the old reprinted editions of frontier colonial exploits—with the veneer of gentlemanly conduct. This was a rugged hinterland where local Pushtun tribesmen carried antiquated *jezail* flintlocks and shotguns dating back to the Anglo-Afghan Wars as they carried out sniping missions and ambushes among the high-mountain ridges.

It wasn't until the mid-1980s that these ancient muzzle-loaders were replaced by AK-47s and .303 Lee-Enfields, brought in by supporters of the mujahideen. These "wily" Pathans, as the British liked to call them, lived in turreted mud-and-stone forts (or *qalas*).

Our main concern was to avoid the Frontier Scouts. No journalist during the Soviet-Afghan war was ever kidnapped and exchanged for ransom while trying to cross into Afghanistan, and most Pakistani tribesmen saw themselves as part of the jihad. So cross-border passage remained possible, though not guaranteed. On one trip with American photographer Steve McCurry (famous for his *National Geographic* picture of the "girl with the green eyes"), *Newsweek*'s Nick Proffitt, and Rauli Virtanen (my Finnish colleague) we got picked up just before the Afghan border. It was frustrating. We all needed "inside" datelines, but the Scouts had good local informants. They deliberately let our bus, which was crammed with tribesmen, slip through, only to apprehend us at the last checkpoint.

"I am afraid that I must put you in the jug," announced a polished Punjabi major after he had taken us into custody at a Mohmand Scouts fort with its whitewashed stones and neatly planted roses. The British, of course, had built the stronghold back in the nineteenth century where it had the best view of the valley. Against a backdrop of brown, craggy mountains punctuated by holly oak and pine, a tumbling river wove its way past villages and fields lined with glittering poplars. "It is not for you to go traversing tribal area without permission. This is not New York, you know."

Walking up the hill toward the gate with its garrison buildings, I noticed what looked like a squash court. I asked the major whether anyone played. "I'm the only one who does," he lamented. Then he eyed me carefully. "Do you?"

"Well," I said. "I believe you've found your man."

The major beamed. "Well then, let us have a game." He immediately ordered his men to take us to the guest quarters instead of the "jug." The court was incredibly dusty and had not been used for months, possibly years. The major and I fought a hard match, but at an altitude of over nine thousand feet it was exhausting. We got through five games and he easily won. As we walked off the court, wiping the sweat with our towels, he exclaimed: "Excellent game. We play again tomorrow morning before I have my chaps escort you back to Peshawar. Now, let's meet for dinner."

The officers' mess was resplendent with old regimental silver and recent mounted plaques commemorating official visits from the United States and Germany. Three other officers were waiting, delighted to have company, even prisoners. A uniformed orderly stood behind each chair, ensuring that we never lacked full glasses of water or Coke and Fanta. I would have enjoyed a glass of wine, but that was unlikely under a military dictatorship headed by an Islamic fundamentalist. At the end of dinner, roast mutton with rice and potatoes, the orderlies served tea. The major winked and whispered in a low voice, "During the British time, it would have been port."

Back in Peshawar, the Arabs were showing intense interest in both the refugee plight and jihad. Pink-turbaned Saudi Arabians or Kuwaitis in impeccably white robes distributed aid as part of *zakat*. Coming out of the Intercontinental Hotel, I watched two Arab businessmen step up to a crowd of three-hundred-odd Afghans. Snapping open their leather briefcases, the Arabs tossed stacks of US dollar bills to the crowd, like bones to dogs. The Afghans grabbed, punched, kicked, and scratched for the money. Moments later, uniformed police surged in with batons to break up the melee and "confiscate" what they could. In time, the Arabs set up Islamic support foundations to build *madrassas*, clinics, and mosques in the camps.

Pakistani intelligence was intent on keeping tabs on the foreign correspondents. I had a code worked out with the *Monitor* for certain types of trips. Heading off for a "tea break" referred to a quick journey into the tribal areas. Going on "holiday" meant crossing into Afghanistan clandestinely. Initially, I referred to the mujahideen as "friends," while the French doctors—who were operating increasingly inside Afghanistan—were known as the "Parisians."

Eventually, cross-border coverage turned into a game. As part of their anti-Moscow stance, the Pakistanis tolerated journalists and aid workers slipping into Afghanistan as long as it was not done overtly. Returning was no problem. The military always seemed delighted to see me and offered friendly chats over tea to find out what I had witnessed "inside." Occasionally, if what I had seen merited more superior attention, I found myself invited to afternoon tea by the home secretary or one of the political agents. Inevitably, there would be two or three short-haired gentlemen—ill at ease in their *shalwar-kamiz* civilian clothes, listening quietly in leather armchairs, their tea untouched.

The ISI was clearly playing its own game. The Pakistanis were quite happy to use journalists as informal intelligence sources. And we were happy to use them if it helped us get across the border. On one occasion, after being apprehended by the Chitrali Scouts near the Afghan frontier and returned to Peshawar with a British journalist, we protested to Her Majesty's high commissioner—who, we knew, would be meeting with General Zia that evening. The next day, two ISI officers appeared at Dean's. "You have twenty-four hours to return," they told us tersely. We immediately headed back, only to bump into the police sergeant who had arrested us. He abruptly turned his back on us and walked off. By nightfall, we were in Afghanistan.

Several months into the Soviet occupation, I had become adept at quick clandestine journeys. But I had yet to witness action. Much of my reporting was based on interviews with the mujahideen or refugees. The various Western diplomatic missions and the aid agencies all had their views, but it was hard to determine what was really happening.

I was not the only journalist bothered by this. Another was Peter Jouvenal, a young Briton with a reticent smile, who had specifically joined the Gunners in the British army to gain experience as a war photographer. Unfortunately, Peter suffered from dyslexia and could never become an officer. On completing his three-year stint, he left with plans of finding a war to cover: Afghanistan.

Quiet, modest, and exceptionally knowledgeable about weaponry, Peter caught a bus from London to Pakistan. When I met him at Dean's, where he lived in a cheap room at the back, he had just begun selling pictures to British newspapers and magazines. We had a similar esprit de corps and we agreed to pool our contacts for a trip inside to see some real "action."

Together we contacted the different resistance groups. The big parties made extravagant promises about major resistance operations. Twice, we nearly left on what were supposed to be key military actions, but these were canceled at the last moment. Finally, Peter and I met a small, obscure group called Afghan-e-Millat, a nationalist Pushtun faction with strong but confused socialist—even Maoist—leanings. I wondered what the tribal equivalent of National Socialism was in Afghanistan. I knew there had been Nazi contacts with Pushtun youth groups during the 1930s and early '40s, but did not know whether Millat was part of it. Peter had already encountered some of their militants inside Afghanistan. They offered to take us in.

At the Millat office in Saddar Bazaar, one of their commanders, a former Afghan army officer, consulted briefly with his men. The mujahideen were stepping up their attacks against Jalalabad in Nangrahar province, he said. How soon could we leave? Immediately, we assured him. "Good, we leave tomorrow," he announced.

The next day we left by bus for Parachinar, about six hours southwest of Peshawar. I had been there before, but always with an official escort. Now we planned to traverse the Safed Koh (white mountain) range into Afghanistan to reach the Jalalabad Plains. We caught a minibus from Khyber Bazaar. The guide sat two rows ahead of us. He would pretend not to know us if we were caught. We covered ourselves with our *patous*. The bus was packed, mainly with tribesmen and -women in purdah returning from town. I was squeezed next to a large woman, who had pushed back her burqa almost fashionably over her head. She kept asking me questions in Pushto—which, of course, I could not answer, so I pretended to be asleep. Peter did the same.

We encountered a good dozen controls along the main Parachinar road. Periodically, scouts or police would board. At one point, a little girl with a runny nose clambered onto my lap. She played with my sunglasses and urinated on me, but I clung onto her as my best bet for not being questioned.

This did not prevent one policeman from noticing my partially concealed camera bag. He made me open it, revealing my cameras—including a small movie camera, which I had brought along for ABC News. He simply nodded and moved on. At another post, a policeman motioned for me to climb out. Peter was pointedly dozing, his face covered, but the officer stepped up to him, too. He barked something, and Peter wearily pulled out a note with Foreign Ministry letterhead that he had "borrowed" from a government desk in Islamabad. One of his contacts had scribbled a *laissez-passer* in Pushto for both of us. Two official-looking insignia were made from an inked-over coin (a British florin), which we had pressed onto paper. It looked tremendously official. The policeman was impressed. He stepped off the bus.

On entering Parachinar, I noticed a significant increase in the number of refugee camps since my previous visit a month earlier. Tents were springing up wherever—in fields, along riverbanks, by the roadside. Afghans were now coming in every day by the thousands. Dozens of World Food Program (WFP) trucks loaded with wheat and other food supplies clogged the streets.

At the bus station, Peter and I followed our guide to the guerrilla compound. It was shared by the other resistance parties, each with its own office. Two Millat militants, high school students from Jalalabad—barely out of their teens—greeted us. They led us into a small room with three beds, party posters, and flags. It was filthy and littered with refuse, the floor covered with dark globules of spittle. The kitchen and squat latrine down the hall were even worse. They reeked of sewage.

The next morning half a dozen guerrillas appeared. We should be ready to leave, they told us. But they first had to make sure that no Pakistani Scout details had been dispatched during the night to monitor the trails. They knew where the troops were positioned near the summit, but it was the forested lower parts that were tricky. We waited as groups of mujahideen left the various compounds in trucks flying green banners.

They were off to war, heading toward Paktia by way of Teri Mangal to the west. Waving their rifles, they seemed boisterously defiant and confident.

At three thirty in the afternoon, our guides returned. They had seen no patrols. They bundled our packs into blankets and slung them into the back of a small Suzuki van. We piled in behind. The van lurched onto a rough track through irrigated fields and stopped at the first stand of trees. We began trekking toward the twelve-thousand-foot-high *kotal*, or col. Beyond it was Afghanistan. It was late spring, but there was still snow at the summit. The sky was intensely azure and the day was hot, but the towering cedars and pines provided welcome shade. I had not expected to find such thick forests. There were numerous streams, sometimes torrents. We had to cross the main river four times, jumping from boulder to boulder or wading through the bitterly cold water holding our packs over our heads. The terrain reminded me of the Alps or the Rockies.

For the next two days, we trekked northward. We followed a trail used by loggers, hunters, and shepherds. I was surprised by the heavy—and wasteful—cutting of timber. The woodsmen, usually in twos and threes, long-handled axes slung over their shoulders, felled the trees and then scaled them down into rectangular blocks. This made it easier to transport them on the backs of camels to Parachinar before being hauled by truck to Peshawar. The rest was left to rot. There were no signs of replanting.

The upper regions of Safed Koh were completely alpine. The climbing was tortuous, sometimes straight up across boulder-strewn fields and landslides. At one point, we descended a huge snowfield by sliding on our anoraks, pulling our packs behind us. I bashed my knee severely on a rock, causing it to throb painfully.

Refugees streamed along the trail. We encountered dozens of families, mainly older men with women and children, struggling across this beautiful but hazardous range. They stepped over rocks or edged their way down precipitous ledges. Some led baggage-laden horses and donkeys, but most carried little or nothing: blankets and a soot-stained teakettle—or a few chickens rhythmically swaying, their legs tied to a shoulder knapsack, while a doleful dog ambled behind. The refugees looked exhausted, their faces etched with resignation. Many were dehydrated from days of walking. Worried about informers, we muttered our greetings and hurried on. We spent the first night in a woodcutter's shed. The guerrillas made a fire. We ate apples and drank water from the river.

Once over the pass and into Afghanistan, we felt safer. The view from the col was astounding. The Hindu Kush, a hazy white band of pink-shaded peaks, marked the horizon—while the plains of Jalalabad, punctuated by dark blotches of irrigated farmlands, stretched out below the mountains. The mujahideen, however, were concerned about aircraft. They constantly scanned the skies for helicopters and MiGs. The Soviets were flying more and more sorties, not seeming to care whether they were attacking resistance fighters or civilians.

The refugee columns increased the farther we got into Afghanistan. We were now encountering forty or fifty people an hour. One woman, carrying a newborn baby in a shawl, stepped in front of me. She held up her shriveled infant, his mouth curling and opening trying to suck milk that was not there. The baby gave a forlorn wail. I had no idea what to do. This mother clearly thought I was a doctor, and she knew that her child would not survive the night. She kept pushing the baby toward me, uttering plaintive noises. There was nothing I could do.

The scenes of desperation were unremitting. Farther on, a small boy, no more than nine or ten, sobbed uncontrollably. His father, himself on the verge of despair, coaxed him softly as they shuffled along. Despite their fatigue, they came up to us to shake hands. I was deeply touched. I could not help but admire the fortitude and grace of these people.

Making our way along river gorges with thick forest rising on both sides, we finally entered our first farming communities, small, scattered hamlets with terraced fields planted with wheat and opium poppies. The houses resembled Navajo villages with flat roofs. Fast-moving sluices cut into mountainsides or lined with hewed timber ran parallel above the torrents to irrigate the terraces below. I had seen similar water platforms in the mountainous Kurdish areas of Iraq and Turkey, but also in northern India and in the Swiss and French Alps. As the forests opened out, walnut, oak, and mulberry groves lined the fields and water ducts, while pomegranate trees with small fruit clung to the more sheltered enclaves or rock overhangs where they would not freeze in winter.

That evening, we entered a large village where we would spend the night. A small boy showed us a rooftop room, normally used for cattle or sheep—which, as we later discovered, was crawling with ticks. He returned a few minutes later with two more boys, all carrying blankets, some glasses, and a kettle filled with green tea. The oldest boy apologized for the lack of sugar. The farmers had shared what little they had with the refugees, but were now running out of supplies.

While our guides were able to interpret for us, I had begun learning Pushto and had studiously brought with me my copy of *Pushto in 50 Simple Lessons*. I wrote down whatever words I learned or needed to know—tree, teapot, snow, mountain, airplane—so that I could at least pick up some of the conversation.

The *malik*, a lively white-bearded fellow, soon joined us and plied us with questions. What was America doing? And what about Britain? Did the world really care about the *Shouravi* invasion? The old man was particularly interested in my watch and shortwave radio. In a loud shrill voice, he demanded that I give them to him. I laughed. I need this for my work, I explained. Otherwise, how was I supposed to tell the world about the war in Afghanistan and know what time it was? He did not seem convinced. A few minutes later, he bade us good night and left.

The next morning, the old *malik*—whose energy astounded me—led us out of the village, bounding down the trail to show us the path to the plain. As I stopped by the side of an irrigation wall, I quickly jotted down the name of this memorable, tick-infested village in my notebook: Tora Bora. Years later, following 9/11, it was the suspected hideout of Osama bin Laden and the scene of a major battle that proved unsuccessful in apprehending him.

Jalalabad, according to my map, was due north, another two or three days' walk. As we descended, the terrain became steadily more arid, eventually changing to a stony, desert landscape. It became hotter. Only when we passed through the irrigated areas with their shady groves did we feel enveloped in refreshing surges of cool, moist air. The farms clung to the edges of the rivers. Glimpsing the city in the distance, I realized that I was now at the foot of the very mountains I had perceived nine months earlier on my bus journey to Kabul before the invasion. At the time, I had wondered whether this was where the mujahideen were operating. Two decades later, this was also precisely where the Taliban and other insurgents would continue their war, this time against the NATO Coalition.

Both Peter and I were desperately thirsty and perspiring in streams. Neither of us had brought salt tablets. Foolhardily but with no other choice, we drank from the irrigation ducts. The water went straight through us. While the water in the mountains had appeared relatively clean, there was little doubt that now it was picking up increasing concentrations of human and animal excrement the farther we walked. I became severely ill back in Peshawar, but with two or three years of such trips my stomach resisted even the most virulent bacteria. I rarely got sick again.

Once, we stopped by a camp of *kuchis*, Pushtun nomads living in broad, black tents made of skins and tarpaulin, to ask for yogurt. A dozen camels and a herd of sheep and goats grazed the edges of a parched stream. My knee was aching painfully and I was glad to rest. One of the guerrillas picked up a stone and carefully approached the tents, halting at a respectful distance to shout over to the women and children. Two powerful-looking, white *kuchi* hounds—often used for dogfighting—lay on the ground, their heads resting in their paws but carefully monitoring the approaching man. *Kuchi* dogs are trained to wait until unbidden outsiders reach a certain invisible line before bursting forth to attack. The stone was a precaution. Two children walked over with metal bowls filled with watery, salted *most*, or yogurt. We sat on the ground, sipping the fermented liquid. The nomads refused to accept payment when they saw that we were foreigners, another example of the extraordinary hospitality I was to come across again and again in Afghanistan.

We were now following the main river toward another distant patch of farmland. This was where their base was located. Occasionally, we could see Mi-8 gunships or Mi-25 transport helicopters moving toward Jalalabad airport. But they were too far off to be of concern. However, just as we were rounding a low hill, two MiG-21s suddenly appeared directly over us at barely fifteen hundred feet. We had just enough time to pull our brown *patous* over us to blend in with the desert rocks. The MiGs roared off and then circled back in a broad, high arch. My heart pounding, I was convinced that the pilots had seen us.

"Don't worry," said Peter calmly. "It's hard to distinguish anything at that speed."

The jets headed directly toward us but then veered off toward Surkh Rod to the west. Several minutes later, we heard two sharp explosions followed by two more and saw a slow-rising cloud of smoke. The two aircraft made another pass, launching more bombs or rockets, and then faded into the western skyline.

Following a network of irrigation ditches marking the edges of the shallow, river-carved valley, we entered a series of tree-lined villages surrounded by checkered fields planted with wheat, clover, and opium poppies. With stepped-up eradication efforts in neighboring Pakistan, the traffickers had begun transferring both poppy cultivation and processing labs across the border. By the late 1980s, there were almost no poppy fields left in Pakistan.

For the first time, I noticed heavy war damage. Walls lay torn and collapsed, while trees bore deep shrapnel marks. Some inhabitants had fled to Pakistan, but numerous others remained. Men and women toiled in the fields, and wherever we passed, children swam with the water buffalo in the murky canals or rushed up to stare at us.

Shortly before dusk, our guides brought us to a cluster of compounds shielded by thick groves of walnut, mulberry, and tangerine trees. Grapevines grew along the walls. Goats, cows, horses, and sheep grazed among the trees, while chickens scratched in the courtyards. Gazing at this bucolic scene, I could have been somewhere in the northern Italian Cinquemille region. But something was missing—then I realized—there were no women or children. The entire village consisted of mujahideen.

A good forty or fifty young men, many of them former students from Jalalabad and Kabul, were based in the compound. Rifles, mainly Lee-Enfields but also Martini-Henrys and Kalashnikovs, were stacked against the trees. Several gray ammunition boxes had been placed alongside a 1938-model Bren light machine gun near the gate. A megaphone hung from a branch in one of the trees. I later learned this was their only form of communication in battle.

The fighters greeted us loudly, immediately offering us cushions to sit on the worn, beautifully woven carpets laid out among the trees. "Hey *bacha*," cried one of the fighters, and a boy—one of the only children around—rushed out with tea, sweets, and cakes. Later, human rights groups maintained that the mujahideen used child soldiers—but other than menial tasks, I never saw or heard of children being deployed to fight. In contrast, the Taliban and al Qaeda would later show little hesitation at using children as suicide bombers.

As the sun set—with the summits of Safed Koh to the south and the Hindu Kush to the north a fiery red—we sat down to dinner, a simple but ample spread of *nan* and rice *pulao* with mutton and vegetables. We chatted about the new Soviet-Afghan war, including the latest situation broadcast on the BBC. The guerrillas were curious to know how Afghanistan was perceived in Europe and the United States. At least four or five spoke surprisingly good English. Zia, a former instructor from the veterinary college in Jalalabad, explained that most of the young fighters around him were his former students. They had joined the mujahideen en masse. "They're missing out on their education. We have no choice but to fight this war," he sighed.

The commander was a thick-bearded twenty-five-year-old with blue eyes and dark blond hair called Ulfat. From Laghman, he had been a cadet at the Kabul military academy, but had deserted in 1978 following the Taraki coup. For the past year, he had been fighting with Millat insurgents in Nangrahar, Kunar, and Paktia provinces. His dream, he told me, was to go back to the academy to complete his studies. "I don't like this life," he said. "But I will fight these Russian parasites for as long as we have to."

How have things changed since the Soviets invaded? I asked him. What about Red Army counterinsurgency tactics? Ulfat laughed. "Oh, they stay in their tanks. They're cowards. Once some of them came up here on their own, but we killed them, including four officers, so others returned with tanks. They destroyed many houses. We have to fight at night because they have helicopters and we have no anti-aircraft guns or missiles."

By eight thirty, the messengers had returned. Ulfat met briefly with them before addressing us. "It is not our turn tonight, but we'll go anyway," he said with a grin. The word was passed. Laughing and joking, the mujahideen readied themselves with their rifles. I was always bemused by the vanity of Afghan guerrillas. Some carefully combed their hair or trimmed their beards, intently staring at themselves in the mirrors of their *naswah* (snuff) boxes. One of them, less than two feet away, casually polished a single grenade, nonchalantly unscrewing the detonator and inserting it back as if doing his nails. For many fighters during those early days of the war, the grenade had become a status symbol, a bit like a Rolex watch. Within months, however, it was replaced by the increasingly available AK-47 Kalashnikov. Two men carried binoculars around their necks, but I saw no night scopes. They all wore a mix of Nuristani *pakuls* and turbans. I was still wearing my constantly unraveling turban but wondering whether I should switch over to a *pakul*. The turban could become a liability.

"So what's the objective?" Peter asked.

"Oh," said Ulfat. "We'll be attacking Jalalabad airport."

Peter and I glanced at each other. While the thought of witnessing military action appealed to my journalistic curiosity, I found myself pausing at the prospect of targeting a Soviet air base. For Peter, however, it was a question of whether there would be enough light to photograph. "I'd prefer a dawn attack," he said matter-of-factly.

Finally, the group was ready to move. They prayed together before separating into units of ten to fifteen men each. Ammunition was carefully counted and distributed, forty rounds per man. Small boys from the next village, fidgeting with their slingshots, watched with admiration as their heroes shouldered their weapons and stepped out into the night. Following the irrigation ditches, we walked quickly through the dark toward the lights of Jalalabad, three hours march to the north. We could hear additional groups deploying on the other side of the river, tracing their progress by the barking of dogs and the shouting repeatedly of *"Allah o Akbar"* (God is great). Occasionally, the glimmer of a flashlight would pierce the darkness.

We walked in single file through the fields and fruit groves, accompanied by choruses of frogs and crickets. The guerrillas moved fast, jumping over the water channels or walls without breaking stride. The closer we got to the city, the more shattered the villages. Rockets and flares arched into the night sky, while farther to the north, in Kunar province, a major battle appeared to be raging. With the intensity of a tropical thunderstorm, explosions flashed and growled into the night. I was enrapt by this pyrotechnic display against the stark Cimmerian outline of the Hindu Kush beyond. It was too beautiful to bear the trappings of war.

"Looks like quite an operation over there," Peter whispered. One of the commanders had mentioned a major Red Army offensive. I was glad not to be there. At the end of February, the Soviets had launched their first big operation in Afghanistan in the Kunar Valley running alongside the Pakistani border. Since then, however, there had been little activity —but there had been reports of the Soviets stepping up their responses to resistance attacks.

Prior to leaving on this trip, Peter and I had met American writer Phil Caputo in Peshawar. Known for his best-seller *Rumor of War*, Caputo had come to Pakistan on assignment for *Harpers' Magazine*. A swarthy man with dark Italian looks, Caputo wanted to do a quick in and out of Afghanistan for his article. He was unenthusiastic about running into any major combat. "I just need the dateline," he explained.

We had suggested Kunar. "It's really quiet there," I noted. "But good for color." If Caputo was now up in Kunar, he was undoubtedly running into some heavy action.

Finally, the signal came down the line to take cover. Peter and I crouched next to an irrigation ditch. I felt reassured by the gurgling of the water and the croaking of the frogs. Judging by the lights, I gathered that the town must be somewhere to our left. Jalalabad airport itself, however, was directly in front of us. Or at least what appeared to be a peripheral military position marked by half a dozen lights. It was difficult to tell.

Amid cries of *"Allah o Akbar"* over the megaphone, the guerrillas opened fire. They blasted their guns indiscriminately and I watched, mesmerized, as red-laced tracers streamed dreamily across the sky. The mujahideen had spread out across the abandoned fields. A Soviet watchtower abruptly switched on a powerful searchlight, playing it in our direction. A lone heavy machine gun began barking intermittently, its tracers slicing over our heads. Peter and I plunged into the canal. The water was warm and tasted earthy. I could feel an adrenaline rush and kept glancing up to determine whether the Soviets were counterattacking, but nothing happened. Peter shot a roll or two of film, then stopped. "This doesn't do me much good," he said. "Why don't these buggers ever attack when it's light?"

At that moment, a flurry of heavy engines started up, no more than thirty or forty yards ahead of us. A barrier of headlights flashed on.

Directly in front of us stood a huge T-62 tank. Its lights illuminated the shapes of no fewer than half a dozen other tanks, lined up like enormous, squatting toads. They, too, switched on their lights. Peter and I immediately backtracked as fast as we could, bullets zipping and cracking over us, before throwing ourselves behind the cover of a mud wall. The wall would never have shielded us, but it felt protective. From there, we ran back toward the last village. The tanks rumbled forward, but then veered westward toward the town. Obviously, the mujahed attack meant little to them. There were far greater incidents of concern to the north.

The attack lasted half an hour. I doubted whether they had inflicted any serious damage. Psychologically for the mujahideen, however, it was important to tweak the noses, once again, of the mighty Red Army. And as for the Soviet conscripts squatting behind their sandbags, it was probably unnerving to listen to these wild tribesmen, defiantly firing and shouting abuse at them from beyond the wire, night after night.

The warm night dried us by the time we reached the guerrilla compound. Exhausted, Peter and I flopped to the ground, falling asleep almost immediately. Shortly after dawn, we were jolted awake by heavy explosions and collapsing pieces of roof. Six tanks were lumbering up the dry riverbed, firing as they went. Two more shells fell close by. The mujahideen were shouting and running, hiding their heavy weapons in garden caches and taking what they could carry. They then ran in small groups toward the Safed Koh foothills. They had no means to fight back against such heavy armor. Hundreds of shouting and screaming civilians, too, were heading in the same direction.

Peter and I grabbed our packs and moved with our guides toward the far side of the river. "The tanks can only see what's in front of them," said Peter. Hiding behind a wall, we watched the vehicles, black diesel exhaust spewing forth as their treads ground across the arid watercourse and through the willow scrub. Every so often, one of the guns fired in the direction of the village, throwing up plumes of smoke and dust. An hour later, the tanks were gone. They had damaged or destroyed a few more houses, killed or injured a few more civilians—but within three hours the mujahideen were back as if nothing had happened.

Peter and I decided to head back to Parachinar via a shorter but steeper route according to our map. We were concerned that the Soviets might pursue both refugees and guerrillas on the trail that so many were now using. But our guides were reluctant to try an unknown route. We realized that they had no idea how to read a map. Reluctantly, we ended up returning the same way. I found myself constantly plotting emergency escapes down through the river should we be ambushed. We had heard that the Spetznaz had not only begun seeding anti-personnel mines along the main mountain passes, but were attacking refugee columns.

Neither of us had brought any food, so Peter and I resigned ourselves to eating nothing for the next two days. But our plight seemed pathetically trivial compared with the refugees. The women, dressed in dark red, green, and black dresses, stood out like flares. There was no way that reconnaissance aircraft could miss these long queues of slow-moving humanity. The weaker refugees paused for water or to rest among the boulders. We passed fresh graves, marked by piles of stones with pieces of cloth tied to branches carefully fixed into the ground.

At dusk, we stopped for the night. We made a fire and sat down with our backs to the rocks looking up at the night sky. The sheer spectacle of the stars immediately banished my concerns of war. There was nothing that could compete with this beauty. Scores of refugees had also stopped. Their fires dotted the mountainside as they huddled around for warmth—their horses, donkeys, and camels standing, unmoving shadows among the trees.

Pulling out my radio to listen to the BBC news, I muttered: "What I would give for a cup of tea." As if in answer to my plea, an old man picked his way toward us holding a silver tray with two glasses of hot tea. There was even a bowl of sugar. We halfheartedly tried to refuse it, but he insisted: "You're guests in our country. And you're journalists. You must tell the world what is happening." Evidently, everyone knew who we were. We drank in silence, both touched and ashamed. As refugees, they had nothing—and yet, once again, I could not help but admire how they retained their dignity.

Once back in Peshawar, Peter and I went for dinner at Doug Archard's, the American consul. He showed films every Wednesday, and tonight was *Apocalypse Now*. His house was the only place where I could get a decent glass of wine. There were a dozen other guests present—aid workers, several Afghan intellectuals who never turned down a glass or more of the forbidden, and one or two diplomatic colleagues. We were almost through with dinner when the butler appeared at the door.

"Excuse me, sir," he announced, addressing Archard. "There is a man at the gate dressed like an Afghan who says he is an American journalist. He is very dirty." Archard pondered for a moment, and then said. "Let him in."

Moments later, Phil Caputo, still dressed in Afghan attire with a thick black beard, stalked in. He saw Peter and me at the table. "You bastards!" he bellowed. "You sent me into a goddamn Soviet offensive." For almost a week, he had been caught in the Kunar operation whose flares and rockets we had witnessed from the south. He had been obliged to cling to tree trunks to avoid marauding helicopter gunships. "So much for a fucking quiet trip into Afghanistan," he spat.

Peter calmly looked at him. "Your mistake for expecting a holiday," he said.

CHAPTER SEVEN

Tracking the Lion, Part Two

Michael, the morning waiter, knocked gingerly at my door, wearing his neatly pressed white tunic and trousers. "Sir, there are Afghan people to see you," he announced. "They are Tajik people." Although always polite, Michael never hid his disdain for Afghans. Nor Muslims, for that matter. He always considered me part of an unspoken conspiracy whereby he, a Pakistani Christian from Lahore, and I—a Westerner and hence he assumed a Christian—had an obligation to join forces against the unbaptized hordes of Central and South Asia.

"That's fine, Michael," I said, weary of his constant asides. "Just show them in and bring some tea."

It was early summer 1981. I had been waiting at Dean's Hotel for over a week for what I hoped would be my first major clandestine trip. My previous journeys into southern and eastern parts of the country since the invasion eighteen months earlier all had been relatively short. The fighters with whom I had traveled, primarily Baluch and Pushtun tribesmen, were neither well organized nor effective.

Jamiat was proposing a very special trip: the chance to join a French medical team accompanying a convoy of horses along one of the old caravan routes to northern Afghanistan. A ten-day journey, this would take us across some of the world's highest mountains. During the snow-free months, dozens of caravans were making their way across many of the three-hundred-odd highland cols punctuating the length of Pakistan's border. Many ancient trade, smuggling, or nomad trails had fallen into disuse during the 1950s and '60s with the advent of tarmac roads, but were now increasingly reemployed by refugees and mujahideen alike.

The trip sounded incredibly nineteenth century. The French had been operating inside Afghanistan setting up clandestine clinics in hidden side valleys and mountain villages since the early months of the occupation. This particular team from AMI, a Paris-based NGO, was heading to the Panjshir Valley to replace a team that had been working there since late 1980. The Panjshir was widely regarded as one of the country's most organized resistance centers. The initial AMI team had returned to France in late spring 1981, leaving a group of Afghan nurses to run the clinic. With the rising number of wounded from Soviet bombings and land mines, the replacement team—two doctors and a nurse—needed to reach this highland region as soon as possible.

I was intent on reporting the situation from "inside." Only a trickle of humanitarian assistance was making it across the border. The bulk of international aid organizations—such as United Nations Children's Emergency Fund (UNICEF), Save the Children, and the International Rescue Committee—were focusing on the still growing refugee problem in Pakistan. But they did little for the millions of Afghans struggling to survive in the countryside, where 80 percent of the population lived. Communist persecution and bombing, including the deliberate destruction of farms, villages, and harvests, was becoming more intense by the day. Many civilians were finding it difficult to remain.

For the hundreds of relief groups flocking to set up refugee operations in Pakistan (it was difficult to work in Iran), it was politically easier to deal with "official aid." Refugee camps were good for fund-raising purposes. Most donor governments and humanitarian groups did not wish to get involved with anything covert. CARE International, one of the world's most experienced aid organizations, had been working in the region since the 1960s. When asked why it was ignoring the needs of war-affected civilians inside Afghanistan, a senior official based in Atlanta retorted: "We're not into clandestine relief."

Ironically, such cautious approaches were only encouraging the overwhelming refugee flow. By setting up camps, clinics, schools, and food distribution points on the Pakistani side, the agencies created a massive relief magnet. Even at the height of the war, no more than a score of groups—such as MSF, AfghanAid, and the Swedish Committee—risked providing serious humanitarian assistance inside. Subsequent wars and crises—whether in Afghanistan, Southeast Asia, or Central and West Africa during the 1990s and 2000s—have shown that people prefer to remain in their home regions even at the risk of military retribution.

At this point in the war, however, I was curious to meet that still relatively unknown guerrilla commander who had taken the nom de guerre of Ahmed Shah Massoud. It was the "Lion of Panjshir" who had invited the "French doctors" to come in. Pierre Issot-Sergent, a documentary cameraman from the south of France, was the first Western journalist to report on this new Afghan Che Guevera. Earlier in the year, he had traveled with the twenty-seven-year-old mujahed leader. "Massoud's more than just bravado," Pierre said back in Paris after showing me some of his recent front-line footage. "He's actually giving the Russians a hard time."

The Panjshiri commander, he told me, was rapidly earning admiration and respect as a leading resistance symbol. Not only had his forces already withstood several Soviet-Afghan offensives waged to take the seventy-mile-long valley, but they were regularly attacking Red Army convoys along the nearby strategic Salang Highway. The Panjshiris represented a guerrilla model that was beginning to spread to other parts of Afghanistan.

Over the past few days, the Jamiat representatives had stopped by to discuss the journey over long bouts of tea. I splayed out my maps and asked them to trace the four-hundred-mile route from Chitral through Nuristan and Badakshan to the Panjshir. As there were no charts with accurate place-names, particularly in the more remote northeastern parts, I used a British 1893 version (which proved surprisingly reliable) from a book I had found in the bazaar. I combined this with two satellite maps, one an aeronautical printout and the other a CIA map slipped to me by a US diplomat. Both provided excellent topographic overviews, but with few names. As I traveled, I was able to write in the names of villages, rivers, and mountains.

By now, I had met the medical team. In their late twenties, they consisted of Fréderique, a romantic but no-nonsense woman doctor from northern France; Philippe, a thin, red-haired volunteer physician from Lyons; and Evelyne, the nurse, from Paris. It was Fréderique and Evelyne's first mission. In typical Afghan fashion, however, the trip kept getting delayed. I would be up at 3 AM, dressed in my *pakul*, *shalwars*, and Timberland boots, backpack at my feet and four or five notebooks with crisp empty pages aching to be filled. And then no one would turn up. By 7 AM, I would be sipping yet another cup of tea and toying with a grim-looking set of fried eggs. Hours later, a messenger would pull up on a motorbike to apologize. He never gave a reason other than that there had been "a problem."

So I was disappointed when Masood Khalili, the Panjshiri commander's personal envoy, asked whether I minded sharing the trip with two French journalists. (This was the same Khalili who was so severely injured in the suicide bombing of Massoud twenty years later.) The Frenchmen were preparing a television documentary, he explained, and it would help to combine our efforts. I reluctantly agreed. Of course, the two cineastes, Christophe de Ponfilly and Jerôme Bony, were equally apprehensive, but we immediately got on well. To be fair, I was glad of their company and they evidently appreciated that I had already done a number of trips.

We finally left Peshawar for Chitral. Apart from the AMI team and the filmmakers, there was Jean-José Puig, a bearded French computer specialist with a gaunt, pixie face. Before the war, Puig had visited Afghanistan to fish for trout in the Hindu Kush, and even got married there. Now, fly-fishing tackle packed in with his gear, he was doing an assessment trip for a French aid group intent on helping the resistance cause. He was also working, as I later learned, with French intelligence.

Chitral was a lively bazaar town. It had its own airstrip—the town's only access during the snowbound months—and a bell, which was clanged to alert waiting passengers that the plane from Peshawar had cleared the Lowri Pass. This was the watershed dividing line between Central Asia and the Indian subcontinent. If the weather was bad, no planes would cross. We stopped at the local Jamiat office, where our guides disappeared to pick up guns. We then proceeded by jeep to Garam Chashma (hot springs), a burgeoning settlement blessed with ancient hot sulfur springs toward the end of a long, narrow valley of farms and fruit orchards. Overlooking the Lutko River, a tributary of the Chitral, the town was hemmed in by terraced fields of wheat and barley bordered by thick groves of walnut, apricot, and mulberry trees. This was where the vaulting Hindu Raj merged with the Hindu Kush, the last range of the Himalayas, before stretching westward across Afghanistan to dissipate into the semi-arid steppes of Herat near the Iranian frontier.

Once serving as a transit point for Alexander the Great's columns— the main body crossed into India through the Khyber farther south—

Garam Chashma was now a major staging base for mujahideen. It was here that Agha Gul, a mild-mannered former policeman with a drooping mustache, took us under his protective wing. His face was in a perpetual state of sadness, only occasionally broken by a sallow smile. He told me that he had spent two years in jail under the left-wing Mohammed Daoud regime for "opposing communism." He had also been tortured. He spoke a little English and would lace his Dari with any other words—French, Russian, even German—that came to mind. Agha Gul explained that he used to be a "detective" with the Ministry of Interior. "Something like CIA," he added helpfully. Following the collapse of the Talib regime in 2001, he became a general with the new Afghan police. He was one of the few who seemed genuinely concerned about the need to provide his men with proper salaries. Only in this manner could one have an effective police force, he said.

A Massoud confidant, Agha Gul was in charge of the medical teams and supply caravans. Ours would consist of fifty horses loaded with medical goods as well as crates of guns, ammunition, RPGs, land mines, food, cooking pans, generators, and boots. The pièce de résistance was a Russian-made ZPU-2 anti-aircraft gun that was being loaded in dissembled parts.

Garam Chashma, primarily inhabited by Ismailis—followers of the Aga Khan—was an "open" area. Nevertheless, Agha Gul insisted on hiding us in a safe house with a view of the bazaar. He did not want the Pakistanis, who had informers everywhere, to know of our presence. The Soviets, too, had their moles. "You stay maybe three, four days," Agha Gul said. He was strict about our going out. "These Pakistanis no good. Police no good. You will be *bandi* (captured), and much *baksheesh* (bribes)," he added, holding up his wrists to indicate arrest.

All we could do was sit or lie on the carpets of our room, drinking tea, chatting, reading, and sleeping. Over the next decade or so, much of my time with the resistance was spent waiting for things to happen. I took notes, wrote letters, or spent hours listening to the BBC, VOA, Deutschewelle, Radio Moscow, and Radio France International on my shortwave. I often came back from my trips far better informed about world affairs than had I been in Paris.

Prior to the war, Garam Chashma had been little more than a hamlet.

Now it thronged with mujahideen and hundreds of packhorses, donkeys, mules, and the occasional camel. With blue smoke hanging over the town, there was a strong smell of charcoal fires, animal dung, and grilled meat. Numerous roadside *dukan* (shops) and *chaikhane* had opened up to cater to this rapidly expanding border trade. Groups of fighters on R&R were constantly arriving from the inside fronts. Fresh men with new guns replaced them. Refugee families also trickled in. Some brought straggling herds of sheep, goats, and cows, which they sold for a pittance to Pakistani merchants waiting like vultures. The farmers needed the money. They had no place to graze their livestock. Local villagers angrily chased them away if they found them on their land.

The conflict was a boon for the Pakistanis. The frontier police benefited handsomely from the *baksheesh* extorted from mujahideen and refugees alike. Islamic compassion only went so far. But then, I have yet to see a war without profiteers. While waiting, I peered cautiously through a small window to glimpse this strange Kiplingesque world outside. Horse drivers tested saddles or checked hooves, with blacksmiths hammering on new iron shoes. Others sat cross-legged on the ground sewing supplies into coarse hemp sacks. Most of the guerrillas stood in small groups, their *patous* wrapped around their shoulders—shouting and talking, embracing each other when they met, some riding horses, others jolting along in pickup trucks, all against an enticing backdrop of glistening snow-blazoned peaks and a deeply azure sky.

Agha Gul saw to it that we lacked nothing. There were always fresh eggs, cream, bread, fruit, and (of course) relentless amounts of green tea, or *kowa*. Late one evening, Agha Gul appeared, his melancholic face exuding the faintest smile.

"Come," he said hastily. "Soap. Wash."

We grabbed our toiletries and he led us through a maze of side alleys to a group of stone huts. Several armed mujahideen were standing vigil. At each wooden entrance, Agha Gul gestured for one of us to go in. Steam sifted through the cracks. Inside, I found a kerosene lamp lighting a small cubicle with a stone tub. It was overflowing with hot water sputtering from a clay pipe. The Greek baths. For the next hour, I soaped myself down, letting the water extract the grime from my pores. The bathhouses had changed little in two thousand years. I imagined that these same stones may have come from the original buildings constructed by Alexander's soldiers and that they, too, had soaked the same way.

The moon already had risen as Agha Gul quietly led us out of Garam Chashma along a disused irrigation duct. This took us through terraced walnut groves and then down to the main trail. The point was to avoid the Pakistani checkpoints on the edge of the town and to wait for the main body of the guerrilla caravan to arrive. The Pakistanis had been paid off.

Wearing disheveled and soiled *shalwar-kamizes*, we tried to look ruggedly Afghan. The men among us had begun growing beards, while the two women sought to look like boys with their hair tucked into their *pakuls*. Agha Gul had even given us Afghan names. Mine was Latif Khan (servant of God). He told us not to say anything if stopped. He would pass us off as Kirghiz or Turkmen from Central Asia who spoke neither Dari nor Pushto. The Pakistanis probably had never seen a Kirghiz or a Turkmen, so they would have no idea.

Several miles up the valley, we waited for the caravan. The mujahideen had prayed by the river at sundown and then returned to their encampments for a final meal of rice, meat, and *nan*. We had a good twenty hours of hiking before reaching the fifteen-thousand-foot-high Diwana Baba (silly old man) pass and the "safety" of Afghanistan. Toward midnight, we finally heard the commanders urging the men forward with whispered commands: *"Boro, boro bakhai!"* (Move, let's go!) Like a steady flow of quicksilver, the first guerrillas emerged, bathed by the moonlight. As many as two hundred men, they walked in loose formation, the plodding horses straining under their burdens. Many were barely out of their teens. They shouldered World War II–vintage Simonov rifles, the result, no doubt, of an aid shipment from Egypt or some other Third World country. All were spartanly dressed in *shalwars*, their personal belongings—including boiled meat and *nan*—slung over their backs in blankets. A few boasted boots, others leather sandals. Most wore cotton sneakers or plastic shoes. The Afghan resistance on the move. I could not help but feel heavily overdressed with my boots, North Face anorak, sleeping bag, and Gore-Tex bivouac gear.

The mujahideen trudged with the eager, self-important air of schoolboys. I wondered how many had the slightest idea about the war they would soon face. And how many would survive. The ICRC hospitals in Pakistan were already filled with severely injured, both civilians and belligerents. Many were land-mine victims. These were the fortunate ones. Those with their stomachs or chests torn by bullets or shrapnel rarely made it to the hospital. The mountain passes were littered with the stone graves—prayer flags fluttering from their midst—of *shahid*, or martyrs, and civilians.

We began walking westward toward the high end of the valley. Rushes of cool, moist air from the thundering river dispelled the powdery dust thrown up by feet and hooves. In the diffused light, I could see the mountains silhouetted like the battlements of some Stygian fortress controlling the gates to a netherworld beyond. Choruses of dogs howled as the snorting horses, their loads moving rhythmically with the rise and fall of their hooves, passed each hamlet or farmstead. Occasionally, we would hear shots. Shepherds scaring off wolves, Agha Gul told me. But the mujahideen liked to fire their guns just for the hell of it. At the same time, I knew of many stories of *shiftas* (bandits) preying on refugees and travelers.

It felt good to be walking again. My colleagues were completely out of shape. They stopped frequently to catch their breath. Christophe was in relatively good condition as he did karate. Jérôme, on the other hand, collapsed groaning every half hour. The guerrillas were not overly fit, either. While most were peasant boys, some came from Kabul. They were not used to the mountains. Whenever the caravan ground to a halt, they dropped to their haunches, their backs propped against the mud-packed walls of the irrigation canals. Hands dropped into gurgling streams to drink or to splash their perspiring faces. The air was thin, and it was now bitterly cold. We had half a dozen passes ahead of us, most of them over sixteen thousand feet.

Soon after 2 AM, the caravan stopped. The drivers slung oat bags around the necks of the animals while the men curled up on the ground to sleep wrapped in their *patous*. We did likewise. But I could not shut my eyes. The moon, the heavens thick with stars, and the outlines of the mountains were too overwhelming.

The false dawn was just beginning to hang over the ridges as the caravan awoke. The mujahideen made fires to boil water for tea, and stood around warming their hands. Agha Gul brought us tea in plastic mugs. We sipped without speaking, lost in our thoughts. Then the men began moving, the horses ambling ahead in groups of three or four. Stiff and cold, we pulled on our packs and started trudging along the narrow track that followed the gradually diminishing river.

The last frontier post flying the green-and-white Pakistani flag consisted of weathered white tents pitched near a stream. We stayed out of sight while the caravan leaders sauntered over to dispense a few more wads of rupees. Agha Gul had ordered his men to place our packs on the horses and to cover them. Our Western gear would have been a dead giveaway.

On reaching the end of the valley, the trail branched off into two directions. We would head into Nuristan and southern Badakshan via Diwana Baba. The other trail led to northern Badakshan and the Wakhan Corridor via the Dorah Pass. Both were heavily used by the mujahideen and refugees. The Pakistanis still operated patrols, but the immediate threat of arrest was over. We began hiking toward a high plateau cordoned off by precipitous escarpments. It was tough going for the horses, many of which came from the northern plains and were not used to such altitudes. The blistering sun was merciless and the drivers, sweat glistening on their bronzed faces, shouted and whistled to egg on the animals. They whipped them remorselessly. One horse stumbled and fell several hundred yards, strewing crates of ammunition. Surprisingly, it was only slightly injured. Two men scrambled down to distribute its load among the other animals.

For the next twelve hours, the caravan, now spread over three miles, climbed steeply. Occasionally, we rested by cascades of snowmelt. Thick copses of willow grew along the edges, providing the men with shade as they brewed up tea and nibbled on nuts or dried fruit. I was grateful for the tea and understood why the Afghans like it so sugared. You needed the energy. Then came the shouts of *"Boro, boro"* and the caravan plodded on.

The film team began shooting. The convoy with its armed guerrillas plodding over harsh terrain was ideal for television. Christophe and Jerôme had pooled their resources to undertake what would eventually become an award-winning documentary, *Valley Against an Empire*. For the next two weeks—swearing, arguing, and laughing between themselves—the two Frenchmen filmed the caravan as it labored up the passes or along narrow, winding trails. Not only did they have to keep up with the column by hiking twelve to fourteen hours a day, but they also had to roam the mountainsides to seek better angles. We finally reached the foot of Diwana Baba, where the mujahideen set up camp. They preferred to tackle the three-hour ascent at daybreak. A penetratingly cold wind whistled among the boulders. The seven of us hunkered down with our sleeping bags behind the stone walls of a sheep corral, the ground thick with dung. Agha Gul brought us banana wafer biscuits and lemon cake with cups of tea for dinner. It tasted as good as a four-course meal at Lasserre in Paris.

We chatted about the next day's journey and the perils of war. The doctors apprehensively contemplated their next twelve months in Afghanistan. Everyone was aware that the Soviets had been stepping up their counterinsurgency. And yet this extraordinary mountain setting appeared totally removed from the new "Vietnam" on the other side of the ridge. Not unlike its sister "French doctor" organizations, AMI saw its role as providing health relief to war victims but, equally important, to act as a witness. This was the principal reason why the founders of MSF, the first of the French doctors' groups, had created the organization during the Biafran war in the late 1960s. The Red Cross had refused to publicly condemn the killing of civilians. Its job was to remain discreet in order to continue operating on both sides. The French medical volunteers, on the other hand, believed that no one should remain silent about atrocities for the sake of humanitarian relief.

It was such testimony that had convinced Christophe and Jérôme to make their film. They were determined to tell the story of the plight these medical groups were dealing with: the farmer with a bomb fragment in his head, the child whose hands were torn off by an anti-personnel mine, or the woman who died in childbirth for lack of access to even the most basic medical care.

Everyone was soon too tired to talk. Tightening my jacket, I pulled out my notebook. I rested my flashlight on a rock and jotted down thoughts from the day. As I wrote, I could hear the mujahideen talking among themselves, huddled around their fires, wherever there was a bit of shelter. The horses, now rid of their loads, stood in small forlorn groups, food bags hanging from their necks. They always looked so sad at night. I searched the night sky. The Pleiades shone directly above me. This had been my father's and my grandfather's favorite constellation. I pondered whether the invading Greeks, who may have pitched their camps at this very spot, had also looked up at these stars, which they knew as the Seven Sisters or Nymphs—providing them, so far from home, with a source of comfort. At one point, the distant rumbling of high-flying jets resonated among the mountains. Soviet planes returning from patrol or a bombing mission? Or a commercial aircraft skirting the no-fly zone on its way to Europe or India? Either way, the war did not seem real.

It was still dark when Agha Gul stood over us. *"Boro, boro,"* he urged as he handed out biscuits and steaming cups of tea. The drivers were loading their animals. A commander was kicking a mujahed who refused to get up. Some of the fighters were perpetually shirking portage duty or sneaking off for a smoke. Nor were they particularly Islamic. We watched as a mullah with a high-pitched voice totally incongruous with his burly stature and thick beard was berating these adolescents for avoiding prayers. He would run around trying to wallop them with a stick as they laughed and skipped out of the way.

The team was already filming as the first horses moved up the zigzag mountain trail. The drivers, shouting and whistling, held the horses' tails to prevent them from falling into the abyss. By the time the first rays of sun broke, I found myself well ahead of the straggling column. It was a tortuous ascent. The path stank of animal dung and urine, and there were bloodstains on the rocks. The horses gashed their legs as they climbed. Every so often, a crumpled, rotting equine carcass blocked the way. They lay mummified, their skin taut from the sun, skulls gaping with pulled-back grins, eyes plucked out by birds. The caravans often lost up to 10 percent of their horses from falls or while crossing rivers.

The Afghans showed little sympathy for the suffering of an animal. The mujahideen and the doctors paid the drivers by the *sir* (roughly seven kilos) to transport goods. The drivers never bothered to put an incapacitated beast out of its misery. Why waste a good bullet? They stared at me astonished when I insisted. Once I got so angry at the plight of one wretched creature that I grabbed a Lee-Enfield and threatened to shoot the driver if he did not dispatch it. Finally, joking with his friends, but nevertheless worried that I might be serious, he took the rifle and put a bullet in the animal's head.

The top of Diwana Baba—a desolate, ice-draped corridor—was cloistered by monumental ridges, like the ruins of a Carpathian monastery. Swathed by swirling mists, it reminded me of a nineteenth-century Caspar David Friedrich painting. Huge, sinister ravens croaked hoarsely from its craggy parapets, and just ahead, a lone eagle soared. The sky opened up, and the sun beat down with vengeance. Behind me lay Pakistan. In front, a sprawling sea of twenty-thousand-foot-high snow-capped peaks and cloud stretching for a hundred miles to the west: Afghanistan. For the next hour, all I could do was blissfully scan this stunning landscape. I had never seen anything like it. I took some photographs and scribbled more notes, but how on earth does one even begin to describe the overwhelming magnitude and beauty of such country?

Once the remaining horses had reached the top, I headed down with Fréderique and a small group of mujahideen into Nuristan. The inspiration for Kipling's *The Man Who Would Be King*, Nuristan was still a heavily forested wilderness. Bear, fox, leopard, Marco Polo sheep, markhor, and even (some maintained) tiger roamed its mountains. At one point, I watched as a herd of high-horned ibex leapt and crashed down a steep slope, while further on I felt myself being observed. When I looked up, I saw three wolves standing high above me. Our eyes met. I turned away briefly. When I looked back they were gone. In little more than a decade, though, the wildlife would grow sparse as lumber trafficking reached even these northerly extremes of the Hindu Kush and much of the game was shot or trapped. The lack of respect for customary rights had eroded any sense of resource management. There was too much money to be made.

Nuristan, which was proclaimed a separate province in the new Afghanistan of the post-2001 era, has always remained a distinct if not insolent entity. By 1981, the eastern part had come under the control of the Islamic Revolutionary State of Afghanistan, or *dawlat* (government) run by an unashamedly greedy Wahhabi warlord, Maulawi Afzal. Until its dissolution under the Taliban, this semi-autonomous state was recognized by the Saudis and Pakistanis. This suited the Soviets, who chose to ignore the region. For the Nuristanis, however, both the Kabul regime and the resistance were still expected to pay homage. This harked back to an earlier epoch when the *kafirs* undertook lighting raids into neighboring areas in search of slaves. Everyone had to pay tribute.

Descending through peaceful alpine meadows interspersed by gurgling brooks and waterfalls, one quickly forgot the war. We could have been in Switzerland. Fréderique and I soon found ourselves too far ahead for comfort. I suddenly realized that the Soviets could have positioned an ambush at any one of more than a dozen points. Peering through my binoculars, I estimated that the main body of the caravan was still a good hour behind us.

"I think it's best we wait for the others to catch up," I suggested, whistling to the mujahideen to halt. As we sat down to rest, a guerrilla suggested they make tea. Two men busied themselves with the kettle, while the others wandered off to find firewood. There was no shortage of dry heather and alpine rosebushes for fuel. Suddenly an explosion ripped across the quiet afternoon. "Down!" I shouted to Fréderique, pushing her back. My first thought was that we were being shelled, a rocket perhaps, or a mortar. But as I lay in the grass, I figured that the explosion had sounded too small. I lifted my head. I could see one of the guerrillas crawling forward on his hands, pulling himself along, crab-like, about twenty yards away. I rose carefully. His foot was dark with blood, completely savaged with bits of flesh and bone hanging from it.

"A land mine," I said to Fréderique, who now stood next to me. The young doctor immediately moved to help, but I grabbed her arm. "No, there might be other mines. We have to tread carefully. Walk only on the stones."

The injured guerrilla, Shah Mansour, was twenty years old. We covered him with blankets and rested his head on a folded coat. It was then that Fréderique realized her medical equipment was back with the horses. The other medics arrived five minutes later. They had heard the explosion, but they, too, lacked their kit. The AMI team began working with what they had. Having kept my gear, I pulled out a shell dressing, bandages, and disinfectant. I also produced my Swiss Army knife. The others offered whatever they had. The explosion had cauterized the wound, so Fréderique sterilized the blade and cut away the dangling strips of flesh and bone. Mansour had lost most of his foot, which was amputated later. He was in shock and did not need anesthetic. The doctors could give him a sedative once the medicines arrived.

Searching the ground, I found pieces of beige plastic, the remnants of a Soviet PFM-1 anti-personnel device—which my journalist friends and I had dubbed "butterfly mines" because of their shape. Children often picked them up thinking they were toys. Mansour's injury was typical of what anti-personnel mines are designed to do, namely to incapacitate rather than kill. Had he died, Mansour's mates would have buried him, and then continued on their way. Now they had to construct a makeshift litter, place him on a horse, and send him back with four other men to the Red Cross clinic in Chitral. From there, he would be driven down by ambulance to the ICRC war casualty hospital in Peshawar, where I would visit him two months later. This meant that one good horse and five potential fighting men, including the victim, were removed from the theater of battle.

The incident was chilling and thrust us back into the realities of war. This was not to be the only time I would witness such a grim event. Several years later, I made my way down a steep mountain to a muja-hed position at the bottom. An Afghan commander ventured down the same trail, but then veered slightly to the left. An explosion and his left foot was torn off. He hopped around on his good leg, cursing loudly for not having been more careful. We found some twenty-five land mines among the rocks in an area barely the size of a tennis court.

On another occasion toward the end of the occupation, a group of mujahideen escorted me into a recently taken government position in eastern Afghanistan. They had not bothered to check the perimeter. I broke out into sweat when I realized that we had wandered into a mine-field. Among the surrounding bushes, I counted half a dozen grenade-like POMZ-2Ms, which we had nicknamed "Noriega" mines after the ex-president of Panama because of their characteristic pockmarks. We carefully retraced our steps. Relieved, I sat down on the ground, rubbing my face. I glanced up. Less than a foot away was a taut trip wire. Another mine. No matter how careful one tries to be, it is impossible to remain constantly vigilant. So much of survival is based on sheer luck. With the escalation of the war, the Soviets were now scattering hundreds of thousands of these anti-personnel mines along the mountain passes and trails, inflicting indiscriminate casualties among guerrillas and civilians.

We arrived in the Bashgal Valley, where the Maulawi Afzal's *dawlat* had its seat. Hundreds of mujahideen and refugees were camped on the outskirts. We did the same while the caravan commanders went over to negotiate. They had to leave some weapons and ammunition as tribute. Agha Gul was nervous. "These people no good," he whispered to me. "Not good Afghans. We must leave tomorrow morning early." The *dawlat* regarded anyone who entered its territory as a source of revenue. During the years that followed, these independent Nuristanis held various foreigners hostage, notably journalists and aid workers, in order to extract as much money as possible from them. Kidnapping was good business.

I strolled over to a group of mujahideen who were charging recklessly on horses across a broad, rocky pasture. They were playing an impromptu game of *buzkashi*, a form of polo using the headless torso of a goat or calf as a ball. One of the men passed me a horse, and I rode with the game before galloping off to a distant hillock savoring the cool wind on my face.

Next morning, the caravan edged off early. We followed another side valley along a tearing torrent, passing terraced villages surrounded by fields of corn and beans cultivated on steep hillsides. We grabbed young ears of corn, sweet and soft, to nibble on. In 2004, I returned to this region. Visiting one of the villages, I was amazed to find that it now had electricity. The locals had transported a hydro generator across the mountains from Pakistan, which they installed in a former flour mill. The man in charge of the generator was paid in wheat on the basis of seven kilos per lightbulb per month.

We climbed two more passes and then descended into a heavily forested region. Occasionally, we would spend the night in villages. At one point, we entered a hamlet of three or four houses. It could not have been more isolated. The doctors treated a small boy whose hand had been blown off by a mine. His wound had been wrapped in a filthy cloth with cow dung, a traditional but dangerous form of treatment. The doctors did their best to clean the wound and instructed the father to bring the boy to the Panjshir clinic for treatment. Although several days' walk, it was the closest place with any form of medical care. They never came. The boy, I later learned, died from infection.

All this provided the film team with the sort of dramatic footage they needed to illustrate the devastating impact of the Soviet-Afghan war. It enabled them to begin telling the story—one that Christophe would pursue for years to come—of how a largely uneducated but resilient peasant people were resisting a superpower against all odds.

The trail often became a veritable highway of human traffic. We passed groups of mujahideen, who, with no horses or little luggage, walked with surprising speed. The problem with encountering large groups of fighters was that you had to shake hands with everyone, sometimes forty or fifty people, and each time murmur the words "*A Salaam Aleikum*" or "*Mandabushi*"—may you not be tired—while raising your right hand to your heart in a sign of respect. If they saw our cameras, they would raise their rifles, shouting "*Allah o Akbar*"—and demand photographs. Usually, their idea of a picture was a formal portrait standing stiffly with their guns at the ready. I would soon dread glimpsing large bands of men coming toward us. In desperation, I tried lying down by the path, pretending to be asleep, but they would stop and prod me awake to shake my hand. Rarely did they seem astonished to find a foreigner "sleeping" by the side of the trail in the middle of the Hindu Kush, as if this were the most natural thing in the world.

Refugees, too, haunted the trails, painstakingly fleeing with small children on their backs, the women trudging behind, while the men wanted to know why we were walking in Afghanistan. When Agha Gul explained that we were doctors and journalists, they nodded gravely, touching their hearts. Sometimes they called back to their group and an ailing child or woman would be brought forward for treatment. They would beseech us to tell the world what was happening. "The *Shouravi* are trying to take our land, our homes, our farms. But they will not take our souls. We'll fight until every last communist is off our soil, until we breathe our last breath," one of the men declared. Everyone nodded in reverential agreement. It was a refrain I was to hear again and again.

On leaving Nuristan, we entered the more semi-arid parts of southern Badakshan. This meant trudging for hours across desert terrain. When Christophe was not filming, he and I often walked ahead, deep in conversation. Sometimes we elaborated on meals we would have on our return to Paris. We went through each course in exquisite detail, conjuring up the succulence of fresh oysters or the taste of a particular Burgundy or Loire Valley wine. We picked out the restaurants and knew precisely which menus we would choose.

The trail took us through villages, their flat roofs a patchwork of yellow and orange from the apricots and corn being dried in the sun. Some of the communities boasted small bazaars, no more than four or five shops. Their offerings were meager: tea, sugar, biscuits, and chewing gum. Even in peacetime, people walked down to the larger valleys that would eventually take them to a town. These days, there was little trade. It was only the old men and the women who dared venture into the communist-controlled zones to bring back supplies.

Whenever we entered cultivated areas, women quickly covered their faces or turned their backs. Men were already harvesting with bullocks and donkeys or winnowing the wheat, tossing it up in the air for the chaff to blow away. Children ran shyly after us, screeching with delight—or in horror—at the unexpected visitors. Small bands of boys traipsed along, shouting, pointing excitedly at our cameras and packs. Somehow, life went on.

Signs of fighting, however, were everywhere—bomb-shattered houses, trees lacerated by shrapnel, and shattered irrigation canals. Some villages were completely abandoned. One quickly realized how dependent these communities were on irrigation for survival and what the canals' destruction meant for the agricultural system. Occasionally, we found the tracks of Soviet or Afghan army tanks, which had driven up the riverbeds to reach the villages. Usually, before the troops arrived, the able-bodied men had bolted into the hills to avoid being arrested as mujahideen or conscripted into the army. There were tales of rape, beatings, executions, and the burning of harvested crops and seed reserves—all of which contributed toward people leaving, either to the government-controlled towns or to Pakistan.

Many of the government *askari* were hapless individuals press-ganged off the streets for military service. They were deployed elsewhere, well away from their home regions. But the desertion rate remained high. This made the Afghan army—except for some crack, well-paid battalions or militia groups—wholly unreliable as a fighting force for the Soviets. The desertions helped bolster resistance ranks, particularly if the soldiers turned up with their guns, which helped curry favor with the commanders. Decades later, the Western Coalition forces found themselves encountering some of the same problems as they sought to train up a new Afghan army and police.

During those early days of the occupation, it was still easy to find food. It was only later in the war that I traveled with my own horses and supplies. I felt it was unfair to expect local populations to feed me. The villagers welcomed us with tea, dried fruit, and nuts. Sometimes we sat in the open in the shade of a mulberry tree in a low-walled enclosure, which doubled up as a mosque. Small boys arrived with carpets, which they spread on the ground. Or they would lead us to the house of a local dignitary, ushering us into a formal receiving room with pillows and rugs. The boys would emerge to set out small individual teapots, Chinese-made copies of the hand-painted Gardner porcelain used during the eighteenth and nineteenth centuries by the caravans, plus bowls of sugared almonds. In the kitchen doorways, smiling young girls and the occasional older woman peeked out at us.

Fréderique and Evelyne would often be taken into the back rooms, where they would meet the female members of the household. There, they told me, the women would feed them and inundate them with questions. Or explain their problems. As a man, of course, this critical part of Afghan society was denied to me. Yet their perspective was crucial to gaining an insight into how things worked, particularly given that women and girls represented more than half the population. So I often used the female doctors as my intermediaries for gaining insights into what was going on. For the French female medics, it was a bit of a chore. "The conversation is far more interesting with the men," complained Fréderique, who preferred sitting with the main group. The men, particularly the guests, were also served the best food. Foreign women often found themselves "neuterized" into honorary men in the minds of rural Afghan males unable to deal with them otherwise.

The turbaned village elders always appeared in delegation to talk with us. While intent on learning what was going on in the outside world, they were adamant about putting across their own points of view. It was important for them, they explained, that the world understand the war in Afghanistan and how they, the Afghans, were resisting. Through the BBC and VOA, they were surprisingly well informed about global events—more so than many Americans with far better access to communications.

For these rural Afghans, it was clearly a matter of prestige to have a Western medical team come to their villages. The doctors held field clinics as people brought their sick and wounded. Agha Gul, however, was not keen on lingering. He was concerned about informers. So just as we were beginning to settle in or catch up on our sleep, he would exhort us to move out. "Harakat! *Boro!*"

We had to be careful about rival factions. While Agha Gul seemed to have good relations with everyone, there were villages where he preferred not to overstay our welcome. "Hezb people," he would mutter. "No good people." Or "Sayyaf people. Arabi people," meaning that a certain village was aligned with Sayyaf's Ittehad and thus beholden to the Arabs. Having privately voiced his displeasure, Agha Gul would nevertheless greet each of the elders as the warmest of friends. He would then make up some excuse, and we would be on our way.

We finally reached the upper reaches of the Panjshir. We had walked over four hundred miles, much of it climbing. We skirted the blue, transparent waters of Lake Anjuman—I counted no fewer than twenty trout in one sweep—before following the winding Panjshir River down to the first patchwork farms and villages. It was like reaching paradise. There were fresh apples, apricots, eggs, vegetables—and small brown cows producing thick milk, cream, cheese, and yogurt. The latter were the remnants of a prewar Swiss dairy project, whose director I had met in Kabul shortly before the invasion.

Roughly halfway down the valley, we halted at a whitewashed house in Dasht Riwat, a small town, for a sumptuous meal. It belonged to Massoud's "minister of finance." Some twenty different types of dishes ranging from roast chicken and mutton stew to eggplant in yogurt, rice *pulao*, and honey-flavored cream were spread out on the "table," a long carpet with everyone sitting cross-legged on either side. We were given the seats of honor and urged to eat as much as we could. "Massoud knows that French like to eat well. We'll eat even better when we meet him," said Agha Gul.

I noticed two men at the far end of the room. One was heavyset with a thick black beard, while the other was thinner, almost haggard. The large one smiled at us, as if hoping to get into a conversation. When I finally approached him, he spoke to me in surprisingly good English. Both were doctors and running one of the Panjshir's three clinics. Were they part of a volunteer medical group? I asked.

"No." He hesitated. "We're prisoners."

The Afghan doctors had been captured by the mujahideen, who accused them of being Khalqis. They may have been, but anyone who chose to work with the government was considered communist. Active collaboration was common, but for different reasons. Sometimes, this was for personal gain or ideological commitment—or because they considered the "progressive" forces of the Moscow-backed factions less abhorrent than the specter of a fundamentalist mujahed government headed by the likes of Hekmatyar, the nightmare of many educated Afghans.

Numerous Afghans, however, supported the resistance. Massoud specifically asked those in well-placed positions, notably senior military officers, to stay on. Throughout the war, they provided him with intelligence ensuring that he was always a step ahead of the Soviets. The same thing happened with the Karzai regime nearly three decades later. In 2011, many working with the pro-Western Kabul administration, including the army and police, were active collaborators with the Taliban and other Islamist groups. Even US forces at Bagram and other bases were known to have employees with ties to the armed opposition.

Over the next several weeks, I regularly saw the two Afghan doctors, who enjoyed relative freedom and worked closely with the French. But this was curbed abruptly months later, when they tried to escape as Soviet-Afghan forces overran the valley. They were recaptured. I never found out what happened or whether they had survived the war. All they wanted to do, they had told me, was to return to their families.

At Astana, a sprawling hillside village where AMI had its guesthouse, we rested for two days. The clinic was a bit farther down the valley. The doctors began working almost immediately. Sidiq, a slightly stooped Panjshiri who had worked once as a cook for a foreign engineering company, had been placed in charge of the doctors. On our arrival, he appeared beaming with huge plates of spaghetti and tomato sauce with fresh salad. He led us to rooms where the beds were covered with sheets and blankets. A further luxury was the chance to take hot showers fired by a wood-burning stove.

Leaving the doctors, Christophe, Jerôme, and I continued on down the valley until we arrived at the town of Bazarak. Here, we were told, is where we would meet Massoud. Most of Bazarak's houses had been badly bombed, but some were still habitable. We were led to a fortresslike compound where our host, Hajji Saduddin (a massive man) welcomed us warmly. A Kabul merchant, he was one of Massoud's principal supporters. Taking my hand in the Afghan manner, he led us into a spacious carpet-strewn room, where we were served green tea, sugared almonds, and *choclit*—or Afghan caramels.

Suddenly the door swung open. Half a dozen men entered, all armed with Lee-Enfields and Kalashnikovs. At their head was a distinctive young man of medium stature, with wavy black hair and sharp facial features. He had the confident air of someone used to dispensing authority and receiving respect. Wearing a green army jacket, white *shalwar* trousers, and a Nuristani *pakul* pushed to the back of his head, he stopped to take stock of the three of us rising to our feet. Then he strode over to shake our hands warmly. I could not help smiling. No doubt, this was the renowned "Lion of Panjshir." With his wispy beard and hawk-like nose, he looked just like Bob Dylan.

He eyed me curiously. "You're Girardet?" he asked quietly in French.

Briefly, we explained the purpose of our trip. Massoud listened thoughtfully, stroking his beard, occasionally nodding. Mirabudin, a young medical student from the AMI clinic who had been loaned to us as an interpreter, translated slowly.

At one point, Massoud broke in. "You're American?"

"Yes, but I live in Paris."

Then, a deep grin breaking across his face, he said: "I hear that you're a good walker?"

"I suppose so. I enjoy it very much."

"Ah, but you have to be careful about walking too fast and leaving our mujahideen behind. If you're caught alone, people might take you for a Russian, and that's not good, particularly if you're an American," he said with a bemused twinkle. Everyone laughed. He seemed pleased with his joke.

For the next three weeks, we traveled the valley, sometimes with Massoud or his men. Occasionally, too, we drove. There were only two operating vehicles—one a Soviet jeep used by Massoud, the other a black Moskvitch that served as the official taxi. Both had been carried over the mountains in parts on the backs of pack animals. The Panjshir had been badly hit during the previous offensives. Many of the villages lay in ruins. Red Army troops had chopped down trees, sometimes entire orchards, to open lines of sight. They had plowed up irrigation systems—causing trees, grapevines, and crops to shrivel. There is nothing as dismal as once verdant trees dying for lack of water. The Red Army troops now contented themselves with controlling the outer ridges, from where they shelled or mortared the guerrillas. Regularly, too, helicopter gunships and MiGs swooped in to attack.

Every time the Soviets sought to take the Panjshir, they dropped Spetznaz on the ridges to control the heights. But they invariably met with fierce resistance. On receiving information of an impending attack, Massoud would order an immediate evacuation of all civilians. As for the mujahideen, they melted back into the narrow side valleys, hid in tunnels (often old lapis lazuli mines) or held key positions on the outer perimeter overlooking the main valley.

The Soviets would send ground troops up the river in armored vehicles. This was to avoid the Chinese anti-tank mines buried by the mujahideen along the only road running the length of the valley. Red Army and Afghan government troops quickly occupied the villages, but the guerrillas began striking from all sides, eventually forcing the communists to withdraw. The wrecked hulks of APCs and tanks half submerged in the water or littering the roadside attested to these assaults. Massoud's mobile mechanics quickly dismantled the vehicles for guns and spare parts.

It was a bizarre conflict between a twentieth-century superpower deploying the latest military hardware and a stubborn peasant people whose resistance profile consisted of customs spanning two thousand years. Despite the Red Army assaults, the Panjshiris managed to pursue relatively normal lives. Just as in Nuristan and Badakshan, we saw farmers harvesting their crops or laying apricots out to dry on their roofs. They used ox-drawn plows to till their fields and oil lamps to light their homes just as their ancestors had done in Bactrian times. They winnowed wheat by flailing it in the air with wooden pitchforks. Then millers ground it to flour using water-churned stones. Some families, too, were rebuilding their houses. Even some shops had reopened, but they only sold what could be smuggled in over the mountains.

Many farmers, who were part of the irregular militia, boasted long-barreled *jezails* and flintlocks. These were soon replaced by more modern weapons brought in by deserters, purchased from the Soviets in exchange for hashish, or carried in from Pakistan. Massoud's main fighting force, however, was equipped with "modern" First World War Lee-Enfields, Second World War Mark IVs, and—increasingly—Chinese-made AK-47 Kalashnikovs. Only the occasional commander had the latest AK-74 Kalakov assault rifle—yet this, over the next five or six years, became the stock weapon of the mujahideen. They also had a ramshackle array of military hardware—whatever came their way—in the form of walkie-talkies, hand grenades, RPGs, land mines, and a few Dashaka heavy machine guns and ZPU-2 anti-aircraft pieces. Ever ingenious, the Panjshiris fashioned rudimentary artillery pieces in hidden side valley workshops out of recuperated materials, such as helicopter rocket pods or tank guns.

Our sorties took us to the front lines at the mouth of the Panjshir, where the river surged through a narrow gorge, eventually arriving at the Soviet-controlled towns of Jabal Saraj and Gulbahar. There was a POW camp where Massoud kept over a hundred prisoners, mainly army officers and party officials. The conscripts were usually released quickly and told to go home. There were no Soviets. It was only later in the war that I encountered captured Red Army soldiers. We managed to send two of them, an Estonian and a Ukrainian barely twenty years old, to Pakistan. Once in Peshawar, they were kidnapped by the ISI—and we never saw them again.

During our stay, we regularly met with Massoud. He was more than just a military leader. He had set up a quasi-government in the Panjshir with its own finance, educational, and social offices to work with the estimated eighty to one hundred thousand people still living in the region. He paid particular attention to ensuring that civilians were not caught up in the fighting. This did not prevent him from continuing his relentless battle from the side valleys. We talked about the war, the Soviets, and his concept of a post-communist Afghanistan.

Massoud was clearly the "boss," friendly, persuasive, and decisive. He commanded respect from all and had an exceptional ability to involve the conservative elders in his decision making. Massoud was both a modernist and a pious Muslim. He sometimes excused himself in the middle of a conversation to pray, peeling off his white-and-black scarf and laying it on the ground facing *qiblah*, the direction of Mecca. Whenever he worshipped, on a riverbank or a hidden mountain position, Massoud usually let someone else lead in prayer. The others—fighters, farmers, refugees, merchants— would fall in beside him. I watched fascinated as Massoud, caught up in his devotion, would solemnly pray—kneeling and bowing, murmuring *"Allah o Akbar"* in unison with the others. Finally, passing his hands over his face, he would climb back onto his feet, refreshed. "Right," he said, striding over. "Where were we?"

What Massoud had achieved during those early years was impressive. The Panjshiri resistance may not have been as well structured as Angola's highly coordinated guerrilla UNITA movement under Jonas Savimbi or the Eritrean People's Liberation Front (EPLF) in the Horn of Africa. By Afghan standards, however, few guerrilla fronts were even remotely comparable. Massoud was organized not only militarily, but politically and socially. He proved himself enlightened and tolerant, constantly curious about life elsewhere. Massoud realized that he had to accommodate the views of all, particularly the more traditional Afghans whose support he needed. At the same time, he consulted closely with the population at large, including the women. Even when he knew what to do, Massoud made a point of letting people feel that they had contributed.

One such area was education. Massoud strongly felt that schooling, including for girls, was the only way forward. This was at a time when many rural Afghans had revolted against the communists precisely because they wished to impose coeducation. More than two decades later, when I visited Afghanistan's eastern tribal provinces, almost every village ran a mixed primary school. This was mainly the result of education in the Pakistani refugee camps until the collapse of the Taliban, a long enough period for even the most conservative Afghans to grasp its benefits. For the Panjshiris, it was already part of their daily lives.

When I asked Massoud about opposition to girls' education, he smiled: "Sometimes, you can't do it in one go. Or by forcing people. But if people gradually understand the importance of education, they will support it. But you have to prove it to them." Then he added: "It's only through education that we can develop this country. We need doctors, teachers, engineers, pilots, lawyers . . . It doesn't matter whether they are men or women."

When presented with the opportunity to bring in the French doctors, Massoud had immediately accepted despite the reticence of certain gray-beards, who worried about the influence of foreign women. Determined that women play a key role in Afghan society, Massoud saw the doctors as a means not only of providing basic healthcare in dire war conditions, but also of training locals as "barefoot" medics. If ordinary Afghan women were made aware of basic hygiene and nutrition, he argued, then one could hope for healthier new generations. This was critical for a society where one in four children died by the age of five, more often than not from easily preventable diseases. Massoud further regarded the French as a means of maintaining relations with the outside world. Whenever he had time, he stopped by to chat or to obtain their reading on international attitudes toward Afghanistan as reflected by the latest BBC or VOA reports.

Massoud asked whether Christophe, Jerôme, and I wished to accompany him on an attack against the Salang. We leapt at the chance. A week later, we received a message to meet him several hours by foot to the west of Bazarak. We set out through a gorge to climb a low pass leading into the next valley. At the top of the col, Massoud sat waiting with a retinue of a dozen men, all armed with AK-47s. These were obviously some of his best troops. Massoud wore a neatly ironed blue shirt, pressed fatigues, and good-quality walking boots. I wondered how he always managed to look so neat. As usual, he sported his *pakul* perched on the back of his head. He greeted us warmly.

Massoud pointed to the ridge opposite. "That's where the *Shouravi* are dug in. They like to shell us. We already have some fighters moving up the mountain to clean them out." I squinted through my binoculars and could make out what looked like a series of bunkers just below the ridge covered with tarpaulins and flying a red flag.

"Is that where the Salang is?" I asked.

"No, that's over there," Massoud said, gesturing to the west. "But the *Shouravi* have positions along the ridges over there," he added, pointing to a series of mountains. "We'll have to go around, not long, maybe five or six hours." Gesturing with a wave of his hand, he added: "First, we go to that village, where I will brief you this evening." I could see a village on the other side of the river, no more than an hour away.

Massoud and I walked ahead as the Frenchmen filmed. The Afghan took large strides up the steeper portions of the trail. His men followed close behind. Every so often, he halted to dictate a message to an aide or to scribble a note to one of his commanders. Sometimes, too, he shouted or replied to calls on the walkie-talkie. For security reasons, he preferred to send written notes via messengers. Finally, Massoud ordered his aide, now armed with a dozen or so missives, to go. The man hastened down the mountain to Bazarak to deliver them. Massoud turned to me. "Are the mountains of Switzerland as beautiful as here in Afghanistan?"

"They're much lower. But I am not sure there is anything as beautiful as Afghanistan," I insisted reciprocally.

Massoud nodded knowingly. "Well, I'd still like to visit Switzerland. The Swiss are very good soldiers, I hear. The next time you come, you must bring me some books on mountain warfare. And road building and hydroelectric power. We could use some of their techniques here." Then he asked: "Is it true that the Swiss fight wars with bicycles?" I laughed. The Swiss, I explained, had not fought a war since the Middle Ages when they were mercenaries. And yes, they did use bicycles for transporting supplies or moving soldiers along roads, but they also relied on trucks and mules in the mountains.

Whenever I returned to the region, I would always bring Massoud books on the resistance wars in Indochina, Algeria, southern Africa, and—equally pertinent—the fighting techniques of Yugoslav partisans during World War II. Massoud had an insatiable appetite for military history as well as the biographies of renowned leaders, such as Napoleon, Ho Chi Minh, and General Giap. He was also intrigued by George Washington, Roosevelt, de Gaulle, and Kennedy. "These were great men," he said to me. "They worked in the interests of their people."

Massoud relied on his own reading but also the expertise of Soviet-trained defectors to develop his strategies. These included two or three former Afghan army officers who had received US military instruction during the 1960s and '70s. He improvised as the war progressed. Later, after my return from covering the Ethiopian and Angolan civil wars during the early and mid-1980s, he questioned me in detail on how their guerrillas operated and how they had organized their support for civilian populations. He was particularly impressed by the EPLF's ability to operate complete surgical units in the mountains of Eritrea. He was also intrigued with how they ran their schools hidden among the rocks of dry riverbeds, implemented humanitarian distribution networks, and even knew how many lactating mothers existed in each camp or village.

By lunchtime, Massoud and I had stopped by a stream to wait for the film team. We nibbled on some *tokhum*, a tightly compressed cake of dried mulberry, which the Panjshiri leader passed around. The black slab of hard fruit dough looked like hashish, but I knew that Massoud was adamantly opposed to drugs. He was even against smoking tobacco and did not allow any of the men in his immediate entourage to indulge. "This is like glucose," said Massoud, tearing off a piece. "It gives you energy."

It was pleasantly warm, and we chatted quietly as the distant thuds of Soviet mortars rumbled across the valley. Occasionally, too, we could hear the barking of a heavy machine gun. Christophe and Jerôme finally arrived. Massoud talked about the strategic importance of the Salang and why his men attacked it so regularly. One reason, he noted, was to obtain supplies, notably fuel and ammunition. At one point, he said with a grin, they had managed to grab the car of the minister of defense. They tried to transport it across the mountains, but the terrain proved too difficult. Often, too, Massoud's mujahideen made hit-and-run attacks against Soviet-Afghan lines controlling access at Jabal Saraj, at exactly the same point where the Taliban later besieged the United Front.

Toward midafternoon, Massoud abruptly announced that he had to leave, but would meet us for dinner. With that, he hastened down the trail—his men following at a jog, their guns slung over their shoulders. Later, as the sun began to slip behind the ridge, our guides took us to a house in the terraced village. These were our quarters for the night. Agha Gul appeared with a kerosene lantern. He had a tendency to pop up when least expected. "*Nan*," he said. Dinner. He led us over to another building with a long room already prepared with food. A red plastic cloth had been laid out on the floor together with large bowls of rice *pulao* and smaller plates laden with chicken and lamb. A half a loaf of *nan* marked each place. "*Pishin,*" he said, bidding us to sit down.

Massoud walked in followed by his men. The guerrillas murmured a prayer, holding up their hands in thanks to Allah, and everyone dug in, breaking the bread to pick up the rice and meat with their right hands. I was not feeling well, perhaps too much sun or an infection, so I ate nothing, except for sugarless tea and bit of plain rice. Massoud asked why I was not eating. "*Mariz hastam,*" I said. I am ill. But you must eat something, he urged. "We've a long walk ahead tomorrow." He then turned to Agha Gul. They should be prepared to leave at dawn, he said in Dari. "You should get some sleep," he told me.

Once we had finished eating, one of Massoud's aides laid out two Soviet military maps. In the soft yellow glow of a hissing pressure lamp, Massoud showed us the Red Army positions and how we would approach the Salang. "There are some *askari* over here," he said, pointing with his finger. "But they're with us, so there won't be any problems. You should be able to film from the ridge." We talked for another hour and then left. A young muj promised to fetch us at first light. "After *namoz,*" he said. Morning prayer. Feeling even more ill with stomach pains, I rolled out my sleeping bag, took my travel knapsack (wrapping my anorak around it to serve as a pillow), and collapsed into bed—boots and all. Christophe and Jerôme took off their gear. I managed to lift myself up. "I wouldn't do that if I were you," I suggested. "Best sleep with your boots and clothes on."

"But that's not very comfortable," protested Jerôme.

"I know, but if anything happens you can move quickly. It's just a gut feeling," I said, half laughing at my unintended pun. They both shrugged and climbed into their bags, without trousers and boots. I briefly listened to the BBC and drifted off. Several hours later, but what seemed like minutes, I was jolted awake by a subway train crashing through the room. This was followed by a flash and a huge crash. A further flash, then another explosion. Pieces of ceiling fell. We were being mortared.

"*Sortez!*" I shouted to Christophe and Jerôme. "Let's get the hell out of here!" I ripped off my sleeping bag and grabbed my satchel and flashlight. The two Frenchmen were now up, swearing loudly as they poked around for their clothes. Two more mortars exploded on the other side of the building. I could smell burning, and the air was thick with dust and smoke.

"Let's move!" I bellowed. Holding my flashlight, I waited by the doorway. "To the river. They're hitting the village." The two men fumbled their way to the door and followed me into the darkness. I avoided using my light outside. I did not wish to attract the Soviets, who had clearly known Massoud's position through their informers. We used the mortar flashes to guide us. Each time one of the rounds was fired from the mountain, it illuminated the valley. Two or three seconds later, the bomb landed. With each explosion, the shrapnel sliced like hail through the leaves of the trees. I could hear the cracking of wood and the shudder of collapsing walls, then shouts and the wail of women and children.

We scrambled through the village. Twice, we ended up in dead-end alleys, forcing us to retrace our steps. The mortars were now bursting at twenty-second intervals. As we ran, I began retching, doubling over with pain and exertion. We broke past the last houses and ran to the river. We plunged blindly into the bitterly cold water, our adrenaline carrying us forward. We waded across, pitching and falling in the current. I was still retching and covered with vomit. I dunked my head, letting the churning water pass over my body. Christophe and Jerôme helped pull me out and we sat by the bank, catching our breath. We looked back at the village where the mortars were still falling. I could see several fires. "There's a farm a bit farther up, over there," I gasped. "I remember seeing it when we came down. It should be out of range."

A few minutes later, we collapsed on a hard mud platform normally used for drying corn. We later discovered that a direct hit thirty seconds after we had left the house had collapsed the roof, leaving three dead. The warm night and the walking had almost dried us, but we were exhausted. Shortly after dawn, a commander appeared—accompanied by three mujahideen and Farid, an Afghan who had lived previously in Germany and sometimes served as our interpreter. "*Boro*," he said. "Are you coming for the attack?" The three of us looked at one another. Pathetically, we decided that we had had enough. "I think we'll give this one a miss," I said. The commander gave us a pitying look and moved off, leaving Farid to take us back to the main valley. I didn't see the Salang again until years later.

It was time to return to Pakistan. I had excellent reporting material, while Christophe and Jerôme had ample footage for their film. We would take no horses, but Massoud promised some mujahideen to accompany us. Massoud came to see us off at a guerrilla post. As we readied to leave, Massoud asked to talk to me in private. We strolled over to some mulberry trees and sat down. Agha Gul sat down with us, as did Mirabudin, the interpreter.

Massoud looked at me carefully. "I don't know who you are, whether CIA or journalist," he said. "It's not for me to judge. But I think that you're a friend of Afghanistan. We want to make contact with the Americans. They believe in freedom and in God. Can you help us?" I explained that as a journalist it was not my job to indulge in intelligence gathering or to become involved with covert support. My job was to report. "However, what I can do is introduce you to the Americans, and you take it from there," I suggested.

Massoud smiled. "Good. Then please introduce Agha Gul to the Americans."

The journey back was like a holiday hike. We even forgot the land mines. We felt fit, and the mountain passes appeared unbelievably easy. At the first Pakistan post, we decided not to avoid the soldiers. I pointed to my multi-entry visa and demanded that they stamp my passport, promising to recommend them to Zia ul-Haq. The two militiamen had evidently expected a bribe but respectfully wrote a note asking me to send greetings to the president. From Chitral, we hired a pickup to drive down to Peshawar. We stopped by the US consulate in the hope of introducing Agha Gul to Doug Archard, but my diplomat friend was away on home leave. Agha Gul was clearly disappointed, so we took him to Islamabad. I would introduce him to someone appropriate at the American embassy. Wishing to show some return hospitality, we took a double suite at the Holiday Inn. I then hit the phones. As I talked, Agha Gul sat timidly on the sofa, sipping tea and nibbling on biscuits. The luxury embarrassed him. So confident in the mountains of Afghanistan, he looked totally out of place in this Western-style comfort.

The US embassy had neither Persian nor Russian speakers, I was told. I found this astounding given that Washington's principal rival was conducting a full-scale war barely four hours' drive to the west.

Yet it was indicative of the often incompetent approach the American intelligence branches were to maintain with regard to Afghanistan. They preferred to rely on the Pakistanis rather than their own sources. Finally, the United States Information Service director put us in touch with a political officer, whom I assumed was intelligence. He arranged to meet us in a building outside the US embassy compound.

The officer, smoothly dressed in a light gray suit and wearing black-rimmed glasses, reminded me of Clark Kent. I explained the purpose of our visit. He jotted down notes with a pencil on a brand-new legal pad. I explained Massoud's wish to make contact. Indicating Agha Gul, I said that we were only here to introduce him. "He's your man," I said, noting that he made up to half a dozen trips "inside" annually. But Clark Kent showed little interest in the Afghan. He preferred to question us, the Westerners. Several times, I reemphasized Agha Gul's importance. Yet apart from occasional patronizing smiles, the American did not address a single question to him. I could see our Panjshiri friend realize that this was going nowhere. That night we took him to the best restaurant in the hotel, but all he would eat were kebabs and rice. Next door was a disco with throbbing lights and lavishly dressed upper-middle-class Pakistanis. "Just like Afghanistan," I laughed. He smiled feebly. It was a poor joke.

The next morning we hired a car to take Agha Gul back to Peshawar with a note of introduction to Archard on his return. "If anyone can put you touch with those you want to talk to, he can," I explained. Years later, when I met Archard at a humanitarian conference in Cape Town, South Africa, I asked him what had happened. Agha Gul had indeed turned up with my letter, he explained, and he had put him in touch with "the right people." Almost until the end of the Soviet occupation, however, Washington never fully grasped the importance of Massoud as one of Afghanistan's key commanders. They never provided him with more than modest support.

CHAPTER EIGHT

The Lion and the Hyena

Amongst the tens of thousands of Afghans who made up the communists, the jihadists, the Taliban, and other battling factions of Afghanistan over the past decades, two figures have dominated the political and military scene: Ahmed Shah Massoud and Gulbuddin Hekmatyar. Of similar ages, the two initially shared the same Islamic tendencies, but they soon were to become bitter rivals. Their animosity led to the deaths of over fifty thousand people in Kabul alone. One was called the Lion, the other the Hyena.

Massoud was Tajik, and Hekmatyar Pushtun. Massoud was a shrewd and persevering guerrilla commander whose heroes were Charles de Gaulle, General Giap, Che Guevara, and John F. Kennedy, and who had proven himself in battle. Hekmatyar was a calculating, deceitful politician whose inspiration was Iran's Ayatollah Khomeiny, but who had started out as a communist. Each had pursued parallel yet completely conflicting careers that profoundly affected not only the future of Afghanistan, but also Russia, the United States, and Europe. To fully grasp the nature of Afghanistan's devastating panoply of wars since the outbreak of civil strife in the summer of 1978, it is crucial to understand these two figures. They represent the strengths and weaknesses of Afghanistan today.

Through my years of reporting in Afghanistan, I was able to get to know both Massoud and Gulbuddin fairly well. But it was only after the collapse of the PDPA regime in 1992 that I grasped how closely the actions of these two had become my barometers for gauging events relating to Afghanistan.

During the 1980s and '90s, Massoud and Gulbuddin stood out as archenemies, each determined to destroy the other. Yet as engineering students during the early 1970s, they were involved in the same conservative Islamic politics. They collaborated as novice jihadists. For several years, the Pakistanis backed both of them as part of their own subversive activities against the Daoud government. Only one, the Hyena—who may have had dealings with the KGB, the Soviet intelligence agency—went on to become the upfront favorite of the CIA and the ISI during the Soviet-Afghan war. And it is Hekmatyar today who is considered one of the most ruthless insurgent figures fighting the international presence in Afghanistan.

Massoud developed into a highly charismatic and politically moderate commander renowned for his prowess at holding the Red Army at bay through a resilient resistance strategy. He ranked as one of the twentieth century's most accomplished guerrilla leaders. His exploits are comparable to Massoud's own hero, General Vo Nguyen Giap, the brilliant North Vietnamese commander who fought against the French during the First Indochina War and then the Americans during the Vietnam War.

As with Giap, Massoud relied on strong grassroots support, but also close cooperation with resistance sympathizers inside enemy strongholds. "Our fight against the *Shouravi* was really not that much different from Giap's with the French or Americans in Vietnam," explained Massoud in Kabul in 1993 in a rare moment of reflection. "The Russians had no idea how plugged in we were with Afghans working within their own military apparatus. We had informers in the highest places, the army, the air force, the police . . . " Two decades later, the Taliban, the Haqqani Network, Hezb, and other anti-NATO insurgents could all claim to have their fair share of sympathizers working within the Afghan government and the security forces—including translators, drivers, and menial laborers hired by the Americans and other Coalition armies.

Unlike the post-2001 armed opposition, however, Massoud retained good relations with the outside world, primarily through the French doctors and foreign journalists. The CIA and the US embassy in Islamabad largely ignored him. Their military support always remained minimal despite later claims that they had been backing the Panjshiri leader all along. In a 1986 interview for the BBC's *Newsnight* with Canadian Arthur Kent, one of the few Western reporters who has relentlessly pursued the Afghan story almost from the very beginning, Massoud maintained that his forces had yet to receive the lethal Stinger anti-aircraft rockets that would help stave off the Soviet helicopter gunships, MiGs, and Su-24 fighter-bombers that were killing so many Afghans.

"I've heard nothing, seen nothing of the Stinger rockets," he told Kent. "My personal view and that of the mujahideen, and of all the people of Afghanistan, is this: The West always talks, but they don't take any practical steps to reduce the problems and pains of my people. We hear on the radio about the help that is on the way, but all we end up with is some medical supplies, or very small financial help. It's negligible."

Only much later in the game did Massoud receive a small number of Stingers. Peter Jouvenal and I encountered some of the horse caravans during the mid-1980s as they transported covert US military supplies across the Hindu Kush. Inspecting their contents, what we found was more reminiscent of the Imperial War Museum in London than the weaponry needed to counter the late-twentieth-century aerial attacks of a modern superpower. Most of the weaponry consisted of US-made Mark I rifles, Egyptian AK-47 Kalashnikovs, and Chinese land mines. There were also some anti-aircraft Dashakas or Zigoyaks, and a few SAM-7 anti-aircraft missiles.

Washington continued to ignore Massoud, even when he warned the Americans and Europeans of the rising influence of al Qaeda and other Arab extremists in Afghanistan in early 2001, only months before 9/11. When the Bush administration finally reacted, it was too late. Hekmatyar, on the other hand, was becoming even more fervently anti-Western despite the overwhelming support he was receiving from the United States. Hekmatyar unashamedly resorted to money, weapons, repression, and murder to assert his aims to become the head of a new Islamic state in Kabul.

The ISI's objective was to establish a regime amenable to Pakistani interests and well out of India's sphere of control. For the Pakistanis, everything related, and still relates, to Kashmir. At the same time, Zia ul-Haq had his own agenda for transforming Pakistan into a more puritanical Islamic society.

Washington's ambition was far more banal. It was to bloody Moscow with its own Vietnam, a policy inspired in 1980 by Zbigniew Brzezinski, the Polish-born and virulently anti-Soviet national security adviser to US Democrat president Jimmy Carter. Brzezinski's approach was wholeheartedly embraced by the two Republican administrations that followed.

Both Presidents Ronald Reagan and George H. W. Bush chose to ignore repeated warnings that support for Islamic extremists would only create monsters. Washington also chose to ignore the ISI's subversive role throughout the 1980s and '90s (and which continues today) by supporting the fundamentalists ranging from Hekmatyar to the Taliban. Even more critical, this approach would lead to a form of terror that would completely change the West's approach to security. In many ways, it proved a disastrous policy directly responsible for the rise of radical Islam in Afghanistan and the ability of foreign jihadists, such as al Qaeda, to use Afghan territory as a place to train and organize terror assaults against the West.

Broadly hated by ordinary Afghans, Hekmatyar ran a tightly disciplined ship. Perhaps because of his communist past, his approach was dictatorially Leninist. This made him even more dangerous than other militants, such as the Taliban's Mullah Omar. As with Khomeiny, Hekmatyar regarded extremist Islam less as a religious ideology than as a tool for power. Throughout the Soviet-Afghan war, he focused on carefully managed disinformation as part of a strategy to convince the international media and foreign political figures, such as US congressmen or high-profile dignitaries visiting Peshawar, that he represented the most efficient of the resistance organizations. He saw little reason, or need, to promote himself through proven successes on the battlefield.

Neither I nor any of my journalist colleagues could point to a single decisive victory against the Red Army based solely on Hezb fighting capabilities. Hekmatyar's forces, however, did attack or otherwise undermine rival guerrilla fronts, a reality that never seemed to bother Washington. The United States provided Hekmatyar with at least half a billion dollars' worth of military and financial support. Some put the figure far higher. The Saudis, Iranians, and other Islamic backers provided much the same. The end result is that Hekmatyar's Hezb probably received more than one billion dollars' worth of backing during the nearly decade-long Soviet occupation. At the same time, Hekmatyar's Hezb (with the help of the ISI) had its own additional sources of income, notably heroin trafficking. The CIA was aware of this, and some say even encouraged it, given that Red Army troops were increasingly indulging in opium abuse.

How much of this massive support was actually used to fight the communists remained another question. A significant portion of Hekmatyar's arsenal, including Stingers, was used to strengthen his position against rival guerrilla fronts during the 1990s. But many of these weapons were also deployed by Hezb militants against NATO forces a decade and a half later.

A 1990 report of the US House Republican Research Committee of the Task Force on Terrorism and Unconventional Warfare severely criticized the CIA and ISI for gross negligence and cover-up regarding Hezb-e-Islami's misconduct. Later reports, such as a 1993 congressional document on the "New Islamist International," highlighted the impact of failed US policy as more militants crossed the border to be trained by the ISI in eastern Afghanistan.

The 1990 report alleged that the ISI had full knowledge of Hekmatyar's involvement with the KGB. It suggested that the picture of Hekmatyar's success was created by KGB-KHAD propaganda, which in turn closely fit the biases of the Zia ul-Haq regime. The report further argued that the new Benazir Bhutto government, which replaced the military dictatorship following ul-Haq's death in 1988, neither dared nor was able to challenge the ISI and had no option but to continue in this track.

Claims of Hezb-e-Islami victories "served the ISI's intrinsic interests so well that it had no desire to doubt them and indeed politically could not afford to," the report said. Moreover, it was in the personal interest of numerous ISI officers and operatives who were embezzling the ever-growing flow of US and Saudi assistance to ensure that the status quo continued. Finally, US State Department sources have since acknowledged that some US intelligence agents liaising with the ISI were personally benefiting financially from the funds lavished on (and heroin trafficking income of) the extremists during this period. As more American diplomats and agents from this period are entering retirement and willing to speak openly, more information is becoming available as to the utter incompetence of the CIA and other intelligence organizations in their handling of the Afghan issue.

As late-twentieth-century resistance figures, Massoud and Gulbuddin each had their own visions of what the new Afghanistan should be. Massoud was the poet and the modernist who ordered his commanders to treat Soviet prisoners humanely and to build schools for girls. Everyone, he argued, should have a role to play in Afghanistan. Gulbuddin was the operator, who relished executing or torturing his prisoners. His concept of a new future was that of a fundamentalist Pushtun-dominated state not unlike the one later created by the Taliban. For him, there was no role for women.

Massoud was a highly charismatic yet very human leader. He openly admitted his mistakes, and indeed had committed some highly egregious ones, such as surrounding himself with a bevy of corrupt cohorts—the Panjshiri Mafia—when the mujahideen took Kabul in the spring of 1992. (Some of these were believed to have absconded with millions of dollars' worth of donor funds during and after the fall of the Taliban.) For his part, Hekmatyar refused to broach any form of criticism. Those who opposed him were killed or otherwise "disappeared." Later, as military head of the United Front, Massoud persevered as the last commander capable of staving off Afghanistan's fast-spreading Talib movement. Hekmatyar fled the country when the ISI dropped him in favor of the Taliban.

Despite the death, destruction, and (above all) intolerance that Hekmatyar represented by early 2010, the Karzai regime appeared to be laying the groundwork for a special deal with him. Already in 2004, Hekmatyar's political wing had begun informal talks with Kabul about involving itself as a principal component of any long-term peace initiative. Hekmatyar, as during the 1980s, was simply indulging in a dual strategy. Hezb's military wing was becoming increasingly active not only in the largely Pushtun provinces of eastern Afghanistan but also in the north.

Traveling to Kunar in eastern Afghanistan in 2009, I met several well-placed local figures, all former Hezb supporters. At least two I had known from the 1980s and early '90s. Each firmly maintained that Hekmatyar was operating from the Pakistani frontier tribal agencies of Mohmand and Bajaur with the support of the ISI. "He crosses over into Kunar for meetings," one of them said. Once again, the Hezb propaganda machine was trying to give the impression that its leader was fighting alongside his men on Afghan soil. Hekmatyar, however, is a cunning politician, not a front-line military commander. It is doubtful that he would go anywhere where his life might be at risk.

Back in the early 1970s when Massoud and Hekmatyar were obscure young engineering students in Kabul, Afghan society was undergoing a dramatic transformation. The country was being penetrated increasingly by foreign trends, both Western and communist. A rising urban middle class was embracing a more sophisticated European way of life, not only in the way it dressed, but also in its attitudes. For these new Afghans, their concept of society included television, electric trolley buses, and jobs. Women were entering the workforce, and not just in the more acceptable professions such as doctors, nurses, and teachers—but also as bank clerks, TV presenters, and civil servants. The Kabul government, at first during the relatively peaceful rule of Zahir Shah during the 1950s and '60s—and then under Daoud leading up to the communists in the 1970s—was rapidly pushing Afghanistan into the twentieth century.

Both the United States and the Soviet Union were competing with huge international aid programs, each trying to out assist the other. They were seeking to develop the country, much of which was still over-whelmingly rural, through improved road infrastructure, education—and large-scale, high-impact agricultural, manufacturing, or mining initiatives. These included major schemes such as the American-backed Helmand River Valley Project, the Kunduz cotton irrigation initiative, and the Soviet olive and orange farms in Nangrahar.

Even while cracking down on both left-wing and Islamic opponents during the 1970s, Daoud began moving closer to the Soviet Union in a bid to fashion a more up-to-date and better-equipped army. Moscow willingly obliged not only by sending in more military and development advisers, but also by stepping up the number of scholarships to young, ambitious Afghan men and women for education in the Soviet Union and Eastern Europe. Whole military cadres were trained in this manner, but so were security services (notably the Amnyiat or KHAD, as the secret branch was then known)—a specialty of the East Germans and Bulgarians. Many returned as card-carrying members of the PDPA, although this did not mean they were convinced communists. Political adherence to a particular ideology in Afghanistan is often a matter of practicality. The same goes for many Afghans purporting to support the post-2001 government in Afghanistan. One never really knows their true position.

Today numerous educated Afghans still speak Russian or other former Eastern Bloc languages. One engineer who fled as a refugee and eventually ended up in Bronxville, New York, was trained in Prague and helped construct Kabul's electric trolley bus system—which was destroyed by Hekmatyar's shelling of the city during the early 1990s. Another, now running a grocery in London, received his medical degree from Moscow University. Many look back to this period with rueful nostalgia. In those days, they maintain, the emerging bourgeoisie genuinely cared about their country. "We were committed to pulling Afghanistan out of the nineteenth century to become a real nation," the former trolley bus engineer said. "When we left, we all intended to come back. And we did. But all that changed with the mujahideen and the Taliban."

The reality was that while Daoud appeared to be embracing a steadily pro-Moscow stance, he played off the Americans and Soviets in a bid to attract more international aid. Not to be outdone, the Americans harnessed some of the country's military talent by sending young officers (such as Rahim Wardak, a former jihadist who became Afghanistan's minister of defense under Karzai) to the United States for training. The French and West Germans, too, sent promising young academics for higher education as lawyers, philosophers, engineers, agriculturalists, and criminologists to universities such as Montpellier and Paris or the Technical University of West Berlin.

Part of this accelerated change was the result of expanding commercial trade, but also tourism—an ideal industry with Afghanistan's rich cultural heritage and rugged landscape. French, Polish, Soviet, and other European archaeologists had unearthed spectacular finds since the 1930s, so there was much to show. Growing numbers of foreign visitors traveled up to the famed Buddhas of Bamiyan, the ruins of the ancient Zoroastrian and later Bactrian Greek city of Balkh in northern Afghanistan, and to trek or hunt in the Hindu Kush. The influxes brought in rock-and-roll and scantily clad, marijuana-smoking hippies on their overland journeys to India and Nepal.

The presence of foreign aid workers helped introduce the country to the outside world. And not just in the cities. "We often spent our weekends staying in villages. People still remember us from this period," reflected David Garner, an American development specialist who first arrived during the 1970s and has continued to work with Afghanistan. Unlike many of the international contractors brought in from 2002 onward, the bulk of these dedicated earlier aid workers made the effort to learn Dari or Pashto. They informed themselves about the culture and often traveled upcountry on their furloughs, forming bonds with Afghans that still exist today.

Another was American Whitney Azoy, a fluent Dari speaker who ventured to Kunduz as a Fulbright scholar in the late 1970s and who went on to become the world's expert on *buzkashi*, the rough-and-tumble Afghan version of polo. He has returned numerous times since as a writer and anthropologist. "The trouble is that Afghan culture is highly alluring. Afghans have a sense of hospitality that is extraordinary. You can't help but sit down and talk with them. Every Afghan, whether a farmer, shopkeeper, or a baker, is a storyteller and a philosopher," he said. The growing obsession with security from 2005 onward has made it more difficult for the international community, even well-meaning aid workers and diplomats, to get to know ordinary Afghans.

What this meant for traditional Afghan society was that an aspiring urban middle class—but also young, educated people from rural areas— were beginning to challenge the centuries-old hold by highly conservative tribal and ethnic leaders and *ulema*. These latter forces strongly opposed anything that was likely to bring about change, including land reform, the elimination of the burqa, or schools for girls. New magazines and newspapers appeared representing a broad array of political doctrines, arts, and literature—above all poetry—to satisfy an increasingly literate society (still barely 30 percent by the outbreak of war) desperate for creative outlets and greater freedom of expression.

During the latter part of the King Zahir Shah era, there had been a relatively open political environment and press. The two PDPA factions had their roots in political journals, the Parcham (Banner) and Khalq (Masses). With their promises of reform, the communists garnered spreading enthusiasm among the bourgeoisie, but also young Pushtuns seeking to break out from the countryside. Later, the profiles of the Khalqis and the Hezb emerged as remarkably similar, with each appealing to radical Pushtuns with little or no education to fill their ranks.

When the PDPA regime finally collapsed in 1992, many Khalqi militants went over to Hezb. Ultimately, many of these Pushtuns joined the Taliban, bringing with them an additional form of extremism, but also fighting experience.

It was in this context of growing openness and liberalism, followed by the conservative backlash, that Massoud and Hekmatyar formed their political ideas. Massoud, who was born in the Panjshiri village of Jangalak near the small riverside town of Bazarak on September 1, 1953, was on the cusp of manhood when the communist movement began to take hold in Afghanistan. A graduate of the famed French Lycée Istiqlal high school in Kabul, Massoud enrolled in 1973 at the Kabul Polytechnic Institute for Engineering and Architecture. It was at high school that he began to develop his close affiliation with France. As Massoud maintained, his ambition since childhood was to pursue an army career. "I always wanted to be a soldier," he said. Like his father, a senior police commander, he wanted to have a role in public service. According to his childhood friends, he was a natural-born leader, constantly taking the initiative and rallying his mates, whether to play soccer or mock battles. However, as he often insisted, he never saw himself in a political role.

"We usually laughed to ourselves when he said this, because he had an extraordinary ability for dealing openly and yet firmly with people at all levels," recalled his longtime friend Masood Khalili, who first met the Panjshiri commander in Pakistan during the late 1970s. "I always remember him as an exceptional person. I was ready to fight with him from the start. And when he asked me, I said, 'Why not?'" During the early 1990s when Massoud found himself pushed by his supporters toward assuming the role of leader, even president, he made a point of telling me that he felt uncomfortable with power. "I prefer being a soldier," he insisted. Until the collapse of the PDPA regime, the Pakistanis feared him as one of the only Afghan nationalists capable of rallying his fellow countrymen toward a united Afghanistan.

As a result, both the ISI and Hekmatyar deliberately torpedoed Massoud's repeated efforts at creating an effective alliance of the inside resistance fronts, which threatened to supersede the corrupt Peshawar-based politicians. Had Massoud survived, many northern Afghans, but also some southern and eastern Pushtuns with whom he had cultivated good relations, believe that he would have made a far better interlocutor for the West than Karzai. Khalili agrees that Massoud would have probably accepted this role, but only during an interim period. "I don't think he ever wanted to become president," he said. Whether Massoud's numerous opponents, notably the hard-line Pushtuns and the Pakistanis, would have accepted this remains another matter.

Very much a romantic, the young Massoud had a passion for Persian poetry. Khalili, then a popular announcer with his own youth show on Radio Kabul, would encourage Massoud, with his gravelly voice, to publicly recite poetry. He was a formidable chess opponent, played soccer avidly, and trained in karate. Often, during the Soviet-Afghan war, we would stop by the banks of a river where there was a natural pitch, the grass cropped short by sheep and cows. The Panjshiri commander would shed his trademark anorak down to his blue shirt and green fatigues and launch into an impromptu soccer game with his troops. His men never hesitated to trip him as Massoud, his face creased with bemused concentration, tried to dribble past.

A northern Tajik, Massoud spoke Dari as his native tongue, but knew Pushto fluently. Later, he learned Urdu during his brief exiles to Pakistan, plus gained a working command of Arabic. He voraciously read French military and political books. This mix of languages served him well. He maintained an open mind and garnered widespread sympathy in France and other parts of Europe during and after the Soviet-Afghan war leading up to his assassination in September 2001. "The thing about Massoud is that he was curious, always wanting your opinion on how the outside world thought. He was constantly exploring new ideas for what might work best for Afghanistan," recalled French doctor Laurence Laumounier.

Massoud's command of Pushto helped his efforts to encourage a nationwide resistance by allowing him to talk with both rivals and collaborators. Select Pushtuns, some of them affiliated with Hezb, lived in his zones of control, including at least one village in the Panjshir plus parts of Gulbahar and Jabal Saraj. He always seemed to have good relations with these groups. I remember stopping at one guerrilla base where the commander, a Hezb, warmly talked about Massoud as a "true mujahed" and then asked me to take a note to him.

Massoud's regret was not speaking English. He had begun picking it up during the late 1990s, primarily through visiting American, British, and Australian journalists—such as Peter Jouvenal, Tony Davis, and Sebastian Junger (author of *The Perfect Storm* and *War*)—but it was too late. "Perhaps the Americans would have been more interested in helping us if I spoke English," he once reminisced. This was probably not far from the truth. I was always convinced that one reason why Washington preferred Hekmatyar was his excellent command of the English language.

Massoud never completed his engineering studies. On entering college, he joined—as did Hekmatyar—Jamiat-e-Islami. During this early period, both men became close associates of Habib Rahman, an ardent Islamist who planned the first armed insurrection in 1973 against the Daoud regime. But it was Hekmatyar who eventually became Jamiat's military leader. While still a communist, he had begun combining his political activism with Islamic extremism. His affiliation with Jamiat was not surprising: The two tendencies, Islamism and communism, were a natural mix.

Born in 1947, Gulbuddin Hekmatyar was a "transplanted" Ghilzai Pushtun of the Kharoti tribe from the northern province of Kunduz. His father originally came there from Ghazni as part of the forced migrations decreed by the late-nineteenth-century Afghan king Abdur Rahman Khan, a Durrani Pushtun, as a means of ridding himself of his enemies. These were designed to move rival Ghilzai from south of the Hindu Kush to non-Pushtun areas in the north in order to disperse and weaken them.

More than a century later, it was the Ghilzai Pushtuns who dominated the Taliban movement. Descendants of some of these same "transplants" are now involved with the anti-NATO insurgency in the north. Hezb became militarily active in Kunduz from 2004 onward and was later responsible for attacks against the German forces operating there. A June 2004 assault by an estimated twenty insurgents killed at least eleven Chinese construction workers as they slept in their tents south of the city of Kunduz. While no group claimed responsibility, later indications suggest it was carried out by Hezb. The victims, most of whom had just arrived in Afghanistan, were part of a road-building team employed by the China Railway Shisiju Group Corporation.

When I traveled to Kunduz in 2004, I found that many villagers approved of the killing of the Chinese workers. As elsewhere in Afghanistan, where the international community has implemented major infrastructure projects, villagers have been angered by the way donor governments hire outside contractors without providing local jobs. As in Africa, the Chinese bring in their own personnel, even drivers and cooks, thus alienating the local population. Hezb and other insurgents have relied on such discontent to expand their support base.

Hekmatyar first became a protégé of Ghulam Serwar Nasher, a successful businessman and Kharoti tribal leader who developed Afghanistan's cotton industry through the Spinzar Cotton Company. This helped make Kunduz, where irrigated cultivation of the crop was introduced in the 1950s, one of the country's richest provinces. Seeing in the twenty-one-year-old a man of talent, Nasher sent him to Kabul's famed Mahtab Qala military academy in 1968. However, Hekmatyar was expelled two years later for his communist activities. It was then that he may have been recruited by the KGB, or at least developed contacts with the Soviets. Hekmatyar went on to Kabul University to study engineering. Although referred to by his followers as "Engineer," he (like Massoud) never completed his degree. Involved in 1972 in the murder of a rival Maoist militant, he was sentenced to two years in prison, but released as part of an amnesty.

Both Hekmatyar and Massoud joined the Nahdat al-Shibab al-Muslim, an underground youth organization and offshoot of Egypt's Muslim Brotherhood (founded in 1969 under Jamiat auspices). The new group included Burhanuddin Rabbani as its chairman and Sayyaf as vice chairman. Although still in prison, Hekmatyar became Nahdat's political director. Evidence suggests that he did this at the behest of the KGB as a means of infiltrating fundamentalist circles. He also hoped to gain an upper hand over his rivals within the Islamist movement. It was then that Hekmatyar reportedly started a campaign to throw acid on female students wearing Western clothes, a tactic later adopted by the Taliban in southern Afghanistan from 2008 onward. The Nahdat youth organization barely lasted four years. When the Daoud regime began cracking down on Islamist groups in 1974, most of its members were arrested or fled to Pakistan.

Habib Rahman's plan to take the Panjshir failed when the Afghan secret police got wind of it. He was arrested. A second revolt was planned in 1974—but this, too, failed. Massoud and Hekmatyar were forced to flee to Pakistan. While in Peshawar, they became part of an exile Afghan group of anti-Daoud activists supported by Bhutto, who opposed the Kabul regime's pro-Pushtunistan rhetoric. For these militant young Afghans, Daoud's policies were too reformist. They opened doors to more liberal outside influences, including overtly pro-communist media linked to different communist factions ranging from the hard-line Khalqis to the Maoists. By then, Hekmatyar was publicly distancing himself from the PDPA and embracing a more extremist form of Islam.

Jamiat split into two tendencies. One was led by Rabbani, who, not entirely opposed to modernism, proposed a gradualist approach for ensuring respect for Islam within a new Afghanistan. This, he believed, could be achieved by infiltrating the country's institutions and persuading Afghans to support the fundamentals of Islam. The other, which emerged as Hezb-e-Islami, was led by Hekmatyar—who wanted a more radical, revolutionary approach. He believed that any reform, regardless of whether it came from the West or the Soviet Union, needed to be halted. If people did not accept Islam, in particular his own doctrinaire approach, it should be forced upon them.

Massoud, then twenty-two, headed back to Afghanistan under the auspices of Hekmatyar's Hezb to attempt a third revolt. He had returned secretly to Afghanistan several times to prepare the ground by talking with potential supporters within the army and police. Backed by the Pakistanis, Massoud and his handful of shoddily armed rebels succeeded in taking the Panjshir Valley in October 1975, but their success was short-lived.

The uprising failed when Hekmatyar betrayed his fellow conspirators. The Hezb politician had promised to carry out a military coup d'état in Kabul by galvanizing pro-Islamist officers. At the last minute, he held back, a tactic he often used during coordinated resistance operations against the Soviets, leaving open flanks for the Red Army to exploit. This led many during the 1980s to wonder whether Hekmatyar was working with Moscow. According to some, he had deliberately torpedoed the uprising in order to neutralize Massoud, whom he already feared as a potential rival. The Panjshiri militant and his fellow fighters barely escaped with their lives. From that point onward, Massoud never trusted Hekmatyar again.

Similar allegations of double-crossing were being voiced in 2010 by the Taliban themselves. Hekmatyar's Hezb, they maintained, was informing on them to NATO forces in order to strengthen its own position.

Massoud's and Hekmatyar's respective ideologies became more defined during the latter part of the 1970s, with the two embracing increasingly divergent approaches. Hekmatyar persisted with his now vehemently anti-left-wing struggle by adopting a hard line marked by brutal intolerance. This included the assassination of government officials, intellectuals, and rival Islamists—some of them former friends and colleagues. Later—notably during the Soviet occupation, the civil war of the 1990s, and the anti-Western insurgency from 2003 onward—this brutal disregard for innocent civilians, both Afghan and foreign, became a trademark of the way Hekmatyar fought his wars.

Massoud rejected such ruthlessness. The Panjshiri militant always maintained that he was not prepared to achieve his goals at any cost, particularly if it involved killing civilians. Like Rabbani, Massoud felt that persuasion through open discussion was the most effective way of turning people around. He wanted to reach out to a broad spectrum of Afghans, from conservative village elders and farmers to the more open urban bourgeoisie.

With the overthrow of Daoud by the communists in 1978 and the spread of armed opposition to the PDPA regime, the two rivals became actively engaged with the new mujahideen, Massoud with Jamiat and Hekmatyar with his own Hezb faction. By then, General Zia ul-Haq, who had overthrown and later hanged Zulfikar Ali Bhutto in July 1977, decided to support Afghanistan's emerging rebel groups by focusing primarily on the fundamentalists. A conservative Muslim with an almost Spartan lifestyle, Zia reinstalled the ISI as Islamabad's principal conduit for dealing with the insurgents. Operating as a military state within a military state the ISI had its own vision of whom to support, and why. It saw Afghanistan's fundamentalists as Pakistan's best bet for supposedly pro-Islamabad militants to take power in Kabul. The last thing the ISI wanted was to enable non-Pushtun commanders, such as Massoud, to gain the upper hand among the inside resistance groups.

For the Pakistanis, Massoud had to be contained. The ISI only worked with those it felt it could control. And there was no way of controlling guerrilla fronts that did not fully rely on outside support for their weaponry and strategic planning. It was this philosophy that attracted the Americans. Some ISI officers had received their training in the United States and maintained good relations with their US intelligence counterparts, a collaboration that continues to this day.

Although the ISI refused to support Massoud, they kept close tabs on his activities. They allowed limited amounts of weaponry to filter through as a means of providing at least some form of oversight. The ISI deployed its informers up and down the frontier as well as in Peshawar, Quetta, and Islamabad. They knew precisely which of Massoud's supply convoys were leaving when and where. ISI agents regularly dropped by for "chats" with Western humanitarian relief coordinators.

From the very beginning, the Pakistanis regarded Hekmatyar as their preferred mujahed leader. His conservative ideals also tied in well with the Zia dictatorship's vision for Pakistan. With enough money and weapons, Pakistanis were convinced that Hekmatyar would serve as their stooge. It was always clear, however, that Hekmatyar had other ideas—and that he vigorously pursued his own agenda. Throughout the Soviet-Afghan war, the ISI and CIA did everything possible to propel Hekmatyar to the forefront of the resistance. Yet in all my encounters with him, never once did Hekmatyar hide his disdain, even hatred, for the United States.

With the outbreak of fighting against the PDPA regime, both Hekmatyar and Massoud consolidated their positions within the new mujahideen. While Massoud emerged as a front-line commander, Hekmatyar became head of his Hezb faction in Peshawar. The Pakistanis pushed Hekmatyar to organize the growing numbers of disparate groups fighting haphazardly and without coordination in different parts of Afghanistan. Hekmatyar started enlisting commanders, many of them tribal chiefs or former army officers, into his ranks. In return, he promised guns and money. Meanwhile, existing training facilities from the Bhutto period were expanded as new ones were established inside the tribal zones. The ISI remained omnipresent, but discreetly in the background, with its agents providing advice and direction. Hekmatyar was often called to ISI headquarters in Rawalpindi to discuss strategy.

As for Massoud, he remained in Peshawar with occasional clandestine trips back into Afghanistan. These included meetings with Nuristani commander Mohammed Anwar Amin, a thirty-six-year-old nationalist and former civil servant from Kunar, who had been arrested and jailed by the Khalqis. Released in October 1978, Anwar Amin immediately returned to Kunar, where he rallied several thousand Nuristanis against the Kabul regime. Massoud linked up with Anwar Amin, and the two became close friends. Equipped only with a small handful of Lee-Enfields and Mausers, they began attacking police stations, military posts, and armories. By spring 1979, Nuristan was completely under rebel control. Elsewhere, other largely remote regions, such as Badakshan to the north and Hazarajat in the Central Highlands, had also revolted and taken control.

Anwar, who was later killed by Hekmatyar, was initially regarded—particularly by the French—as the most charismatic and promising of the new resistance leaders. Following the Soviet invasion, however, he and other Nuristani leaders lost out to extremist Maulawi Afzal, who established his own Wahhabi government with Saudi and Pakistani backing. Afzal remained the central figure in Nuristan throughout the 1980s and much of the '90s. Hekmatyar's Hezb, on the other hand, had always cultivated support in the region and soon emerged as the lead insurgent body.

During those heady days of 1979, it was Anwar Amin who introduced Massoud to organized guerrilla revolt. Anwar gave him a Nuristani hat, the *pakul*, which soon became the trademark of the Panjshiri leader and his northern resistance. While trekking through Kunar in 2004, I encountered Anwar's son, a government commander. He gave me a bed for the night in his *qala*, or compound. I did not realize he was Anwar's son until we began talking about Hekmatyar. He then made it clear that he would track down and kill the man who murdered his father. "He has much blood on his hands. He knows there are many who would like to kill him, so he is afraid. But I will get him," he announced quietly.

As fighting spread, Massoud began to organize his own armed opposition. In 1979, together with some twenty men, he returned to the

Panjshir, where he queried the elders to determine local willingness to fight the communists. Most agreed to support him. As many as thirty thousand Afghans—whether nationalists, Maoists, intellectuals, or even rival Parcham communists—are believed to have been killed by the Khalqis from April 1978 to the Soviet invasion nearly a year and a half later. Many were Panjshiris. Some of the valley's wealthy merchants, such as Hajii Saduddin, whom I first met in Bazarak, pledged to support the insurrection financially. "Massoud was a young man, but he was determined and we recognized in him a leader. There was never any question that we should not support him," recalled Saduddin, who died in 2009 after having served for years as an éminence grise for Massoud.

Not unlike Anwar Amin's operations in Nuristan, Massoud's forces quickly ousted the Khalqis from the seventy-mile-long Panjshir Valley by overruñning the local police stations and army garrisons. From then onward, the Panjshir became a symbol of defiant opposition for the entire country. When the Soviets invaded, they made a point of securing the valley, with only limited success. They launched no fewer than eight major offensives between 1980 and 1984, when Massoud negotiated his much-criticized truce with the Red Army. After that he used the opportunity to expand his resistance fronts across the north, but also to unite with other key resistance commanders elsewhere in the country. Constantly undermined by the ISI and Hekmatyar, however, he never managed to establish the broad-based alliance of inside guerrilla fronts that he had dreamed of.

For Hekmatyar, it was a different story back in Peshawar. There it was a matter of securing a leadership position among the mujahideen. He made a point of intimidating any intellectuals, commanders, and refugee leaders who criticized his dictatorial approach. Hundreds of Afghan exiles are believed to have been murdered in Peshawar alone by Hekmatyar's orders. Aided and abetted by the ISI, their killers were almost never brought to justice.

Hekmatyar also sought to undermine international aid activities that might put a more favorable light on other commanders. In 1986, Thierry Niquet, a French coordinator for two Paris-based relief agencies, was murdered by Zabet Toufan, a renowned Hezb commander. Niquet was traveling by foot toward Mazar-e-Sharif on a mission to bring cash to destitute communities for purchasing subsidized grain in government-controlled bazaars. A year later, Médecins sans Frontières reported that Hekmatyar's men had hijacked a ninety-six-horse caravan bringing aid into northern Afghanistan. According to Juliette Fournot, the outspoken MSF coordinator who had been brought up in Afghanistan by her archaeologist parents, this represented a year's supply of medicine and cash. When confronted, Hekmatyar denied responsibility.

By 1987, Hekmatyar's Hezb was being increasingly criticized not only for subverting other resistance fronts, but for negotiating with pro-communist militia in areas where he had no control. Hezb regularly maintained that it had good relations with all mujahideen. Its officials often invited me to travel with their fighters to prove this. While I had gone in with Hezb groups during the early days of the occupation, I refused to travel with them unless I had the right to hook up with other fronts inside. What I wanted to avoid was to become an "embed" with one particular group.

Mangal, the Hezb spokesman, insisted that I commit to his organization. "If you travel with us you have to remain under our responsibility. We have to protect you. What would happen if you traveled with another group and you were injured or killed?" he declared. What Hezb was trying to ensure was that any news coverage, which was always rebroadcast back into Afghanistan via the BBC and VOA, focused solely on its operations.

In October 1987, American documentary filmmakers Lee Shapiro (a member of the Unification Church of Korean Sun Myung Moon) and Jim Lindalos (a cameraman and paramedic) joined Hezb on a trip to eastern Afghanistan. Shapiro had already made a feature-length film, *Nicaragua Was Our Home*, on the guerrilla struggle of the Miskito Indians, which was broadcast on PBS in the United States. Hekmatyar's propaganda people were savvy enough to know that an American profile of Hezb guerrillas would help clean up their image. Several major documentaries—including de Ponfilly's and Bony's *Valley Against an Empire* but also films by ITV's Sandy Gall and the BBC's John Simpson with Peter Jouvenal—had already been broadcast on Massoud, making him the hero of the Afghan resistance.

While traveling inside, however, fighting broke out between the Hezb guerrillas and a rival Jamiat front. Tragically, both journalists were killed. Hekmatyar and the US embassy tried to claim that the two Americans were victims of a Soviet ambush. However, according to our own sources, including their translator (who survived) there had been no Red Army troops in the vicinity. By then, it was known that Hezb fighters regularly attacked other groups, so the incident came as no surprise. Jouvenal and I were threatened by Hezb for questioning the official position.

A further example of Hezb's effort to control information was the murder in October 1987 of a highly accomplished British cameraman, Andy Skrzypkowiak. He brought out rare images of guerrilla attacks against the Soviets, mainly by Massoud's forces. Hekmatyar was furious that journalists were largely ignoring American and ISI efforts to promote him. A tall former SAS soldier known as "the Pole," Andy was a driven man. Interviewed in *Last Images of War*, the 1992 Emmy Award–winning PBS film by Stephen Olsson and Scott Andrews, he said: "This war will go down in history, and I want to be there—close—getting it all on film." Andy knew how to take care of himself. Yet he was apprehended by Hezb mujahideen near the Nuristani village of Kantiwah on his way back from the Panjshir. He was killed at night in a cave while sleeping when his "hosts" crept over and crushed his skull with a rock. Trekking in this same area during the 1980s, I had twice encountered Hezb fighters who—while never physically accosting me—regarded me with cold suspicion. I never hung around.

Our own efforts, and particularly those of Andy's wife, to bring his murderers to justice were ignored. His killers were even rewarded by Hekmatyar. Polish Foreign Minister Radek Sikorski, a former journalist and close friend of Andy's, called for Hekmatyar to be tried for war crimes in response to the murder. "Let's hope we get him," Sikorski noted to me in a conversation in January 2011 at the World Economic Forum in Davos. "Hekmatyar's a very nasty man."

The most prominent Afghan to be murdered by Hezb was Professor Sayid Bahauddin Majruh, one of the country's most highly respected resistance intellectuals. Majruh, an old friend whom I regarded as my Afghan mentor, came from a distinguished family of Sufis from the

Kunar Valley. He was the former dean of philosophy and a professor of literature at the University of Kabul and had also served as governor of Kapisa province under Zahir Shah. Two months after the Soviet invasion, Majruh fled Kabul by foot across the mountains to Peshawar.

A dedicated academic, who had received his doctorate in France, Majruh realized that he now had a vital new role to play. He established the Afghan Information Centre (AIC), which published one of the few truly independent Afghan journals monitoring the Soviet-Afghan war. He continued to write books, notably *Ego Monster*, his life's work and an extended poetic allegory. Majruh enjoyed chatting about writing and was impressed by the "Anglo-Saxon" approach to journalism, notably straight reporting. He wanted to do the same with his monthly bulletin. While Majruh's sympathies clearly lay with the moderates, he saw himself as a free-thinking independent. He never hesitated privately to express his opinion (but rarely in his journal) or to question American or ISI support for the extremists. He criticized Hekmatyar's excesses and regularly warned the Americans about placing too much reliance on the increasingly corrupt Peshawar-based politicians. This proved his downfall.

Balding, his graying longish hair curling over his collar, and perpetually squinting through his black-rimmed glasses beneath thick eyebrows, Majruh walked with a limp from a car accident earlier in life. Ironically, his name, *Majruh*, means "one who has been injured." Leaning on his walking stick, he was a regular guest at international functions in Peshawar. He constantly badgered the Western embassies to provide funds for his publication. He wrote up his stories with a portable typewriter, and his magazine was often poorly printed. Yet it served as an indispensable information source for journalists, aid workers, and diplomats. He was as excited as a child when he received his first computer, significantly easing the editing of his journal.

What made his AIC magazine so unusual was that in the seventy-odd editions published up to his death, Majruh made a point of maintaining a staunchly neutral stance. Part of this neutrality was a family tradition. His grandfather, Pasha Sahib-e-Tigari, was a principal deputy of the mullah of Hadda, who lived in the Upper Kunar near the Pakistani-Afghan border. As a Sufi Pir, he mediated in the often bitter strife between the Safi and Mohmand tribes of the region. Majruh's home and office in Peshawar became a contemporary variation on this service.

People who came to see Majruh knew that their accounts would be treated with respect and in confidence. His journal reported events and quotes, rarely commentary. He was constantly interviewing new arrivals from across the border or Afghans from the refugee camps to glean news of what was happening inside Afghanistan. We often shared information and spent long hours discussing the war. At his house, I would be sure to bump into visiting commanders (from all parties), academics, former government officials, and merchants who had recently fled the repression.

In November 1987, Majruh published a survey that his researchers had conducted among two thousand of Pakistan's three million refugees, most of them Pushtuns from eastern Afghanistan. Despite Hezb's claims—and those of the ISI and the American embassy—that Hekmatyar was the most popular resistance figure, the results showed that the overwhelming majority had no confidence in the Peshawar politicians. They preferred ex-king Zahir Shah. Even Hezb commanders supported this sentiment. While not necessarily representing any great love for the former monarch, Zahir Shah stood for a nostalgic period of peace that none of the resistance leaders—with their constant bickering, corruption, and inability to unite—could offer.

As soon as the survey came out, Majruh received numerous death threats. When I spoke with him from Paris, he was evidently worried. Indeed, many of us had been concerned for Majruh's safety for some time. Until the report was published, there had been an undercurrent of understanding among the political parties that Majruh was off limits. Even the ISI respected this, primarily because the AIC served as a useful source of information. Now, however, Majruh's journal questioned the very existence of the Peshawar Seven.

Radical opponents, who bitterly opposed the return of Zahir Shah, considered Majruh a monarchist. Nevertheless, Majruh had always made it clear that he foresaw the ex-monarch returning only as a figurehead for rallying support and an interim step for paving the way for a new democracy once the Soviets had withdrawn. The AIC survey came at a time when the UN-backed agreement for Soviet withdrawal was being negotiated in Geneva. The BBC quoted Majruh's report and interviewed the exiled king in Rome regarding a possible future role in this settlement. Zahir Shah, who rarely commented on Afghan politics, declared that he was fully prepared to return, but only at the request of the Afghan people.

Among the many foreign visitors who came to see Majruh was Felix Ermacora, the UN investigator for the Human Rights Commission. Majruh had been helping compile data on abuses by the Soviets and the mujahed groups. UN officials based in Islamabad and Peshawar, or who came in on assignment from Geneva or New York, regularly met with Majruh to obtain his views. In my own conversations with them, several asked whether I thought Majruh would make a good mediator, acceptable to both the international community and the resistance.

A key issue was how to bring together the different players and how to incorporate the desires of ordinary Afghans. There was even talk of involving PDPA elements (much like today's concern about incorporating the Taliban for ending the NATO war). It was this prospect for a far broader platform for reconciliation to avoid a political vacuum that worried those who had everything to lose, notably the Peshawar parties and the ISI. In early 1988, I found myself back in Peshawar. I phoned Majruh, telling him that I planned to stop by to see him over the next few days. "Just come when you like. There are people I would like you to meet," he told me.

On the morning of February 12, I rode over to Majruh's house on my bike. Pakistani police and a group of Afghans were standing outside. I walked up to the door. The threshold was splashed with blood. Seeing me, one of Majruh's assistants quickly walked over. "They've killed the professor," he said. Later, his son Naim told me what had happened. On the afternoon of February 11, Majruh had been expecting the French chargé d'affaires. The gunmen had been watching the house. They waited until Majruh's cook had left to buy fresh *nan*, or bread, for dinner before going to the gate to ring the buzzer. Majruh opened the door. The assailants, believed to be as many as four, opened fire with one or more Kalashnikov assault rifles. The force of the bullets threw my friend back, killing him instantly.

Naim took photographs of his father's body lying drenched with blood. He was determined to record as much evidence as possible before it disappeared. The Pakistani police, while assiduously playing the roles of diligent Scotland Yard detectives, dusting for fingerprints or questioning witnesses, always seemed to "lose" leads in awkward cases. This probably had little to do with the performance of the detectives themselves. One of them hinted to me that directives had already come down from above, notably ISI. It was not long before the investigation ran into the usual dead end.

Majruh's killing shocked Peshawar. Yet no one has ever been brought to justice. Nor have any credible official details of his murder ever been released. Many suspected Hekmatyar, but the Hezb politician denied involvement. Eventually, unsubstantiated reports began to filter through that Majruh's assailants had been picked up. According to one senior European diplomat, it was never clear whether they were Pakistani or Afghan. The suspects then disappeared. One report suggested that the ISI had taken the suspects into the mountains where they shot them, disposing of the bodies in the Kabul River. Other reports said that the ISI had ordered the men to disappear into the tribal area. No one was to talk. And no one would probably ever find out what happened.

It became increasingly apparent that neither Hekmatyar nor the ISI were going to tolerate any form of criticism that might undermine the Hezb image. Nevertheless, as a journalist, I never hesitated to refer to Hekmatyar's abuses. Once, in early 1987, I was invited together with Peter Jouvenal and Afghan cameraman Habib Hayakani to speak at a seminar on Afghanistan hosted by a Washington-based think tank. My book *The Soviet War* had recently been published, so I was considered an "expert," while both Peter and Habib were known for their exceptional film coverage of the war for the BBC, CBS, and other networks.

The gathering brought together specialists to discuss support for the mujahideen. At least half a dozen CIA agents, all with name tags, were present. At one point, CIA director William Casey quietly entered the room to listen. Peter, Habib, and I were utterly astonished when the bulk of the participants persistently stressed the effectiveness of Hekmatyar and argued he was the key resistance politician to back. When we pointed out that Hezb did not have the on-the-ground support that they claimed, several speakers repeatedly refuted our views.

Later, during a coffee break, one of the CIA delegates rudely accused me of being politically naive and said that I had no idea what was going on. "Hekmatyar's the best commander out there. He's the one the Afghans support." Cynics dealing with Afghanistan have noted that such attitudes were not surprising given that the United States never had any intention of supporting a resistance that was too effective. The long-term idea was to have the Soviet-Afghan war drag on for as long as possible.

Not long afterward, I attended a formal garden party in Peshawar hosted by USAID for honoring a visiting congressional team from Washington. I found myself discussing Hekmatyar with Tom Gouttiere, an old acquaintance and the highly experienced director of the Center for Afghanistan Studies at the University of Nebraska at Omaha. He strongly disagreed with me. "You know," he said as we chatted over drinks, "Hekmatyar's not as bad as you make him out to be. He's one of the most effective of the mujahideen."

Having lost several close friends and colleagues at the hands of Hezb, I found this hard to take. Almost shouting, I told him: "I can accept stupidity, but what I can't accept is ignorance. You should know better." There was a sudden silence as startled faces glanced in our direction. I stalked out of the compound, thoroughly embarrassed by my behavior, but also disgusted by the ongoing blindness of so many US policy makers. All one needed to do was visit the refugee camps or travel to find out what was happening. The trouble was that all too many visiting Americans were relying on the same unreliable sources lined up by the Pakistanis and the US embassy in Islamabad.

It was then that I realized that I, too, was beginning to walk a very fine line. In late 1988, Mike Malinowski, the American consul in Peshawar, stopped by my house in University Town. He had come to warn me. "We're hearing that Hekmatyar is out to get you," he said. "As you're an American citizen, it's my duty to warn you." Apparently, Hekmatyar was unhappy that I had been focusing so much of my reporting on his abuses. The reports were being picked up by the Afghan-language services of the BBC and VOA.

Malinowski had always been helpful toward the foreign press corps. He seemed genuinely concerned. He suggested I leave as soon as possible. "I really don't want a dead American reporter on my hands," he added with a faint smile. Despite Washington's support for the Hezb politician, Malinowski was never a particular fan. During one of our conversations at the American Club—after a hard day in the field and everyone drinking too much—he had confided, "We all know the guy's a real fuck. But that's the way it is."

I pondered Malinowski's warning. "Well, you know what Hekmatyar can go do with himself," I told him. I was determined not to become unnerved. At least, not in public. Nevertheless, I was fully aware what Hekmatyar and the ISI could do. As I walked back into the house, I contemplated my next move. I had no intention of backing down, although I knew that if I informed my editors, they would insist I leave. I decided to confront Hekmatyar in person. But not alone.

Together with two of my colleagues, I headed over to Hekmatyar's house, which was only a few streets away. As usual, a good twenty or thirty Afghans, including several Pakistanis, milled around in the courtyard. We entered the building, a spacious villa behind the railroad track leading to the Khyber Pass. We were shown into Hekmatyar's office. Wearing a black turban, he was sitting behind his desk, carefully sifting through papers. Another five or six militants sat drinking tea. He looked up, surprised to see us.

"Good morning, Mr. Gulbuddin. I hear that you're trying to kill me," I said, holding out my hand, which he took in his usual limp manner.

He smiled wanly. "Please. You are mistaken. Please sit down. Have some tea." His men immediately vacated their seats, while an aide poured green tea and placed bowls of raisins and nuts on the table.

"So where do you hear this?" he asked serenely, as if questioning me about the weather but clearly somewhat perturbed. It was a pleasure to witness Hekmatyar's discomfort.

"From good sources," I said firmly. I tried not to make my nervousness felt. "You know, of course, killing me would not be good for your image." The reality, of course, was that if something did happen, Hekmatyar would easily get away with it. He had murdered enough people to land himself before any international tribunal, yet probably never would. He was too well protected. We continued with our false chitchat. The mere presence of my colleagues made it clear that his intention to kill me, whether true or not, would be publicized. At least this might make the

Afghan warlord think twice before dispatching his henchmen to deal with me. On leaving, I felt somewhat better, but hardly secure.

When I got back to my house, I realized that Malinowski's warning had been dead serious. A good dozen mujahideen, several cradling AK-74s, were standing by the gate or sitting under the trees in the garden. Two were even holding watch on the roof. They were Massoud's men. My friend Agha Gul walked up to me. He had heard the same reports in the bazaar of Hekmatyar wanting to kill me. "I have sent these men to protect you," he explained. "It is important to show Gulbuddin that we are here."

I was grateful, but shocked. For the next two weeks, several of Massoud's men remained at the house. Two followed me wherever I went. Later, when these were pulled off my detail, I discovered that Agha Gul still had one of his men tail me at a discreet distance. Nevertheless, for months afterward, whenever I heard the sound of a motor scooter or car changing gear behind me, I tensed up to throw myself into the gutter.

The CIA's extraordinary decision to back such a vitriolic anti-American was hard to understand. Despite repeated advice by well-informed State Department officials, but also journalists and relief operatives working inside Afghanistan, Washington insisted on ignoring the on-the-ground realities regarding the extremists. If ever there was an American Foreign Service hero in the Afghan arena, it was Edmund, or Ed, McWilliams, who made the issue (as he put it) his personal Rubicon.

Having served in Southeast Asia and, from 1983 onward, Moscow, McWilliams worked out of the US embassy in Kabul, shuttling back and forth to Islamabad and Peshawar during the latter half of the 1980s. He was posted to Islamabad in 1989 in the wake of the Soviet withdrawal. His blistering attack on US policy—with its support for Hekmatyar and other radical Islamists, but also its reliance on the ISI for direction—drew the ire of American Cold War warriors based at the US embassy in Islamabad.

Angered by McWilliams's critical assessment of the situation, US ambassador Robert Oakley and CIA station chief Milt Bearden launched an unsubstantiated internal investigation concerning the foreign service officer's integrity. The investigation proved groundless, yet McWilliams was sidelined within the State Department. According to McWilliams,

Oakley and Bearden were fully aware of the problems that Hekmatyar, Sayyaf, and others were generating. McWilliams, whom I met on several occasions in Peshawar and Islamabad, said they knew that Hekmatyar was sabotaging resistance groups inside Afghanistan.

"They were also frustrated by the reality—which they acknowledged internally—that the fundamentalists were attacking Afghan intellectuals in Peshawar and menacing journalists and foreign NGOs in the Peshawar area and of course inside Afghanistan," McWilliams wrote to me in late 2010. It was Bearden who played a principal role in funding and training the mujahideen from the mid-1980s onward. Ironically, Bearden became an adviser to the Mike Nichols film *Charlie Wilson's War*, based on the book of the same name by author and CBS producer George Crile. While the book correctly talks about Wilson's involvement in supporting Hekmatyar, Hollywood whitewashed the US role by replacing Hekmatyar with Massoud.

Oakley, a career diplomat, may have genuinely believed that Hekmatyar was the most effective commander. Bearden, on the other hand, undoubtedly knew better. Given that so much aid was being provided to the extremists through the ISI by the Saudis, both government and private, the challenge of confronting the Pakistani military intelligence agency came too late in the game. It was, as McWilliams put it, "a bridge too far." With the Soviets indicating their readiness to withdraw, it proved far easier to continue serving as apologists for Hekmatyar by refuting journalist or aid agency reports and by misinforming Washington, including Congress.

According to McWilliams, this came in a specific form: "We clearly weighted arms delivery to Hekmatyar and the worst elements, but we were also prepared to use food and humanitarian assistance to pressure the more moderate mujahideen to stay in line." Acknowledging that the support for Hekmatyar helped create the base of wealth, arms, and power from which he operates today, he also noted that it was widely known that the Hezb leader never had any significant power inside Afghanistan and that his power always flowed from the outside.

Even Afghans supporting Hekmatyar had little understanding of their supposed leader. McWilliams recounted a visit to meet Afghan commanders in the town of Zhob, known as Fort Sandeman under the

British, in the Baluchistan desert during the late 1980s. The CIA had organized the trip to persuade the US diplomat to shift his views. He questioned the Hezb representative about his "leader," but the response sounded scripted. McWilliams then pressed toward the personal side: What kind of man was Hekmatyar? "There was silence around the circle. Finally, the most senior commander responded with a question to me: 'Do you know who Gulbuddin's father was?' I confessed that I did not know," McWilliams told me. "Neither do we." There was laughter all around.

CHAPTER NINE

Crossing the Tar

Y ou're never going to make it if you don't get fit," I admonished my friend from *Time* magazine. He had begun staggering after less than one jog around the leafy lanes of the Parc Monceau in the seventeenth arrondissement of Paris. "Even if we're taking the southern route, you've got mountains to climb."

It was early May 1982. William Dowell, who was barely in his forties and distressingly overweight, grabbed hold of a park bench. "Don't worry. I'll be ready," he rasped hoarsely. Bill was the man who had initially advised me to head off to Afghanistan to cover this emerging "little war." Now, almost two and a half years later, he had decided to join me on one of my clandestine treks. It was my fourth major trip inside. The plan was to head up to the Panjshir Valley to meet Massoud. I had received information that the Soviets were preparing to launch yet another offensive—their fifth—against the Afghan commander's mountain stronghold. It would be interesting to have Bill's perspective based on his years in Vietnam. I found myself constantly grappling with the need for comparative military references with Afghanistan. But the last thing I wanted was for him to die on me.

There was no way that he would survive the more precipitous northern route across the Hindu Kush. So I opted for the less arduous southern one. Stretching over 170 miles, this way would still take seven days of solid walking or riding. Massoud's messengers could do it in less than four. But they walked fast, even ran. The Panjshiris normally used this trail to send mail or smuggle in the French doctors. Furthermore, it was passable during the winter months when the northern routes were closed by fourteen-foot-high snow.

The circuitous southern trail would take us through the pine-forested mountains of eastern Paktia past Ali Khel before descending into the low, undulating hills of western Nangrahar. From there, we would proceed westward via Jagdalak before reaching the Kabul River and the main Jalalabad highway. Once across the "tar," as we called the asphalted road, we would have to skirt the dangerously exposed eastern fringes of the plains of Shomali, where the heavily guarded Soviet air base at Bagram was located. Then came yet another fluvial crossing, this time the Panjshir River at its widest point. Only then would we find ourselves at the foot of the Hindu Kush within a day of Massoud's first front-line positions.

The Soviets rarely monitored these routes during the early 1980s. Apart from their reconnaissance overflights, they did not have the same satellite capacity or drone predators of their post-2001 Western counterparts. When Red Army troops began stepping up their interdiction of guerrilla supply routes, they occupied vital mountain passes and deployed Spetznaz to lay mines or stage ambushes. Helicopters would drop special forces teams a few miles away so that no one would hear their engines. The troops would quickly march to their targets, lay the mines or conduct their assaults, then return. The guerrillas would have no idea what hit them. The Red Army night operations caused severe casualties among mujahideen and refugees alike.

As the war wore on, I became increasingly concerned. First thing in the morning when no one had used the trails, I found myself warily checking for trip wires or disturbed ground. As a precaution, we would put one or two horses in front. I prayed that there was no ambush-in-waiting as we trudged through the narrow defiles. Everyone relied on the first travelers to test the trails. As trekking became more hazardous, the mujahideen were forced to take more difficult routes. The cost per kilo of supplies transported by horse and camel rose fourfold.

This meant I had to be especially careful to plan trips properly and travel only with the most experienced guerrillas. I was able to work like this until the Soviet withdrawal in early 1989 and the general pullback of communist forces in the year that followed. However, given NATO's ability to track guerrilla movements remotely, I would not risk doing the same today with the Taliban. Western surveillance can rapidly call in airpower. The Americans did this with devastating consequences during their 2001 bombardments of the Taliban. Even more lethal, they can direct a drone to destroy any sinister-looking band of individuals walking along a mountain trail or even sleeping in a village compound.

Two weeks after our Paris jog, Dowell and I were in Afghanistan. In an effort to get a glimpse of the Soviets—my visa requests with the Afghan embassy in Paris had been rejected—we opted to take the regular DC-10 Ariana Afghan Airways flight from London and Paris to Delhi via Kabul. As we flew over the Hindu Kush, Bill got nervous when I pulled out my Scotch-taped and heavily marked-up CIA map. I peered through the window to figure out where we were. "My God, there's the Panjshir," I pointed out eagerly. "And that's the northern route through Nuristan, right over there."

"For Christ's sake, be careful," Bill whispered harshly. "Do you want to get us arrested?" He was convinced that we would be hauled off as spies as soon as we landed. For my part, I thought an arrest would be a superb way to see the city. I doubted that anything serious would happen other than pro forma interrogations and then deportation.

With the aircraft maneuvering into a corkscrew descent to avoid missiles, I pinpointed the Kabul River plowing its way through the eastern gorges. I wondered which of the many trails meandering through the semi-arid, rocky terrain below would be ours. As we taxied toward the terminal, we could see Soviet Mi-24 helicopter gunships bristling with 57mm rockets line up along the runway in groups of six. They threw up clouds of dust that drifted slowly across the airfield. We watched as the helicopters lifted briefly in a trial hover like metallic gray ballerinas before veering northward, presumably to attack guerrilla positions beyond the crusty, ocher-tinged mountains that overlook the Afghan capital.

Farther down the tarmac, heavy transport planes and MiG jet fighters stood along the runway aprons, while shirtless Soviet soldiers wearing khaki overalls and floppy bush hats unloaded supplies. The troops, mainly conscripts, stopped to watch the commercial passenger plane, which did this trip twice a week—possibly trying to remember what it was like to be a civilian. One or two ventured a casual wave.

The scene reminded me of the footage I had seen of Vietnam. These young men looked just like American GIs, some barely able to grow mustaches. They shared the same ambivalence toward a war in which they had little interest. Thirty years on, as I visited Coalition bases such as Camp Bastion in Helmand or Bagram, I saw very similar young soldiers, simply in different uniforms.

Only a sprinkling of passengers moved toward arrivals. These included a few Afghan embassy personnel, a team of UNESCO officials, three French Communist Party militants, and several Russians. The rest of us ambled off to the transit lounge. Our few hours at the airport provided little more than a glimpse of life in the capital. Traveling with the mujahideen, I walked within a few miles of the city in the nearby hills, but was unable to get closer. The Soviets maintained three security perimeters around the Afghan capital. My only sources of information about Kabul were interviews and informal discussions with the few Western diplomats and foreign nationals who still lived there.

"Hardly a night goes by when you cannot hear some shooting or explosions in the city," one US diplomat told me while passing through Islamabad. Curfew ran from 10 PM to 4:30 AM, but the streets were virtually empty by 7:30 in the evening except for armed military patrols. Kabul's yellow taxis charged exorbitant rates toward the end of the day, but stopped running before darkness set in.

Nighttime assassinations in Kabul of PDPA members were commonplace, but the mujahideen were not necessarily responsible. The feuding Parcham and Khalq posed as much of a problem for the Soviets in forging a united government as did the Peshawar political parties to the Pakistanis and Americans. They liked to settle their accounts during the shadowy curfew hours. The mujahideen tended to warn their victims first, such as the female radio announcer who was ordered to halt her derogative broadcasts. When she refused, they killed her. Similar perils emerged during the post-2001 period, with attacks or kidnappings of Afghans and foreigners just as likely coming from the Taliban or Hezb insurgents as from disaffected elements within the government ministries or warlord factions.

Curiously, the Russian advisers who walked around in armed groups were less vulnerable than their PDPA counterparts. People shouted at them or refused to give directions, while small boys threw stones. Occasionally, though, Red Army soldiers were murdered, and in late 1981 the guerrillas shelled the Soviet ambassador's residence. Nevertheless, as one Russian, who was with the Soviet embassy during the 1980s but who returned to Kabul as a UN staff member in 2009, said: "It was risky in those days, but we went shopping in the bazaars and met with our contacts. We knew things were bad, but we were never as holed up as we are today."

By mid-1982, however, the mujahideen were promising to go on the offensive in Kabul in order to prove that they were more than just a disparate force operating in the countryside. In one attack witnessed by Anglo-Dutch journalist Aernout van Linden in eastern Kabul, a thirty-seven-man unit lead by Abdul Zabil Halim—an able resistance commander with over three hundred urban guerrillas at his disposal— attacked a communist supply base and killed or wounded thirty Soviet and Afghan soldiers and destroyed forty-two trucks and tankers, plus a police post. The explosions sent huge fireballs into the evening sky. Several days later, Soviet forces killed Halim in a punitive ambush.

Abdul Haq, another commander, was stepping up his operations in the capital—notably assassinations and rapid action attacks. "We've got to show the communists and the people of Afghanistan that we're not just a minor nuisance. We can make life for the Russians very uncomfortable," he told me in Peshawar. He used to ride up with his sputtering 250cc Honda and signature Soviet helicopter helmet. We would have tea, and he would brief me on the latest military operations. Once he came with a small boy, the son of another commander who had been killed. When it was time to leave, this swarthy man with the look of a huge teddy bear— but who was a self-admitted killer—awkwardly picked up the boy, who had fallen asleep on the sofa. Not quite knowing what to do, he held the child outstretched and shook him like a beanbag. "There," he said with accomplishment as the startled lad opened his eyes. "He's awake."

Bill and I finally made it to Parachinar at the beginning of June 1982. As before, I had arranged to accompany an AMI replacement team of two doctors and one nurse to the Panjshir. It was a good way to learn more about military actions, as the wounded or their families had stories to tell. In the early 1980s, there were still only three French medical organizations (the other two were MSF and MDM) operating with a total of twenty-five medics providing relief in eight provinces. The AMI team would be replacing the two women doctors who had been running the Panjshir clinic for the past several months. With the war forcing more civilians to leave the valley, the plan was to set up new clinics elsewhere.

Traveling with Assad, a close confidant of Massoud and an incredibly thin Panjshiri, we headed up to Parachinar. There we met up with some twenty mujahideen, all from Massoud's Jamiat-e-Islami faction, and we rode by pickup along a rough track to Teri Mangal. This was a border supply town for the guerrillas. It was also where all the trafficked lumber from Afghanistan was brought for onward shipment into Pakistan.

There was a romantic Wild West atmosphere in Teri Mangal. It was a rambunctious settlement of two-story mud-and-stone buildings, rickety bazaar stalls, smoke-filled *chaikhane*, and tents. Hundreds of horses, donkeys, and camels were tethered in groups amid the mud and squalor, the horses with oat bags tied to their mouths. Groups of armed fighters, but also smugglers and refugees, picked their way through the bustle, loaded up animals, or sat around the teahouses. We spent the evening in a *chaikhana*, but left shortly after midnight. We trudged slowly up the pass toward Jagi on the Afghan side. The mujahideen had brought eight horses, all loaded with weapons and ammunition, including Soviet-made RPGs, Chinese anti-tank mines, and giant dewlap sacks filled with loose bullets. By the time we reached the last Pakistani military post, I could see that Bill was seriously flagging. Gasping, he constantly stopped to rest as our armed mujahideen and beasts of burden moved past. Some of the rebels laughed and Bill wearily waved his hand, like brushing off a fly. I was worried.

My principal concern, however, was the Pakistanis. Assad, who had done this journey many times, strolled over to the frontier scouts standing by a wrought-iron archway that symbolically demarcated the two countries. He slipped them some *baksheesh* and we moved past. There was no way the Pakistanis could have failed to notice the tall, red-faced, and gasping Westerner with his ill-fitting—and new—Afghan garb.

As the sun came up, we could see a broad dirt track with men, camels, and horses walking in both directions through mountainous pine forests. We could have been in the Grand Tetons in Wyoming. There was also the rusting hulk of a Soviet APC as well as a large complex of bombed-out buildings, a former school.

We soon left the main road and took a well-trodden trail northward. There were fewer people now, sometimes farmers and mujahideen but also refugees. We always stopped to talk with the refugees. Most were from

Kabul. Some tried to retain their dignity by wearing suits, city shoes, and even ties, not the most appropriate gear for fleeing through mountains and deserts. With some speaking English, German, or French, they all told us the same story. The repression under the Soviets was becoming overbearing. People were being arrested, beaten, and killed.

Most of the four thousand government schools had closed, with only those in Kabul and other cities still operating. Many university professors had fled, causing the academic quality to drop. With male students liable for conscription, young men disappeared overnight. They were either press-ganged by roaming militia or had fled to Pakistan. Many joined the resistance. One of the refugees, Mustapha, an eighteen-year-old boy from the French Lycée Istiqlal, was carrying his textbooks and wanted to complete school. At that time, the Pakistanis were still reluctant to build educational establishments in the refugee camps, and only those Afghans with money could afford the private schools. Even then, they often had to pay more, including bribing teachers to pass their exams.

Discipline at Istiqlal had completely collapsed, recounted Mustapha, whose French was precise and eloquent, improved by regular listening to Radio France International. Out of thirty pupils per class, at least two or three were Parchami, he said. "They carry guns and can do what they like. They order teachers around and inform on other people in the school. We have no respect for the [communist] teachers, only the five French who still teach there. As for the principal, he walks around with a Kalashnikov and knows nothing about education."

Some of the Western embassies were offering advanced studies in Europe or North America, but to no more than a few hundred Afghan students. It's a real dilemma, said one British diplomat, whose government provided twenty-eight student grants in 1982. "On the one hand, we want to give a lot of these young people a chance to educate themselves. But then, quite frankly, once they leave, it seems highly unlikely that many of them will ever return . . . It will only cause a brain drain, and there will be no one to put the country back on its feet."

The trail ran along the sides of mountains, overlooking occasional farms and villages in the valleys below. Some had been badly hit by the war—with walls collapsed and roofs caved in, fruit orchards torn by shrapnel, and sections of the forest completely burned. But many fields

were still being cultivated. Being so close to Pakistan, caretaker farmers, mainly old men and boys, tended the land while the women and
children sought shelter at the refugee camps in Parachinar. In many
parts, however, the Soviets waited for the crops to be harvested and then
attacked the farms to burn the harvest.

By the end of the sixteen-hour hike on the first day, Bill could barely
move. He was exhausted and dehydrated. He seemed to be visibly growing emaciated as the day wore on. I had never seen anyone deteriorate so
quickly. Several times, he collapsed by the side of the trail. "Just leave me
here to die," he moaned.

"Forget it," I said. "It'll get easier."

I had distributed his gear to the mujahideen. In this state, he was
not going to get much farther. Without being overly dramatic, I feared
that he might well die. I eyed the horses to see if I could repartition the
loads and use one of them to carry Bill, but they were already top-heavy.
Finally, a passing farmer trotted up on a shabby-looking horse, and I
immediately asked Assad to negotiate for the animal. For the next several
days, Bill walked and rode the horse. He looked more like a sorry version
of Surgeon Brydon arriving in Jalalabad following the annihilation of the
1842 British expeditionary force than a veteran journalist heading out to
cover the wars.

At night, we stayed in *chaikhane* or villages, but the farther away from
Pakistan the less food there was. All we had was tea, *nan*, and sometimes
a broth with pieces of meat and potato floating in it. A big treat was
lemon or banana biscuits. One quickly got used to this frugal diet. The
chaikhane were filthy with fleas, the mattresses smelling of sweat. For
Bill, the conditions did not matter. He simply flopped down and went to
sleep. The only thing he could consume was heavily sugared tea mixed
with a bit of salt.

At one mud-and-stone inn dominated by a huge steaming samovar
and packed with local peasants and mujahideen, the men loudly debated
the prospects of the Soviet offensive against the Panjshir. In a country where causerie still constituted a major pastime—the introduction of
satellite television in the 1990s and early 2000s more or less brought an
end to this—travelers represented a source of gossip and news. At 5 PM,
the group fell silent as the innkeeper placed a large transistor radio in the

middle of the room. The familiar strains of "Yankee Doodle" emerged from the crackling and hissing of the shortwave and then we heard the authoritative announcer of the Voice of America Farsi service introducing the main points of the news. An excited muttering arose when the speaker mentioned the Panjshir operation. Preceded by a week of heavy bombardments, the Soviet-Afghan force of twelve thousand men had entered the valley on May 17. By the end of the evening, these largely illiterate people would have also listened to other versions of the news on the BBC, Deutschewelle, Radio Moscow, Radio Kabul, and Radio Tehran.

Assad used conversations with returning commanders to obtain the latest intelligence. The Sorubi region with its parched desert terrain along the Kabul-to-Jalalabad highway was particularly dangerous. Though it was heavily Hezb, it was never clear which side the mujahideen were really on. Deals had been made with the PDPA regime to protect the electric pylons from the Sorubi dam, which served the capital. Assad was wary of these fighters. "They're more like bandits," he explained. He preferred that we move through as quickly as possible.

One commander who began operating at Sorubi toward the end of the Soviet-Afghan war was Faryadi Zardad Khan, a sadistic fiend who used to keep a hairy "human dog" on a chain to savage his victims. The "dog" was actually a mentally challenged Afghan whom Zardad kept in a cage. Between 1991 and 1996, Zardad conducted a reign of terror by robbing, brutalizing, and kidnapping travelers. When the Taliban came, he fled to Pakistan. In 1998, he made his way to the UK using a fake passport, eventually ending up in South London running a pizza parlor. Scotland Yard arrested Zardad in July 2003 after Peter Jouvenal tracked down the Afghan commander for the BBC's *Newsnight*. In a landmark case involving two trials at the cost of over $4.5 million, including witness testimony by satellite link from Afghanistan, Zardad was found guilty of a "heinous" campaign of torture and hostage-taking and sentenced to twenty years in jail. This was the first time that a UK court had convicted a foreign national for crimes committed abroad.

Giving a wide berth to the shimmering blue lake in Sorubi created by the West German–built dam, we walked through a sprawling mud-and-stone village. There were still families living in the houses. I tensed when we rounded the corner of a building to find a group of *askari*, all in gray uniforms, playing "kick the can" with military vehicles parked a few yards away. They simply waved to us. "Our friends," grinned Assad. Many government employees put in place by the Soviets had made arrangements with the mujahideen. Some, particularly the conscripts, but also a few officers, wanted to cross over to the resistance, but the guerrillas preferred them to remain. At least that way they knew these areas had been neutralized, plus they had access to the latest intelligence.

By the fifth day, with Bill beginning to recuperate, we reached the top of a narrow defile leading down to the Kabul River. "We'll walk all night," Assad announced. "We have to cross the river but it's dangerous. There are *Shouravi*." The horses would be taken to another crossing in daylight and meet us later. The terrain had become far more rugged. Escarpments of sand and gravel made the walking difficult, and we had to climb down steep ravines in the dark. Sometimes blasts of hot air would hit us as we descended into a particular pocket where the rock had not yet cooled from the heat of the day. Finally, I could hear the rushing of water and see electric lights to our right. We were in the Kabul River gorge with the highway just on the other side. Assad told us to be quiet. We would have to cross a weir, which was part of a hydroelectric installation at Moi Pan. This, in turn, was being guarded by Red Army troops.

It was hard to see in the dark. I could just distinguish some stone buildings. We carefully approached and soon found ourselves walking along the parapet of a concrete wall with the waters swirling below. I could hear a radio and voices. They sounded Russian. The soldiers were less than twenty or thirty yards away, probably inside the guardroom. I could feel the adrenaline pumping. The parapet branched left and suddenly the river was below us. We now had to tread across a loose wooden board-walk. I was amazed that they had no guards in position. Only later did Assad explain it was the *askari* who were on duty. Obviously, they had been "persuaded" to look the other way. In 2011, similar arrangements were being made by Afghan army soldiers and police with the Taliban along this same route.

On the other side lay the tar, that long ribbon of darkness combining both comfort and fear. Stepping onto the tarmac was a bizarre sensation, a completely different texture from the semi-arid terrain we had been crossing for the past few days. I knelt down to touch it. The asphalt felt warm, even sensual. It was only when Assad whispered "*Boro.* Let's go!" that I quickly stood up. A steep goat path led up from the road to the ramparts of the gorge above, and we proceeded to climb.

Heading north, we walked for the rest of the night before settling down to sleep in a dry sand-river, making sure that we were not visible from the air. The first outposts of the Red Army's outer security rim around Kabul were only a few miles to the west. One of the French relief teams had been trapped here by advancing Soviet tanks during a night operation two months earlier. They barely escaped.

As the sun rose, we trudged across more low hills until we could see, in the distance, Bagram air base. Beyond that lay the Hindu Kush. Several *kuchi* families were grazing sheep and goats in the higher reaches of the plain. We immediately made our way to their low, black tents pitched like scattered leaves at the mouth of one of the side valleys. Wary (as usual) of the dogs, we called for some *most* or yogurt. Four or five children came rushing over with large metal bowls and pieces of bread. They placed them on the ground and we sat around dipping the bread into the yogurt, as the children eyed us curiously. Despite the strong sun, the yogurt—which had been mixed with water and *namaq* (rock salt)— was blissfully cool, savory, and refreshing. I asked Assad how much we should pay. He shook his head. It was their hospitality. I asked him to thank the *kuchis* for us. Again, he shook his head. It was not expected. As before, I could only marvel at the generosity of these ordinary people, even in time of war. Sated, as if we had eaten a huge meal, we stood up and continued on our way.

As we got markedly closer to Bagram, Bill grew nervous. If this had been Vietnam, he said, we would already have been pinpointed. We were barely half a mile away and we could clearly see the runway with its planes and helicopters. Every so often, a pair of jet fighters or a cargo plane would rise into the sky, or slowly descend toward the air base. Bagram was the principal launching pad for air assaults against the Panjshir.

Several weeks earlier, a force of mujahideen from the Panjshir and Gulbahar had raided Bagram with mortars and an 88mm recoilless rifle. They cut through the perimeter, reportedly destroying twenty-five helicopters and three MiGs. They also overran the base hospital, where they

Ahmed Shah Massoud, the "Lion of Panjshir," holding a newly captured Soviet AK-74 Kalakov, 1981. Massoud went on to become one of the country's most effective resistance leaders and among the world's greatest guerrilla strategists of the 20th century. PHOTO BY EDWARD GIRARDET

A Mujahed commander praying with his men during the height of a Soviet offensive, 1984. Many guerrilla leaders were civilians who developed their skills with experience, while others were former Afghan officers who had changed sides. PHOTO BY EDWARD GIRARDET

A United Front (also known as Northern Alliance) official seeks to reach Massoud by radio in early September, 2001. The author had travelled to Khoja Bauhuddin to meet with Afghanistan's last significant commander to oppose the Taliban, but had to return to Pakistan before seeing him. Several days later, Massoud was assassinated on September 9 by two Al Qaeda operatives who had been staying in the room next to the author. PHOTO BY EDWARD GIRARDET

Baluch guerrillas, early 1980. Already fighting in southeastern Afghanistan against the communists prior to the Soviet invasion, these defiant tribal Baluch were not so much effective as fierce-looking. PHOTO BY RAULI VIRTANEN

Mujahideen undertaking an impromptu game of *buzkashi* (the traditional Afghan "polo" using the torso of a calf or goat as a ball) in the mountains near the Pak-Afghan border, 1987. PHOTO BY JEFF CARMEL

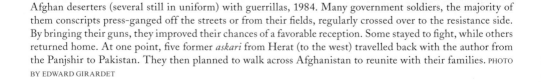

Afghan deserters (several still in uniform) with guerrillas, 1984. Many government soldiers, the majority of them conscripts press-ganged off the streets or from their fields, regularly crossed over to the resistance side. By bringing their guns, they improved their chances of a favorable reception. Some stayed to fight, while others returned home. At one point, five former *askari* from Herat (to the west) travelled back with the author from the Panjshir to Pakistan. They then planned to walk across Afghanistan to reunite with their families. PHOTO BY EDWARD GIRARDET

The author (right) meeting Ahmed Shah Massoud in a hidden cave in a narrow side valley, late 1980s. They spent several days together while Soviet planes bombed the Panjshir Valley. PHOTO BY MOHAMMED SHUAIB

The "French Doctors"—Capucine de Bretagne (left) and Laurence Laumounier—of the Paris-based volunteer health agency Aide Médicale International, who (together with Médecins sans Frontières) first began operating clandestinely inside Afghanistan in the summer of 1980. PHOTO BY WILLIAM DOWELL

British journalist Julian Gearing and cameraman Peter Jouvenal filming new refugees from northern Afghanistan making their way to Pakistan, 1984. PHOTO BY EDWARD GIRARDET

American producer Ian Woods (brother of Tom Woods), British journalist Tim Weaver, and the author under arrest by the Pakistanis near Terimangal, 1988. Western journalists and aid workers were often arrested by the Pakistanis, held for a day or two, and then released. It was simply a matter of waiting it out. The author always travelled with reading material, a couple of good books and magazines (in this case *The Economist*), precisely to deal with such moments. PHOTO BY TIM WEAVER

Renowned journalist Rory Peck smoking in Eastern Afghanistan, 1989. Charming, adventurous, and impetuous, Peck was killed by a sniper's bullet on October 3, 1993, in Moscow during Russia's constitutional crisis. PHOTO BY TIM WEAVER

Osama bin Laden. The author first met the Saudi extremist in the eastern province of Kunar in February 1989 on the eve of the Soviet pull-out. Unknown to the outside world at the time, the tall Arab threatened to kill the author if he saw him again. Less than a week later, Girardet was back—this time with American producer-cameraman Tom Woods. Confronted by bin Laden and his foreign Islamic legionnaires, the two journalists only barely escaped with their lives.

Gulbuddin Hekmatyar, Afghanistan's most nefarious resistance politician during the Soviet-Afghan war. Knowingly backed by the Americans as an Islamic extremist as part of a disastrous and highly naïve CIA-inspired policy that has come back to haunt the West, Hekmatyar today stands out as one of the most ruthless insurgent leaders fighting the US-led Coalition. PHOTO BY DONATELLA LORCH

Jalaludin Haqqani, once an American ally, now a bitter opponent. Haqqani (right) began fighting the communists around Khost in 1978 and finally took control of the city in 1992. Today, his network is still fighting—this time based in the Pakistani tribal area of North Waziristan with his main foe, NATO. As with numerous other Islamic fundamentalists, he received major support during the Soviet occupation from the United States. He also traded opium with Red Army soldiers in return for weapons. By 1992, his group was heavily infiltrated by foreign fighters. PHOTO BY TIM WEAVER

6

Refugee graves along the caravan trail in eastern Afghanistan, mid-1980s. Some refugees (particularly the young or the old) succumbed to exhaustion, cold, or injuries as they walked—sometimes hundreds of miles—across the mountains to Pakistan in a bid to escape the war. Their graves often littered the trails also used by the mujahideen. PHOTO BY EDWARD GIRARDET

Refugees from northern Afghanistan crossing the Hindu Kush mountains with camels and horses, 1984. Some of these were killed or wounded in Soviet aerial attacks against their columns, which often took hours to cross the rocky passes. PHOTO BY EDWARD GIRARDET

"Dr. Tom," the low-key optometrist from Delmar, New York, who had dedicated his life to helping Afghans. The American eye doctor was executed together with nine other Afghan and foreign aid workers of International Assistance Mission (IAM), a US NGO, by unknown assailants in Badakshan in the summer of 2010. COURTESY OF TOM LITTLE FAMILY

Mujahideen loading rockets in the Pakistani border areas for transport by horse into the interior during the mid-1980s. When the Americans there stepped up their resistance support in the mid-1980s, the amount of weaponry entering Afghanistan from the outside rose significantly. Scores of clandestine caravans of horses, donkeys, and camels crossed over the frontier in numerous places during the summer months when the mountain passes were open. PHOTO BY EDWARD GIRARDET

One of the last known photographs of four members of the IAM team executed by unknown assailants in northern Afghanistan in the summer of 2010. From left to right: Tom Grams, Glen Lapp, Tom Little, and Dan Terry. COURTESY OF IAM/TOM LITTLE FAMILY

View of the Safed Koh mountains as guerrillas walk the road along the Kunar River, summer 1989. The Afghan government frontlines were only several miles further on. PHOTO BY EDWARD GIRARDET

Afghan Uzbek refugee girls in northern Afghanistan, 2001. PHOTO BY EDWARD GIRARDET

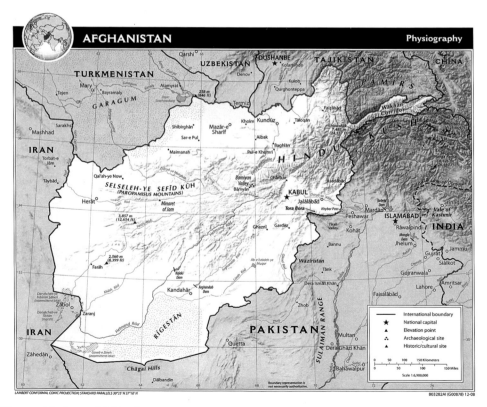

Topographical map of Afghanistan. COURTESY OF UNIVERSITY OF TEXAS

shot wounded soldiers as they lay in bed. How could they kill patients? we asked. Assad looked at us in astonishment. Because they're a lot easier to kill, he replied. Captured Soviet prisoners later independently told us that the attack had been a traumatic shock for the Red Army. Crushing Massoud had now become a priority.

Bill continually expressed concern over what he considered to be the total insouciance of the mujahideen. While we had now spread out for security reasons in spaced single file, one of the guerrillas (a boy in his teens) insisted on loudly playing music on his radio. Bill shouted at him to turn it off. When the boy laughed, Bill grabbed it, threatening to throw it to the ground. Assad had to step up, angrily explaining to the boy that it was dangerous. The mujahed reluctantly stuck the radio into his blanket bundle. To make matters worse, our single-file policy was shattered when we were joined by other fighters. We were now sixty men with over thirty horses. Bill and I cringed. We could only hope that the Soviets did not send out any helicopters or tanks.

By midday, we had reached the Panjshir River at a ford shallow enough to wade across. We were being increasingly joined by other groups on their way to help Massoud. It had the air of a social gathering as heavily armed commanders came up to pay their respects. There was a veritable traffic jam of men preparing to traverse the river. They hooked arms against the strong waist deep current and then, in groups of fifteen or twenty, gingerly edged their way across. Others clutched horses against the current. Occasionally, huge Huckleberry Finn–style rafts of trees, branches, and lumber tied together shot past, steered by a man or boy clinging on from the rear.

Once on the other side, we marched along a wide track toward Gulbahar. On the left lay the river, and beyond that, the poplar-bordered and fertile irrigated fields of Shomali planted with wheat, fruit orchards, and vineyards. It was near sunset. A lone horseman came galloping toward us, flaying his mount left and right with his reins. He had an elaborately embroidered saddle that shone in the evening light. Thundering past, he galloped for sheer joy, extolling the spirit of liberty. The mujahideen, now in their scores, moved silently through the streets. As we passed the first adobe houses—the warm sun on our faces—women, small children hanging on to their skirts, emerged throwing sweets and sugared almonds in our path. Murmuring the traditional greeting of "*Mandabashi*, may you not be tired," they had come to greet the fighters. It was an exhilarating moment, and we felt that this is what it must be like to be part of a liberating army.

I found it hard to believe that the first government installations, a factory and some administrative buildings, were only a few hundred yards farther on. The Soviets, too, had a fort beyond these. The Red Army had even massed its tanks and APCs along the main road west of Gulbahar as they prepared to move into the Panjshir. And yet, not even bothering to hide, several hundred armed mujahideen were filtering through the outskirts before peeling off into the mountains.

Assad took us into a high-walled compound close to the government buildings. It was the house of a local commander. A tall Pushtun with a thick, black beard and a green West German army-surplus anorak, he greeted us warmly and led us into the guest room thick with carpets and a smoking samovar in the corner. We collapsed on the pillows that lined the walls, while a boy brought us tea. Half a dozen fighters, all shouldering Lee-Enfields, entered and sat down cross-legged with us. There were other groups operating in this area, the commander told us, but most—a mix of Tajiks and Pushtuns—had gone up to the Panjshir weeks earlier to reinforce Massoud. I was surprised to learn that our host was with Hekmatyar's Hezb. Assad assured me that they were friends, and everyone laughed when he translated my concerns. "Massoud is a great man," the commander laughed loudly. "We fight together." When I asked about the government forces down the road, he tsked dismissively. "They're not a problem. The *Shouravi* come here sometimes but they have no idea. Everyone's with the mujahideen. Even the *askari*."

The next morning, well before dawn, we started our climb into the Hindu Kush. We could already hear the dull thud of distant artillery or aerial bombardments. The challenge now was to find Massoud. It was now May 30 with the Soviet-Afghan offensive in the Panjshir well into its second week. Prior to the assault, Massoud had begun evacuating the entire valley of most of its remaining fifty thousand civilians. Many had made their way to Pakistan, while others preferred to wait out the fighting in the side valleys. We encountered scores of the displaced Panjshiris living like troglodytes in the gorges with cows, goats, and chickens—

less than a day's walk from the main valley, now in the hands of the Soviets. They had built shelters among the towering landslides or inside concealed caves, some emerald or lapis mines. Everyone was waiting for the offensive to end.

"They [the Soviets] have never stayed so long," lamented a teacher, who had been separated from his family during the evacuation. He had no idea where they were, or whether they were even alive. Food supplies were running low, so Massoud had ordered his men to share rations. These consisted of wheat, sugar, and tea, which he had previously placed in hidden caches. Afghans from nearby provinces were also sending in supplies—but Spetznaz had taken some of the passes and side valleys, blocking access routes. The Panjshir was now occupied as far north as the Anjuman Pass, with Massoud's most experienced front-line guerrillas attacking from the twelve- to seventeen-thousand-foot upper ridges.

For the French medical team, their main objective was how to connect with their colleagues, Laurence Laumounier and Capucine de Bretagne. No one had any idea where they were. Assad took us to a nearby village still held by the mujahideen. "Apparently, there is an Englishman and Dutchman there, both journalists," he said. I figured that one of them could only be Peter Jouvenal. I knew that he had headed in weeks earlier.

The village had been badly bombed, but there were still intact houses. Groups of mujahideen, their weapons resting on their knees, were sitting under the mulberry trees. All were wearing Nuristani *pakuls* plus military anoraks and black Czech boots, now the uniform of northern forces. At least two ZPU anti-aircraft guns were placed among the rocks above. Entering a house, we walked into a large room with shattered windows. Sipping tea out of one of several flowered china cups, Peter was sitting with several mujahideen. Huddled gloomily in a corner was another man, a tall European with straight blond hair dressed in a light beige *shalwar-kamiz* and wearing a Red Army hat. Peter looked up. "Hello, Eddie, I heard you were around," he said. "Some tea?" Nothing ever seemed to surprise this low-key Englishman.

We shook hands and I turned to the other man, whose name was Wicher, a Dutch journalist. He had injured his knee while climbing. "You're looking a bit Russian," I said. "I wouldn't advertise that hat too much. Might get yourself shot."

"I wear what I like," he retorted.

"It's okay. He knows everything," Peter volunteered. Obviously, there was a bit of tension between the two. We spent the night in the house and prepared to move up to the front lines in the morning. Peter had already been to one of the nearest positions and knew the direction. Wicher would stay to wait for the French doctors.

Well before dawn, we followed a narrow path leading up through the mulberry and walnut trees. Just as first light was breaking, we could hear the ominous drone of the helicopters. Tiny specks on the horizon, they began to sweep over the Hindu Kush in waves. Mainly Mi-8s and Mi-24 gunships—but also heavy Mi-6 and Mi-25 transports—they arrived in twos, fours, and sixes. By the time we reached the crest, they were flying directly overhead. By the end of the morning we had counted no fewer than two hundred helicopter sorties, some of them probably running relays back and forth from their bases. The gunships peeled off to attack targets in the mountains, while the others proceeded to specific locations to disgorge more troops and supplies.

Heavily armed with Kalashnikovs and RPG launchers, a squad of fighters were lounging among the ridgeline boulders. Massoud had over two thousand regular fighters at his disposal, not counting another fifteen hundred who had flocked in from other parts with promises of weapons and the chance to fight the *Shouravi*. With their long hair, thick beards, and tough looks, however, these were his professional *motoraks*, or flying commandos. They were well trained and paid. They had already repulsed Red Army efforts, sometimes with hand-to-hand combat, to take these crests. Massoud was one of the few resistance commanders in Afghanistan to have put together such an elite force. They reminded me of Cuban revolutionaries.

Massoud's men bade us take cover among the rocks so as not to be too obvious to the helicopters, which flew close enough to see the gunners' helmets. Grinning, the fighters brought us glasses of green tea and *nan*. It could not have been more civilized. With the high-altitude sun beating down, we sat with our backs against the rocks.

The scene in the main valley below was like a nineteenth-century oil painting with picnickers watching a showpiece battle consisting of different scenarios. With their tanks, APCs, and heavy weaponry, the

Soviets clearly controlled the valley floor. Toward my left, I could see a long column of tanks slowly churning its way amid plumes of black exhaust up the river to avoid land mines. On an open field where only a year earlier I had watched Massoud train his men and play soccer, there were several helicopters plus a dozen APCs and self-propelled artillery pieces parked alongside trucks loaded with BM-21 Katyusha multiple rocket launchers—the modern equivalent of World War II Stalin's organs. Periodically, one would open fire to hammer a guerrilla position, a hidden machine gun perhaps. But the rockets seemed to have little impact. Before the smoke and dust had cleared, the machine gun would start up again.

Over to my right, I watched as six gunships circled like sharks before veering in, one by one, to fire rockets from their pods at guerrillas entrenched among the slopes. Intermittently, pairs of MiG-23 jetfighters or the highly maneuverable Sukhoi Su-25 fighter-bombers known by NATO as Frogfoots shrieked across the skies to dislodge their loads in the side valleys.

From where we sat, we could see the town of Rokha, while farther up was Onaba, where the Soviets had established a large base; beyond that was Bazarak. It was outside Bazarak on a low hill overlooking the Panjshir River where Massoud would later be buried in a white mausoleum with a green dome. Peering through my binoculars, I could see Red Army soldiers sunbathing with their shirts off on looted carpets laid out on the flat house roofs. They seemed oblivious to the shooting and bombing around them. Nearby, other soldiers redeployed, jogging single-file through the shrapnel-torn mulberry or apricot trees.

Bill, Peter, and I all were eager to see Massoud. The area commander, who was in regular radio contact with "the Lion," would only reveal that it might take several days' trek to reach him, as he was on the other side of the main valley. This meant that we would have to slip through Soviet-Afghan lines, not an appealing thought. The commander sent a message to Massoud to garner his views.

Massoud maintained a unique communications system with daily situation reports, issued by all his commanders, brought in by runners. He would then add his own input in a highly personalized letter and make dozens of copies on a mimeograph machine. Messengers ran with these to all the villages and troop positions. At night, commanders and village elders met with their men for communal dinners. Whoever was literate would then read out Massoud's missive, and a discussion would ensue. We were always welcome to sit in on these meetings. There was never any suspicion that we might be spies. As far as they were concerned, if Massoud agreed to have us here, then we must be part of his resistance strategy. Indeed, Massoud relied on journalists to keep the outside world informed and provided every means to help us.

Massoud's writing style was highly personal and candid. He did not hesitate to voice his uncertainties and comment on setbacks. It was as if Massoud were in the room talking to them directly. This helped bind the Panjshiri commander with his men and incited far-flung loyalty. At the same time, as all those who knew Massoud well were fully aware, Massoud was always the one to make the final decisions.

On the second day, we visited another front-line position and, once again, watched the battle unfold. Prior to the main offensive, Soviet aircraft had dropped leaflets promising amnesty to any civilians prepared to support the government. Then began two days of intensive bombing. At the same time, for the first time and in a move that surprised Massoud, helicopters began dropping Red Army commandos along the entire length of the valley. The French doctors later told us that Massoud had warned them a day before that an attack was imminent. With such advance warning, the guerrillas and civilian population suffered almost no casualties. The Soviets managed to round up some old people who had refused to leave and tried to force them to reveal the guerrilla hideouts. A few old men agreed and took them up into the mountains, but then disappeared, leaving the Russians to stumble around on impassable rocky trails.

Soviet efforts to take the ridges failed. Massoud had about a dozen Chinese heavy machine guns and anti-aircraft guns positioned on the summits. Helicopters had problems operating at peak efficiency at such altitudes. When they tried to land commandos, they encountered heavy fire. This forced the Spetznaz to assault the ridges from below, but it became more like a duck shoot with concealed guerrillas firing down from above. Soviet and Afghan government troops suffered severe casualties during the first few days, with some estimates putting the number of killed or wounded at over one thousand. Although it was impossible to verify such figures, diplomats in Kabul reported large numbers of trucks taking bodies back to Bagram and Kabul airports for shipment home.

The Soviet bombing was not that efficient, either. On one day, 223 bombs fell on the town of Parandeh. Total casualties: one villager dead, one wounded, and one blown-up cow. Many of the bombs did not explode. One of the reasons could have been that the Soviet soldiers during the previous freezing winter had opened the bombs to steal the explosives inside for fuel. Another possibility was that the mountainsides were so steep, the bombs ricocheted off. Each bomb that failed to go off was a potential source of materiel for guerrilla land mines. The Soviets became so frustrated that they finally began unloading bombs with small parachutes so that they would hit at the correct angle.

In an effort to establish a long-term presence in the valley, but also to support claims of victory, the Soviet-Afghan forces set up a provisional administration in Rokha at the southern end of the valley. A number of civilian PDPA officials were brought in, including a leading party member, Abdul Rahim, who was supposed to act as the valley's district commissioner. Within a week, Rahim had been shot dead and the other officials had fled. No one else agreed to assume the new positions.

Days passed with no word from Massoud. But eventually, I spotted several mujahideen walking quickly toward us. One was Mirabudin, the former Lycée Istiqlal student who had translated for me on my first trip to the Panjshir. He had a personal message from Massoud. Given the seriousness of the situation, Massoud wanted me to take the French doctors and nurses, plus any other Westerners, back to Pakistan. He could not risk us being captured. The threat was not just Soviet military operations but that the KHAD would inform the Soviets that there were foreigners in the vicinity.

Mirabudin asked me to help retrieve Laurence and Capucine, the two women doctors, who were hiding out in a high-mountain cave. We needed four hours to reach them. I would then have to take them back to Pakistan. His men would round up everyone else, and we would rendezvous at a nearby pass. We had to hurry, as Massoud had intelligence the Soviets might begin penetrating the side valleys. The humanitarians were not a liability he could afford to assume.

I quickly briefed Bill and Peter. Neither was keen on having come all this way and not seeing Massoud. I felt the same, but also felt a personal obligation to the French doctors. Finally, Bill decided that he had enough for a good story. Returning with the doctors might make an even better one. In any case, we needed to file our stories, and neither of us could risk being stuck here for weeks. Peter, however, needed more footage of the offensive. He opted to stay.

Leaving Bill with the mujahideen, I followed Mirabudin. The Soviets had positioned a machine gun at the entrance of a nearby side valley, which we had to cross. Peering through my binoculars, I could see the gunner with his striped shirt hunched behind his weapon. I figured that if I could see him, he could probably see me. The mujahideen began firing to distract him, enabling Mirabudin and me to bolt across.

It was a hard climb across loose scree toward a series of jagged ridges. By early afternoon, we had reached the cave. I knew both doctors from Paris. Exhausted, they were dozing in sleeping bags. The two French women had been forced to evacuate their hospital as heliborne commandos landed several hundred yards away. Capucine was in the process of amputating a man's leg when the door flew open. She saw a Soviet helicopter about to fire. She quickly dived to the side. The building blew up, killing the patient on the operating table. "If only the Russians had done this before I amputated the leg, it would have saved him the agony," she said.

As guerrillas held off the advancing commandos, the doctors and their staff moved their patients by placing them on horses and donkeys. They had to evacuate twice more, and each time they only barely escaped, losing a number of patients in the process. The two women only had sneakers to walk in. They had no time to return home to retrieve their walking gear—nor their passports, which the Soviets later found.

The Red Army was fully aware of the French medical teams working in the Panjshir and that most were women. As part of their propaganda, they dropped leaflets claiming that Massoud had brought in French whores. Based on the two passports, the Kabul government also announced that they had captured the doctors. Furthermore, the communists claimed to have apprehended two journalists, Peter Jouvenal and me—probably obtaining our names through informers. Back in Paris, the US embassy scrambled to deal with inquiries, some of which became embarrassing. The press attaché had to call a friend, Mike Barry, a well-known American specialist on Afghanistan based in France, to determine which of the three women who were calling repeatedly regarding my fate was, in fact, my real girlfriend. In the end, Doug Archard, the Peshawar consul, put an end to Kabul's claims. If the Soviets had indeed caught four Westerners, he argued, they would have put us on television. The KGB may have determined that we were in the region, but there was no evidence that we were being held.

By evening, I found myself preparing to lead a group of five doctors and nurses, plus Bill and Wicher, back to Pakistan. Bill and I, however, decided to stay on another day or two with Peter, and then catch up with the group. I explored the possibility of an even shorter eastern route, which I had taken before. This would trace the southern slopes of the Hindu Kush back through the Pech Valley in Kunar, but the Panjshiris did not have good contacts in these parts. There were too many villages known to be pro-Khalq or pro-Hezb. But as usual, Afghanistan proved the land of contradictions. Just as we were preparing to leave, filling our water bottles from an alpine spring, a group of Hezb fighters from Laghman, some thirty to forty men bristling with guns, entered our camp. They had come to reinforce Massoud.

Bill and I soon reached the medical team, which had been moving slowly. We returned much the same way, except this time we crossed the Kabul-to-Jalalabad highway farther east. Bill was in better shape. He had lost thirty pounds and grown a beard. Laurence and Capucine, however, were suffering badly. The constant fleeing, the patients killed in the evacuation, and the fear of imminent capture had been traumatic. The three other medical team members, who had come in with us, were philosophical—even happy—about returning to Pakistan.

The Dutchman, on the other hand, was a real problem. The French loathed him. In his late forties, Wicher had the arrogance of someone who always knew best but was actually quite inexperienced. The Afghans, too, had no respect for him. Wicher insisted on wearing his khaki *shalwar-kamiz* with his Russian hat, so none of the mujahideen wanted to be seen with him. The mere fact that he looked *Shouravi* sufficed. He had paid them to carry his pack because of his injury, but they repeatedly abandoned his bag by the side of the trail. Wicher only made matters worse by repeatedly berating, even punching, them.

I had nothing personal against Wicher. I simply wanted to ensure that we all got back safely. Every few hours, I had to renegotiate with the Afghans. Unfortunately, Wicher would soon say something that would make the Afghans abandon his pack yet again. "He has a bad leg," I explained. "And yes, he's an idiot. But he'll give you ten dollars to carry his bag. Massoud wants him back alive." Then I would turn to Wicher. "I've negotiated it once again. Don't screw it up."

Wicher, of course, could not leave it. On one occasion, he spread-eagled himself across a high-mountain pasture fully visible from the air. He would remain like this, he informed me, until the Afghans treated him properly. "You're a fool," I told him. "If you insist on lying here, I guarantee you'll be killed. Either the Russians will get you, or the Afghans will tear you apart, piece by piece, as a Russian soldier. If they're feeling merciful, they'll just shoot you." The French berated me for help-ing him, while Bill suggested that we abandon him. "Let him die if that's what he wants," he proposed. Tempting though it was, I felt I could not leave him. I waited until he reluctantly climbed to his feet.

Passing through the villages, it became clear we were only five or six hours ahead of the informers. Friendly tribesmen warned us the word was out that a group of foreigners was making its way back to Pakistan. I doubted that the informers had two-way radios. Their only option was to send a message by car or by bus to the next military base. Twice, however, we had to change our route when locals maintained that Khalqis or Spetznaz had positioned themselves farther ahead. I never knew whether this was rumor, but we could not take chances.

We continued walking at a pace much quicker than on the outward journey. I was worried about Laurence and Capucine. They were both clearly distraught. At one point, the strain became too much. Laurence, a tough and resilient woman by any standard, collapsed sobbing. Capucine immediately knelt down, taking Laurence in her arms. "Weep, *ma cherie,* weep," she murmured soothingly. "Don't hold it back."

Group relations with Wicher only grew worse. By now he was completely ostracized by the French, while Bill only talked to him when necessary. I was growing tired of being constantly forced to intervene.

"Why don't they like me?" Wicher repeatedly asked me.

"Look," I said, "everyone's under a lot of pressure, so make an effort to be nice. And shut up."

The Afghans were the most intolerant. By now, they positively savored tormenting Wicher. Stopping for the night in a hut by the side of a stream near the Pakistani border, we all lay down to sleep. Several hours later, I was woken by Wicher whimpering outside. He had been suffering from a bad case of the runs. Taking my flashlight, I found him squatting with his trousers down trying to go to the toilet, surrounded by the Afghans. They were throwing little stones at him, repeatedly whispering his name in unison: "Wicher, Wicher,"

"Oh God, help me. I can't even shit in peace," he moaned. I ordered the Afghans to leave, which they did with smirks on their faces. Even this did little to remedy the situation. Every day, there was at least one Wicher crisis. But at least we were nearly in Pakistan. Once in Teri Mangal, I promised everyone, we would hire a vehicle to take us directly to Peshawar. Even if the Pakistani military arrested us, the last thing they wanted was a bunch of Western journalists and aid workers in the tribal belt.

On approaching Jagi, we could hear loud explosions and heavy machine-gun fire. My immediate thought was that the Soviets were attacking the mujahed positions along the border. But the fighting came from inside Pakistan. Guerrillas told us that a Sunni village was fighting against a rival Shiite one. It had been going on like this for two days. The astounding thing is that they were using weaponry, such as 82mm mortars and rockets, that even the mujahideen did not readily command. It was a regular war. Years later—from 2008 onward—these same tribal areas became no-go zones, with Pakistani Taliban fighting pitched battles against the Islamabad military. But in 2010, some of the Shiite villages refused to allow Taliban to pass through, a move that irritated the ISI—which, as usual, was playing its double game.

I was in no mood to let this little conflict prevent us from getting back to Dean's Hotel, a nice hot bath, clean clothes, and a solid meal. "We're going to have to go to the nearest army post and surrender," I explained. "The Pakistanis will take us through. They don't want us witnessing this sort of thing." I paused. "And most important of all, they'll probably give us a cup of tea." I could see Wicher glaring at me. He raised himself to his full height. "As the oldest person here," he declared grandly, "I will decide what to do. We'll stay here until the fighting is over."

My patience had run out. "We're going through whether you bloody like it or not," I told him. "If you want to stay here, be my guest. I'm no longer responsible for you. I've gotten you this far, alive." Wicher immediately went quiet, muttering that he had never seen me like this before. Demonstratively, I picked up my pack and stalked across the Durand Line. I walked straight to the old British frontier picket fort flying the Pakistani flag. Several scouts with Kalashnikovs emerged. I demanded to be taken to the officer in charge. Evidently perplexed by the sudden presence of these foreigners, they debated heatedly among themselves and then pointed to a pickup. We all climbed in and they drove us to the nearest command post, lined with the usual whitewashed stones and rosebushes.

A Pakistani major came to greet us. I explained that we had come from Afghanistan and were heading to Peshawar. He took all this in his stride by inviting us to tea. Chatting amiably, we sat in white garden chairs sipping from china cups and nibbling biscuits while watching the shelling in the valley below. "These tribal people are having a bit of a spat," the major explained magnanimously. "Nothing much we can do. I'm afraid we'll have to wait until they're finished."

Noticing several armored vehicles parked in front, I pointed to them. "If you could take us through, then we could become the problem of the political agent," I explained sweetly. The major agreed and ordered his men to accompany us. We drove straight through the battle zone, with artillery shells hurtling overhead, to the PA's office. Several hours later, we were in another convoy escorted by armed militiamen to the edge of the tribal agency. From there we rented a vehicle to Peshawar.

A day later, Wicher appeared at my room door back at Dean's Hotel. He had a case of beer in his hands. "I've come to offer an apology," he said. "I appreciate what you did. Afghanistan does strange things to you over which you have no control." *Finally*, I thought, *Wicher has said something with which I can agree.*

During the weeks that followed, it became clear that Moscow's fifth offensive against the Panjshir failed. But this did not stop the Soviets from proclaiming victory. Massoud's forces continued to hold most of the ridges and the side valleys. His guerrillas suffered few casualties and, within days, launched repeated assaults against the entrenched occupiers. They also isolated government garrisons. Afghan *askari*, poorly paid and disheartened, slipped out at night with their weapons to join the resistance—or to walk home, sometimes across the whole of Afghanistan. By the end of June, the Red Army had pulled out, leaving behind two government garrisons. These did not last, either.

The Red Army launched another operation in September, but got nowhere. Massoud's flying commandos fought back hard, killing a reported four hundred Red Army infantrymen and Spetznaz. In the end, the Soviets inflicted a total of nine campaigns against the Panjshir, none of which really benefited their occupation. The 1982 Soviet offensive we had witnessed was a case in point. Where the Soviets did succeed, however, was in making life unbearable for the civilians. The bulk of them could no longer return. The Panjshir was not unique in this regard. The same thing was happening in resistance-held areas throughout Afghanistan.

Overwhelming retaliatory raids were causing immeasurable suffering and low morale among Afghans. The Soviets bombed farms and villages, deliberately destroying the irrigation systems. Once rustic fruit orchards and farmlands were turned into windswept wastelands littered with withered trees. Furthermore, the Soviets stepped up their campaign to seed suspected guerrilla zones, both trails and agricultural areas, with anti-personnel land mines. "The Soviets have succeeded in shattering the economic and social bases of certain strong resistance areas by applying constant pressure," noted Jean-José Puig, president of the Paris-based Friends of Afghanistan Association, following a ten-week trip through eight provinces toward the end of 1982.

The situation became so bad that Massoud and other inside commanders appealed to the international community for urgent humanitarian aid. Unless Afghans living within Afghanistan were given the means to survive, they warned, even more people would have to flee. The plight of the "inside" Afghans, however, failed to ignite the humanitarian concerns of the West in even remotely the same degree as the millions of Cambodians caught up in Pol Pot's killing fields several years earlier. Most international agencies providing "official" aid within Pakistan preferred to ignore what was happening across the border. It's quite simple, maintained Etienne Gille, head of Afrane, a French NGO running food, clothing, and medical caravans to the interior. "The less aid the Afghans receive in Afghanistan, the more refugees will be forced to flee."

The Soviets continued with their assaults against the Panjshir. To the surprise of many, Massoud entered into a yearlong truce with the Soviets in 1983. During this period and the years that followed, I made several trips to the Panjshir. I spent many hours talking with Massoud trying to understand his strategy. I was always struck by his shrewdness and ability to assess the strengths and weaknesses of the Red Army in order to conduct his own war. In one interview in a hidden cave a few hundred yards from Soviet positions in 1984, he explained to me that the Soviets had initially come to Afghanistan with World War II tactics, notably heavy weaponry and training totally unsuited to conditions in the country.

"They've improved a great deal," he told me. "They're making better use of helicopters and more mobile troops with lighter equipment specifically geared to the mountains and this sort of warfare. They're a much more difficult enemy." At the same time, Massoud was fully confident that given their available resources and manpower, there was no way that the Red Army could control anything more than the cities and a select number of fortified bases in the countryside. "Some of these," he added, "one can ignore. There's no point in attacking them. Eventually, they'll have no option but to leave."

While the 1983–84 truce enabled the Red Army to adopt a "take and hold" policy—not unlike the Americans in southern Afghanistan in 2010—with several garrisons established in the valley, this also tied them down. The bases had to be supplied by helicopter. Some civilians returned, while the guerrillas manned their own concealed positions in the side valleys and in the mountains. It was an absurd situation whereby we could walk with the guerrillas within sight of the Soviet garrisons, and then head off into the mountains where the resistance could indulge in operations against the Red Army elsewhere.

Twice during this year of truce, the Soviets tried to capture or kill

Massoud. On one occasion, they attempted to lure him into their heavily fortified garrison at Onaba for further negotiations. A government interpreter, however, warned the Panjshiri leader of plans to arrest him. He did not go. The second time, the KGB sought to bribe one of Massoud's men, a cook, into poisoning his food. Again, an inside informer alerted the Panjshiris, who later executed the would-be assailant.

Finally, KHAD chief Dr. Najibullah, later president of the PDPA government, personally ordered a hit on Massoud. The man to do the job was Kamran, captain of the Afghan national soccer team, who had gone to school with Massoud. He was sent to the Panjshir to assassinate his former classmate with a silencer-equipped pistol. On meeting with Massoud, Kamran was so impressed that he revealed the KHAD plans and, with Massoud's help, managed to escape to Pakistan. Kamran eventually ended up a refugee in West Germany. Ironically, it was Massoud who protected Najibullah's life once the mujahideen entered Kabul in April 1992.

The Soviet-Panjshiri truce was much criticized by rival resistance parties. But this was part of the northern commander's long-term plan, namely to create a more coordinated nationwide resistance by uniting the different fighting fronts. The arrangement allowed Massoud to keep the Soviets tied down while operating elsewhere. He regularly attacked fuel and supply convoys along the Salang, causing severe shortages in Kabul. He also captured key government bases in the north. In the years that followed, Massoud built up a highly proficient regional force, denying the communists whole swathes of the countryside.

CHAPTER TEN

Peshawar: Aid Workers and Assassins

It was when the Islamists hanged three dogs with telephone wire and left their lifeless bodies to rot on a rubbish heap outside the American Club in the summer of 1988 that I realized the atmosphere in Peshawar was becoming nasty. Killing the dogs was the fundamentalists' way of showing just what they thought of the Western *kafirs* who were living in Peshawar and frequented this University Town club. For me, the sight of the dogs lying rigid—with their tongues sticking out, wire cutting tightly into their necks—was one of the most horrific I had witnessed as a journalist covering Afghanistan, primarily for the callousness that it represented. What do dogs have to do with religious ideology?

Most weekends, dozens of foreign aid workers, volunteers, diplomats, spies, mercenaries, adventurers, Drug Enforcement Agency (DEA) agents, and others converged on the club to eat, drink, and take it easy. For me, it was an informal oasis where I could relax and get a decent meal or cup of coffee. Many who stopped by were aid workers who labored in the refugee camps and frontier areas or who had just returned from Afghanistan. Then there were the hacks, looking tough in their Banana Republic vests and stubbled beards, swaggering in and whispering: "Just back from inside." Usually this meant that they had just driven back from the border where they had spent, at best, a few hours inside Afghanistan.

The American Club was the only place to get a proper drink in Peshawar. It even had surprisingly good Californian wines. Though the Muslim bartender, Masud, mixed the best martinis this side of the Khyber, Muslims were not allowed into the American Club as customers on orders from the Pakistani government. John Soden, a poised aid consultant and my squash partner at the Peshawar Club, refused to join because he felt it was discrimination. He was not even allowed to bring in American Muslims. He felt strongly about this. "We're no different from the colonials," he said.

Soden was right, of course. But most of us, me included, were willing to overlook it, and simply smuggled in our Muslim friends.

The night before we found the dogs was a Friday and the Muslim Sabbath, and the club had hosted a particularly raucous rock-and-roll party. Although surrounded by high walls, the compound was hardly noiseproof. Huge outdoor loudspeakers blared Dire Straits, the Rolling Stones, Fleetwood Mac, and Phil Collins across the suburban roof-tops. The Western music was in competition with the drumming and gunshots from a tribal wedding on the other side of Canal Bank Road, two or three blocks over. For the Islamists, it was the sound of decadence.

Shortly before midnight, I decided to head home. A group of drunken Brits and Scandinavians were staggering along the road. It was then that I noticed the Arabi, all wearing body-length white *jalabiyas*, by the streetlamp opposite. There were a good half dozen, probably volunteer jihadists from the Middle East with one of the Islamic organizations that had established its offices by the nearby Momin Khan mosque.

The Arabi glared with disdain at the inebriated men. Then they began hissing and hurling guttural epithets at them. The Pakistani police had already warned the American Club to tone down its parties. Some of the foreign jihadists had complained about allowing such godless people into the country. Looking back, I realize now that they were probably working with Osama bin Laden, whose own organization Maktab al Khidamar (Office of Services, or MAK) had its headquarters only a few hundred yards down the road.

"Oh fuck off, will ya!" muttered one of the Englishmen. His friends laughed, and they continued on their way.

Prior to leaving the club, I had noticed a group of women, all European and American aid workers, preparing to walk home. I decided to return to accompany them just in case the Arabi accosted them. There had been a rise of incidents with jihadists verbally abusing Western women—many of whom wore shawls, making the effort to dress modestly so as not to offend the Pakistanis and Afghans. But this was not good enough for the jihadists. When I left the compound with the girls, the Islamists were waiting. They immediately began spitting and throwing stones. We hurried off until out of sight.

It was the next morning, when I casually rode over on my Chinese bike—a cheap but functional affair—to grab a quick breakfast that I found the dogs. I also wondered how long it would be before the Islamists started killing and dumping human bodies. Peshawar during the 1980s was the quintessential war town. Prior to the expanding of the Soviet-Afghan war, Americans in Peshawar were modestly represented by Doug Archard (the American consul), a smattering of USAID officials, and a couple of DEA operatives, who were always complaining about how corrupt their counterparts were in the Pakistani police. But as the war became more intense, the number of Americans and other foreigners—mainly aid workers—spiraled.

For many of us, it was the most exciting place on earth—a frontier city that exuded an atmosphere of 1940s Casablanca intrigue combined with twentieth-century Cold War rock, emergency sex, and TV bravado. Everyone felt a part of history in the making. Unusual, too, was this staggering mix of individuals and backgrounds—aid, journalism, military, diplomacy, narcotics, espionage, trafficking, artists—from all over the world. By the early 1990s, with the departure of the Soviets in Afghanistan and the civil war in Kabul, this extraordinary atmosphere had disappeared.

One of the largest establishments in Peshawar was the American Center run by what was then the United States Information Service (USIS). Air-conditioned and cool, the American Center reading rooms were where Afghans (both men and women) went to read newspapers, learn English, or study quietly. Here, too, USIS would hold courses on democracy for mujahed commanders; a waste of time perhaps, but it put these tribesmen in touch with ideas from the outside world and forged friendships that remain today. The Center's "Afghan Contacts List" was invaluable to anyone visiting Peshawar. Inevitably, the USIS officer would invite newcomers, regardless of their nationality, for a drink to introduce them to new people.

The French had their idiosyncratic cultural advisers attached to the Alliance Française, which had a library and showed films. The Pakistanis and Afghans loved these films; they never got to see kissing in the local cinemas. My friend Raza Khan Khattak, a scion of one of Pakistan's leading families, was the honorary French consul, but could not speak the language. "I haven't the faintest why they chose me," he said. "All they want me to do is host parties or help track down lost Frenchmen."

We always suspected that the head of the cultural center was working with French intelligence, but no one cared.

Finally, there were the old Brits who had stayed on with the end of the Raj. One of the most extraordinary was Hubert M. Close, the English professor at Peshawar's Islamia College—one of Pakistan's most renowned schools—who first came to India in 1937. I would sometimes see him quietly riding his bicycle to and from class. Occasionally, too, we would meet. Close's students, who affectionately called him Hajii Mohammed, regarded him as a true Pushtun. Every summer, he would troop out with his students to inoculate children against smallpox or to hand out insect sprays against malaria. Profoundly but unobtrusively Christian with a deep respect for Islam, he was the only teacher on the campus who would stop lecturing during *azan*, the call for prayers.

Close steered clear of the international Afghan crowd, but once he invited me for a long chat over tea at the college. He lamented the erosion of educational standards, and the failure (including his own) of helping to change society for the better. No one was investing properly in education, particularly among the refugees, he warned. Noting that Islamic extremists were assuming this role, he feared that this would undermine basic decency and tolerance among the different communities.

"There is too much lip service but not enough substance. We'll have to pay for our lack of commitment in the future," he said. These were chilling words given the increasing influence of hard-line *madrassas* that were turning a whole new generation of Afghans and Pakistanis into religious bigots and future Taliban. Incredibly modest, kind, and devoted, Close represented—as one of his former students, S. Amjad Hussein, now professor of surgery at Ohio Medical College, put it—"the noblest of the Christian tradition of serving others." When I heard of Close's death in 1999, I sadly thought that Peshawar had lost one of its most committed citizens.

Peshawar in the 1980s was dramatically affected by two overwhelming trends. The first was the gradual and then rapid arrival of international aid agencies in response to the exploding refugee problem. Then came the growth in international narcotics and weapons smuggling. War was good business. Peshawar's hurtling expansion of trade, residential areas, and offices was established not only on foreign aid, but also drugs

and other forms of trafficking—including pornography and the prostitu-
tion of Afghan boys, girls, and women. The breadth of those involved
in all the illicit trade was staggering: the ISI, Pakistani military, police,
government officials, business community, Afghan political parties,
Saudis, truckers, Islamists, Afghan merchants—and indeed, some of the
Western internationals.

When I first arrived in the fall of 1979, the main road leading out
to University Town and the Khyber was bordered by idyllic rice paddies
and the occasional house. In less than four years, the entire area had
been transformed into a tangle of new compounds, car dealerships, repair
workshops, restaurants, video outlets, and office blocks with whole slews
of new "import-export" businesses. Elaborately built villas with ostentatious marble facades, iron-gate latticework, and ornate fountains were
referred to as "the house that hash built" or "the house that aid built."
From the very beginning, it was clear that much of the international
assistance was not going where it was supposed to and that different
interests were taking huge rake-offs. As with Kabul today, there was
simply too much money.

It was around this time that Pakistan's once thriving opium poppy
cultivation, including the tribal heroin labs, started moving across into
Afghanistan. Until the mid- or late 1980s, one could drive through
Pakistan's tribal areas and marvel at the purple-and-white patchwork
poppy fields, perhaps some of the most beautiful but deadly flowers in
the world. By the end of the decade, they had all disappeared. Today the
same flowered patchwork fields are scattered across southern and eastern
Afghanistan.

Soon after the Soviet invasions and massive exodus from Afghanistan,
hundreds of NGOs began to establish themselves in Peshawar. Most
were run by expatriates from the United States, Canada, West Germany,
United Kingdom, France, Italy, Scandinavia, Japan, Australia, and elsewhere. These included IRC, CARE, Oxfam, Save the Children, MSF,
Médecins du Monde, Aide Médicale International, Caritas, the Swedish
Committee, and Shelter Now—the latter a Christian proselytizing
group. Eventually, these groups created the Agency Coordinating Body
for Afghan Relief (ACBAR), an umbrella organization designed to help
coordinate NGO activities. Various Saudi, Kuwaiti, Jordanian, Egyptian,

and other Middle East nationals set up their own organizations, such as Islamic Relief. Many Muslims had a genuine concern for the plight of Afghans, and most of their humanitarian organizations were bona fide. Some, however, particularly those funded by the Saudis, focused primarily on the construction of new mosques and *madrassas*.

The Afghan crisis helped transform international relief. It was no longer the domain of twenty-odd veteran organizations that had emerged from the rubble of World War II; new agencies were popping up not just in Peshawar, but in response to humanitarian crises and conflicts elsewhere—including the French doctors who were seeking to reach beyond the frontiers of conventional humanitarian aid. "It was a time when we were trying to help those who were left out. These were the civilians caught up in the no-man's-lands and conflicts of Angola, Afghanistan, Eritrea . . . They were not being reached by the big humanitarian agencies," noted Dr. Rony Brauman, a Maoist during the Paris student revolts of 1968 and later president of MSF France during the 1980s.

Filming with Christophe de Ponfilly, I had traveled widely with Brauman in places like Angola, Congo, and El Salvador. Today, still involved with MSF, he ranks as one of the most respected—and radical— thinkers on humanitarian action. Constantly exploring the hazards facing the international aid community, he condemns the way media are increasingly co-opted by the agencies for fund-raising purposes. He is highly critical of NATO efforts in Afghanistan to draw in the humanitarian organizations, severely compromising their neutrality and ability to work.

Some of the organizations based in Peshawar were specifically tailored to Afghanistan, such as Britain's AfghanAid—or the Hawaiian relief agency Freedom Medicine (FM), which trained Afghans to provide primary medical aid and started over 150 clinics inside guerrilla-controlled parts of Afghanistan.

For the Pakistanis, the refugee problem was a burden, but also a source of revenue and opportunity. With barely a hint of a smile, the Zia ul-Haq regime acknowledged that the Soviet invasion had put Pakistan "back on the map." It provided his dictatorship with a respectability it could never have achieved otherwise. In the beginning, the Islamabad authorities were determined that the refugee presence remain a temporary one. The last thing they wanted was a Palestinian-type situation.

Pakistan's refugee situation quickly became the largest international relief operation since the end of World War II. The Pakistanis had set up a comparatively efficient administration infrastructure, which was run along military lines with seven thousand employees. Almost all the senior camp officials were former army officers.

For the first three years, the camps existed as tented towns, with aid agencies providing relief such as tents, blankets, water, and basic food items. Only reluctantly did the Pakistanis allow the construction of adobe walls to block off the heat, wind, rain, and snow. Anything that signaled permanence was discouraged. But the camps became more established as refugees replaced their windswept, decaying tents with *katchas*, traditional mud-and-stone dwellings. By 1984, there were over three million Afghans, the bulk of them living in the 380-odd refugee towns and villages that had emerged. Many had also moved in with friends and relatives in the tribal areas, while the wealthier ones went to Islamabad, Lahore, or Karachi.

A source of friction with the local Pakistanis, however, was that Afghans began moving into local business, notably transport. Where previously Pashto had dominated, Dari Persian was now heard in all the bazaars. Even with such transformations, the authorities still sought to retain the illusion that this was temporary. "We no longer discourage them from making *katchas*. It only reflects their style of living and does not imply permanent residence," insisted the Pakistani refugee coordinator in Peshawar.

Before long the numerous aid agencies in Peshawar were competing for donor funds being dispersed by the Americans, Europeans, Australians, Saudis, and others. As with Rwanda during the 1990s and the Haiti earthquake in 2010, international media were crucial to their fund-raising and PR image. There was no shortage of subject material in Peshawar to attract journalists.

According to author Mort Rosenblum, a former senior correspondent for the Associated Press and editor of the *International Herald Tribune*, events in Peshawar often left him stunned. In one incident, a refugee family asked a Pakistani paramedic to examine their ailing daughter. When he emerged from the tent, the elders stoned him to death for being alone with the girl. "That sort of thing was still new to us infidels," Mort added.

During the early 1980s, I normally stayed at Dean's, but I moved to

University Town when the traffic became impossible. Many Pakistani owners had rented out their homes. As the international presence grew, they crammed in new buildings. When I returned to Peshawar during the mid-1990s, I could scarcely recognize my former abode, a seven-room villa that I had shared with four other foreigners. The once pleasant garden was built over with new apartments. Even the American Club had expanded to include a swimming pool and a new tennis court.

The perception of the international community as one huge milk cow attracted the usual scams. Operators of the PTC, the Pakistan Telecommunication Company, made deals for cheap calls by tacking on the charges to the internationals, sometimes thousands of dollars every month. My phone bill surged with scores of calls to Libya and Egypt, some of them hours long. When I complained, an accountant quietly proposed to "remedy this matter" in return for a five-hundred-dollar "service charge." He would simply add it on to someone else's bill.

Peshawar drew an unusual out-of-the-box crowd of kindred spirits. As with so many humanitarian crisis zones during their early stages, there was a powerful pioneering element. Some of those who came had been in regular jobs in the United States and Europe, but were regarded as misfits. In Peshawar, they found their niches.

In many cases, they also found love. Juliet Crawley, a British staff member of AfghanAid, arrived in Peshawar at the age of twenty-four and soon after met her first husband, Dominique Vergos—a flamboyant French fashion-photographer-turned-war-reporter-*cum*-spy. The daughter of an English pastor, Juliet was attractive and infuriating with a dry, cutting sense of humor. She soon became the head of AfghanAid, which was operating clandestinely inside Afghanistan. With shortish blond hair and a jutting face, Juliet was scathing about US support for Afghan extremists.

She made an unlikely pair with Dominique, who was tall and suave with his groomed shoulder-length hair, always carefully dressed in front-line chic. He wore silk scarves, Mongolian riding boots, embroidered Turkmen waistcoats, and tribal turbans.

Dominique found that he could do better financially as a spy for a consortium of NATO intelligence organizations than as a journalist. Whenever he traveled, he carried a revolver and a curved, Ghazni sword. He was also never without his huge Damascus bowie knife, which he used to take out while chatting in restaurants or at parties. Taking his sense of adventure to the extreme, Dominique was an excellent horseman and would disappear for months on end deep inside Afghanistan—ostensibly to shoot photographs, which he still did, but also to record rifle serial numbers to determine weapons' distribution among the guerrillas.

Dominique and Juliet married, but on Christmas Day 1988, while returning from the American Club, Dominique was killed. The official version was that the *chawkidar*, night watchman, had shot him twice in the back of the neck with his Kalashnikov. Dominique always became combative with too much alcohol and loved nothing better than to fire off AK rounds in the garden, or even in the *chawkidar*'s gatehouse. They had grappled, the story went, and the gun had gone off. However, given Dominique's intelligence dealings—and often aggressive attitude—there were other, darker versions.

Another Peshawar figure was Rory Peck, a former British army officer and adventurer par excellence. Tall, tempestuous, and charming to the bone, Rory was born in the United States, but brought up in Ireland. He embraced excitement—and women—whenever possible. Divorced with two sons, Rory came out to Peshawar to try his hand at filming. Once, my friend Charles Norchi arrived with a dark-haired Armenian American female assistant to conduct human rights research. Hoping to seduce her, a drunken Rory sauntered out at night with a pail of black paint and a brush to plaster the walls of Canal Bank Road with LONG LIVE ARMENIA. SOVS OUT NOW! The graffiti episode was preceded by a motor-scooter rickshaw race from the Old Town to VIP house, as the house where a group of us lived, was known with several contenders ending up wallowing in the filthy canal in front of the house.

The fact that the canal bottom was littered with live anti-aircraft rounds and mortars did not seem to perturb anyone. These were explosives that Rory had once perched over the fireplace in the house; all were souvenirs from Afghanistan. One night, feeling the tremors of an earthquake, I tossed them into the canal—not exactly the brightest thing to have done, as these sluggish-moving water channels are emptied and cleaned every few years. I sheepishly went to the police informing them that some irresponsible idiot had thrown in live ordnance. Several months later, the military sent in a team of sappers to remove them.

Later, Rory proved himself one of the most intrepid camera-men around. While I was covering the front line with him in eastern Afghanistan, he insisted on moving closer toward the PDPA govern-ment positions—ignoring the fact that they could see us and had already begun launching mortars. He laughed uproariously as one mortar after another whistled overhead, exploding dangerously close by.

To my surprise, Rory and Dominique's widow, Juliet, developed a relationship and got married. Juliet later helped Rory set up the Moscow branch of Frontline News, the London-based TV agency. Rory was killed in 1993 when filming in Moscow. Juliet set up the Rory Peck Trust, which was designed to help the families of freelance journalists killed in action.

Several years after losing Rory, Juliet and I met for tea in London. She had not lost her sense of humor. When I gently asked whether she would ever consider marrying again, she retorted: "Oh for God's sakes. Who the hell's going to marry a woman both of whose husbands were shot dead? He'd be constantly wondering whether he'd end up a hat trick." Fate was unusually harsh on Juliet. She developed cancer, which caused the loss of her right eye. She wore a black eye patch, which gave her a stunningly defiant look. The cancer went into remission, but returned, finally killing her in 2007.

Another Peshawar character was Steve Masty, a rotund and utterly brilliant writer, singer, raconteur, and cartoonist. An American who had studied for his doctorate at St. Andrews in Scotland, he had also worked as a speechwriter for Reagan. Masty became manager of the American Club, and no evening in Peshawar was complete without Steve picking up his guitar to regale us, Elvis-style, with his latest songs mocking the mujahideen, the foreign aid workers, the US government, and others:

> In the back of Peshawar where nobody's been
> There's a *chawkidar* and his teeth are green,
> He's the meanest man that you ever seen
> But his boss is meaner, and he's Gulbuddin . . .

Steve's drawings were to the point and hilarious, a far better rendi-tion of what happened during the Soviet-Afghan war than anything we could write. I saw him again in Kabul for dinner toward the end of 2009. He remained the same irreverent, humorous Steve, voicing his latest jibes—this time against the international community and its failure, yet again, to deal with Afghanistan. "Oh, it's all the same again. The foreigners trying to do everything without letting the Afghans have a say in their future. Lots of words, lots of money, nothing to show," he lamented.

Peshawar attracted various "Soldier of Fortune" types, who wanted to fight. Many made quickie trips inside but found the going tough, particularly when coupled with paltry diets of tea and *nan* dipped in a bit of gravy. Some, too, had to shuffle back with dysentery or hepatitis. It was also hard to find Vietnam-style combat. The truth was that Afghanistan was simply not an action-oriented war involving regular contacts with the enemy. It had more to do with lots of walking and distant bombardments. Nevertheless, they all came back with pictures of themselves posing with Kalashnikovs and the mujahideen. The number of "mercenaries" who actually operated with the resistance on a sustained basis—similar to what John Walker Lindh, the American Talib, did in 2001—could probably be counted on two hands. I only knew of one American, two Germans, Muslim converts—plus a number of ex–Red Army soldiers who had deserted or been captured.

Some seemed to be part of an ongoing tragic comedy. Rudolf, an American of East German background, was bitterly anti-communist and wanted nothing more than to fight the Soviets. He arrived in Peshawar with all sorts of military gear. Flak jacket, bayonet, metal-soled boots, night scope, camouflage netting, canteens . . . everything purchased at an army-surplus store back in the States. He had never been in the military but knew all the right language. He was constantly negotiating with the different groups about going inside. I would see him sitting in the coffee shop at Green's Hotel. Waiting. He was becoming increasingly depressed. The mujahideen had already taken several thousand dollars off him to "buy horses" for the journey. As far as I know, he never made it across the border. And he never saw his horses.

Then there was the Italian photographer with the neatly clipped beard and dark green fatigues straight out of a Milan fashion magazine. He wanted to cover the war but also fight. He trained every day in the garden of Dean's Hotel—looking tough as Rambo, doing pushups and executing precise karate moves. Finally, after weeks of negotiating, the mujahideen took him into Paktia. But he was back within three days, virtually in tears. On crossing the border, they had been attacked by Soviet MiGs. The horse carrying the Italian's luggage—and cameras— was blown up.

Several of the journalists covering the war had military backgrounds, which may have helped them handle the stress of conflict. Once, in a typical Peter Jouvenal encounter, I found him having lunch in a dining room. On sitting down, I noticed that he was picking little black things from his arm. What's that, I asked.

"Oh, nothing, just a bit of shrapnel."

"What do you mean, shrapnel?" I asked incredulously.

"Oh, this chap next to me had his head blown off," he said cryptically. He had been filming a Soviet operation when a rocket exploded near him. It killed two people and he was only protected by his camera, which was shattered. That was all he would say.

Things got wilder in Peshawar toward the end of the 1980s. Several delegates from the ICRC turned one of their residences into a weekly social watering hole with the creation of The Bamboo Bar, where people could meet and drink. They even set up an illicit gambling casino attracting aid workers, diplomats, and anyone else to its tables. Eventually, the ICRC discreetly closed it down when it began to become too known about on the outside.

Much of the social focus always reverted to the American Club. The conversations at the bar were entertaining, if not always believable. On one occasion, a tall American nebulously involved with counternarcotics explained that he and his team had been smuggling anti-aircraft guns into Afghanistan by horse, "right under the goddamn noses of the Pakistanis." When I queried how he had managed to slip them through the lines, he leaned over, the warm smell of whiskey on his breath. "We plastered the goddamn things with horse manure," he said conspiratorially. "No fuckin' Pakistani is gonna stick his nose into horse shit." I was skeptical.

One evening, one of the MSF coordinators entered the restaurant and, on seeing me with some friends and a bottle of wine, came over. "May I?"

he said, grabbing a glass and pouring himself a drink. "Sometimes," he announced with a thick French accent, "it just gets too much."

Apparently, while arranging a humanitarian relief caravan, he was approached by an Afghan helping them with the loading. He wanted to borrow some MSF supplies—three or four horses would be enough, plus throw in some guns from his own sources—so that he could stop off at a village along the way. He needed to meet with the commander. There was a particular girl from that village now living in his family's refugee camp. He liked her (he had seen her face only once) and wanted to marry her. But his own family was poor and could not afford a dowry, so it was up to the commander to decide. He thought the horses would do the trick. But if that did not work, the young man suggested, could he instead have one of the French nurses? He had heard that dowries were not a requirement in France—and besides, he added, he had also heard that they "liked love." The MSF doctor said he felt sorry for the boy. Many mujahideen wanted to get married but had no means to do so, at least as long as there was war. Islam or not, there were a lot of frustrated young men among the mujahideen.

"I think *le petit con* [the little idiot] just wants sex," he said. Of course, he admitted, it did not help that so many of the French volunteers were constantly having sex with one another, and they were not married. "These things don't go unnoticed."

Many aid workers who came to Peshawar were just out of high school or college, but others were professionals who had grown bored with their jobs and wanted new challenges. One was Anders Fange, the blond pipe-smoking head of the Swedish Committee for Afghanistan (SCA). A former journalist with a husky voice and trimmed beard, he had come out during the early 1980s to report on the new Soviet war. I met him in Peshawar following his first trip inside. So affected was he by what he had witnessed that he returned to Stockholm to help set up in 1983 what soon became—and still is—one of the most effective NGO operations in Afghanistan. Anders left Afghanistan on repeated occasions to work in Ethiopia, Palestine, and elsewhere, but kept getting drawn back.

"It's a matter of dealing with individual commanders," he later said. "You need to forget the affiliations. They're all human. They want the best for their families, for their kids." Fange joined UNAMA, the UN

Assistance Mission in Afghanistan, following the collapse of the Talib regime, but eventually left. He was bitterly disappointed with the way the UN was handling the recovery situation, notably its willingness to bring the warlords into the 2002 Emergency Loya Jirgha.

Never mincing his words, Anders became a thorn in the side of the Americans. By the mid-1980s, international aid for Afghanistan had become heavily politicized. The US government was placing enormous pressure on the aid agencies to tow the anti-Soviet line and to expand their humanitarian efforts, regardless of whether the initiatives made sense. There was no shortage of funds. This same no-holds-barred approach was adopted by the United States and much of the international community during the post-2001 recovery effort, with billions of dollars senselessly thrown at inappropriate projects within a matter of four or five years.

Anders rejected American efforts to persuade the SCA to double, even triple, its activities inside Afghanistan. When USAID chief Larry Crandall proposed unlimited funding to the SCA, which had implemented a highly transparent monitoring process among its cross-border programs to assure that their aid was not being squandered or otherwise abused, Anders refused. At the time, the SCA's annual budget was roughly eleven million dollars. Anders noted that he might be able to increase his operations to twelve or thirteen million dollars. Beyond that it was pointless.

"There was no way we could have monitored such expenditures," Anders explained in an interview with US producer Tom Woods and me on international aid for America's leading TV current affairs program, the *PBS MacNeil-Lehrer NewsHour.* "It would have been a complete waste of time and money." Crandall was furious. He found it hard to understand why anyone would wish to turn down good American money.

"They never learn," Anders said to me over dinner at his house in Kabul in December 2009, referring to the US penchant for throwing money at the Afghan problem. "They did not learn during the 1980s and they haven't learned now." By then, too, he had become totally disheartened with the entire international recovery process.

When twenty-eight-year-old Michael Keating arrived in Peshawar in 1988 as a special envoy for UN diplomat Prince Sadruddin Aga Khan to explore setting up Operation Salam, a UN-coordinated operation providing humanitarian and economic assistance to Afghanistan once the Soviets left, the United Nations was not very popular. Many NGOs considered it arrogant, incompetent, and out of touch. For the new initiative to work, it needed someone to get the NGO community on board.

A somewhat disheveled Englishman with a disarming smile, who wore suits when he had to but no socks, Keating was an obvious choice. Born in Uganda and a Cambridge graduate, he had worked or met in Africa with inspiring individuals such as George Adamson of *Born Free* fame and British explorer Wilfred Thesiger. Charming, witty, and culturally perceptive, Keating was equally at ease negotiating his way through a diplomatic soiree in London and a tribal ceremony in northern Kenya's Lake Turkhana. I had met him briefly in a refugee camp on his first trip to the region, when Mark Malloch-Brown—a friend and former journalist for *The Economist*, then working as Sadruddin's PR director; he later became deputy secretary general of the United Nations—introduced me in jest: "This man Girardet is precisely the sort of person you should not consort with." Needless to say, Michael and I became good friends. The first thing he asked me was how he should deal with the NGOs. My advice was for him to spend the next two weeks visiting all the organizations and, above all, to listen. The last thing these people want is someone from Geneva telling them what to do, I told him.

I helped arrange a number of meetings and personally accompanied him to several. Michael's principal objective was to find out what the aid community thought the UN should be doing. I took Keating for dinner to meet French doctor Laurence Laumounier, the doyenne of the "inside Afghanistan" aid crowd. Living in Peshawar with her Flemish husband (Paul Ickx, a former MSF doctor) she was now working with an American health organization. She knew Massoud well and had a good sense of how ordinary Afghans viewed both the resistance parties and the international community. On entering their house, I suggested to Michael that he take off his shoes. I forgot that he had no socks. Laurence glanced down at his feet and turned to me in an aside. "Is this what you call an eccentric English?" she asked with a wry smile.

Based on these meetings, the UN established Operation Salam, which immediately pulled in over one billion dollars in pledges for coordinated humanitarian and economic assistance to Afghanistan; at that time, this was an enormous sum. "One of the problems was that the Russians offered four hundred million dollars' worth of support, but in kind," recalled Keating. "Obviously, as the UN, we had to take this, but it did raise serious questions." Operation Salam began dispatching teams to most of Afghanistan's provinces to set up pilot aid projects focusing primarily on health and agriculture. It also started training Afghans, eventually over twenty thousand people in less than two years, in land-mine clearance and awareness—one of the most lethal problems facing Afghanistan at the end of the Soviet occupation and still a problem over two decades later.

Michael, who had at first come out on short exploratory trips from Geneva, was soon based in Peshawar and stayed there for a year and a half until September 1989. He also got married to his longtime girl-friend, Kim, with three weddings—one Pakistani, one Afghan, and one Catholic in Peshawar. Although Keating was one of the more junior UN representatives in Peshawar, everyone came to him because of his rela-tionship with Sadruddin. They figured that he must be the one to hold the purse strings and make the decisions—which, he insists, was never the case. His credibility was strengthened by his trips inside Afghanistan, notably to Kunar, where he met local commanders and encountered Arab Islamic legionnaires who had firmly entrenched themselves in the province. They refused to have anything to do with the UN team. On one occasion, remembers Michael, "a Saudi Wahhab—in retrospect, al Qaeda—dropped his kit and waved his penis at me to prove a point, to the utter horror of my local Afghan hosts." Michael left Afghanistan soon afterward, but returned to the region again for two years—this time with his wife and four young girls—during the late 1990s. And in early 2011, he was back in Kabul as special adviser to the head of the United Nations in an effort to work out a new transition policy for when the NATO troops pulled out. "The trouble with Afghanistan is that one just can't leave it," he quipped. "One keeps getting drawn back in."

Probably the most influential foreign organization operating out of Peshawar was the International Committee of the Red Cross. A Swiss organization, the ICRC has always operated in war zones. Traditionally, it has sought to ensure that prisoners of war are properly treated and can

receive food packages, mail, and other forms of relief. It also deals with
the tracing of relatives missing in war and provides emergency medical
care to civilians and belligerents.

The ICRC was able to set up offices in Peshawar and Quetta, plus
establish a temporary presence in Kabul. One objective was to visit mujahed POWs held by the Kabul regime. Another was to deal with any
Soviets or Afghan soldiers captured by the resistance. In less than six
months in 1980, the ICRC visited 427 political prisoners at the city's
notorious Pul-e-Charkhi prison. It also distributed two tons of medicine to different hospitals and dispensaries. But by June of that year, the
Kabul regime forced the ICRC to leave. It was only in 1986 that the
ICRC was able to open a full-time Kabul office.

The ICRC saw its principal task as one of upholding the applica-
tion of international humanitarian law. The Geneva Conventions clearly
stipulate that captured members of a resistance movement who belong
to an organized armed force are entitled to POW status. Yet neither the
PDPA regime nor Moscow considered the mujahideen to be covered by
this protection during the Soviet occupation. Later, during the US-led
invasion, the Bush administration similarly thwarted the conventions—
detaining thousands of Afghans and foreigners fighting with the Taliban
as "unlawful" combatants, claiming that with their informal dress they
did not constitute a formal or legitimate force.

"This was a complete travesty of justice and lack of respect for humanitarian norms," noted one ICRC delegate in Geneva. "The Americans
have done themselves a lot of harm with this approach." Even US military lawyers dealing with terrorist suspects held at Guantanamo during
the post-2001 period agreed, arguing that this could endanger the lives
of American soldiers captured by the insurgents. In the end, some believe
that this policy contributed to the brutal executions by al Qaeda–linked
groups in Iraq and Afghanistan of Western contractors, humanitarian
aid workers, and journalists—including American reporter Daniel Pearl
in Pakistan.

Claiming that it could not work inside Afghanistan without permission of the "host" government, the ICRC opted to set up two front-line
war hospitals—one in Peshawar, the other in Quetta. These would deal
with the perpetual stream of injured civilians and fighters brought by

foot, horse, camel, truck, rickshaw, ambulance, taxi, car, and bus from the border.

Afghans—including many now with the Taliban, Hezb, Haqqani Network, and other insurgents—still remember these hospitals today. In fact, such memories and recognition of the Red Cross emblem have prevented kidnapped or hijacked ICRC representatives from being killed in the NATO war. The Geneva organization is able to work in parts of Afghanistan where even US and other Coalition troops do not dare operate. The ICRC teams saved thousands of Afghan lives during the jihad conflicts of the 1980s and '90s, and then in Kabul and other parts of the country with the spread of the Taliban. What is more, they have saved lives on all sides.

From the beginning, these ICRC establishments ranked among the best war trauma units in the world, with surgical teams rotating in from countries such as Switzerland, West Germany, Finland, Denmark, Italy, and New Zealand. Much of their time was spent dealing with victims from land mines or trauma inflicted by aerial bombardments, artillery shelling, frontal assaults, or shootings. The overwhelming majority of the injured were civilians. Sometimes I would pass by the hospital to check on casualties, which was one way of determining how the Soviet-Afghan war was unfolding. The wards were overflowing with men, women, and children with torn bodies waiting to be operated on—some crying, their bandages soaked with blood, or lying in stoic silence. Some were mujahideen, just carried in from the war, with their comrades sitting quietly around them.

Journalist colleagues and I sometimes referred mujahideen and refugees to the hospitals. I knew that Red Crescent ambulances were waiting at select border crossings, or at least by the main roads in the Pakistani tribal areas. The French doctors, too, forwarded their more complicated cases to the ICRC hospitals, as their survival depended on getting them as quickly as possible to Pakistan.

It was always hard to behold these injured, yet I remember them vividly: the young girl without a face, victim of a helicopter bombardment; a woman whose right leg had been twice amputated following a severe ground assault against her village; a small boy, his foot blown off by a butterfly mine. Outside, the paraplegics struggled to exercise from their wheelchairs, while others hobbled about on crutches, waiting for a new foot or leg to be made at the prosthesis workshop. Later, during the NATO war, I would witness similar scenes—but then the victims would be at the ICRC rehabilitation center in Kabul, which was coping with civilians wounded in insurgent attacks (notably by IEDs).

What placed me in a peculiar relationship with the ICRC, however, was the plight of Soviet prisoners held by the mujahideen. During the first eighteen months of the war, I often heard about captured Soviet prisoners. My understanding was that most of them had been executed, often in a horrific manner, so great was the hatred of their Afghan captors toward them. In the first documented case of a Soviet being captured (and kept alive) by the mujahideen, a Ukrainian MiG fighter pilot was shot down over Afghan territory. Hezb guerrillas (Khales faction) smuggled him across the border into Khyber Agency and then to a safe house in Peshawar. Aware of the publicity he could attract, Youris Khales, head of one of the two Hezb factions, showed him off to the international press. For the sensitive Islamabad government, the last thing it wanted was a Soviet POW on Pakistani soil. It pressured the mujahideen into handing him over. Discreetly, the Pakistanis passed him on to the Soviet embassy, which promptly bundled him back to the USSR.

The fact that the Pakistanis had forced the guerrillas to hand him over did not help matters. The guerrillas were not likely to offer up their captives again. By 1982, there were more reports of Red Army prisoners in hideous conditions, with their captors repeatedly trying to convert them to Islam or deliberately starving them before shooting or beating them to death. Some reports, too, suggested that Red Army prisoners, particularly pilots, had been skinned alive. In one incident, a video captured two Soviets being forced to remove their boots, jackets, and overalls, and then being shot.

It often seemed that the guerrillas did not know what to do with them. They could see no point in keeping them alive. Nor did they have any idea about the Geneva Conventions. Not only that, but for a mujahed (or Talib) to kill a *kafir* meant becoming a *ghazi*, a hero.

I broached the issue with Jean-Michel Monod, the chief ICRC delegate in Peshawar during the early 1980s. Monod—a tall, good-looking Swiss with a thick mustache—had been hearing similar reports, and the ICRC was now exploring options with the guerrilla leaders. One of Monod's main concerns was to persuade not only the leaders to respect the Geneva Conventions, but also to persuade the rank and file—who were largely illiterate. We agreed to share information as long as it did not compromise the ICRC's time-honored position of confidentiality, the main reason why belligerents allowed the organization to inspect prisoner conditions under the Geneva Conventions. Monod provided me with specially produced comic books in Pashto and Dari explaining the purpose of the conventions. While the distribution of humanitarian "propaganda" was not exactly a journalistic responsibility, I considered it part of my own basic humanity. I would always carry a few copies with me, which I would hand out to guerrilla commanders inside Afghanistan.

On their own, I do not think the booklets had much impact, or that they saved POW lives. Nevertheless, they always prompted discussion, particularly over tea or meals while traveling inside the country. The illiterate commanders could not understand why on earth they should waste good food and accommodation on captured enemies. In the end, the most persuasive argument was that a powerful commander was also a merciful one. By handing over POWs to the ICRC, they would receive international publicity—and even be mentioned on the BBC. The unison murmur of "Ahas" from the guerrillas would always indicate that this had touched a nerve, or least their vanity.

The POW issue soon became a major dilemma for the ICRC. For the first time in its history, the Geneva organization was faced with a new concept of prisoner responsibility, namely the proxy internment of POWs on neutral territory from a conventional army captured by a nonrecognized guerrilla movement. Since the late nineteenth century, the ICRC has assured the proper treatment of POWs by visiting internment camps, engineering prisoner exchanges, and even mediating the release of captured civilians in rebel-held areas.

Afghanistan, however, was not a typical war. Prior to the Soviet invasion, captured rebels or "bandits" were summarily shot, or thrown into jail by the PDPA regime. Reciprocally, the mujahideen disarmed captured soldiers conscripted by Kabul, while Communist Party militants and army officers were tried by shari'a courts and executed. The ICRC was not allowed to visit the notorious Pul-e-Charkhi prison nor any of the KHAD-run detention centers in Kabul, Kandahar, Jalalabad, or other locations. Furthermore, given that the 1977 Geneva Protocols did not grant POW status to guerrillas in a purely civil conflict, international norms could not be applied, even given the "internationalization" of the war with the presence of thousands of Soviet military advisers.

This changed with the invasion. Concerned by repeated reports of prisoner executions ranging from captured Red Army soldiers with their throats slit to trussed-up Afghan partisans being run over by Soviet tanks, ICRC representatives in Peshawar had begun negotiating with the various resistance parties from almost the very start of the war. "We would meet with Hekmatyar, Rabbani, Mojadeddi, Mohammadi, Khales, Pir Sayed Gailani, Mansour, and a few others on a daily basis if necessary, trying to convince them to keep prisoners alive," said Monod. Finally, Moscow made a formal request to the ICRC for assistance in recovering captured personnel.

Several months after the guerrillas were forced to hand over the Ukrainian MiG pilot, Khalqi commander Abdul Haq organized a daring daylight raid in the middle of Kabul to kidnap E. R. Okrimyuk, a senior Soviet geologist. Having learned their lesson, the mujahideen did not take him to Pakistan. Instead, Haq—a tough, heavyset Pushtun who was becoming increasingly versed in dealing with internationals—approached Monod. He proposed exchanging the geologist, whose own driver had betrayed him, for fifty Afghan prisoners—one of them Khales's own son. "He used to come discreetly to the house in University Town in the evening, on a moped, wearing the helmet of a Soviet helicopter pilot, to negotiate," remembers Monod.

This posed a severe predicament for the Soviets, who did not wish to be perceived as dealing with "terrorists." If they did, it might encourage further kidnappings, particularly the more vulnerable Soviet civilian advisers. But if they did not, they risked demoralizing Red Army troops in Afghanistan. The ICRC was all for negotiations to save Okrimyuk's life, but against prisoner exchanges. Monod argued there was nothing to prevent the Kabul authorities from abusing existing prisoners or grabbing people off the street, calling them rebels, and then using them as collateral. "Obviously a political matter, this sort of thing could easily snowball out of control," he said.

In the end, the Kremlin refused to bargain. To illustrate their intention of never negotiating with the *basmachi*, or bandits, they executed the fifty Afghans on the mujahed list. Six months after Okrimyuk's capture, a bitter Khales announced that they had executed the Soviet adviser. Other reports, however, indicated that he had died of natural causes.

Pressure was growing as fighting became more intense and more reports emerged of Red Army soldiers being captured or having deserted. By the end of 1982, several hundred Soviets—primarily Russians, Lithuanians, Estonians, Ukrainians, and Central Asians—were said to be in guerrilla hands. International humanitarian organizations had put together a detailed list of at least fifty known prisoners, some of whom had already been executed. Sometimes these killings were prompted by Soviet assaults against villages where the captives were believed to have been held, with the mujahideen shooting their prisoners as the Red Army troops advanced. The Red Cross persisted in its attempts to find a solution. ICRC delegates made regular visits to the different mujahed offices but also talked with the inside commanders, drinking innumerable cups of tea. Sometimes, impressed by the medical care provided by the ICRC hospitals, particularly care of their wounded, commanders would themselves approach the Swiss. One of the options discussed was the transfer of captured Soviet personnel to a neutral third country for internment. This would conveniently provide the mujahideen with a means of abiding by the Geneva Conventions. In return, the ICRC would have the right to visit resistance prisoners held by the government. For the Afghans, constant contact with Western doctors, journalists, and human rights activists had made them aware that working with the ICRC would not only enhance their stature, but also significantly embarrass the Russians. It would offer a reminder to the world that there was a war going on.

In May 1982, the ICRC finally managed to work out an arrangement for the transfer of Soviet POWs to Switzerland—following twenty-four months of negotiation involving the Soviet Union and fourteen resistance organizations. It represented the first comprehensive agreement between the ICRC and the USSR since 1945. In accordance with the Geneva Conventions, the ICRC would assume full responsibility for the prisoners for two years, or the duration of the war. The Swiss government was to provide internment facilities guarded by Swiss soldiers with Moscow paying all the costs. In return, the ICRC would receive access to the Kabul prisons to visit captured mujahideen and other political inmates.

In effect, the ICRC suddenly found itself in a highly unusual predicament for a humanitarian organization: It would be in charge of interning prisoners of war. The first transfer took place in June 1982 as Monod was preparing to leave Peshawar. "This was also something completely new . . . it was the first time since World War II that Soviet prisoners were detained in such circumstances," he said. Despite these well-laid plans, by early 1985 only eleven Soviet POWs had been flown to Switzerland. Afghanistan's war was clearly not a conflict that would slot into carefully elaborated initiatives designed to make it more "humane." Nor was it one that would proceed unnoticed by outside players determined to impose their own often alien agendas.

CHAPTER ELEVEN

Arabs, Islamic Legionnaires, and Satanic Verses

Sympathetic Arabs and others from the Muslim world responded to the plight of Afghans from the very start of the Soviet occupation. Within days, money and humanitarian aid were flowing in. Businessmen from Saudi Arabia and the Gulf dressed in their white *thaubs* with red-and-white *keffiyeh* headdresses often flew in to Peshawar to disperse relief or cash in person among the refugees. Some did this as a social obligation through *zakat*, or alms giving, the contributing of a small percentage of one's possessions or surplus wealth to charity. Others genuinely wanted to help. I often encountered Arabs in the offices of the mujahideen with their luxury four-by-four, tinted-glass vehicles parked outside. Such generosity quickly became more organized with the establishment of new Islamic aid agencies, but also the setting up of operations for various Middle Eastern Red Crescent societies, the Muslim equivalent of the Red Cross.

Many Afghans initially saw the Arabs as easy funding. This soon changed when the often haughty Saudis or Kuwaitis, who tended to look down on the Afghans, began only offering support with strings attached. "It is very clear what they are doing," said Hezb (Khales faction) commander Abdul Haq. "They give you everything you need and when you don't do what they want, they cut off the aid."

One Saudi sympathizer who arrived shortly after the invasion was the young Osama bin Laden. As a fabulously wealthy Saudi, he often donated his own money to various groups. Later, like any good investor, he raised funds from other sources, including like-minded Arabs from Saudi Arabia and the Gulf. It was only well into the Soviet-Afghan war and during the 1990s that he became, as American writer Jon Randal shrewdly characterized in his 2004 book, *Osama*, "a cross between the president of the Jihad Incorporated money machine and the head of a maverick Ford Foundation dispensing seed-money grants of a very special nature." During those early days, bin Laden met all the Afghan leaders to discuss their needs, but collaborated with those already enjoying strong Arab connections, notably Sayyaf. As pro-Arab, the Afghan fundamentalist politician received the bulk of his support from the Saudis. In turn, Sayyaf helped promote Wahhabism in the eastern Afghan border provinces.

Bin Laden soon returned to Saudi Arabia to solicit support, which (at least in the beginning) was primarily for humanitarian purposes. He made numerous trips back to the South Asia region and was soon delivering both relief and weapons to the resistance. This was made easier once the Americans, Saudis, and other outsiders had worked out logistical details with the ISI for the smuggling in of support. Middle Eastern military and other nonhumanitarian aid was provided in discreet coordination with the CIA and ISI. Saudi Arabia's aid, however, was organized by Prince Turki bin Faisal al Saud—who as head of the al Mukhabarat Al A'amah (or General Intelligence Directorate) had close relations with the CIA. Bin Laden became, in effect, a CIA asset.

The Pakistanis did not want to make it too obvious to the Soviets that they were aiding and abetting the resistance with arms. Weapons and ammunition were brought in with blackout flights to Peshawar airport. I could hear the planes roaring in late at night or in the early hours of the morning. Suitcase loads of dollars were splashed out to the different Afghan political parties. Saudi money was also used to purchase difficult-to-trace weaponry such as Egyptian Kalashnikovs, Soviet RPGs, and Chinese land mines in the open markets. Nevertheless, the Saudi government steadfastly maintained that it had nothing to do with the Wahhabi even though the political fortunes of this strictly puritan sect have been linked to the country's ruling al Saud royal family for nearly two centuries. Saudi Arabia's principal support, Turki stressed, was meant to go to the Afghans themselves.

During the first several years of the occupation, the only Arabs I saw were those managing on-the-ground operations of the Islamic aid agencies. They had their offices in University Town, and also in Islamabad. Their presence in the Pakistani capital was primarily to cultivate relations with the government. They also met regularly with ISI agents—sometimes with CIA operatives present—given that the Pakistani military intelligence organization was headquartered just down the road in Rawalpindi. The US embassy clearly regarded the Arabs as an asset to America's subversion of Moscow. I sometimes sought to interview the Saudis and Kuwaitis, but they were reticent about talking with Western journalists. My most forthcoming diplomatic sources were the military attachés at the Egyptian embassy, who seemed positively delighted to talk. Yet they rarely divulged anything of interest, particularly if I started probing weapons shipments.

By the mid-1980s, I began to notice more Arabi and black African Muslims dressed in *Julubiyas* or *thaubs* and sandals wandering around University Town. Some of them, barely out of their teens, could not even grow beards. These were no humanitarians. They were the first real jihadists, whose goal was to march into Afghanistan and combat the godless Russians, and even die in the holy war. Self-righteous and zealous, they were the Islamist equivalent of the International Brigade against Franco's fascists in Spain except that they were not fighting for freedom and democracy. Rallying against the Crusades in the eleventh and twelfth centuries might have made a better analogy. As one Arabist with the US State Department in the late 1980s pointed out: "Basically, the Afghan Jihad suits their purposes. It's the only one they've got. It's the first real Jihad since the Middle Ages."

A few appeared to come from sophisticated, well-to-do backgrounds—while others were just out of the *madrassas* with half-baked educations. They spoke mainly Arabic and almost always walked in groups. While some had come as part of organized initiatives back in Egypt, Sudan, or Algeria, others had arrived on their own.

None looked as if he had picked up a gun in his life, and as it later turned out many did not prove to be particularly good fighters. It was only with the rise of the Taliban during the 1990s that the training camps set up by al Qaeda and other radical groups in the Pakistan tribal zones or deep inside Afghanistan began to turn out full-fledged combatants.

Occasionally, I managed to get into conversation with some of the English speakers, but they harbored a deep loathing for the *kafirs*. It was always a struggle to find out why they were here and where they came from. It was like dealing with a recalcitrant religious sect. Probably, too, they considered me a spy. Even if personally amiable, they were nervous about how they would be perceived by fellow Islamists. They had their own stringent norms of political correctness. They almost never gave their names—or, if they did, these were clearly noms de guerre. Nor did they ever shake hands, as if the pagan filth would contaminate them.

Once, I succeeded in chatting with a Briton of Pakistani background. He had a Yorkshire accent from the north of England and seemed grateful to be able to speak in his native tongue. He had come to fight because of what he had seen on television and read in the papers. Afghanistan was discussed in the mosques back in the UK, and some had talked of joining the jihad. What the Russians were doing was wrong, he said. They had no religion. He also thought that only through Islam could one bring true assistance to Afghanistan. Clearly a True Believer, he seemed decent enough and even wished me good luck when we parted. However, he would not take my hand and appeared embarrassed by his own refusal. I had the feeling that even if he did not drink, he would have liked to go off and have a jar with me at the pub. He was homesick.

Others with whom I talked were less friendly. One man in his late twenties with thin spectacles and a scornful look could have been Algerian. Passing him in the street as he and two other jihadists were returning from the mosque, I heard them speaking French. I assumed them to be North African or even second- or third-generation French nationals of Maghreb origin. Quite a few, I was aware, had come out from the Paris suburbs or cities such as Marseille where there were large Muslim populations. I immediately greeted them with an enthusiastic "*A Salaam Aleikum*." I asked one if he was French, but he pretended not to understand.

When I persisted, he suddenly blurted out: "*Qu'est-ce que tu veux?*" What do you want? I explained that I was a journalist exploring the jihad, trying to create the impression that I was really on their side. But he was having none of this. "We don't like you people," he said in no uncertain terms. "You have nothing to do here." We talked for a few more minutes as other jihadists sauntered up to the French group asking them in Arabic what was going on. My "Algerian" was becoming increasingly uneasy. It was then that I realized neither he nor his French companions could speak Arabic. Obviously, being in my presence and speaking French was awkward. They hurriedly walked away.

Many of these jihadists lived in an array of guesthouses located in different parts of University Town. These served primarily as stopping-off points before heading into Afghanistan. One was run by bin Laden's own Maktab al Khidamar (Office of Services). I never managed to enter any of these compounds and could only assume that—much like the Afghan quarters for visiting mujahideen—they must consist of rooms with mattresses and carpets for people to sleep, eat, and pray. It was only later as their numbers grew that bin Laden established camps in the tribal areas and inside Afghanistan. One of these was Jagi, overlooking Teri Mangal in Kurram Agency. This is how the name *al Qaeda*, or the Base, emerged—such logistical facilities came to serve as the launching point for many militants.

It was only from 1987 onward that we began to notice growing numbers of Arabs inside Afghanistan itself. It was as if they had only been dabbling with jihad up till then. Massoud had a few in the north and welcomed them as fellow Muslims. The bulk of the Arabi, however, focused on the Pushtun border areas. They did not mix readily with the Afghans, who often complained of their arrogance. The Arabi had their own commanders. The Afghan mujahideen operating directly with them were hired guns. The Arab attitude was that money and weapons could buy everything, including allegiance. "It sometimes amazes me that the Afghans have [tolerated] such attitudes for so long," said a European aid worker operating in eastern Afghanistan. "Money speaks loudly but it is not in the Afghan character to take this sort of thing lying down."

Some of the mujahed factions, such as Hekmatyar's Hezb, had received Saudi backing for years, but they were at political loggerheads with the more religiously strident Wahhabi, who were pushing for the creation of a "new Islamic man." The Islamic legionnaires considered themselves better Muslims than their Afghan counterparts. Given their traditionally independent nature, many Afghans deeply resented being told what to do by outsiders—whether Muslim, communist, or (as during the post-2001 period) Western. Above all, they begrudged being told that they were not true followers of Islam.

This did not stop the foreign Wahhabi from trying to dominate the jihad. They sought to impose their own will through intense proselytizing and the buying off of mujahideen with money, guns, uniforms, and other forms of support. Most of the Afghans I met who had ostensibly embraced Wahhabism did it for cash. They never appeared to give any great thought as to what problems such affiliations might cause in the years ahead. "The Arabi have *besiaw paise*, much money," laughed one guerrilla from the Safed Koh region. In Afghanistan, it is the present that matters, not the future. And if there is cash to be made from these Arabs, then why not?

In many ways, such attitudes set the scene for al Qaeda and other extremist groups to firmly establish themselves in Afghanistan a decade later. The problem with the Taliban in 2001 was that they were never sophisticated enough to see the big picture. On a local or regional basis, some Talib commanders realized that in return for their money, weapons, and satellite phones, the Arabi—who also had ISI support—had the run of the country in order to reinforce their own agendas. In the end, however, the Taliban had no real control over their activities. Until the collapse of the Talib regime, these foreign fighters operated parallel existences by running their own camps, eating out on their own in local restaurants, and conducting their own operations. For the Taliban to simply kick out al Qaeda because of US and other outside pressure was probably impossible at that late stage of the game.

The friction between the Wahhabi and the mujahideen began to cause serious rifts within the resistance. Commanders such as Abdul Haq warned that relations with the Arabs were running the risk of breaking out into open conflict. "Something is going to happen and it is best that it happens sooner rather than later, so that Afghans realize how dangerous these Arab Wahhabi are," he said. Such attitudes were shared by other leading inside commanders. In early 1989, angry delegates at a resistance council in Islamabad hijacked the microphone—demanding that the Arabi be thrown out. These Wahhabi were only here for themselves, they declared, not Afghanistan. It was because of such sentiments that the Afghans finally expelled bin Laden and other foreign Islamists during the early 1990s.

During the Soviet-Afghan war, however, Afghans were bemused by the Arab obsession for wanting to die in the jihad, while the mujahideen themselves clearly did not seek the same fate. One of the most common terms used by the Afghans to describe their Arabi Muslim brethren was *diwana*. Crazy. The concept of suicide bombers had yet to be introduced to Afghanistan by these outsiders. I sometimes saw groups of Arabi in the *chaikhane* or at Afghan bases, but they kept to themselves. While Afghans inevitably came up to greet us or offer us tea as part of their traditional hospitality, the foreign jihadists would deliberately and disdainfully turn their backs or walk out. The Afghans considered this rude. On one occasion in Paktia province, we filmed a group of some sixty Arabs accompanied by several mujahideen shouldering Kalashnikovs walking back along a dusty track to Pakistan. There was nothing military or disciplined about them. Their clothes were torn and dirty, and they wore rags on their heads. They completely lacked the pride that Afghans always seemed to exude. None of them had guns.

When they saw the camera, they immediately raised their fists, shouting *"Mard au Israel, Mard au America."* Death to Israel, Death to America. Several spat at us. I caught the eyes of one of the Afghans with them. He shrugged apologetically. I had never heard Afghans lambaste the United States to one's face, even if they disliked the West. Even Hekmatyar held back his personal feelings when talking with Western journalists or visitors. It was un-Afghan to insult one's guests.

In early 1989, the Soviets were in the process of conducting their final withdrawal from Afghanistan after nearly a decade of costly and futile war. Both *The Christian Science Monitor* and the *PBS NewsHour* in New York wanted me to do a report that could run as the last Red Army troops crossed the Oxus River back into the USSR. My normal partner for the television side was Tom Woods from Paris, who would come in with a film crew once I had completed a "reccy," or reconnaissance trip. I decided to do a first sortie across the border in Kunar with *National Geographic* photographer Steve McCurry. While the Soviets had already pulled out of Kunar, there was still heavy fighting between the mujahideen and Afghan government troops down toward Jalalabad. We should be able to obtain some good footage, I felt.

As Kunar was now largely in the hands of different mujahed factions, particularly Hekmatyar's Hezb and Arab-backed Afghan Wahhabi, I decided to travel with my own Pushtun guards and translator so as not to be beholden to any one group. I hired Abdul, a teacher from Asadabad, the capital of Kunar, who often worked as an interpreter for journalists and aid workers. Abdul had learned his English at the American Center in Peshawar, and I knew him well. I asked him to bring along two trusted men. We drove by car to Nawagai, the main bazaar town in Bajaur, the smallest of Pakistan's seven tribal agencies. Two decades later, in 2008, this is where the Pakistani army launched a major offensive to rid the area of Taliban, reportedly killing over a thousand militants with two hundred dead of its own in bitter pitched battles. Bajaur was supposedly where bin Laden had taken refuge following the collapse of the Taliban in 2001.

Afghanistan was just on the other side of the Nawa Pass, which in those days was still a rough, unpaved track. Now it is an asphalted road leading from Asadabad into Bajaur. So we needed a four-by-four pickup to cross the rugged frontier hills into Kunar. The two guards immediately went to their homes in a nearby refugee camp, where they kept their Kalashnikovs. Driving up toward the low-lying mountain pass, which was surrounded by thick pine and cedar forests, we came to our first "checkpoint," a rope laid across the road by armed tribesmen. We had to pay a "toll" of a few rupees and then continued. A few hundred yards before the final Pakistani checkpoint, Steve and I had to get out and walk while the car drove ahead. The Frontier Scouts were checking the cars, but in our Afghan gear no one appeared to notice us.

Once on the Afghan side, we jolted down the nine-mile track toward the Asadabad bridge over the Kunar River. As part of a tacit agreement with the mujahideen, no one attacked it during the Red Army occupation despite the presence of a nearby Soviet-Afghan army base. Nearly a decade and a half later, the Americans, who established forward operating bases with special forces troops in the area in late 2001, built their own heavily fortified Provincial Reconstruction Team (PRT) compound overlooking the main road only a few hundred yards away. They faced exactly the same problems as the Soviets. The Red Army "controlled" the town, but the mujahideen operated at night with relative impunity the length of the valley.

During the Soviet-Afghan war, I had trekked through Kunar to the Pech Valley, now an insurgent stronghold, and on my return from the

Panjshir took the route running along the southern edge of the Hindu Kush. The river was too fast and too deep to wade, so we had to traverse at select points in the marshes using truck inner tubes tied together. Young men and boys from the villages operated these ferries with up to a dozen mujahideen crossing at any one time. They also transported animals, such as cows and sheep. During one of these traverses, two Soviet helicopter gunships suddenly appeared. Hugging the river, they thundered past us no more than three hundred feet overhead and on to Jalalabad. I plunged for cover among the surrounding reeds. The mujahideen laughed but I nearly retched with fright.

Asadabad, which had been taken by the guerrillas when the Soviets pulled out months earlier, had two resistance governments, or *shure*. One was an alliance of local mujahideen, while the other consisted of Afghan and Arab Wahhabi. Sayyaf's Ittehad was in strength here, as was Jamaat Ulduwaat, a local group. The Wahhabi-allied mujahideen, who were paid fifty dollars a month—not a paltry amount for Afghans—were easily recognizable by their lavish weapons, expensive vehicles, Banana Republic vests, and camouflage fatigues. Like the more moderate National Islamic Front of Afghanistan (NIFA) guerrillas, they too were known as "Gucci guerrillas." With the Arabi intent on imposing their own form of extremist Islam on Afghanistan, which had nothing to do with local culture, many of these enlisted tribesmen prayed in the Wahhabi rather than the Afghan fashion. During the 1990s and 2000s, some became key supporters of the Taliban and other anti-NATO insurgent groups.

At the time, however, some observers felt that the Afghans would simply play along by taking the Wahhabi dollars and then eventually dropping their patrons when they were no longer needed in the old "you can rent an Afghan" manner. Others were not so sure. Looking back, it is evident that this was when such outside influences, which ran counter to traditional values of the Pushtunwali, were beginning to embed themselves. Their biggest influence was among the younger fighters, many of whom had been brought up in the refugee camps and attended local *madrassas*. This period, too, was when the Taliban as a political rather than a military movement began to emerge.

The two *shure* ruled uneasily side by side. Steve and I met with both of them as a matter of courtesy. Ten days later, when I returned with the

TV team, we were in the middle of shooting an interview with a local teacher about the lack of books and basic educational materials when a group of Afghan Wahhabi entered the school and began removing chairs and desks. They needed the furniture for their offices, they told us. When the teacher protested, they ignored him. "This happens the whole time," he said. "These Arabi don't care about education."

The local mujahideen were not happy at the way the foreign Islamic legionnaires were seeking to turn Afghans against non-Muslim foreigners, particularly the humanitarians and journalists. A major topic of debate at the Afghan *shura* had been a recent incident when several Arabs had confronted a visiting UN team by threatening to shoot them unless they left Kunar immediately. As one Hezb commander angrily told me: "These Arabi are not Afghans. They have no right to insult our guests like this." Shortly afterward, a French photographer was beaten up, purportedly by three Black Muslims from New York.

We headed toward the front thirty miles to the south along the main Asadabad-to-Jalalabad highway. This ran the length of the Kunar River down to the plain, where it joined the Kabul River as it surged eastward toward Pakistan and the Indus. Untouched by frost but surrounded by snow-covered mountains in the winter, this part of the valley is a warm, agriculturally rich region with irrigated wheat and cornfields, citrus orchards, and even rice paddies—plus wetlands attracting an overwhelming array of bird life, such as Siberian cranes, egrets, and ducks. While tens of thousands of villagers had fled across the border, much of the land continued to be cultivated by caretaker farmers. Madera, the French agricultural NGO then known as Bureau International pour l'Afghanistan (BIA), managed to provide clandestine farming support even during the height of the war.

Some villages and farms had been deliberately destroyed as part of punitive raids by the Soviets because of local support for the mujahideen. Their shattered walls and rubble surrounded by torn-up and now arid fields with ruptured aqueducts provided a constant reminder as to the brutality of this war. A few small towns and districts, however, were known to be pro-Khalqi. This had less to do with Marxist-Leninism than the relations the families enjoyed with senior party members in Kabul. One town was even dubbed "little Moscow"; it was protected by heavily armed militia officered and paid for by pro-government military. About forty of these PDPA militants were being held in a makeshift prison just off the main road. According to the mujahed commander who was accompanying us toward the front, they would be tried and—if proven to be godless—shot. Those who were true Muslims would be released.

Throughout much of the occupation, the Soviets "held" the highway but could only travel in armored convoys protected by patrolling helicopters. I had even walked part of the road with a group of mujahideen for fear of land mines, while seeking a safe route to cut down toward the river. We did not see or hear a single Soviet vehicle. By the time the mujahideen took the valley, the road had deteriorated into a series of deep potholes, jagged corrugation, and undulating humps—so that one drove it like a small craft rolling on the high seas. Even before arriving, we could hear the front lines near Abdel Khel, where the river swings to the east. The air echoed with the repetitive booms of mortars exploding a few miles to the southwest. The mujahed commander indicated a dirt track off the main road for us to follow. "We can go to the trenches," he explained. "You can see Khalqis from there, but right now there's not much fighting. Maybe tonight." For the next twenty minutes, we swerved and bumped toward a clutch of low hills protruding from the river plain like the kopjes one sees in southern Africa. Over to the left, on the other side of the river, was the sharp green of one of four large-scale orange plantations that the Soviets had established east of Jalalabad. It now lay abandoned with no one to water it. Dying trees have become tragically symbolic of Afghanistan itself.

We finally halted at the foot of the largest hill. A network of trenches ran off toward the right. These were manned by Afghan mujahideen, who waved to us, offering us tea. A guerrilla agreed to take Steve up to the ridge to see if he could get any shots of the government lines on the other side. They had been shelling each other for weeks. To the left, I noticed another series of excavated furrows. Several men were sitting by an entrance supported by wooden beams with clothes hung up to dry in the sun. They did not look Afghan, so I strolled over with Abdul. They were Arabi. One of the men shouted something in Arabic and a strikingly tall man—a Saudi it later turned out—with a thin black beard, perhaps in his mid- or even late twenties, stepped out. He was evidently the leader.

"Who are you and what are you doing in Afghanistan?" he demanded in good English, with a slight American accent as if learned at school. Wearing a military fatigue anorak and billowing trousers with black boots, he scarcely hid his contempt for the *kafir* a few paces away. He talked with the confidence of someone who enjoyed an affluent background, but who also sounded like a spoiled brat who always got his way. Within minutes, a good dozen other Arabi—some Arabic-featured, others black, all bracing or shouldering AK-74 assault rifles and RPGs—had stepped behind him. Most seemed to be in their late teens or early twenties. In turn, a good dozen fighters from the Afghan trenches gathered behind me.

I immediately realized that this was a confrontation that needed to be handled deftly. I resented the way he addressed me, but I also had to hold my ground. It is crucial to save face in Afghanistan. It was important to show this lofty Arab, another foreigner, that he had no business demanding to know who I was or what I was doing. So, for the benefit of my Afghan companions, I turned to Abdul and loudly asked him in English what the man was saying. This was simply a ploy to remain aloof from the Arab and to establish my own position among both the Arabs and the Afghans with me. Abdul glanced at me quizzically given that the tall Arab had spoken to me in English. "He wants to know who you are and what you are doing here," he said.

Tell him, I declared as grandly as possible, that "I'll leave if our Afghan friends no longer consider us their guests, just as I'm sure you'll leave if they no longer consider you their guests." Now grasping what I was doing, Abdul dutifully recounted with amusement what I had just said back in English. He then immediately translated the same in Pushto to the Afghans, all curious to know what was unfolding between these two foreigners. To this the Arab, who gave his name as Abu-al Kakar, retorted, "This is our jihad, not yours. Afghanistan does not want you." Again, Abdul translated for me in English.

By now, however, I had made my point and directly addressed my interlocutor. We began to debate—at first heatedly, then guardedly—about what each of us was doing in Afghanistan, and why. At one point, it even became somewhat of a relaxed conversation. First of all, as I always did when embarking on a religious conversation, I explained that I was *"ali Kitab"*—of the book, the Old Testament. I had been covering the war since the very beginning and had never seen him or any of his colleagues. The Arab glared at me angrily when I pointed out that the French doctors—most of them women, I emphasized—had been risking their lives and helping Afghans since 1980. I also noted that most Afghans welcomed the international aid workers and journalists who had come to their country to help or report.

"Where were you people then?" I could not help adding. "You just throw money and pretend that you are fighting jihad." It was probably not the wisest thing to say, particularly given that they had guns, but I felt compelled to make the point. I could hear a few giggles from the Afghan side as soon as Abdul had translated this. They were delighted with this wonderful piece of trench theater. They clearly did not like the Arabs.

The Arab commander, who referred to me as a *kafir* to my face, claimed that he had been helping Afghanistan since the early days of the Soviet-Afghan war, but that he and his men were now fighting as part of the jihad. "Afghanistan does not matter," he said. "It is Islam that matters." Raising both hands to the sky while peppering his discourse with Koranic references, he explained why he and several thousand other militant Arabs and other Muslims had descended on the region: "We are here because of Allah. The Afghans are our brothers of Islam, but we are here to fight all our enemies. Americans, Russians, Israelis . . . " By now, our discussion had become like a contest, each with our own team of supporters holding the rear, listening and commenting among themselves on what was being said.

The tall Arab continued. "We are here to release our brothers from East and West. We have to show them the true Islam. Many are uneducated and do not know the true path. This is our duty in the service of Allah, the all-merciful."

We talked for nearly an hour. By then, Steve had returned and I was wary of overextending my discussion. The atmosphere was still tense and could easily deteriorate. I told the Arab that it was time for us to go and I wished him goodwill with his jihad. But as I moved forward to shake his hand, he stepped back, refusing to touch it. "Ah well," I sighed. "You see, you keep saying how uneducated these Afghans are, and what poor Muslims . . . But for me, these people are true human beings. They understand civilization, hospitality . . . An Afghan, even if he dislikes you, will always shake your hand. That is the difference between them and you. That is why this is such an extraordinary country and why this extraordinary people will never be like you."

Of course, I was saying this for the benefit of the Afghans standing behind me, but I also meant it. Throughout my years of reporting in Afghanistan, I had almost always been welcomed with exceptional hospitality. Whether in comfort or under fire, I had shared tea, food, and water with my Afghan hosts—and even slept in mosques at the request of villagers struggling to survive in a war-torn country. I wanted to mention this to the Arab and was tempted to add that I had probably spent more nights sleeping in a mosque than he had, but decided that might be a bit too childish—and dangerous. Under the extreme rule of the Taliban during the late 1990s, to allow a *kafir* to sleep in a mosque was unacceptable. But that was because the Taliban, too, were abandoning their traditional forms of respect and benevolence toward strangers.

However, now standing at the front lines near Jalalabad, I realized that this was the first time that I ever felt uncomfortable in Afghanistan. As I turned to leave, the Arab shouted after me, as if none of our conversation had ever happened. "If I see you again, I'll kill you. Don't ever come back." I ignored this. Waving my hand with a slight nod, I walked away.

A week later, I was back with Tom Woods, the tall, blond American producer from upstate New York based in Paris. Together, we would be filming for the *NewsHour*. This would be his third time to Afghanistan; he'd first come here in 1980 to film a French cross-border aid agency, and then had come for NBC News to shoot the new Russian war. It had been a nasty experience, with a Soviet tank firing directly at the TV crew. Shaken, Tom had not been back since, but over time he developed a strong feeling that we needed to make a good documentary report on what was happening to this country after nearly a decade of war. Given our tight budget, we quickly trained Abdul to become Tom's assistant, teaching him how to hold the microphone or deal with lights and batteries.

We first spent several days filming around Asadabad and Chagaserai. I also wanted to visit the massacre site at Kerala, which I had never seen before. We did the usual stand-uppers and cutaways, plus spent a day filming the bazaars and the surrounding villages. By then, Asadabad had become, once again, a bustling town with traders setting up new businesses almost daily. Sitting at large outdoor tables in the warm sun, we drank tea in the main square watching the taxi services of minivans and pickups shuttle fighters to and from the front lines. Several years later, this same square was destroyed by a massive bomb set off by unknown assailants, killing and wounding scores. Some thought the bombers were the communists; others blamed Hekmatyar.

As before, we headed down the main road toward Jalalabad, filming as we went. At one point, we halted at a large guerrilla compound for tea and to do some shots. Suddenly a stocky guerrilla with a thick black beard saw Tom and immediately went over to hug him. This was the same man who had helped Tom and the NBC team film back in 1980. Safi, a former teacher, was now a commander. He arranged for us to meet with the mujahed *shura* of commanders at the front. They could help us get anything we wanted, he maintained. He also sent several of his men with us to ensure that we were properly treated.

At the *shura* command post, we stopped for the night. Over dinner with about twenty commanders and their aides, they briefed us on the situation at the front, noting that the PDPA forces were fighting far harder than they had expected. "Now that the *Shouravi* have gone, they cannot rely on outside help," said the lead commander. "They're afraid we'll kill them. But if they are good Muslims, we'll treat them well. They will have nothing to fear." Sitting with the group were two men who were clearly not Afghan. The style of their haircuts and darker, South Asian features gave them away.

"Are you Punjabi?" I asked. They both smiled awkwardly.

"No, we're Afghan," one of them said quietly in English.

"Really? But you don't speak Pushto?"

The Afghans looked at them with grins. They were, of course, Pakistani military advisers, probably ISI. They were already in the process of seeking to organize the guerrilla offensive against Jalalabad, which, they hoped, would propel Hekmatyar into power. At least half the commanders of this frontline *shura* were Hezb. The rest were Jamiat, Khalqi Hezb, and Harakat. For months afterward, I would encounter ISI Pakistanis along the border areas and inside Afghanistan with the mujahideen. We asked them where we could film on the front line without running into the Arabs. I did not consider it a good idea to suddenly appear with a television camera. When I mentioned my concern, the commander shot back angrily: "This is Afghanistan and it is our country. These Arabi don't tell us what to do. If we want to take you there, we'll take you there!"

The next morning we piled into two pickups and drove toward the front. I realized that we were heading to precisely the same place I had visited before with Steve McCurry. The only difference was that this time, the area was being heavily mortared. I could see the plumes of dust and smoke rise from the other side of the river near the orange tree plantation. Sometimes the bombs struck the river, sending high fountains of water. I also noticed that the mortaring was creeping steadily closer.

Arriving at the front-line trenches, I warned Tom to be discreet. He flicked on his camera, but kept it at knee level as if carrying it, yet filming as he walked. Suddenly we heard a deep shout. "I told you not to come back!" It was the tall Arab. Wearing a beige *shalwar-kamiz* and white headscarf, he was walking toward us with a bevy of armed fighters with him. He was also looking very angry. He demanded to know why we had returned.

"Not good, not good," muttered Tom.

All the Arabs were now shouting at us—and the Afghans—for having dared to come back. The Afghans shouted back. Within seconds, all were pointing their weapons at one another. At that moment, the tall Arab noted the red recording light on Tom's camera. He walked up to Tom, demanding: "Why are you filming? I know that you're filming. Turn that camera off." This was no unsophisticated Arab who did not understand the workings of a TV camera. Tom tried to deny it, but carefully cut off his camera. "These are crazy people," he said, turning to me. "We'd better go."

"Who are you calling crazy?" bleated a fat Arab with thick curly hair. "Who are you calling crazy?" He cocked his Kalashnikov and thrust it into Tom's back. The situation was getting completely out of hand. At the same time, I could not help noticing that the mortars were moving closer and closer—and these people couldn't give a damn. More than anything else, however, I feared that shooting would break out between the two groups. I was certain, too, that Tom and I would be the first to be killed. I had managed to make it this far through the war and was now going to be gunned down by a bunch of mad Arabs.

At that moment, our Afghan commander stepped in between the rival groups. He held up his hands. "Stop, stop!" he appealed in Arabic and Pashto. "This is not good for Islam. We must stop. We are brothers of Islam."

All the fighters were still pointing their weapons at one another, but the shouting had subsided. Two mortars exploded less than 150 yards away. I glanced at the vehicles, wondering whether we would have time to jump in and head out before the bombs came closer. The commander shouted something to one of his men, who immediately began ushering Tom and I toward the pickups. Several of the fighters climbed in with us, still pointing their guns defensively at the Arabi. The other Afghans began backing away toward the remaining vehicle. We lurched forward and careened down the track just as two more mortars crashed in the same place where we had been parked, showering earth and stones on us. The other pickup, now jammed with the remaining mujahideen, appeared not to be touched and pulled away.

Both Tom and I were shaking. We had not expected this. I had been in touchy situations before, but this was the first time that I had felt death so close, and only a trigger away. The Arabi were mad enough to kill us, even at the risk of being gunned down themselves. They wanted the pure satisfaction and honor of having destroyed an infidel.

As we jolted back, deep in our thoughts, we passed an ICRC clinic in a mud-and-stone compound. A Red Cross flag was flying from its roof. An ICRC Land Cruiser with a high antenna was parked outside. This forward medical base must have been set up that morning, because we had not noticed it coming out. I stopped the vehicles and told the commander that we needed to warn the Red Cross people. They would be killed if they went to the front with such heated tempers simmering in our wake. We turned around. Two Swiss delegates with ICRC badges came out, and we shook hands. I told them about the Arabs at the front line. "They'll kill you if they see you," I warned.

"Oh no," insisted one of them in English with a strong Swiss-German accent. "You see, we're ICRC."

"I don't think they give a shit who you are. You're foreign and that's enough."

We later heard that the two aid workers had ignored our advice and driven up toward the front lines. Their Land Cruiser was shot up, and they barely escaped with their lives. Farther down the track, we stopped again, but this time at the orders of the commander. He gestured to me. "Come and look."

We walked into an arid cornfield still littered with bits of husk and stubble from the previous harvesting. It was then that I saw what he wanted to show me. Mummified hands, feet, and other pieces of human bodies sticking out of the ground. "Khalqis," said the commander. There were about sixty bodies here, he explained. The Arabi had captured the government soldiers and had executed them here in the field, he said, slashing his finger across his throat. "They slit them. With knives." He paused with disgust before adding. "You don't kill a man like a dog. You shoot him." I was never sure whether he opposed the killing of prisoners, some of whom had been hapless conscripts, or whether he simply abhorred the method used.

Tom and I decided that we had enough for our report. The incident had so shaken us that we figured we would be tempting fate if we stayed longer. We bade farewell to the commander and his men. He was furious at the way we had been treated by the Arabs. The Afghans considered this an affront to their honor. Several days later, a force of heavily armed mujahideen returned to the front and arrested half a dozen Arabs. According to the information I received weeks later, but which I have never been able to confirm, the Afghans executed the Arabi by shooting them as a warning. One of the key factors was that these Islamic foreign legionnaires had not only insulted and threatened us, their guests, but had shamed them as Afghans.

We drove back toward the border. The vehicle, however, had to return to Asadabad, so we walked the last few miles. We would pick up a "taxi" on the other side. As we trudged up the mountain, it began to snow. The huge, wet flakes partially obscured the hills and forests around us. It was exquisitely beautiful. The track, now muddy and slippery, was crammed with a constant flow of traffic: pickups, men, horses, and donkeys heading in both directions. Much of it carried mujahideen deploying toward the front. But more Arabi were coming in, all heavily armed. Some shouted at us, making vile gestures with their hands.

It was then that I noticed three or four trucks grinding up the hill in low gear toward the Pakistani side. They were packed with women and girls. Each one was guarded by one or two armed fighters sitting at the rear. As the vehicles drove past, the women, wrapped in dark shawls and blankets, stared at us blankly. What was strange was that none of them was covered. Being a heavily Pushtun and conservative region, this was what one would normally expect. I turned to one of the mujahideen walking next to me. "Khalqi zan, Khalqi women," he said in Dari, making a sexually jerking gesture with his arms. "Karachi. Arabi . . . "

I later confirmed this with Abdul. What we were witnessing was the human trafficking of sexual slaves, in this case the womenfolk of the Khalqis who had been captured or killed by the resistance and the foreign Islamic legionnaires. The Arabs were forcibly taking them back to their own countries. The Pakistanis were fully aware of this trafficking, as were the Americans, but no one dared bring pressure on the Saudis or the jihadists to stop it. They were the booty of war. Tom managed to grab a few shots before they disappeared into the tribal area. This blatant trafficking, which we and other journalists highlighted, never really became an issue except in the reports of select advocacy organizations, such as Human Rights Watch.

On reaching the border, we decided to talk with the Pakistani officers at the picket fort observing the Afghan side. There was no risk in being arrested, and we wanted to broach the topic of the Arabs. One of the Frontier Scouts escorted us up. When we reached the post, which directly overlooked the frontier barrier, we found three Punjabi officers—a major and two captains—intently watching the Pakistan-India cricket match on a small black-and-white television powered by a car battery. They immediately invited us for tea, offering us seats to watch the cricket. This was far more important than monitoring cross-border movements into Afghanistan.

I recounted what had happened and asked why Pakistan was allowing all these Arabs to enter Afghanistan. The major immediately and good-naturedly denied this. When I pointed to yet another group of Arabs walking across just below us, he said: "Oh, those are Afghans, Pushtun people. They look very similar."

No, I insisted, they're Arabs.

He shook his head. "You're mistaken."

When I referred to the women being trafficked, he again denied this. "They're simply refugees returning to Pakistan."

Obviously, they were under orders to shut their eyes to such movements. We thanked them for tea and headed down to Nawagai. Once in the main bazaar, we piled all our equipment in one place to wait for the Afghans to return. They had gone back to their homes to drop off their weapons. I sat down next to our gear to write up my notes from the past day. It had been a rough twenty-four hours. Tom wandered off to look at the gun shops.

So intent was I with my writing that I failed to notice the tumult that had begun to erupt around me. I heard shouting and looked up to see a man's finger pointing angrily in my face. A group of men were screaming at me in Pushto, clearly accusing me of something heinous. I kept hearing the word "*kitab, kitab*"—book, book. The crowd kept growing. Some of the men were making slicing gestures with their fingers or shaking their fists at me. I had no idea what was going on. Abdul had still not returned, so there was no one to translate. While I knew sufficient Dari, my Pashto was dismal.

Finally, a middle-aged man wearing a tweed jacket and brown-rimmed prescription glasses stepped up to me.

"Excuse me, sir. But I think it is best that you leave," he said. The crowd quieted down. He was a civil servant on vacation and had come to visit his family in Bajaur, he told me. He just happened to be in the bazaar.

"Yes," I said. "I can see that. But what on earth is going on?"

"Well," he said, enunciating his words carefully, "the fact of the matter, sir, is that these people would like to kill you."

I fully agreed with him, particularly given that at least two men had appeared brandishing swords, while the little boys—who had been crowding around so curiously only minutes before—were picking up stones. It all had the markings of an emerging lynch mob.

"But why?" I asked nervously.

"Well, sir," he began again—I was getting impatient with his studied politeness—"these people—and I have to say they are uneducated people—would like to kill you. They think you are Salman Rushdie."

I was stunned. Salman Rushdie? "But I don't even look like Salman Rushdie!" I exclaimed. Of course, this was when Rushdie, the British-Indian novelist based in London, had published *Satanic Verses*—a thick novel that had upset the Muslim world, causing numerous protests. Pressured by Pakistani radicals linked to the ISI, Iran's Ayatollah Khomeiny had only just declared a fatwa against him, inviting anyone to kill him.

"Well, sir," continued my civil servant friend, "these people see that you are writing in your book. They think you're from London because of your camera. Therefore you must be a writer from London." He gave a theatrical pause. "And therefore you must be Salman Rushdie, and that is why they would like to kill you," he added grandly.

It all made sense. Or sort of. Anyone in the news business had to come from London. The BBC, which most Pakistanis listened to, always opened with the words: "This is London." While these tribesmen had probably never even seen a picture of Rushdie (otherwise they would have realized that his hair was neither curly nor blond), they had listened to the same fire-and-brimstone lectures delivered by every mullah in every mosque in Pakistan. The irony was that I was undoubtedly one of the few people in Pakistan who had actually read *Satanic Verses*. I had already had conversations with Pakistanis in Islamabad and Peshawar regarding the book; none had read it, yet they bitterly chastised Rushdie for his purported blasphemy.

These largely illiterate frontier Pakistanis probably could not believe their good fortune. Here was the very man whom all good Muslims should kill, now standing in their midst clutching a roller pen and a little black notebook. Tom had by now returned and was trying to gather up his equipment just in case we had to make a run for it. The crowd had grown to about a hundred angry, shouting men who were becoming increasingly aggressive. My civil servant friend tried to reason with them, but could not make himself heard above the commotion. I was getting seriously worried. This was not looking good.

Just then, our three Afghans returned, with their guns. They had heard the shouting and had rushed back to grab their weapons. The two gunmen leapt on top of a car and pointed their Kalashnikovs at the crowd. Abdul leapt up with them—bellowing that if anyone dared touch a hair on our necks, they would shoot to kill. The crowd parted, and the Afghans escorted us out. We immediately began searching for a vehicle to hire. The first three drivers, on seeing the melee of angry tribesmen behind us, refused. The fourth agreed, but only if we headed north. He considered it too dangerous to drive through the town. We did not even bother to negotiate a price. We flung ourselves with our equipment into the back and tore off—the crowd running behind us, shouting and throwing stones.

We drove two hours north and then doubled backed via another route to Peshawar. As usual, we had picked up other Afghans—mainly mujahideen—along the way. We were about a dozen when we finally arrived. Tim Weaver, one of my housemates and a British journalist, had just returned from Khost where he had been reporting with Haqqani— the Afghan fundamentalist, supported by the Americans and Saudis, who later created the Haqqani Network operating against the NATO forces out of North Waziristan. He was calmly sitting in bed reading a book. Tom and I walked in to say hello, as did all the Afghans, each filing in to shake Tim's hand.

Tim looked up in surprise: "Ed, who are all these people?"

"Oh, just a bunch of Afghans, but they did save our lives . . . "

Ten minutes later, Mike Malinowski, the American consul, came to the door. I could see that he was fuming about something. "Girardet, what the fuck have you been doing in Bajaur? The whole agency is up in revolt!" Following our hasty retreat from Bajaur, the crowd had rampaged through the town in search of foreigners. They began hunting for aid workers working in the nearby refugee camps. The Frontier Scouts had to be called out to restore order.

Although we had enough material, Tom and I decided to do a bit more filming to finish off the report. The mujahideen were holding a *buzkashi* match to celebrate the Red Army withdrawal, with several hundred horsemen near the Peshawar army stadium. It should provide a superb final touch for the *NewsHour* report, we thought, with thundering steeds and fierce-looking Afghans whipping their way toward the headless torso of a calf. This would represent the spirit of Afghanistan.

We were about to leave when Donatella Lorch of *The New York Times*, whose boyfriend was a Swiss Red Cross aid worker, stopped by with an ICRC vehicle. They could give us a ride. Jolting toward the stadium, I sat behind Dony with the camera across my lap, while Tom preferred to sit on the pickup side in the back. Along the way, we collided head-on with another vehicle. I managed to reach forward and prevent Donatella from flying through the windshield. She still injured herself, but I had dropped the fifty-thousand-dollar camera in the process. It broke in half. Tom struck his head in the back.

Fortunately, there was a US embassy vehicle right behind, which I commandeered to take everyone to the ICRC war surgery hospital. The driver was more concerned about getting blood on the seats than helping. In the end, no one was too seriously injured. But it had been a trying past few days. That evening, I went to the American Club bar—where I chatted with P. J. O'Rourke, the American satirist, who was writing a column about Afghanistan for *Rolling Stone* magazine. He was less intrigued with the crazy Arabs trying to kill us than my being mistaken for Salman Rushdie.

"Yeah," I said. "If I ever do bump into Rushdie, he's going to owe me more than just a drink. I certainly don't want a signed copy of *Satanic Verses*. I've just experienced it."

It was just over a decade later in Pakistan that I met one of the commanders who had been with us in Kunar. The Afghan capital was then in the control of the Taliban; he was working with one of the international aid agencies. We chatted about the Arabi fighting with the mujahideen in those days. Do you remember that tall Arab commander, he asked. How could I forget? I replied.

"Well, that was Osama bin Laden. He was the main Arab in Kunar in those days," he said. "Everyone knew him."

This confirmed what I had already suspected. Following the August 1998 embassy bombings in East Africa, I had seen photographs of the al Qaeda leader. I realized that the tall, arrogant Arab commander we had encountered on the front lines of Jalalabad had to be him. In the late 1980s, of course, there was no reason to know bin Laden. He was just one of those foreign Islamists trying to edge in on the jihad.

What was becoming clear then, however, was that bin Laden and his fellow Islamists were already directing their attention toward the West. Based on my conversation with him, he did not differentiate between Soviets and Americans. They were infidels, and his hatred for each was just as venomous. With the Red Army gone from Afghanistan, the jihad had to spread to new frontiers. This was precisely what many of us dealing with Afghanistan feared. Where do the jihadists go from here? The Afghan war provided them with an invaluable battle experience that they could apply elsewhere—which they did in Bosnia, Chechnya, Sudan, Somalia, the Philippines, the United States, Spain, and the United Kingdom.

Even my friend Tom Woods, no expert on the Middle East or militant Islam, put his finger on the ugly potential of these extremists immediately after our Kunar incident in 1989: "It's really frightening meeting these people. They're the sort of people who blow up planes or plant bombs in airports," he said.

Once the Soviets had gone and the war was more focused on ousting the Kabul PDPA regime, relations between the Arabs and the mujahideen deteriorated steadily. With the taking of Kabul in April 1992, the Afghans expelled most of the remaining Arabs as disruptive, unwanted guests. What many ordinary Afghans had come to understand was that, in the end, the Arabs were no different from the Pakistanis, Americans, Chinese, Russians, Iranians, and other outsiders. They had all come to Afghanistan and the region ostensibly to help the Afghan resistance, but in reality to pursue their own agendas.

The extremism espoused by bin Laden and other foreign militants represented a form of Islam totally alien to Afghan tradition, culture, and religion. But even with the ousting of the Arabs, their long-term influence was not halted. A significant portion of the hundreds of millions of Arab dollars that the jihadists, but also the Saudi government, had poured into the Afghan cause during the 1980s went toward the creation of Koranic schools, clinics, and orphanages in the refugee camps. A whole generation, or two, of Afghans were indoctrinated in the *madrassas*. Even the much-respected Saudi Red Crescent Society was used as a surreptitious front for introducing Wahhabi concepts to the Afghans. By the time many of these young men emerged from the camps, they had lost their sense of what it meant to be Afghan. They provided the new fodder for the Taliban and, eventually, the suicide attacks—which were so un-Afghan and rarely used as a tactic during the Soviet-Afghan war.

For bin Laden and many of his Afghani—as they were called when they returned to Saudi Arabia, Egypt, Syria, or Algeria—Afghanistan had proved a crucial and invaluable experience. But their involvement in forcing the Soviet withdrawal also went largely unrecognized by the Saudi and other governments. This left a bitterness that colored bin Laden's approach to the Western world in the years to come. When Saddam Hussein invaded Kuwait during the first Gulf War, the Saudi government did not turn to bin Laden and his jihadists to engage the Baghdad regime. Instead, Riyadh chose the United States as its ally, inviting it to deploy its troops on Saudi territory.

Bin Laden saw this as a historic betrayal for which he never forgave the corrupt royal family, which maintained closer ties to the Bush family than its own people. Expelled from Saudi Arabia in 1991, he went to Sudan for five years to organize and develop his anti-Western terrorist activities. But he did not forget Afghanistan. With the emergence of the Taliban and its spread across the country from 1994 onward, he foresaw new opportunities with a conservative Islamic movement that could be coaxed with money and other support to provide him and his al Qaeda organization a new base. In 1996, bin Laden returned to Afghanistan.

CHAPTER TWELVE

The Battle for Kabul: A Mad Dogs' War

It was only from the mid-1980s onward that the Soviets began to grasp that Afghanistan was an unwinnable war. The arrival of Stinger and Blowpipe missiles and other forms of outside support for the resistance was having an increasingly devastating impact on their ability to hunt down the mujahideen. Forced to alter their tactics, the Soviets began to deploy more mobile commando-style units. They also introduced equipment specially geared to mountain and desert warfare, such as lighter mortar launchers, plus seismic cluster bombs triggered by vibration along guerrilla trails.

Equally lethal, they adopted more surreptitious approaches, such as the assassination of guerrilla commanders. The Red Army approaches inflicted severe losses among many of the key resistance fronts. By the end of 1985, the mujahideen had lost over half their best officers. Aided by informers and equipped with silencers, Spetznaz were dropped near known guerrilla routes, where they would set up ambushes. Amin Wardak, a noted French-speaking guerrilla commander from Wardak province, said he lost eighty-two men with sixty injured over a single three-day period. They had been attacked at night and did not know they were being shot at until fighters started dropping.

The Soviets also significantly improved their war from the air. While fixed-wing aircraft flew higher to avoid being hit by shoulder-held missiles, helicopters learned to maneuver at far lower altitudes, often hugging the valley floors. The mujahideen could fire up, but not down.

Not to be outdone, the resistance fine-tuned their ability to fight back through more coordinated and better-prepared assaults. They also sought to disseminate intelligence on Soviet operations among other fighting fronts, such as plans to deploy Spetznaz in specific areas. However, given the lack of effective communications equipment, such as two-way radios, such information often arrived too late.

In the north, Massoud's expanding regional alliance was proving far more adept at attacking, and taking, major government bases. In the Central Highlands, the Shiite Hazaras, once the underdogs of Afghan society, were distinguishing themselves as highly proficient combatants. Many tribal Pushtuns were still focusing on traditional hit-and-run attacks, but with limited effectiveness. These commanders made little effort to develop regional strategies beyond their districts and valleys. "Too many groups are fighting a local war," said Peter Jouvenal. "They don't see the importance of moving outside their valleys and hitting targets that count."

Only certain Pushtun commanders such as Haqqani in the Kandahar region or Abdul Haq operating east of Kabul excelled. Haq, a specialist in urban guerrilla warfare, openly admitted that the Soviets had made impressive progress. For this reason, it was crucial to counter the effectiveness of the Spetznaz and other highly professional troops. Haq set up dummy caravans. The reconnaissance planes spotted them, and the Soviets would dispatch their commandos. Haq's men, however, observed where the helicopters were putting down, how many troops were dropped, and the type of equipment deployed. "Then we would ambush their ambush positions," he told me in 1985. The only way for the resistance to say ahead of the game, he stressed, was to concentrate on a real guerrilla war that hit specific military and economic targets. The long-term goal was to force the Soviets to focus their troops on a few main locations, notably Kabul and other cities. Only by increasing their occupation strength from 120,000 troops to figures more comparable with the Americans in Vietnam (550,000) would the Red Army be able to continue operating in the countryside. Politically, Haq believed, the Soviets were unwilling to do this.

Halfway into the occupation, the war had become a gruesome stalemate, with casualties mounting on both sides. Even the efforts by the PDPA regime to develop well-armed and well-paid militia contingents were backfiring. While proficient in maintaining security in the cities, these militia contributed little toward garnering popular support; many became powers unto themselves. In 2010, when the United States and NATO began backing the creation of similar militia initiatives of "local police," observers with experience of the Soviet-Afghan war warned that the West could run into similar problems. Operated by local warlords, such as Abdul Rashid Dostum in Mazar-e-Sharif, they were hated by ordinary Afghans. Nor could they be trusted by the regime. Some made their own deals with the mujahideen. When Soviet support withered in the winter of 1991–92, loyalty to the PDPA dissipated.

Overall, the cost of Moscow's war was becoming prohibitive. Conditions in Kabul and other cities were often better than back in the USSR, with the PDPA government propped up by subsidized food, fuel, and other supplies.

Even more critical, the rising number of sealed coffins shipped back to the USSR could no longer be ignored. Soviet mothers' groups were holding candlelit vigils and singing songs in the cemeteries of Kiev, Vladivostok, Tannin, and Leningrad over the graves of their sons, husbands, and brothers. They were demanding to know why their men had died. As more *Afghansti*—as Soviet-Afghan war veterans were known—returned home, some joined the women at the graves, bringing tales and songs of a futile conflict. Even American Vietnam vets were sympathizing with these former Red Army soldiers by taking up contact and sharing experiences.

Gradually, the Soviet media began to report the war more candidly. My Soviet counterpart, Artyom Borovik, was one of the first journalists allowed to question the war through his front-line reporting. Film footage released on state television was becoming more harsh, including the depiction of Red Army casualties. The reportages, which used to show new Kabul factories or hospitals being opened to the applause of grateful, flag-waving Afghans, had changed. Now they ran combat segments revealing Red Army convoys under attack in river gorges and on mountain passes. Pinned-down conscripts crouched behind road barriers, firing back. With the realities of the Afghan front seeping back, ordinary Soviet citizens were coming to grasp that the much-vaunted internationalist duty of their soldiers was no longer a matter of crushing counter-revolutionary bandits in order to create a new socialist society. The war had become pointless, a lost cause.

None of this, however, did anything to alleviate the draconian nature of Moscow's occupation. Numerous reports were emerging of a systematic terror campaign. More Afghans were being killed and injured daily.

Huge swaths of countryside were rendered uninhabitable as the security forces deliberately destroyed villages, crops, orchards, and irrigation canals. The ICRC hospitals in Pakistan were witnessing a constant rise in the number of wounded, while the French doctors, Freedom Medicine, and other groups struggled to deal with fresh casualties inside Afghanistan itself. "We've never had so many women and children as in the past year," said François Ruffinen, chief ICRC delegate in Peshawar at the end of 1985. "We were completely overrun during the summer . . . we had to set up a secondary hospital tent just to cope."

My repeated trips into southern, eastern, and northern parts of Afghanistan during this period only reinforced my own perception of the sheer brutality of this war. Previously, communist attacks had been directed against communities suspected of supporting the resistance. Journalists and aid workers were now coming back with accounts of assaults specifically targeting fleeing civilians.

I encountered one such incident in the summer of 1984, while traveling through the southern fringes of the Hindu Kush. Some five hundred refugees were making their way from Kunduz province toward Pakistan. Mainly Kandari nomads, they were struggling to cross the fourteen-thousand-foot-high Chamar Pass dominated by the towering snow-covered peak of Mir Samir. They told me that they were leaving because of repeated Soviet attacks against their homes and livestock. The government was also using heavy-handed tactics to press-gang men, both young and old, into the Afghan army. Fathers and sons often disappeared, kidnapped from the fields or in the bazaars.

For nearly four hours, I waited with Peter Jouvenal, Julian Gearing (another British journalist), and French reporter Patrick de Saint-Exupéry as the straggling caravan—spread out over two or three miles and laden with teakettles, pots, rugs, and tents—crept through a narrow defile. We had set up our camera to film as the refugees edged from one valley to the next. Flanked by women dressed in embroidered red dresses and dark shawls shepherding small children, the men prodded reluctant camels, donkeys, horses, and sheep to negotiate the final ten yards. We gave the children sweets. Exhausted, they numbly took the toffees, quietly unwrapped the paper, and stuck them into their mouths. Apart from the shrill whistles and shouts of the drivers or the occasional roar of an affronted camel, the only other sound to mar the tranquility of the sunny afternoon was the constant drone of a two-propeller Soviet Antonov reconnaissance plane.

Once over the pass, the refugees clambered down to the Pashai Valley, a high plateau with a rushing river, where they set up camp. Toward the end of the day, we finally managed to descend into the next gorge. It was then that the first pair of MiG-27 ground attack fighters appeared. Thundering up the nearby Panjshir Valley from Bagram, they swooped to bomb the refugees amassed on the other side. As they drew out, a second pair emerged from behind Mir Samir. For the next twenty minutes, we heard the dull thud of explosions. Our first instinct was to return, but then a unit of guerrilla commandos dispatched by Massoud told us of planned Spetznaz landings on the ridges. Reluctantly, we continued down toward the main valley.

For the next three days, the Soviets bombed and strafed the refugees. The attacks were followed by the dutiful return of the lone Antonov to photograph the damage. Ten days later, as I headed back to Pakistan with Saint-Exupéry plus five Afghan army deserters who had adopted us, we followed the same route. Because of Soviet troop movements, we trekked back up the Chamar at night. The first signs of tragedy were the dead horses and camels at the base of the pass. The people killed had already been buried. By dawn, I reached the summit to discover that the MiGs had attacked the tail end of the very column that we had filmed.

At least forty men, women, and children had lost their lives. Scores more were wounded. I realized that some were those to whom we had given the sweets. I found their wrappers discarded by the trail. The Soviet planes had deliberately attacked the camp with its distinctive black nomad tents, open fires, and herded animals. Each time the swing-wing bombers finished—at first dropping two five-hundred-kilo bombs, then returning to strafe with rockets and 23mm Gatling guns—the Antonov would reappear. There was no way the Soviets could have mistaken these civilians for mujahideen.

One who had witnessed the attacks was Hajii Saduddin from Bazarak, the Panjshiri merchant who had hosted me on my first meeting with Massoud in 1981 and was coordinating humanitarian relief for the resistance. Sheltering with several families at the end of the valley, he immediately began dealing with the dead and wounded. "It was horrible," recounted Saduddin. "We've seen a lot of war but nothing like this. People were screaming and lying all around. Many had lost their hands, their feet, arms, and legs. The tents were burning, and there was an awful smell in the air."

Dozens of mutilated animal cadavers, twisted metal pots, scorched clothing, torn saddles, and a tattered boy's slingshot littered the ground, churned by shrapnel or ripped into long furrows by machine-gun bullets. With the little they had, Saduddin and his fellow Panjshiris helped treat the victims. Then they buried the dead in a yawning bomb crater, covering the bodies with a tarpaulin and piling stones on top in the Muslim manner. A single prayer flag—a green, pink, and orange piece of cloth hanging from a wooden tent pole—and an inscription quoting the Koran marked the massacre. More refugees died of their injuries. We found their graves on our way back to Chitral, the first major town on the Pakistan side of the border.

Later trips in eastern Afghanistan confirmed the same sort of premeditated attacks. By the time the Soviets announced in 1988 their decision to withdraw, many areas had become free-fire zones. The civilians had long since left, so anything that moved was a legitimate target. This included Western journalists and aid workers. Afghanistan remained one of the least covered conflicts in the world, but the presence of these outsiders always stood out as uncomfortable reminders of what was happening.

The Soviets had already succeeded in capturing a well-known French TV journalist, Jacques Abouchar, who had walked into a Soviet-Afghan ambush. First threatening him with death, the Kabul court sentenced him to fifteen years imprisonment for operating illegally inside Afghanistan. Through their ambassadors in different countries, the Soviets made it clear that the next time they might not be so lenient. The message was that the Red Army was now under orders to kill reporters and relief volunteers. This was confirmed to me after the war by a senior Ukrainian officer from the military academy in Kiev. "We knew that you people were in the mountains. We would have lined you up and shot you had we found you" was his chilling assertion.

Improved military equipment and tactics were soon making a crucial difference for the resistance. While not seeking to overrun Soviet bases, the principal objective was to maintain the pressure of a nationwide guerrilla war. Toward the end of 1987, Peter and I accompanied mujahideen descending in captured trucks, on horseback, and by foot to hit communist positions in Nangrahar and Paktia. A striking improvement since the early 1980s, their gear consisted of machine guns, mortars, assault rifles, and a rocket launcher—but no Stinger missiles. Throughout the war I only saw about half a dozen Stingers. In one such operation, the guerrillas wanted to attack a government fort about ten miles southwest of Jalalabad. According to the commander, Mohammed Ashnarar, they did not have enough ammunition to capture it. "We just like to keep up the pressure," he said.

The assault came shortly before sunset. For two hours, a fiery exchange of 107mm Chinese rockets, mortars, and red tracer bullets erupted across the evening sky. A single Soviet tank fired shells in our direction. The guerrillas withdrew for the night, but returned the next morning. The fort had taken several direct hits. Several additional tanks appeared, clattering down the road and lobbing shells as they drove. I would first see the flash of their guns before the shells slammed into the hillside in front of us or whistled overhead, hitting the ridge behind. Not able to move forward or backward, I spent the rest of the morning reading a novel and listening to the history of rock-and-roll on the BBC. Occasionally, I raised myself to see how the attacks were going.

In what proved to be the last big battle involving the Red Army prior to its withdrawal, the Soviets were forced to intervene in the winter of 1987–88 to save the garrison at Khost. Following a three-month siege, the Afghan army was on the point of surrender for lack of food and ammunition. The Soviets had to dispatch thousands of extra troops, bringing the total to nearly forty thousand—as much as one quarter of the entire force in Afghanistan. Over the Christmas period, they sought to clear the eighty-mile-long route between Gardez and Khost. But the road had been heavily mined by the guerrillas, who were rushing in more fighters from nearby provinces, while stepping up attacks elsewhere.

For the Soviets, Khost became a matter of prestige. In the end, however, it only underlined the absurdity of this protracted war. While admitting heavy fighting, the Soviets gave the operation massive coverage on the home front. The Soviet public viewed evening news broadcasts that bragged that fifteen hundred Red Army commandos had been deployed to inflict severe casualties against the mujahideen. Some reports maintained over two thousand guerrillas were killed.

Proclaiming victory, the Red Army eventually reopened the road. The communists may have broken the siege, but as a major operation to crush the insurgency, they had achieved nothing. Hezb (Khales) commander Maulawi Jalaluddin Haqqani, a favorite of the CIA and ISI and later head of the anti-US Haqqani Network, finally captured Khost on April 11, 1991. Little fighting was involved. After negotiations with the Afghan army garrison, the mujahideen entered the city. It was the first major population center to be captured by the resistance prior to the fall of Kandahar, Jalalabad, and finally Kabul.

By the late 1980s, the Soviets were exploring how to extricate themselves from their hopeless war in Afghanistan. With the UN-sponsored Geneva Accords, which were signed bilaterally on April 14, 1988, by Pakistan and the communist government of Afghanistan with the United States and the USSR acting as guarantors, the Soviets were able to start their pullout. They achieved this in less than ten months, with the last Red Army soldier crossing the Oxus River on February 15, 1989.

Although the Geneva talks paved the way for the Soviet withdrawal, they completely failed to take into account on-the-ground realities. The Pakistanis, Americans, and Soviets were all making deals but neglected to include the Afghan resistance—which rejected the agreement. "The big problem as I see it," noted Mohammed Eshaq of Jamiat-e-Islami, "is that Pakistan will decide what they think is best for the Afghan people. We are the ones who have been fighting this war, not the Pakistanis. Afghans have the right to a peaceful and new future." The talks also failed to involve Iran, China, India, and other key regional players. "It's as if the Vietnam peace talks had not included the Americans or the Viet Cong," noted one West European diplomat.

Resistance commanders, such as Abdul Haq, warned that only with a comprehensive agreement could future war be avoided. "It is not just a question of the Soviets leaving," he said. "It is what they will be leaving behind." Some guerrilla representatives stressed the need to consider the nature of government to be established once the Red Army pulled out. A few even hinted at a willingness to accommodate former PDPA members as long as they accepted Afghanistan's "true interests." These could include "good Muslims" and members of government who had helped the resistance, among them select senior PDPA officials. Others maintained that only the "heirs" of the jihad had the right to run Afghanistan.

The Geneva Accords encouraged the government of former KHAD chief Najibullah, who had replaced Babrak Karmal as president in May 1986, to seek the creation of a broader government that might appeal to ordinary Afghans tired of the war. To achieve this, he announced a unilateral six-month cease-fire. This put the Peshawar parties into an awkward position. They realized that they could not ignore Najibullah's offer, particularly as he was trying to involve the former king. They also knew that many people were open to compromise if it promised to bring an end to the turmoil. Numerous urban Afghans, too—the very people with the qualifications needed to help rebuild the country—were suspicious of the mujahideen.

UN special negotiator Diego Cordovez hoped that the mujahed parties would agree to some form of shared interim government with the PDPA, but this proved wishful thinking. "The Geneva Accords proved little more than a sham and a disaster for any possibilities for long-term peace in Afghanistan," recalled American international law expert Charles Norchi in 2011. While the Peshawar leaders discussed various options, they failed to come up with anything substantive. As for the inside mujahideen, they condemned the accords as "unjust" and "unrepresentative" and hence incapable of ending the fighting.

However, the possibility of a compromise agreement lingered. It was an option that needed to be considered, particularly if the only future proposed by the Pakistanis, with Saudi backing, was a new regime to be headed by Hekmatyar. Some feared that Hekmatyar might pursue a double track of fighting the Kabul regime militarily, while seeking to do his own deals with the PDPA police and KHAD. In this manner, if and when he came to power, he would have a repressive security apparatus already in place.

The Soviets recognized that pulling out of Afghanistan with nothing left in its place would leave a political mess that would reverberate for years, if not decades. Moscow could not afford to have an Islamic catastrophe on its doorstep. The Soviet glasnost leader, Mikhail Gorbachev, admitted that although Afghanistan had become his country's "bleeding wound," he also believed that it should be considered a global problem. He appealed to the Americans to work together to prevent even greater catastrophe. The Reagan administration refused to budge.

Select US intelligence, State Department, and USAID officials warned Washington that Afghanistan could not simply be abandoned. "It was not that we weren't telling the US administration what was going on, and more importantly, what could happen. The information was there, staring them in the face, but they chose to ignore it," one former American intelligence analyst told me in 2009. A USAID source acknowledged back in 1988 that few people were under any illusion that the fighting would end with a signed agreement. "Yet, whenever we talk with Washington, they do not seem to understand that," he complained.

While the resistance political parties talked of setting up a temporary government in the "liberated" areas, the bulk of the country's by now estimated 850 guerrilla "commanders of the interior" were in the process of strengthening their own local and regional fiefdoms in preparation for the Soviet departure. The concept of a coordinated and united approach for a new Afghanistan was crumbling.

Following the Soviet departure, the mujahideen succeeded in pushing back the Afghan communists. The various guerrilla factions captured numerous front-line positions, often because the PDPA troops, most of them conscripts, had crossed over to the mujahideen side. These defections were based on intense negotiations between the two sides, sometimes via radio or loudspeakers. The government soldiers wanted to ensure that there were no Arabi among the mujahideen. Word of massacres perpetrated against captured PDPA troops by the foreign Wahhabi had reached their lines.

Meanwhile, friction among the mujahideen became steadily worse. The term *watandar*, or countryman, which had become so symbolic of unity and emerging nationhood during the Soviet-Afghan war, was fading. Apart from the more enlightened commanders, few seemed to share the vision of a united Afghanistan.

The change in attitude among the mujahideen and the government forces was apparent in different ways. At times, there was uneasy cohabitation. While on the outskirts of Jalalabad in early 1989, I was less than one hundred yards from the nearest government positions. Several armed PDPA soldiers entered my compound. For a moment, I felt my stomach tighten. But the communist soldiers appeared to know the mujahideen I was with. They had slipped through the lines to bring supplies to their families. They shook hands, drank some tea, and headed back. Nevertheless, only minutes later the Afghan commander ordered us to move out. Khalqis, he explained with a grin. Even though he knew them, he did not trust them. The KHAD were offering substantial rewards for information regarding the presence of foreigners. One could not fault a poor conscript for selling out.

For the first time since covering the war in Afghanistan, I felt that I could not trust the guerrillas. The sense of solidarity had gone. Previously, the mujahideen had understood that reporting the war was a crucial part of making their plight known to the rest of the world. I had never worried about my belongings. The only items of value were our cameras and gear, but these we could always entrust to the guerrillas. Two months following the Soviet withdrawal, we were filming in the eastern parts of the country barely five hours' walk from the Khyber Pass. Returning to Pakistan, we traversed the Kabul River with a small ferry, a roughly hewn wooden boat. While waiting for our guide to walk up to the main road (a good hour or two away) to find a vehicle, we lounged by the river drinking tea and sleeping. The commander had shown repeated interest in my battered Sony transistor shortwave radio, my lifeline to the outside world. I had used it since the start of the war. I always kept it in the pocket of my shoulder satchel.

When I woke up, I found the radio missing. I immediately suspected the commander. But I could not accuse him. So I pointed out that the radio was gone. For years, I told him, there had been a sense of honor among Afghans, and this was why I had persisted in reporting their war. If Afghan pride no longer mattered, I said, then Afghanistan was no longer a country worth knowing. With that, I climbed to my feet and headed off along the banks of the river. When I returned, the radio was back in my bag. I never mentioned it again. But this never would have happened during the Soviet-Afghan war. While this may have seemed a paltry matter, it represented a turning point. Afghanistan at the end of the 1980s was entering a new phase. It was an era of greed, selfishness, and lack of respect among Afghans—with regard to not just foreigners but also fellow citizens. The Afghans themselves must shoulder much blame for this period, just as they must for what is happening today.

The main fault, however, lay heavily with the Americans and Pakistanis. Of course, other players ranging from the Saudis to the Chinese were also involved, all seeking to manipulate the Afghans. But the complete abandonment by the Americans of Afghanistan barely two years after the Soviet withdrawal was a key factor. For some observers, this indicated the utter failure of the United States to fathom the complexities of the Afghan situation. As one European analyst noted, it had taken the Americans years to get involved—and then suddenly they knew it "better than anyone else." And yet, in the end, he added, "they understood nothing."

Washington thought it could remove itself from the Afghan scene without any implications for the future. Afghanistan had served its purpose, notably to shove it to the Soviets with their own Vietnam. Suddenly, earlier statements such as President Reagan's December 1985 declaration that "the United States stands squarely on the side of the people of Afghanistan and will continue its support of their historic struggle in the cause of liberty" sounded hollow. Ironically, twenty years later Afghans were wondering whether the Americans would do the same thing again once the proposed NATO deadline to remove all foreign troops by 2014 had been reached.

Furthermore, despite warnings that the current political vacuum would provoke a vicious civil war, the new Bush administration (of the senior George Bush, that is) believed it would only be a matter of weeks or months before the PDPA regime collapsed. Hence, its willingness to continue backing Pakistan's position until a new government was in place. There seemed to be little concern that Pakistan was endorsing a ruthless Islamic fanatic, dictator, and killer as the future head of the country. As noted by American Steve Keller, head of the IRC in Peshawar toward the end of the 1980s, the original idea had been to support the more independent commanders of the interior and eventually cut off the corrupt

Peshawar politicians. Instead, he said, "The United States surrendered to the Pakistanis on every point."

From the Pakistani perspective, there was the belief that with the Soviets gone they could fully manipulate the war in their favor. For years, they had encouraged Hekmatyar to undermine the other resistance factions. "By supporting the fundamentalists, we are artificially giving them an influence which they should not command," complained Bernard Kouchner, who later became French foreign minister, when he was head of the Paris-based aid group Médecins du Monde in December 1987.

Many mujahideen wanted nothing to do with Pakistan's push for victory through Hekmatyar. They deliberately pulled back their forces. What the ISI's meddling showed was that, once again, while outside interests could wreck local aspirations, they did not necessarily control Afghans themselves. The Pakistanis had rented their Afghans for the past decade, but the relationship was now ending. The ISI, however, continued to use every means to bring pressure. When the people of Kandahar refused to accept Hekmatyar, who had sought to make a triumphal entry into their city, the ISI retaliated with a cut of trade and aid flow. This shut down many vital NGO efforts in the region. The United States just stood by and watched.

As for the Peshawar parties, they still had no vision for the future. They were rapidly losing any form of influence inside Afghanistan. Everything they did was based on money and power. As Mohammed Gul, a former civil servant from Jalalabad, told me: "They do not care about the people, only themselves. They make money, have big cars, and are not hungry. They have never fought the war."

A vision was not necessarily lacking among the inside commanders. Some had thought hard about the future. While Massoud's Northern Resistance Council—as his alliance was then called, representing seven different provinces—had always discussed what needed to happen once the PDPA regime was overthrown, it had limited impact among the Pushtun groups to the south and the east. Other factors were also entering the equation. One of the most important was drug trafficking, which had now moved from Pakistan to the Afghan side of the Durand Line. Even though cultivation and production locations had changed their geographic position, the industry continued to be manipulated by the same outside syndicates.

The KGB had been heavily involved in trafficking. Much of this was officially sanctioned by Moscow as a means of subverting the opposition. But some of the agents were also in it for themselves. With the rise of the Russian mafia in the 1990s, many of these old Afghan connections proved good for business. "A lot of the Russian drug mafia go back to the Soviet invasion of Afghanistan," noted one narcotics specialist with the Lyons-based Interpol in 2009. Similarly, opium cartels involving high officials in Turkmenistan, Tajikistan, and Uzbekistan date back to this same period. Russia, however, is now paying for this affliction. By 2010, heroin addiction based on narcotics smuggled from Afghanistan had hit epidemic proportions—with well over 2 million addicts (6 million according to unofficial estimates) out of a population of 124 million. This made the addiction rate eight times higher than in the European Union.

As the walls began to cave in for the PDPA regime, the late 1980s and early '90s were marked by a mad rush among the mujahed groups to garner as much government loot as possible. In June 1988, I traveled up to Jagi in the wake of the PDPA regime's sudden departure from the district—some four thousand army troops, militiamen, and militarized KHAD. They had abandoned their fortifications (spread over six miles) almost overnight. Crates of rocket and mortar rounds, gas masks, field telephones, helmets, mobile kitchens, chairs, tables, ration packs, documents, and a sewing machine littered the ground as groups of guerrillas, some wearing Russian helmets, rummaged what they could. Then, outside the badly scarred buildings that once served as base hospital and cookhouse, they divided their booty.

"We share whatever we find among the seven parties," said Zabid Shahboz, a Hezb (Hekmatyar) commander claiming to be in charge of six hundred men. "We have good unity here, not like in Peshawar." Groups of Afghans swarmed over two dozen Soviet-made APCs, shouting to one another over the roar of the engines as they prepared to drive or tow them away. Several other commanders from other parties standing next to me agreed that they all had good relations. When I mentioned Peshawar, they all laughed heartily as if I had just told a good joke. No one seemed to take the Peshawar politicians—or the Pakistanis—seriously.

It was not so unified a year later when I toured eastern Nangrahar immediately after the Soviet withdrawal. Rival factions in late 1988 had taken the four state-run model farms at Ghaziabad on the eastern approaches to Jalalabad. Established in the late 1950s and '60s with Soviet assistance, these sprawling orange and olive groves, livestock breeding centers, and crop research stations were to serve as agricultural models for the rest of Afghanistan.

When first visited by Western aid workers shortly after their capture, most of the equipment and facilities were still intact. Within months, they had fallen into complete dereliction. While sabotage and aerial bombardments by the Soviets may have caused some of the devastation, the bulk was the result of guerrilla plundering. All usable tractors and harvesters as well as prize cattle had been removed. Gardens shaded by towering eucalyptus trees lay strewn with rubbish—broken refrigerators, smashed furniture, strewn documents, and torn mattresses—while inside the modern, concrete workshops, office blocks, residential buildings, and conference halls, the guerrillas had smashed windows, torn off doors, and used bedrooms as cookhouses with soot-stained walls. Human excrement cluttered every corridor.

When I asked why they had done this, Faqir Mohammed, a local commander, first insisted that the communists were responsible. But then he admitted that they wanted to grab their share. Another commander explained that they had carted off the spoils for distribution among the local population or for safekeeping by the parties. Finally he said: "If we don't take them, the others will." For some concerned resistance and international aid representatives, such forms of infrastructure destruction raised serious doubts about the ability of the Peshawar parties to take over the country. Never before had I witnessed such wanton and rapid ruin, not even in Somalia. It did not bode well for the new Afghanistan.

Meanwhile, the bitterly divided resistance parties continued to grope for a united strategy. Without a government, the commanders of the interior feared that the battle for Kabul and other communist-held cities would be long and gruesome. "We want to avoid what happened in Kunar," commander Abdul Qadir told me as we shared a curry lunch in a small restaurant on the outskirts of Peshawar in early 1989. He was referring to the killing and looting by local tribal guerrillas and Arab Wahhabi. "What is now in the hands of the government belongs to the resistance, so we should be careful not to destroy it." Both he and other commanders were now leaving fighters behind to protect facilities they had captured. They also feared that if the guerrillas behaved badly, they would lose popular support.

A key question was what kind of government a new Afghanistan should have after the formation of a broad-based interim administration. "No one in Washington is really thinking about this," warned American anthropologist Louis Dupree, one of the foremost authorities on Afghanistan not long before his death in 1989. "What I see emerging is a federated system with considerable provincial autonomy . . . a nation based on Islam but not dominated by Islamic leaders." This probably remains one of the most realistic approaches today if Afghanistan is ever to succeed as a workable nation.

By mid-1989, the mujahed factions were in disarray. Still supported militarily and economically by the Soviets with an estimated three billion dollars a year, at least until the end of 1991, the Najibullah regime was holding its own. It had been receiving equipment no longer used by Red Army units in Eastern Europe. Located ninety miles to the west of Jalalabad, Kabul launched a barrage of medium-range Scud missiles against the mujahideen in eastern Afghanistan. While in Kunar, we used to hear them land with enormous thuds farther down the valley. This boosted the morale of the PDPA regime. Defections also dropped. The war entered another form of stalemate.

In true Afghan manner, however, there were divisions within the ranks of the PDPA. In 1990, the Khalqis sought to take control of Kabul through a coup d'état, believed to be supported by Hekmatyar and the ISI, but this failed. Politically, Najibullah was finding himself in an increasingly weak position. The Soviet Union—already in the process of collapsing—was unable to continue with its economic aid. There were severe food and fuel shortages in Kabul. With Moscow out of the picture, the regime suddenly lacked the means to maintain its costly military apparatus, including paying the powerful militia groups. Factions and militia began to defect.

Whole regions of Afghanistan were now in the hands of the guerrillas. Faced with growing mutinies and defections, Najibullah held UN-brokered talks aimed at a compromise agreement with Massoud. In

March 1992, he agreed to stand down as soon as a neutral transitional government was established. The next day, in a serious blow to Najibullah, Dostum and his militia forces crossed over to join Massoud's coalition. This consisted primarily of three groups. Foremost was Massoud's Jamiat force; the second group was the mainly Shiite Hazara fighters of Abdul Ali Mazari's Hezb-e-Wahdat; finally, there was Dostum's Junbesh-e-Melli-ye Islami or National Islamic Movement. Within days, the mujahideen took Mazar-e-Sharif.

With the UN still seeking a compromise solution, Massoud was rapidly approaching Kabul. Together with some Junbesh forces and his own Panjshiris, he had overrun Bagram air base and the strategic towns of Jabal Saraj and Charikar less than thirty miles to the north. Most of the plains of Shomali were now under his control. He could be inside the capital within two hours. At the same time, Dostum's forces were quickly moving toward Kabul airport.

Meanwhile, in an operation planned by the Pakistanis, Hekmatyar had moved his forces to the south of the capital. PDPA forces were now defecting en masse to different resistance factions. Each of the guerrilla leaders had his own contacts and cultivated defections in his favor, often along ethnic lines. Officers and civil servants within the Ministries of Defense, Foreign Affairs, and Education dominated by the more educated Parcham, many of them Tajiks, tended to prefer Massoud. The Pushtun Khalqis within the Ministry of Interior were more amenable to Hekmatyar. Dostum, too, had his own former relationships and drew the Uzbeks and Turkmen. The great majority of ordinary Kabulis, however, seemed to prefer Massoud as the least of all evils. For many, the Lion of Panjshir was still a legend and a hero.

On April 15, Najibullah resigned. But in a last ditch attempt to work out a deal, he tried to meet up with Benon Sevan, the UN representative, who had flown into Kabul airport. Najibullah still believed that he could play a role in the new Afghanistan. He drove out to the airport in an armed convoy, but found his way blocked by Dostum's forces. They had already reached the main road leading into the city and probably would have killed him.

Najibullah headed to the UN compound near the French embassy. Later, once Massoud had entered the city, he protected Najibullah when rogue mujahideen sought to capture the former Afghan president. Massoud foresaw the possibility of bringing in Najibullah, whom he had known since their youth, as a possible partner for a future government of national unity. Najibullah was still a popular man among many Kabulis. In fact, in 2011, many Kabulis were looking back nostalgically to the Najib period as one of peace and security. Prior to fleeing the capital as the Taliban approached in late 1996, Massoud offered Najibullah safe passage. The latter refused, fearing that this might be misinterpreted by the Pushtuns, who provided much of his dwindling support. However, once the Taliban were in Kabul, they arrested, tortured, and shot Najibullah and his brother, Shahpur Ahmadzai, before hanging them in front of the presidential palace.

By mid-April 1992, Hekmatyar had still not given up on capturing Kabul. He had made deals with the Khalqis, who began letting Hezb fighters into the city. On April 24, as Hekmatyar prepared to enter the capital and set up offices at the presidential palace, the northern troops rapidly moved in. Massoud's coalition took most of the ministries and attacked Hezb forces entrenched at the Ministry of Interior and the presidential palace. For the next two days, there was bitter street fighting and shelling. By April 27, Hezb forces were edged back into the southern suburbs, but still within artillery distance of the downtown area. Hekmatyar was never able to make his grand entrance.

On April 26, 1992, the resistance politicians-in-exile finally announced a new power-sharing agreement, the Peshawar Accords. Initially, this was supposed to consist of revolving presidencies, with Mujaddedi appointed for the first two months. Rabbani was next, ostensibly for four months. A *shura* was supposed to select a transitional government for eighteen months, followed by elections. Rabbani, however, succeeded in having his mandate prolonged, much to the anger of the other parties. The post of prime minister was handed over at Pakistani and Saudi insistence to Hekmatyar, but he never dared enter the capital for fear of being assassinated. Instead, with his headquarters at Char Asyab to the south, he proceeded to launch another campaign to take the capital. Massoud was appointed minister of defense but agreed to stand down in a bid to encourage agreement among the feuding politicians.

Within days, all the different mujahed parties had entered the city.

The PDPA regime had collapsed and the Afghan capital was now firmly in the hands of the guerrillas. There was relatively little damage to the city itself. Within less than a week, however, the Battle for Kabul had resumed, with different factions fighting over local turf. Heavily armed gunmen prowled the streets, defending their city blocks against rival and often ethnically opposed groups. Terrorizing the population, they looted houses and stores—killing and raping the inhabitants, regardless of sex or age.

As head of the northern coalition, Massoud could control his own fighters but not those of his allies. The Wahdat fighters established themselves in the southwestern part of the capital in districts where there was already a strong Hazara civilian presence. Dostum's unruly Uzbeks knew the city well, having protected it while still in the pay of the communists. They immediately moved into different sectors. As for Hekmatyar, he still had designs on taking the capital. By early May, his forces were heavily shelling Kabul.

The Northern Council's rule of law was chaotic. Factional rivals within the PDPA administration, particularly the Khalq, had deliberately released the estimated twelve thousand prisoners languishing at Pul-e-Charkhi prison. While the majority were political detainees, three to four thousand were common criminals. Many were armed, and they mingled with the mujahideen. They were responsible for a significant proportion of the horrific abuses committed against the civilian population. Among the worst offenders, however, were Dostum's own Uzbeks.

The Battle for Kabul represented the culmination of the long-standing rivalry that existed between Massoud and Hekmatyar. The others were side players. Pushed by the ISI, Hekmatyar proved more determined than ever to play the spoiler if this was the only way to achieve his goals of a strict Pushtun-dominated Islamic emirate. The Americans could only look on helplessly. As one senior US diplomat in Islamabad admitted: "Afghanistan was landed with a powerful, well-armed, and artificially created Frankenstein over whom no one has any real control."

For the next four years, the jihadists fought bitterly over Kabul with a merry-go-round of constantly changing alliances. Sayyaf's Ittehad, which was based in Paghman to the west, initially joined Hekmatyar in his shelling of the Afghan capital. Six months later, in November

1992, Sayyaf changed his support to Massoud—while Wahdat went over to Hezb. This was later followed by another Massoud alliance with Wahdat. By January 1994, however, Dostum's Junbesh had joined with Hezb-e-Islami, resulting in even more bloody fighting. Caught between all these was Kabul's hapless civilian population of two million.

In the summer of 1993, Christophe de Ponfilly and I traveled to Kabul to shoot a documentary on the city's spiraling madness. We flew into the Afghan capital in early July on Ariana Airways, which (according to Western drug enforcement agencies) had been running narcotics to Czechoslovakia during the Soviet period—but was now back in operation as part of the new government. Despite the rocketing, regular flights carried backpack tourists traveling from Paris and London via the Afghan capital to Delhi. Somewhat to our embarrassment, Massoud had sent an official car to pick us up and bring us straight to one of his guesthouses in Wazir Akbar Khan, the diplomatic quarter of Kabul. While certainly intending to meet with him, we had hoped to remain more neutral in our approach. We wanted to visit other leaders, notably Hekmatyar.

The purpose of the film was to explore why such carnage was being visited on the Afghan capital. Throughout May 1993, Hekmatyar's Hezb had been lobbing up to a thousand rockets and artillery shells daily at the mainly northern districts, where most of the government ministries were located. The southwestern part of the city, the Hazara quarter, became the front line. Since early summer 1992, whole swaths had been devastated by street fighting and long-range artillery duels. Huge parts of the Old City looked like Dresden, with shattered buildings and strewn rubble. According to the ICRC, as many as twelve thousand people, most of them civilians, had been killed since the mujahideen first arrived. Another sixty thousand had been wounded. By the time the Taliban pushed out the jihadists in November 1996, the death toll had risen to over fifty thousand.

Elsewhere in Afghanistan, however, cities such as Herat had managed to avoid major ethnic, tribal, or religious strife. Only in Kandahar had limited clashes broken out between Jamiat and Hezb fighters in August 1993, resulting in over a hundred deaths. For the Kabulis, the only logical reason for such unbridled destruction was that it had become a war of total madness, a "ludicrous battle of the chiefs" as one Afghan doctor described it.

Madness was the word that kept cropping up in all conversations. "We have all left our senses," said one mujahed in a lively *chaikhana* filled with fighters near the Ministry of Finance. "We have become a people of madness."

During the three weeks we were in Kabul, a relative lull had descended. Only occasional flurries of rockets could be heard, primarily in the front-line areas. Wandering groups of fighters on the outskirts were continuing to fire their long-range weapons against the besieged capital or at one another. It did not matter where the rounds landed. It was only toward the end of our visit in early August that the shelling started again in earnest. One morning just before five o'clock we counted sixteen incoming (plus several outgoing) rockets that crept closer and closer. Christophe and I lay in our sleeping bags trying to judge from the shaking of the windows whether to take cover under the concrete stairwell.

On so-called quiet evenings, according to Peter Stocker—the robust, long-haired, "seen it all" ICRC chief delegate whom I had last met in Mogadishu—at least a thousand Kalashnikov rounds were being fired over the city. "Everything becomes relative the longer you see this stuff," said the German-Swiss relief representative. "It is hard not to become cynical. The abnormal becomes normal." The ICRC and MSF were the only two humanitarian organizations to remain in the city during the most bitter days of shelling in the Battle for Kabul.

One night, I was having dinner with a dozen Red Cross workers, men and women, most of them Swiss aid veterans from conflicts elsewhere. Listening to rock music, we drank red wine and sat outside by the unused swimming pool in their shared compound. The main discussion was the war. While chatting, I watched fascinated as orange tracers streaked across the night sky. Most mornings, the Red Cross people found two or three spent rounds in the pool. It was difficult to determine whether they were being fired in anger or boredom. For most of the armed groups, the only way to resolve disputes was by the Kalashnikov, machine gun, or tank. Every day, the few hospitals operating had to deal with the innocent victims of "stray bullets." "We only shoot up in the air," explained one Jamiat commander. His men laughed when I dared suggest that bullets must also come down.

When it came time to return to our guesthouse just behind the US embassy, Christrophe and I groped our way back through dark, empty streets—swearing as we tumbled into potholes and shell craters. Every two or three hundred yards there was a checkpoint manned by one of the factions, sometimes Dostum's Uzbeks, sometimes Massoud's Panjshiris. It was well past curfew. Every time we approached a barrier, sometimes just a row of stones across the road or (if more elaborate) barbed wire, we could just make out the fighters with their RPGs. We put our flashlights Halloween-style up to our faces, loudly shouting *"A Salaam Aleikum"* and *"Kharbarnigar."* Journalist. The Junbesh fighters were largely illiterate, and we always guffawed as loud as we could to show that we were having fun and therefore not hostile. They usually laughed back, but I was always concerned that they might think it amusing to fire a bullet or grenade at us.

The irony of Afghanistan's nearly decade-long occupation by the Soviets was that Kabul itself had suffered little damage. In the months that followed the arrival of the mujahideen, their infighting had inflicted more death and destruction than occurred during the entire Soviet-Afghan war. The shelling forced tens of thousands to flee. Refugee encampments sprang up in the "safer" parts of the city, which were never really safe. The rockets could hit anywhere. Some refugees took over former schools, government buildings, and residential compounds on barren hillsides and on the dusty plains of Kabul.

For those who knew the city, the devastation was heart-wrenching. Once pleasant suburbs lay abandoned, the house interiors burned out, corrugated iron roofs torn and twisted as they banged in the hot summer wind. Collapsed or shrapnel-pocketed walls overlooked ordnance-littered streets. Shells, used or live, lay everywhere. The only inhabitants in the battered southwestern sectors were armed fighters and a few scattered families or caretakers willing to risk the daily threats of war to prevent looting.

Numerous symbols of the Afghan capital's once sophisticated past lay wrecked. The ruined University of Kabul, situated in the Shi'a-controlled Wahdat zone, served as a base for front-line mujahideen. Even the nearby Kabul Zoo, formerly a favorite outing for Kabulis, was torn apart by rockets and shrapnel. Held by Massoud's government forces, it pathetically boasted a neurotic lioness, a brown bear, two Himalayan bears, three ragged vultures, a wild boar, an emaciated tiger—and a shrieking, traumatized baboon. Later, there were tales of Taliban feeding prisoners to the lion and tiger. At the start of the recovery process in 2002, the renovation of Kabul Zoo was one of the first—and best-funded—projects to be undertaken, largely supported by a concerned, animal-loving British public.

Farther down the road into no-man's-land, the former Soviet cultural center had become a concrete wreck with a collapsed auditorium. The polytechnic college, also built by the Soviets, on the other side of the city's bullet-riddled grain silos and the Intercontinental Hotel, stood out as little more than a torn and empty shell. One of its professors took me on a slow, sad tour of its vandalized buildings—marked by smashed windows, broken doors, and floors lined with looted or ruined equipment, furniture, and books. It was as if those who did this wanted nothing to do with education. "I can understand, maybe, the need to fight from behind walls, but to deliberately destroy books? What have we come to? What madness are we embracing?" the professor said, tears welling in his eyes. "This is our country's future, but we haven't even got a present."

Many residents showed little love for the mujahideen, particularly the brutish Uzbeks from the north. While some had formerly supported Massoud, I detected a distinct nostalgia for the Soviet occupation days. "At least we had security then," a female teacher said. Food had also been available, and people were not being constantly robbed by armed men. Maybe for some, the city's senseless destruction had a rationale. But for most, the Battle for Kabul encapsulated the incredible single-minded greed for power and financial gain that has now come to characterize so many of Afghanistan's politicians, tribal leaders, guerrilla commanders, and warring groups. This helps explain why so many ordinary Afghans turned to the Taliban as their last hope for an end to the fighting.

During my stay in Kabul, I met with Massoud on a regular basis. The last time I had seen him was in a hidden mountain cave near the Panjshir while being bombed by Soviet planes six years earlier. As de facto minister of defense, he looked tired and drawn. Nevertheless, he retained his normal optimism and determination to continue with his goal—namely, as he put it, "to bring real peace to Afghanistan." For him, the fall of Kabul had come "two years too early." The mujahideen, he said, were not ready to take over. "Nothing was organized properly and there were too many armed gangs acting on their own but in the name of the Afghan resistance." As Massoud pointed out, no Kabuli dared question a man with a beard and a gun. Girls and women could not venture outside unless accompanied by at least two or three male family members.

When asked why he had done nothing about the abuses, the northern guerrilla commander said he fully understood the growing animosity toward the mujahideen. "Many have misbehaved and should be punished, but we have no control over them. They have abused people and wrecked property. There is no proper unity among the mujahideen," he explained.

Massoud did not think much of the Peshawar politicians, but was reluctant to criticize the resistance government openly. Reading between the lines, it was clear that he considered them greedy, irresponsible, and incompetent. Several years later, he told Christophe that in retrospect he should have intervened against the party leaders because they did not represent the Afghan people. However, he added warily, "this would have meant a coup d'état and that might not have been good for Afghanistan."

The reorganized Kabul police force was trying to crack down on the banditry, some of it highly organized—such as car theft, rake-offs, and checkpoint robbery. Corruption was rampant, and there were simply too many guns. While Massoud commented on the lack of rule of law, he did not mention the graft that was already growing among his own entourage, the Panjshiri Mafia. It was only later, shortly before his death, that he regretted not having kept his followers on a tighter rein.

As Massoud but also some of the international organizations realized would happen, there was a severe shortage of Afghans capable of running a government. Most of the high-ranking PDPA officials had long since fled, many of them to India, the former Soviet Union, and the West. Massoud explained that he had no problem incorporating qualified former PDPA members as long as they agreed to work for a new Afghanistan. The overwhelming majority of mujahideen were from rural areas and had learned only how to fight and kill. "It is difficult to teach peace to people who have known war most of their lives," he said. Many commanders, too, he pointed out, "may have proved their worth launching guerrilla operations, but they have little idea how to run a government office."

Despite the fighting, the government was making headway with the UN to provide public services and rebuild the city. Kabul's war was far from over, and yet its inhabitants were diligently rebuilding. The bazaars were bustling once again with goods brought in from Pakistan and the former Soviet Union. Small-scale repairs were being undertaken on Kabul's basic infrastructure. Potholes were being filled in, sewage gutters re-concreted. With the threat of cholera hanging over the city, water engineers were grappling with the overwhelming task of ensuring safe drinking supplies.

Schools, too, were being reopened. Women teachers, in particular, were anxious to have the schools up and running as soon as possible. One of the biggest problems, they explained, was obtaining the salaries, books, and other basic essentials. Numerous qualified teachers existed in Peshawar, but they had to be convinced to return. We stopped by the French Lycée Istiqlal to film the damage. It was considerable, but a French embassy official from Islamabad thought it could be put back into shape without too much difficulty. Pupils were enthusiastically determined to get back to their classes as soon as possible.

Even the city's fire department (headquartered behind the Ministry of Defense) was operational. Its 20-odd firemen wore donated uniforms, including shiny steel helmets and black coats, and their firefighting equipment was a hodgepodge from West Germany, France, Poland, and Czechoslovakia. There were at least four functioning fire engines dating back to the 1970s. Two others had been wrecked by the shelling. Sitting on the fire chief's desk was a gray telephone emblazoned with gold stars. "We respond to fires when the phone rings," he explained with no uncertain pride.

So how often does the phone ring? I asked.

"Oh, it doesn't," he said helpfully. "The phones aren't working." He admitted that they went out when people ran to the fire station for help or if they saw smoke. And then, he added: "It depends if we have petrol." What happens if you don't? I asked. "Oh, we take a taxi," he said.

Despite Massoud's waning popularity, he remained one of the few credible leaders. His guerrilla credentials still held him in good stead with numerous Afghans, and not just in the north. Throughout 1993 and even right up to his retreat from Kabul in the face of the Taliban in November 1996, he persisted with his efforts to broaden the government's base among regional commanders and tribal leaders. Only in this manner, he felt, could he weaken Hekmatyar and bring an end to the fighting. Nevertheless, as he also made clear, a "final" military confrontation with Hekmatyar might prove the only solution. As many Massoud supporters believed at the time, Hekmatyar was the last obstacle to peace. Once he was out of the way, they felt, Afghans could embrace a new future. As usual, however, nothing would ever prove to be so simple in Afghanistan.

As part of our story, Christophe and I decided to follow Suzy Price, the BBC correspondent in Kabul. The BBC's Pashto and Dari services functioned more as a local radio station, even if broadcast from London. One could be sure that millions of Afghans were listening to the station at the same time, every night, throughout the country. No commander's claim of victory was taken seriously until reported on the BBC. Nor would any press conference begin before the BBC correspondent had arrived. For a largely illiterate country, the BBC remained the only authoritative source for news.

As Suzy—an exceptionally courageous young British woman with long, curly hair—explained, she had to be extremely careful about what she and her team of Afghan journalists reported. They had to remain credible. They were out every day reporting. "If there's a bombing and five people are killed, you have to be accurate with your figures. Someone will always find out and then accuse you of getting it wrong or deliberately putting out misinformation," she said.

Planning to head down to Hekmatyar's headquarters south of Kabul, she suggested we join her and Mirwais Jalil, a local BBC reporter, for the trip. They tried to see Hekmatyar at least once every two weeks. After all, he was the prime minister. But this meant driving through the lines. Terence White, the Agence France Presse correspondent, would also be coming. A tall New Zealander with a long beard, gray *shalwar-kamiz*, and a contagious sense of humor, he was having a hard time with the constant pressure and looked forward to such trips as a welcome break. Hekmatyar's comments and lies always made good copy.

We drove there in two four-by-four vehicles with BBC plastered on the side. Not that it made much difference. Most of the fighters could not read, but they understood readily when you told them at the checkpoints. I was quite happy to be hiding behind the BBC, as I was not sure how I would be welcomed by Hekmatyar. In Peshawar, at least there were the constraints of the Pakistanis and the Americans. Here, in the middle of a war zone, he could do what he liked.

On arrival at Hekmatyar's heavily guarded compound about thirty minutes out of the city, we had to leave our vehicles at the gate and walk in. The Pushtun politician was terrified of being assassinated. Massoud never took such precautions—one reason, no doubt, why eight years later he was dead and Hekmatyar was alive. At least two long-range D-30 122mm artillery pieces stood in a field next to the compound. Just then, the Iranian ambassador's black Mercedes flying his country's flag drove in ahead of us. We went up and shook hands, but he was clearly embarrassed to have been seen—and filmed—by a group of journalists. Iran, which was supporting Wahdat, was also a key backer of Hekmatyar's Hezb, providing him with much of the weaponry now being used in the Battle for Kabul. Hekmatyar first met with the ambassador and then had us come in. He greeted Suzy and Terence and proceeded to answer their questions. I sought to remain in the background, keeping my face concealed behind the camera. I did not want him to know that I was there.

My precautions were not overdone. I was part of a 1987 Hezb hit list of a dozen Western journalists. Among these was the ubiquitous BBC correspondent in Islamabad who was branded as "the voice of demon," while I was vilified as "the enemy of Islam." We were warned of "dire consequences" if we did not desist from our "calumnies." These threats proved to be legitimate. A year later, on July 29, 1994, Mirwais (the young Afghan working with Suzy) drove out of the city with a visiting Italian journalist to interview Hekmatyar. The Hezb politician complained bitterly about Mirwais's coverage and threatened him. Heading back to Kabul, their car was stopped by four armed fighters, their faces hidden by scarves. This was firm Hezb territory, so they were almost certainly Hekmatyar's men. They dragged off the twenty-five-year-old BBC correspondent. The next day, his body was found dumped by the road with no fewer than twenty-four bullet wounds.

Christophe and I finally left Kabul in early August with a feeling that this war would drag on for years. From the human rights point of view, all the factions involved in the Battle for Kabul had blood on their hands. All were responsible for the enormous abuses that resulted in thousands of innocent men, women, and children being killed—and huge areas of the capital destroyed. For months on end, meaningless battles erupted over streets and buildings, many turned into rubble with little left to control. Seeking to neutralize the Wahdat forces that had aligned themselves with Hezb, Massoud's troops often fired on anything that moved. For this reason, Massoud, too, bore much of the responsibility for high civilian casualties during this period.

But it was the constant shelling by Hekmatyar that caused the bulk of casualties. There was no question that Hezb forces had intentionally fired on civilians. As one ICRC delegate told me: "It was quite simply coldhearted, terror bombing. There are no other words for this." A 2005 Human Rights Watch report examining the 1992–96 period documented much of this flagrant abuse, which it considered in violation of international humanitarian law. "Conditions were such that anyone in Kabul could be killed at any time, almost anywhere: rockets and shells would hit homes, offices, bus stations, schools or markets," said the report.

In mid-1995, I returned to Afghanistan as part of a trip organized by the International League for Human Rights in New York. The closest I got to Kabul was the western outskirts of Jalalabad. Here the former mujahideen were still in firm control, but the road toward Sorubi was unsafe. Refugees were making their way eastward by skirting Kabul completely and then walking or riding through Laghman to the Nangrahar provincial capital.

By then the Battle for Kabul had turned into a far broader war. Mullah Omar's Taliban had now firmly emerged as a new military phenomenon in response to the rampant insecurity that had raged throughout much of the country. Its largely illiterate Pushtun fighters were rapidly moving against the former jihadists, taking new territory daily. They had already occupied Wardak province to the southwest and had forced Hekmatyar from his headquarters at Char Asyab, obliging him to flee to Sorubi in the direction of Jalalabad. Bin Laden's Arabi were also making a comeback in support of the Taliban, whose principal objective now was to take the Afghan capital.

The war had now spread to Mazar, Kandahar, Badghis, Baghlan, and Nangrahar. The fighting was producing thousands of casualties plus even more refugees, many making their way to eastern Afghanistan. There were also serious food shortages. Hekmatyar's and Dostum's forces, which still controlled the access routes to the north and the east, had blocked the international agencies from dispatching food convoys to the capital. By mid-March 1994, at least two hundred thousand people had fled, while another three hundred thousand were displaced in and around Kabul.

By early 1996, the Taliban were operating south of Kabul, where they confronted Massoud's highly experienced forces for the first time. Massoud still represented a government recognized by the United Nations and most other countries. In a bid to initiate a peace process while still in a position of strength, the Panjshiri leader traveled to Maidan Shar, a largely Pushtun town twelve miles south of Kabul. His purpose was to meet secretly with senior Talib commanders. It was a daring risk. While his safety was guaranteed by traditional words of honor based on the Law of the Pathan, it was not certain that the pledge would be honored. But following talks in which Massoud proposed a joint interim government leading up to democratic elections, he was allowed to return to the Afghan capital.

The Talib leader with whom he had negotiated then sought to persuade his Kandahari allies to accept Massoud's proposal. Instead, they killed the Panjshiri leader's former host for not having executed Massoud while he had the chance. What this showed was that these new Pushtun fundamentalists, influenced by outside extremists, no longer respected the traditions or norms of the past. Over the next several weeks, Massoud's forces attacked the Taliban, inflicting a severe defeat. Nevertheless, months later—with strong support from Pakistan, Saudi Arabia, and al Qaeda—the Taliban relaunched their offensive with massive shelling. The Taliban were believed to have been backed by as many as thirty thousand Pakistani nationals, some unofficially seconded by the ISI as military advisers and active combatants. Bin Laden's organization also helped bring in several thousand foreign Islamic fighters.

On September 26, 1996, Massoud declared Kabul an open city and withdrew his forces to the plains of Shomali and then the Panjshir. As he later explained, the destruction and civilian casualties would have been too devastating had he chosen to remain. On the morning of September 27, the Taliban entered Kabul.

CHAPTER THIRTEEN

The Taliban, Al Qaeda, and the War on Terrorism

The capture of Kabul by the Taliban marked a new stage in Afghanistan's wars. The new Islamic movement had been sweeping up from the south since late 1994, when groups of former mujahideen coalesced around Mullah Omar, an ex-Hezb (Khales) commander, in his home district near Kandahar. Given that these fighters consisted primarily of students and teachers from the Pakistani *madrassas* affiliated with the Jamiat-ul-Ulema-e-Islami party, they called themselves *Taliban*, or Islamic scholars. Many who later joined the movement were former mujahideen, but there were also former Khalqis from the PDPA regime in Kabul.

Ever since the collapse of the PDPA regime, former mujahideen, warlords, and bandits had terrorized whole regions by stealing, looting, killing, raping, kidnapping, and extorting hapless civilians. People were fed up. As an organized body, the Taliban had already existed at the provincial level since the late 1980s. By late 1992, some of the Taliban were prepared to confront the mujahideen militarily, but then opted to give them more time to try to form a common front. Various concerned *ulema* and elders regularly appealed to the former jihadists to halt their excesses and establish a proper government, but to no avail.

Finally, the Taliban decided to respond to the increasing chaos in Kandahar, when the *shura* of ex-mujahideen who had taken the city had fallen apart. Rival groups terrorized the local population with killings, beatings, extortion, and kidnappings. Angered by this anarchy, the "scholars" took physical control of Kandahar city by placing it under a single new authority.

Encouraged by their success, the Taliban announced their intention to restore Islamic law and order throughout the country. The movement quickly gained support, its ranks swollen by new recruits from both sides of the border.

Numbering several thousand by late 1994, the Taliban took Zabul and Uruzgan provinces with little fighting. In a widely used ploy, the movement relied heavily on bribery to convince commanders to join its forces or to step aside. Helmand proved more difficult but soon fell because of tribal rivalries. By January 1995, Ghazni to the east had succumbed. The constantly expanding Taliban were now moving northward toward Kabul. At Maidan Shar, capital of Wardak province, they confronted Hekmatyar's forces, which were forced to pull back. Several key commanders—pressured by the Taliban to the south and east, and Hezb to the north—opted to join the movement. Two years later, I asked one of them, a moderate Pushtun tribal leader from Wardak, why he had become a Talib. He shrugged: "What choice did I have? I had to decide what was best for my people." When these new Islamic forces attacked Kabul, however, they were decisively thwarted by Massoud.

Within the year, however, most of southern and southeastern Afghanistan was in Talib hands. At the same time, when they sought to move into the western provinces in the summer of 1995, they encountered bitter resistance from Ismail Khan—a Massoud ally. His forces even managed to push the Taliban back into Helmand and Kandahar. But the Pakistanis intervened with more weapons and even air strikes. The Afghan truckers and merchants of Quetta, who had been heavily taxed by Khan, poured in funds to buy off commanders. Many who joined the movement did so because it was in their interests, because they had been paid off, or because they had no other option. Talib retribution was harsh when dealing with recalcitrant warlords and brigands.

Overstretched, Ismail Khan was eventually forced to flee to Iran with eight thousand men. Two years later, while regrouping to fight the Taliban in northern Afghanistan, he was betrayed and captured by Abdul Majid Rouzi, a senior Dostum commander who had defected to the Taliban in 1997. In March 1999, however, Ismail Khan managed to escape, eventually exerting his revenge against the Taliban following the US invasion, when he retook Herat.

The Taliban soon seized Paktia and Paktika provinces to the east. They also launched several more offensives against Kabul, but each failed. They then began rocketing the city. The Taliban claimed to be shelling only military objectives, but ordinary people were being killed and wounded every day. International human rights groups believed that, just as Hezb had earlier, the Taliban were carrying out indiscriminate bombardments. Following the Serb siege of Sarajevo in Bosnia, one of the most brutal of any conflict since the end of World War II, a damage assessment showed that 60 percent of the buildings had been damaged. The devastation of Kabul after four years of fighting was far worse. What I saw in 1993 was catastrophic. But when I returned in 1997 with the Taliban in power, aid organizations estimated that as much as four-fifths of the city had been damaged or destroyed. Even more was wrecked when the Americans bombed the capital in late 2001.

Much of the imagery produced by the international media during this second battle for Kabul was deemed simply too horrific to be shown. Filming one seventeen-year-old girl at an ICRC hospital in Kabul in 1996—her legs shattered after stepping on an anti-personnel mine—the BBC's John Simpson maintained that, even though his team had no constraints on what they could shoot, "no television audience could bear the sound of the girl's screams or the sight of her wounds." But the girl's ordeal did not end there. Recovering from her surgery, her face thin and shadowed by pain, the girl realized her future was shattered. "She would always be a burden to her family. She would never be able to marry or have children; the best she could hope for was charity," observed Simpson, who began covering the Afghan wars with the Soviet invasion and remained one of the most enduring foreign correspondents.

The Taliban committed numerous massacres, particularly against non-Pushtun opponents. They were particularly brutal against the Shiite Hazara population whom they considered no better than *kafirs*, or nonbelievers, and therefore not worthy of life. Many Hazaras fled northward to seek refuge within the United Front–held areas. Hezb-e-Wahdat, the main Hazara faction, which had previously fought against Massoud with Hezb, now joined the northern side. Many other groups—including leading Pushtuns such as Abdul Haq, Abdul Qadir, and future president Hamid Karzai—also aligned themselves with Massoud. Allegiances shifted constantly.

For many Afghans, but primarily the Pushtuns, the Kandahari-based Taliban initially had brought much-needed security to their country. Tired of war and lawlessness, people simply wanted to get back to their normal lives. Harsh as these new jihadists were with their radical Islam and shari'a justice as set out by the Holy Koran, the Taliban put a partial end to the trauma that had replaced the Soviet occupation. What these self-righteous Islamic scholars were offering was not only law and order, but a return to the purity of the teachings of the Koran and the sunnah, the practice of the Prophet. From their valleys, farms, and villages, many conservative Pushtuns saw nothing wrong in the Islam the Taliban were imposing. Issues such as women's rights or education for all did not even enter their thoughts. Nor did they see anything bizarre with local militants hanging smashed television sets and videocassettes in the streets like criminals on a gibbet. The Taliban believed that to show the human face on television was to create a graven human image, which was tantamount to idolatry.

The popularity of the Taliban during the first several years, however, was not shared by most urban dwellers and Afghan moderates. These included ethnic groups in the countryside, such as the Hazaras and the Tajiks—traditionally at odds with tribal Pushtuns who make up the bulk of the Taliban. According to Wakhil S., an Afghan senior aid consultant who has worked with the Soviets, Americans, Taliban, and the current Karzai government, the wars in Afghanistan have nothing to do with religion. "All Afghans are Muslim and no man is better than the other. It is about greed, power, and self-interest. After so many years of death and destruction, there is deep frustration among ordinary Afghans, who dislike the foreigners who tell them what to do and the Taliban whom they fear. People are grasping for straws because there is no one to trust. Neither the government, nor the warlords, nor the Taliban. Instead, all they are left with is hopelessness."

Prior to the fall of Kabul, Afghanistan was functioning as an increasingly fragmented state. The country was breaking up into ethnic and tribal components. Local power centers without any central authority were on the rise. Some were controlled by individuals who cared little for their people, while others operated as relatively well-organized mini-states. The breakdown of central control meant that they operated without any outside support other than what the UN or the NGOs could offer.

Afghanistan was also edging toward a north–south divide between Pushtuns and other ethnic groups, a notion pushed by the ISI. Nevertheless, this split was never clear-cut. Pushtun communities still lived in Kunduz and other northern parts, and not all Pushtuns joined the Taliban. Many of the more moderate commanders supported Massoud; so did select fundamentalist figures, such as Sayyaf, who regarded the Taliban as a threat to their own power base.

Most Afghans who supported the Taliban did not necessarily perceive the movement as being foreign-influenced. Few were even aware that the Taliban were being backed, and increasingly manipulated, by the Pakistanis—or that other outside interest groups such as al Qaeda, Saudis, and Qataris were involved. The ISI had abandoned Hekmatyar as part of Pakistan's "forward policy" with Afghanistan when it realized in 1994 that his chances of taking Kabul were slim.

The Taliban, who officially changed the name of the country to the Islamic Emirate of Afghanistan in October 1997, were now officially based out of Kabul. Their main concern was to bring the rest of the country under their rule. In May 1997, the Taliban had sought to capture Mazar-e-Sharif, but were routed with their worst defeat so far. Thousands of their fighters were killed or summarily executed. The Taliban made another attempt in September, but were again pushed back. Nevertheless, they established bases in Baghlan and Kunduz where there were significant populations of "transplanted" Pushtuns.

By 1998, Pakistani and other outside influences began to dominate the overall Talib strategy. The Pakistanis were finally getting what they had sought for so long, notably a Pushtun-dominated government. Thousands more Pakistanis from the Northwest Frontier tribal belts flocked in to help. Entire *madrassas* shut down in order to send their students across the Durand Line to take part in the new jihad. Foreign Islamists, too, were making their way to Pakistan and then Afghanistan.

Bin Laden, who had returned from Sudan, was able to take advantage of the situation by establishing his training and operations bases on Afghan soil. He moved to Kabul, where he took several houses for his wives, and then traveled to Kandahar, where he developed an increasingly close relationship with Mullah Omar. His camps, mostly located around Khost with others later set up in more isolated parts of southern Afghanistan, were geared to training militants in pursuit of his own global objectives. The Americans attacked several of these camps in August 1998 with missiles, following their claims that bin Laden was involved with the US embassy bombings in Nairobi and Dar-es-Salaam.

At the same time, the Taliban phenomenon began to take hold in the frontier areas of Pakistan. Encouraged by the success of the jihad, but also by well-funded Arab Islamists and Wahhabi, the Pakistani Taliban sought to impose their own version of shari'a law on their areas of control. These included punishments such as stoning to death for adultery and the amputation of limbs for criminals. They forced local populations to adopt the Talib way of life, which (for many) was little different from what they had known before. The principal difference, however, was that this outside form of Islam was undermining Pushtunwali. An entirely new generation of rootless "scholars" influenced by a more global form of Islam now considered themselves no longer bound by centuries of local tradition and tribal codes.

By the summer of 1998, the advancing Taliban had finally captured Mazar-e-Sharif, a bustling and relatively well-organized Central Asian city. They murdered over two thousand civilians, mainly Hazaras, in reprisal for their earlier losses. They also shot dead eight diplomats and intelligence officers, and one journalist, at the Iranian consulate. Dostum only narrowly escaped to Iran.

Many people were not aware that the Taliban were entering Mazar until they heard the shooting and saw the telltale white flags on their vehicles. According to Human Rights Watch, the Taliban were involved in what witnesses described as a "killing frenzy." Many civilians were murdered as the Taliban moved through the streets firing machine guns mounted on pickups, just like the "technicals" in Somalia. In the days that followed, the invaders carried out systematic searches for male members of the Tajik, Uzbek, and particularly Hazara communities in the city. During the house-to-house searches, "hundreds of men and boys were summarily executed, apparently to ensure that they would be unable to mount any resistance to the Taliban," the November 1998 Human Rights report *Massacre in Mazar-e-Sharif* noted.

From 1999 onward, the Taliban increasingly adopted a policy of collective punishment against non-Pushtuns. Their destruction of

villages, cultivated lands, and bazaar shops forced massive displace-
ments, with thousands of refugees fleeing to already overcrowded towns
in opposition-held zones. Others fled to Pakistan and Iran, often via the
north to avoid Talib lines.

Humanitarian organizations reported the systematic use of economic
blockades as a means of overcoming resistance. When I traveled to
Hazarajat in 2002, local inhabitants showed me where Talib checkpoints
had barricaded the roads to prevent vehicles or caravans from carrying
food into the interior. Those who tried to sneak past along the nearby
mountain ridges or goat tracks were shelled and even bombed by helicopters and planes, the latter believed to be piloted by the Pakistani air force.

Various international human rights reports refer to one mass killing after another against non-Pushtuns during this period. One was the
Ab Khor-Achabor Massacre on February 2, 2000, when the Taliban
arrested ten men, all civilians, whom they executed with assault rifles.
Only one injured survivor managed to escape and tell his story. Another
was the "Khassar Elders Massacre" on February 12, 2000, when a group
of villagers sought to negotiate security guarantees for the local population but were taken off and shot dead.

Outside Kabul, in the plains of Shomali, the Taliban destroyed
villages and killed or expelled the bulk of the population. Arab militants murdered hundreds of civilians captured in United Front areas,
often by slashing their throats or cutting off their heads. The Taliban
press-ganged thousands of boys and young Kabulis to chop down fruit
orchards and uproot entire vineyards. The latter were considered blasphemous although none were grown for wine. Only during the time of
King Zahir Shah were limited amounts of wine produced.

Despite their brutal activities, many Pushtuns and even the Americans
welcomed the renewed security that the Taliban were bringing to various parts of the country. Since the end of 1995, the United States was
involved in secret negotiations with the government of President Rabbani,
the Taliban, and Dostum's Junbesh for a proposed gas and oil pipeline
from the Caspian Sea and Central Asia region through Afghanistan
to Pakistan, India, and the Persian Gulf. This new project would frus-
trate the route the Iranians were pushing with Indian backing through
their own territory. The project, whose estimated cost was three billion

dollars—plus another two billion dollars to extend it through Pakistan—involved a consortium consisting of America's UNOCAL, Saudi Arabia's Delta Oil, and Gazprom of Russia. The competing Argentinian group, Bridas, was also negotiating with the same parties. The prospects for dealing with a single government commanding firm control over the whole (or at least most) of the country was enticing.

The official US position called for an end to the fighting and backed UN efforts to form a broad-based interim government. Heroin trafficking and opium cultivation had been expanding steadily since the end of the 1980s, with thousands of farmers planting the crop in provinces such as Helmand, Kandahar, and Nangrahar. Afghanistan soon overtook Burma and the Golden Triangle as the world's principal source of heroin. The Vienna-based UN Drug Control Program (UNDCP) estimated the 1996 opium crop in Afghanistan at three thousand metric tons, much of it destined for Europe, Russia, and the United States. The US foreign policy in Afghanistan was focused on "drugs and thugs," as one official quipped.

By early 1996, perhaps regretting America's decision following the Soviet pullout to drop Afghanistan, the Clinton administration began showing renewed interest beyond just a determination to block Iran's efforts to construct its own pipeline. It wanted to see an end to the anarchy and wished to ensure the creation of a moderate regime, which would curb the training of Islamic extremists in the southern and eastern parts of the country. By paying off the Taliban—and with the encouragement of the ISI—al Qaeda and other Arabi (including Islamic legionnaires from countries such as Chechnya, Central Asia, Bangladesh, Indonesia, Turkey, Germany, and Britain) were returning to the region. Washington sought to get back into the game, but this time with a more regional approach.

As Robin Raphel, US assistant secretary of state for South Asia, observed at the time: "We believe the instability in Afghanistan is progressively more dangerous to our own interests. There is a concern it will spill over the borders to Central Asia and Pakistan, and that the poppy growing, the heroin production and the trafficking will become more embedded into Afghan society and the economy." While expressing concern for terrorist training camps in Afghanistan, but also a need for the UN to negotiate with all parties, she did not see a need for a more direct US role. Instead, Raphel foresaw the involvement of a "neutral" force to maintain peace in the event of an agreement.

Congressional conservatives in Washington opposed a UN-led multi-lateral approach. Instead, they pushed for a more unilateral American policy that would address suspicions that Iran was behind the training of extremists in Afghanistan. These same conservative senators and congressmen, many former supporters of Hekmatyar and other Islamic hard-liners during the 1980s, were also advocating the return of former king Zahir Shah as if they had suddenly discovered that he was key to the new Afghanistan. Afghan moderates had been proposing just such a solution less than a decade earlier.

At the same time, a group of American diplomats and scholars were seeking to develop a more coordinated policy with the Russians. Moscow was becoming increasingly suspicious that the United States was tacitly playing along with Pakistan's support of the Taliban, which it saw as another fundamentalist threat to Central Asia. In the end, the US policy proved limp and unimaginative, never contributing to peace in Afghanistan—and ultimately paving the way for 9/11.

Despite the rise of the Taliban, and since the collapse of the PDPA regime, hundreds of thousands of the estimated six million refugees—many born outside Afghanistan's borders—had returned in a bid to reconstruct their country and their lives. Many of the internally displaced also went back to their villages. Huge portions of Afghanistan—particularly in the northeast, east, and south—were actually peaceful.

During the Soviet-Afghan war, travel around Afghanistan was nearly impossible. With the fall of the communists, aid agencies were able to establish more regional operational bases and the UN and numerous NGOs began to set up rehabilitation programs, some with impressive results. This included combating crop infestations by pests and restoring shattered or neglected irrigation systems. In numerous areas, such projects helped bring rural populations from marginal survival levels to food self-sufficiency. Previously only able to work with the mujahideen, the Western aid agencies were now operating in most towns. They were also now involving local populations more closely in their programs rather than just the political leaders or commanders, who had previously skimmed off much of the aid.

Assistance programs could only be implemented in zones where security was good. Countless roads were inaccessible, particularly in winter, or barely traversable because of war damage and neglect. Numerous Afghans lacked the financial means to do any proper rebuilding. Over 60 percent of schools had no walls, and barely one-quarter of school-age boys were able to attend class; for girls, the figure was a dismal 3.7 percent.

Many rural areas lacked doctors and even the most basic primary health centers. Nevertheless, the World Health Organization (WHO), UNICEF, and other agencies managed (with the help of the BBC) to conduct a Mass Immunization Campaign of over two million children against preventable childhood diseases between November 1994 and June 1995, operating in both Talib and government-controlled areas. This involved negotiating cease-fires among the warring factions, reinforced by incessant radio appeals. The guns—which had been raining death for weeks and months on men, women, and children—fell silent, enabling the health workers to jab the long lines of kids who had gathered with their mothers in villages and along roads. "Even the most hardline commanders had families and understood the need for their children to be vaccinated," noted former BBC producer Gordon Adam.

The BBC continued to play a high-profile role in Afghanistan in this period. A radio soap opera, *New Home, New Life*, was created, based on the highly successful post–World War II radio show *The Archers*, initially designed to help British farmers. The Afghan version was a huge success. With the country almost coming to a standstill when the program was broadcast, it was used to promote health, land-mine awareness, agriculture, and reconciliation through "real life" entertainment. When one of its characters had to be killed off because the actor had been granted an Australian visa, people held memorial ceremonies.

Overall, international aid programs for Afghanistan varied enormously from the late 1990s up to the US intervention, in the quality of their design and implementation. The arrival of the Taliban in many communities posed a host of new challenges and predicaments. While certain organizations worked with local communities whether or not they were controlled by the Taliban, other NGOs refused—often primarily because of the movement's traditionalist attitudes toward women.

The Swedish Committee and ICRC, which chose to work on all sides during the 1990s, have proved the most capable of operating in Afghanistan today. Both organizations demonstrated that while the Taliban were difficult, they were not necessarily hostile—nor were the Talib rules hard and fast. There were some perfectly reasonable commanders and progress could be achieved, but it required a lot of legwork. Anders Fange of the Swedish Committee noted that success required constant negotiation to provide at least some aid, even if everyone did not receive it. In this way, the Swedish Committee continued to open and run girls' schools in Talib areas.

The ICRC managed to negotiate the opening of a new hospital in Kandahar with the Taliban's minister of health, Mullah Baluch. A striking figure with a long face and close-set eyes, he wholeheartedly supported grassroots access to health. But he was also a hard-line Talib who advocated the implementation of shari'a, notably the cutting off of hands and feet of criminals. He believed this should be done humanely, and he encouraged Afghan "surgeons" (often little more than barely trained "barefoot doctors") under his control to do the job. The ICRC, which sought to work in Talib-controlled areas, had to deal as tactfully as possible with such extremist individuals without surrendering basic principles.

Some organizations, however, maintained that there could be no middle road. Working with the Taliban, they argued, would condone the implementation of cruel and inhumane forms of punishment, even if the severity and frequency varied depending on local commanders and mullahs. Prisoners were often forced to clear land mines or dig trenches in areas known to be contaminated by ordnance. This resulted in an unknown number of victims being killed or injured.

Unacceptable, too, they pointed out, were Talib attitudes toward homosexuals. Men accused of "unnatural" acts were punished by having a wall toppled over them. If they survived half an hour under the rubble, they would be pardoned. In one case in Kandahar in 1998, three accused were placed under a stone wall that was then knocked over by a tank. All three were alive after thirty minutes, but two died in the hospital later that day. It is not known whether the third survived.

When asked whether there was ever a precedent for this in shari'a law, or even how or why anyone could even imagine such a punishment, a Talib Ministry of Information representative in Kabul told me in 1997 that he considered it appropriate. When I asked him why not amputate a limb or shoot the man, he seemed shocked. "No, that is not a correct punishment for someone who commits blasphemous acts," he said sternly. I was tempted to question him further as to the hypocrisy within the Taliban itself, particularly given the reputation of Kandaharis within Afghanistan—as also extolled through renowned poems—for homosexuality. Many tribal Pushtuns, including Taliban, traditionally indulge in sexual acts with young boys brought into the family compound specifically as servants or to provide favors. However, I thought it prudent not to pursue this form of questioning.

Until May 1996, UN efforts at mediation among the different Afghan factions had foundered under the largely lackluster leadership of Mahmoud Mestiri, the UN special envoy for Afghanistan. A Tunisian political appointee and crony of UN secretary general Boutros Boutros Ghali, he had managed to alienate rather than bring together Afghan rival leaders and parties. As the Taliban secured new territory and the fighting became more intense, the UN had to do something about stimulating renewed global interest in Afghanistan.

By then, I had started my own organization, the International Centre for Humanitarian Reporting (later Media Action International), and soon UN representative Alfredo Witschi Cestari approached me in Geneva to see whether the center could help put Afghanistan back on the map. I had set it up as a means of promoting the use of credible media to highlight critically humanitarian action. Cestari viewed this to be an initiative organized by an independent outside group unhindered by political constraints. I suggested holding a two-day brainstorming session in Switzerland with experienced Afghans and expatriates. Held in the Lake Geneva town of Morges with about thirty experts who knew the country well, we pragmatically explored different aspects ranging from how to work with the Taliban on women's issues to helping better inform international workers, diplomats, and journalists about Afghanistan itself.

One of the projects to emerge was *The Essential Field Guide to Afghanistan*, designed to inform the international aid community working with Afghanistan. The Morges initiative helped stimulate other long-term goals, such as the need to involve credible media, like the BBC and VOA, more directly as a means of promoting mediation among the belligerents. This could be done through practical information outreach aimed at making fighters and local populations more aware of on-the-ground humanitarian needs.

When the Taliban took Kabul in the fall of 1996, a whole new set of rules began to apply. For sophisticated Kabulis, but also other non-Pushtun ethnic groups, the arrival of the Taliban was bad news. The Taliban immediately began enforcing new edicts, which basically cut off more than half the population, notably women, from normal life. They also persevered with their war against Massoud and his United Front forces. Talib troops, reinforced by growing numbers of foreign Islamic legionnaires, ground their way through central and northwestern Afghanistan—massacring Hazaras and burning villages.

In the summer of 1997, I returned to Afghanistan to research the *Essential Field Guide.* Together with my co-editor Jonathan Walter—a cheerful and unflappable former British Gurkha officer, who had been working in humanitarianism for the past several years—we flew from Peshawar to Kabul on the daily ICRC plane. Our goal was to visit as much as possible of Afghanistan. In Kabul, we stayed at the BBC house and spent weeks interviewing international aid workers and Afghans.

The Taliban we encountered in Kabul were haughty, but also clearly uncomfortable in this urban environment. At the Herat Restaurant opposite the Park Cinema, one of the first cultural centers to be closed down by the new occupiers, I watched as a group of Taliban sauntered in with their black turbans and sat down at a special area at the far end. The locals simply ignored them.

As journalists, we had to register on arrival with the Ministry of Information, which then issued us with a long list of what we could do and not do. No photography, no reporting of military targets, no playing of music, and no secret interviews with women. A special feature of the regime was what we referred to as "Tali-Bans," decrees issued by the Religious Police, otherwise known as the Department for the Promotion of Virtue and the Prevention of Vice (or Amr Bei Maruf wa Nai Az

Munkar). Some were incomprehensible and would have been amusing had Talib rule not been so vicious and repressive. The "Tali-Bans" included, verbatim:

> **To prevent sedition and female uncovers:** No drivers are allowed to pick up female who are using Iranian Burqa (chador). In the case of violation the driver will be imprisoned. If such kind of female are observed in the street, their house will be found and their husbands punished.
>
> **To prevent keeping pigeons and playing with birds:** This habit/hobby should be stop. After ten days this matter should be monitored and the pigeons and other playing birds should be killed.
>
> **To prevent kite flying:** Advise the people of its useless consequences such as betting, death of children and their deprivation from education. The kite shops in the city should be abolished.
>
> **To prevent washing cloth by young ladies along the water streams in the city:** Violator ladies should be picked with respectful Islamic manner, taken to their houses and their husbands severely punished.

Absurd as these decrees were, they deprived ordinary Afghans of their traditions and basic rights. Not able to travel alone by taxi meant that women, particularly those without menfolk such as widows or wives whose husbands were imprisoned, could not travel across town. The decree regarding young ladies not being able to wash clothes by village wells or street gutters (often the only source of running water) meant that many households could no longer have clean clothes.

According to the Kabul foreign correspondents, however, the farther away from Kabul, the easier things got. The front-line fighters at the base of the Panjshir Valley even begged to have their pictures taken. They all played music. The rules did not stop us from meeting with female aid workers and recipents, including widows, at meetings organized by the relief agencies. They were eager to speak and discuss their survival strategies.

Afghanistan's women had much to be demoralized about. The negative impact on their lives was immediately obvious to anyone traveling to Talib-controlled areas during the late 1990s. Shattered, bereaved, and often disabled by years of war, many women coped silently with post-traumatic stress. They struggled daily to feed their families and to keep them warm in the freezing winters. Officially prevented from going out unless accompanied by a male member of the family, women were barred from schools, universities, and employment.

The Taliban intimidated women if they stepped out of line. The fighters, who patrolled the streets in vehicles with Kalashnikovs, would not dare to touch them physically. Instead they would announce over loudspeakers that the women should go home. Only expatriate female aid workers could show their faces, but few dared walk in the streets for fear of being jeered or spat on by the fundamentalists.

Not unlike the mujahideen and Arabi during the latter years of the PDPA regime, Talib forces abducted women, particularly among non-Pushtun populations. Well documented by human rights groups, the fundamentalists coerced families into handing over their daughters for forced "marriages" to Talib soldiers. Furthermore, they kidnapped or detained men and women (based on their ethnicity) for ransom. Al Qaeda and other foreign Islamic legionnaires engaged in similar behavior by absconding with women and girls for onward shipment to Saudi Arabia and the Gulf countries. Some were taken to Pakistani tribal areas, where they were forcibly kept for personal use by Arabs, Chechens, and others who had settled there.

Once in Kabul, the Taliban immediately started to close down schools and women's development programs. They threatened women who persisted in working, and the aid agencies that insisted on employing them. This meant that professional women, such as teachers and secretaries, could no longer hold jobs—even if they were the sole bread-winners. While some organizations deliberately modified their activities as the Taliban requested or bargained and compromised with the Taliban in order to remain operational, others refused.

One organization to continue operating in Talib-controlled areas was MSF. A combination of isolation, destruction of health services, and appalling health care for women led the international medical organization to establish a primary health project in southwest Afghanistan's Uruzgan province in the Pushtun heartland.

From the outset, it was clear that the Taliban were not interested in initiatives that focused on women. In Uruzgan, where traditional Pushtun culture is strongest, most families observed purdah. They sequestered women from the onset of puberty for the rest of their lives. As British doctor David Wickstead (who had been working in the region for MSF Holland) noted, opportunities for women to leave the family compound were limited. Education outside the home was virtually unthinkable. "Women are meant to be seen only by the men of their immediate family and should never be seen, much less medically examined, by another man," he observed.

The challenge in Uruzgan was that most health workers had either fled the Taliban, or preferred to stop working for "cultural reasons." In an effort to encourage at least some of the women health workers to return, MSF brought in two expatriate midwives plus two female health workers from Jalalabad. This prompted several former employees to come back. Even though they could only function out of specially walled-off compounds, this limited initiative made a marked difference for improving health care. Without MSF, there would have been no clinical support for women and children at all. Many Pushtun families would have preferred to see their women die rather than have a male treat them.

Even if the Taliban had brought improved security to the region, Wickstead pointed out, "anarchy, violence and repeated robberies do nothing for under-five mortality rates or the health of children." Some officials were more liberal or cooperative than others, but Talib policies changed repeatedly. This forced the aid workers to constantly work out new ways of providing relief.

The question of whether to work with the Taliban or not posed a severe predicament for the international community. Some organizations, such as Save the Children (SCF)–UK, opted to partially or fully suspend their operations in Talib-controlled areas. In Herat, SCF pulled its support for schooling programs in areas where girls and women were denied access to education. It also halted its non-emergency initiatives where female employees were prohibited from working. Angela Kearney, a New Zealand nurse and SCF's Herat representative, pointed out that after working for fifteen years in war zones, she had never expected such restrictions imposed on her by the Taliban. "When you are banned from a meeting to discuss humanitarian aid because you are a woman, there is no escape. Experiences like these introduced me to the realities of the powerlessness of women in Herat," she said.

SCF, which had been operating in Pakistan since 1980, had opened its Herat office in 1994. For Kearney, it was exciting to be working with local communities to build rural primary schools. "The people were so positive about making a difference in their lives. Parents had hopes for progress and development for their children," she noted. And this despite often traditional opposition to the construction of girls' schools in isolated rural areas. Many teachers, too, were women.

All this changed radically with the Taliban. They closed all the girls' schools in Herat and, with female teachers banned from working, even boys were suddenly denied education because there were no more teachers. Mullahs and fundamentalist "scholars" often stepped in to meet the demand, but many of these could themselves barely read or write. In January, the Taliban issued a decree banning all women from working except in the health sector. If they persisted, the new regime warned, the women would be punished according to Islamic law.

Collaboration between SCF and the Taliban became impossible. Overnight, SCF could no longer talk to women. Unable to employ female translators, local women could not share their ideas with international staff. Nor could Afghan men and women meet for professional purposes unless they were family members. Furthermore, many women, such as widows with no means of support, could no longer take part in income-creating programs.

Forced to deal with men only, SCF felt that its humanitarian and development initiatives failed to benefit the community as a whole. One example of this, Kearney noted, was the need to discuss where to place a village well. The men proposed the mosque. However, because women in many parts of Afghanistan were banned from the mosque, they would not be able to benefit from the new clean water source. As the traditional water carriers, women and girls would have to continue collecting their water from the old polluted sources.

Despite such problems, Afghan women were still finding ways to demonstrate their courage, resilience, and even resistance. It was the female students of Malalai High School in Kabul who were the first to demonstrate against the communists in the late 1970s. Many believed that the international community should not give up on Afghanistan, even if it meant working with the Taliban. As Dr. Shaiza, a Soviet-educated female physician and a widow, pointed out to me in Kabul, "the Taliban are very ignorant people. Even with all their restrictions, they cannot put us down. What they don't realize is that we can work against them while working with them, subverting them every day in the smallest of ways. Just because they are now in control, we shouldn't give up."

In the end, it was the reaction of Western women's and human rights groups that severely curtailed international aid operations in the country, and forced numerous agencies to reduce operations. As pointed out by some international relief representatives, this overwhelming focus on women's issues only made life more miserable for ordinary Afghans—particularly women. Vital projects were closed down because they were linked in one way or another with the Taliban.

It was time for Jonathan and I to leave Kabul. Our findings were depressing, and I was eager to start writing about Afghanistan under the Taliban. What we did not know, however, was that we needed to have exit visas in order to leave. On the morning of our departure, we dutifully headed out to the airport to catch the ICRC flight. When we tried to board the plane, the police informed us that we did not have proper stamps. With a dismissive wave, the Talib official ordered us to return to the city. We would have to apply for a visa the next morning at the ministry. As we sullenly watched the ICRC plane taxi down the runway, I decided there was no way that we were going to be defeated. "We'll take a taxi and drive to Pakistan," I told Jono. I was sure the border guards at Torkham had no idea what an exit visa was.

Our usual driver was more than delighted to do the trip. The Pakistani gate closed at 1600 hours, so unless we intended to spend the night out in the desert, we needed to make the journey in less than six hours. It was doable, but only just. The road trip gave us a chance to see the countryside. For me, it was the first time that I'd traveled along the "tar" since my first venture into Afghanistan as a journalist in October 1979. All my journeys since had been by foot. As I had suspected, no one on the Afghan side even checked our passports. The gate had just closed—I had forgotten about the time change, half an hour ahead of Afghanistan—but one of the Pakistani Frontier Scouts opened a side portal to let us in. We passed through immigration and headed down to Peshawar.

For the next three years, until the summer of 2001, I remained closely engaged with Afghanistan, but primarily from my home base in Europe or in neighboring Pakistan. The biggest problem was getting a Talib visa. After publishing the *Essential Field Guide*, my organization set up a radio program with the BBC Trust—Radio Education for Afghan Children (REACH), a distance education initiative deliberately tailored to help educate girls unable to attend school. Broadcast by the BBC's Pashto and Dari services, it provided homeschooling out of the firing line of Talib dictates. Books were smuggled in to accompany the programs, and were even brought in from Peshawar by Talib commanders who wanted education for their own children, including girls.

As the aid community sought innovative ways to provide support to the beleaguered population, Massoud continued his military struggle against the Taliban. Although ostensibly serving under President Rabbani in Faizabad, the Panjshiri was the de facto leader of the north. By now, very few Talib victories were based purely on combat capabilities. Most military advances were due to the Talib ability to buy off commanders still fighting with Massoud. The Pakistanis, the Saudis, and bin Laden himself ensured that the flow of cash and weapons continued and that Talib coffers were bulging. They even tried to bribe Massoud with promises of positions of power—first as prime minister, and then president.

By 2000, Massoud was trying to persuade the West to understand that without Pakistani support, there was no way the Taliban could continue. Despite repeated denials, Pakistan had backed the offensive against Mazar-e-Sharif by sending in advisers to plan the operation. Saudi Arabia, too, provided pickup trucks, communications equipment, and money. By exposing Pakistani support to the outside world, Massoud felt, Islamabad would be forced to withdraw its overwhelming backing for the Taliban. Without ISI backing, there was a good chance that the Taliban would begin to fall apart. Such appeals, however, fell on deaf ears.

Western journalists continued to visit the north, and their reporting was largely sympathetic to Massoud's war of resistance. While admonishing the Pakistanis in private discussions, the US government under President George W. Bush, however, was reluctant to confront the Saudis for fear of damaging relations. Largely because of the pressure brought about by the women's and human rights groups—but also the failure of the rival petroleum consortia, UNOCAL and Bridas, to make any headway with the oil and gas pipeline—Washington's ability to influence Afghanistan had severely weakened.

In January 1999, the Clinton administration imposed unilateral economic sanctions against the Taliban, but this proved a largely decorative measure that only affected international aid operations. Nine months later, the UN Security Council imposed limited sanctions through Resolution 1267, demanding that the Taliban end the use of Afghanistan as a base for international terrorism and hand over bin Laden. This included a freeze on Talib assets and an international ban on their aircraft, notably Ariana Airways. The Security Council imposed further sanctions in December 2000 (Resolution 1333), including an arms embargo and travel restrictions for senior Talib officials.

Pakistan, however, chose to ignore the resolutions and continued to transport weapons and ammunition shipments across the border. According to Human Rights Watch, these consisted of as many as thirty trucks a day in April and May 2001, with some convoys loaded with artillery shells, tank rounds, and RPGs. On Vice President Cheney's orders, the US government also provided the Taliban with a grant worth forty-three million dollars. While US attorney general John Ashcroft later relentlessly pursued the "American Talib" John Walker Lindh, a twenty-year-old Californian, as its scapegoat for consorting with the enemy, no action was ever taken against those within the Bush administration who supported the Taliban financially or with other means—including American intelligence "observers" operating with the ISI. With the young American Talib sentenced to twenty years imprisonment coupled with a gag order, the Walker Lindh affair has been considered by some legalists as a shameful and politically inspired travesty of justice by the Bush administration. In 2011, he was still lingering in a federal prison.

By now, most of Massoud's own outside support was coming from the Russians and Indians, with a limited dribble provided by the United States, France, and other Western countries. Cracks, however, were beginning to emerge among the Talib fronts, with some commanders deeply resenting the continued dominance of the Kandaharis. They also disliked the incessant expanding of Pakistani and Arab involvement in their movement, which they found derogatory. Furthermore, the Taliban were increasingly distancing themselves from ordinary Afghans, including those who had initially welcomed the Islamic "scholars" during the early and mid-1990s.

The overall situation for Massoud began to look exceptionally bleak in 2001 as fighting spread toward the northeast of the country. At one point, the Lion of Panjshir had to retreat from his former military headquarters at Taloqan, capital of Takhar province, to Khoja Bahauddin along the Tajikistan border. Time appeared to be running out. The front line had now moved well beyond the outskirts of Taloqan to the low mountains and dry riverbeds to the east.

Elsewhere, the behavior of the Taliban was increasingly outraging the international community. Two years earlier, Hezb-e-Wahdat forces had sought to retake the central province of Bamiyan—but their resistance eventually collapsed, forcing them to retreat to the more isolated areas of Hazarajat. The Hazaras repeatedly tried to regain their lost areas. Then on December 29, 2000, Hezb-e-Wahdat recaptured the Hazara town of Yakaolang, which was retaken by the Taliban a week later. According to human rights reports, they executed 176 men in reprisal for having risen against their Pushtun occupiers. In early summer 2001, the Hazaras again took Yakaolang only to see it fall five days later. Fighting continued, and the Taliban were forced to retreat again. As they left, however, they adopted a "scorched earth" approach by burning over four thousand houses, shops, and public buildings. When I visited the region in 2002, I could still see the scorched villages, farms, and bazaars.

One of the most heinous acts of deliberate destruction by the Taliban was the blowing up on March 11, 2001, of the world-famous seventeen-hundred-year-old Bamiyan Buddhas. Not unlike the Serb shelling ten years earlier of the historical port city of Dubrovnik during the Balkans War, it was, as one UNESCO official described to me, akin to "slashing a woman's face" to show one's contempt by destroying what is dear and beautiful to a country's culture. The rocketing and then dynamiting of the 180- and 125-foot statues shocked many, including numerous Afghans. Despite countless appeals, the Taliban persevered until they had rendered the sandstone effigies to little more than rubble and dust.

Public outrage at the shattering of this irreplaceable world heritage was still not enough to persuade the American and European governments to adopt a firmer position with regard to Afghanistan's plight. It was then that Massoud was persuaded to make his first trip to Europe to personally alert the international community. Speaking to a European parliamentary group in Strasbourg, he condemned the destruction of the Bamiyan Buddhas and warned that Islamic extremists were preparing a significant strike against the West. He also went to Paris to meet with members of the French government, but was not formally invited by the Elysée Palace. In addition, he held secret meetings with US officials, where he made clear his position, notably the urgent need to pressure Pakistan to halt its connivance with the Taliban. "The Taliban would not last a year without Pakistan's support," he said. He also warned of an impending attack by al Qaeda against the West.

While his visit was regarded as a success, he privately noted that he was disappointed with the lack of a decisive response by Europe and the United States. Christophe de Ponfilly, who met with him, said that Massoud had been somber about his meetings. It was only on September 10, one day before the attacks against the World Trade Center, that the Bush administration agreed to militarily intervene against the Taliban unless they handed over bin Laden.

Looking back, it appears obvious that the events of 9/11 or the current NATO war might have been avoided had Washington taken firm steps against Pakistan for its direct military involvement in Afghanistan. What was clear in the summer of 2001 was that the Bush administration, despite all the intelligence at its disposal, lacked any sense of vision for dealing with Afghanistan and the entire region.

By early summer 2001, I was preparing to make another big trip to Afghanistan, this time for *National Geographic* magazine. I was planning to cover both sides of the war. Following months of waiting, I finally received my visa to cover the Talib side and I was looking forward to writing a comprehensive story that might finally engender US interest in the country. But first, I made arrangements to visit the north in order to meet with Massoud and explore his own views of what was happening in the country.

I never got the chance.

CHAPTER FOURTEEN

Enduring Freedom: Missed Opportunities and the New Occupation

---

"What have you learned since the British and Soviets invaded this country during the nineteenth and twentieth centuries?" I asked a British colonel on the tarmac of the former Soviet air base at Bagram north of Kabul.

"Never to occupy Afghanistan," he replied.

His American counterpart, an army colonel, pondered the question. "We're here to do a job. To bring peace and stability to this country. And to do whatever it takes."

—Bagram, northern Afghanistan, April 2002

Officially, America's longest war began on October 7, 2001, when US and British warplanes started bombing suspected Talib and al Qaeda positions in Afghanistan. In reality, it started when the United States began supporting the mujahideen, especially the extremists, and engaged with bin Laden. Washington's "war on terrorism" has become a full-fledged counterinsurgency and the country has descended steadily into chaos and insecurity that is far worse than during the Taliban.

Washington's "Operation Enduring Freedom" purportedly aimed to punish the Taliban for welcoming those suspected of involvement with the 9/11 terror attacks. More specifically, its declared objective was to capture bin Laden and put out of action the training camps and operational bases believed to be preparing future assaults against the West. By collaborating with the United Front (Northern Alliance) forces, the military Coalition also intended to help install a more moderate, broadbased, and (above all) Western-style government in Kabul.

Perhaps the most glaring weakness of this strategy was the role of Pakistan and Saudi Arabia. Neither Washington nor London sought to admonish publicly the Islamabad government for its backing of the Taliban and al Qaeda right up to the time of the US invasion. This support enabled bin Laden and thousands of other foreign Islamic legionnaires to operate on Afghan territory. Nor did the United States reprimand Saudi Arabia, which had recognized the Talib regime. Furthermore, many questioned whether the United States really was intent on capturing bin Laden given the awkwardness of relations during the 1980s.

For many Afghans, however, the Western intervention promised the possibility of a peaceful resolution, once and for all, to over two decades of war—which had already cost over 1.5 million lives and destroyed much of their country. As during the Soviet invasion, much of the world's mainstream media had descended on northern Afghanistan as Coalition warplanes pounded the Taliban in the fall of 2001. Although several media outlets such as Fox TV broadcast propaganda-style coverage, others including Britain's BBC, ITV, and Sky TV—as well as German, French, and other European networks—were of a far higher standard. The Arab network Al Jazeera also provided interesting perspectives, which one simply did not see on Western television. This was possibly a reason why the Al Jazeera news bureau in Kabul received a direct hit by a US missile in November 2001. No one was hurt and US officials apologized, claiming that they had believed it to be a "terrorist site."

On the morning of November 13, 2001, Peter Jouvenal, the BBC's John Simpson, ITV's Julian Manyon, and other Western journalists entered Kabul at the forefront of the United Front troops. Two days prior to 9/11, Peter had been in Peshawar negotiating with the Taliban to set up a BBC office in Kabul. When news of the terrorist attacks came through, Peter immediately began preparing the logistics for its coverage over the next three months.

"As we drew nearer to the city we could see the grim evidence of battle," reported Simpson as he traveled with Peter and the BBC team. "The roads were littered with the bodies of former supporters of the Northern Alliance who had switched sides and joined the Taliban—no mercy for them."

Thousands of jubilant United Front troops surged toward the capital, but were ordered to halt as part of a deal with the Americans not to move beyond the outskirts. Most obeyed, forming a gigantic traffic jam of troops, tanks, trucks, and APCs. The journalists continued on foot, even ahead of the troops. They were welcomed by rejoicing people shouting "kill the Taliban." Most Taliban had fled, but lying in the streets were the bodies of foreign Islamic legionnaires, mainly Arabs and Pakistanis. Particularly loathed by the Afghans, they had been lynched or shot. On a hillside above the city, shots rang out as soldiers hunted down remaining Taliban. The men surrendered and were led away to face Northern Alliance justice. Many were executed.

With the Talib regime gone, I was keen on returning to Afghanistan as soon as possible. I wanted to set up journalism programs as part of an international initiative to develop a new and independent Afghan media. Like everyone else, I assumed that with the Taliban gone, and al Qaeda dismantled, a new and open government would be installed to oversee a vibrant recovery process.

The international aid community was also stepping up operations. My wife, Lori—an American aid worker and former journalist from Indiana—and I decided to move to Islamabad. She was working with WHO, while I would represent Media Action International plus continue with my reporting. We rented a large house in a pleasant, leafy suburb, sent our two children to the international schools, and proceeded to take turns traveling between Islamabad and Kabul.

In December 2001, the German government asked me to take part in the Bonn Conference on Afghanistan. Held under UN auspices, this brought together donor representatives, independent experts, and prominent Afghans to decide on a plan for the new Afghanistan. I was part of a group that would explore the constitutional and legal aspects. On December 22, the conference inaugurated a thirty-member Afghan Interim Authority (AIA), which would operate with a six-month mandate. This would be followed by a two-year Transitional Authority leading to a Loya Jirgha (Grand Council) and the country's first free and fair elections. The Bonn Agreement also proposed the creation of a NATO-led International Security Assistance Force (ISAF), which would help oversee security as well as begin the long process of building up a new Afghan army and police.

It soon became apparent that the Bonn accords were establishing a highly centralized government, with a top-down framework that was putting back into place a lot of the old players (former mujahed politicians, warlords, imposed outsiders, drug traffickers, and so on). Unfortunately, Afghans had little confidence in the old crowd of politicians. The Peshawar parties had long since disgraced themselves with their corruption, bickering, and vested interests.

Another problem was the question of justice. Based on various human rights assessments, an overwhelming majority of Afghans said they wanted to see those responsible for past atrocities brought to account. This meant the perpetrators from the PDPA, jihadist, and Talib periods—but also, more recently, those who had indulged in crimes against humanity since the US invasion. As has been seen during similar post-conflict situations elsewhere in the world (such as in South Africa and Cambodia), if reconciliation is to succeed, societies cannot afford to ignore what has happened in the past—particularly if those responsible remain in positions of power.

The decision of Lakhdar Brahimi, the UN special representative for Afghanistan, that justice could be delayed until the country was rebuilt was calamitous. Brahimi believed that compromise was key to a future stable Afghanistan. For this reason, he allowed the warlords to participate in the 2002 Emergency Loya Jirgha. He believed that making them part of the process would help ensure they didn't join the insurgents.

Many Afghans and internationals involved with the Bonn process were genuinely sincere in their attempts to come up with a recovery approach that would respond to the needs of this battered and traumatized nation. However, the pressure from Washington to tailor the process according to its own interests was enormous. The Americans were obsessed by the threat of terrorism and the ostensible need to capture bin Laden.

In the months that followed, I regularly took part in telephone conferences hosted by the Council on Foreign Relations in New York. Many of those participating had longtime experience with Afghanistan. Some recommended that all strategies should be implemented with a long-term perspective. Above all, they warned, vast sums of money should not be thrown at the country. Equally crucial was to avoid bringing in costly outside consultants with little or no knowledge about the country.

It would be far better, they suggested, to work slowly and carefully with Afghans. Above all, the bulk of international recovery operations should focus on rural areas, where 80 percent of Afghans lived. Too much emphasis on Kabul would only draw returning refugees and displaced populations from the countryside in search of jobs. This would overwhelm existing infrastructure. It could also discredit the overall recovery process. Afghans needed to feel that recovery was changing their lives. In the end, few donors paid attention to this advice.

Even more disastrous was the centralized government imposed by the West. Many Afghan experts familiar with the country during the 1970s, '80s, and '90s argued that the only workable scenario was a federal system adapted to Afghan traditions. This would give people in the countryside more of a say over matters that directly concerned them and would prevent Kabul from imposing its own stalwarts.

Providing more autonomy to the regions is precisely what the late Louis Dupree and others had suggested when the Soviets announced their planned pullout in early 1988. Regional resistance commanders such as Ismail Khan and Massoud had already shown that this could work relatively well.

Many donors, however, feared that federalism in such a diverse country would undermine their concept of nation-building. Some Pushtuns also expressed concern about losing their historic control over the country if other ethnic groups began making their own decisions.

Another question plaguing the recovery process was whether those now in positions of power—including the Peshawar politicians, the warlords, and special favorites of the Americans—should really be running the country. By 2011, the corruption within the Afghan government was overwhelming. One pundit compared it to a throng of spoiled brats let into a candy shop to ransack what they could, their parents looking on tolerantly, while the poorer kids were held back at the door.

The first several years of the recovery process were riddled with lost opportunities. An overwhelming majority of Afghans, particularly from the countryside, had far more confidence in the United Nations than anything else, except the ICRC. In retrospect, it is likely that there would have been a broad willingness among ordinary Afghans to support a UN-run administration operating for at least four or five years. A more

Afghan "face" could have been incorporated with the return of the former king as a figurehead leader. At least this would have given the bulk of the country's war-weary population a much-needed breather.

Much of what finally emerged from the Bonn accords was a recipe for disaster. The Western idea of democracy has largely failed because of corruption. The 2009 presidential elections, the country's second, enabled Karzai to regain power fraudulently, while the September 2010 parliamentary polls overseen by a supposedly independent election committee showed that it is almost impossible to gain office without ballot rigging. By early October, as many as one-quarter of the election results had been considered invalid. The international community still insisted that democracy was working in Afghanistan. For many on the ground, however, it had become a joke.

Equally farcical is the legal system that eventually emerged. Although it is supposed to be based on Islamic principles, international standards, the rule of law, and Afghan legal traditions, it has largely failed to translate into a justice that people trust. Despite brand-new courthouses and an overhauled constitution approved in January 2004, the justice offered by the Kabul government lacks transparency. It harbors judges who are widely regarded as corrupt, while those who have committed crimes against humanity are still walking free and even in government. Hence it was no surprise that ordinary people began to seek out the shari'a courts of the Taliban rather than those established by the Kabul regime.

Even rule of law specialists working with the Coalition forces in 2009 admitted that government justice, which worked in favor of he who pays the most, was failing. As Nora Niland, an Irish human rights representative with the UN, put it: "Everyone knows the judges and police working with the government are corrupt. And then there are the warlords . . . And we're supporting such people. While the Taliban and others are responsible for horrific acts of violence, perpetrators of impunity are also those who are in power. So how do you expect ordinary Afghans to have confidence in what is going on?"

My first trip back to Afghanistan was in early January 2002, when I drove with Peter Jouvenal to Kabul. He had already rented a large house, which he planned to turn into a guesthouse, Gandamack Lodge, for international journalists and aid workers. The house, in fact, had been previously rented by bin Laden for his third wife.

Peter had found it in an unusual way. Nearly a year before 9/11, he had been operating "runners" between Kabul and Pakistan as a means of tracking potential stories for the BBC, CNN, and other networks. One of these was a twenty-two-year-old Afghan called Massoud, who had been working for al Qaeda. He came to see Peter over Christmas 2000, seeking political asylum in the West. "He had also been working for ISI and the CIA, and had probably got in over his head with al Qaeda," explained Peter. "He was desperately afraid, so I suggested that if he worked for the media, we could probably help him."

ABC News in New York was the first to be interested in the runner's information. The network proposed that he be properly debriefed. In the spring of 2001, four months before 9/11, Peter flew with him to Kuala Lumpur. The reason for this was that the runner was convinced he would be killed by any one of his three former employers if he remained in Peshawar. Once in Malaysia, he revealed that al Qaeda was planning to hijack aircraft as a means of attacking the West. ABC never used this information because of pressure brought about by a "certain intelligence agency," presumably the CIA which wanted the runner returned. During the briefings, the young Afghan had also showed Peter various locations, including Talib and al Qaeda houses, in and around Kabul on satellite maps.

Bin Laden's wife and entourage had vacated the house three months previously. All that was left was a bra, a pile of ash where paperwork had been burned, and a promotional VHS video for the jihad. On viewing the video, Peter found images of himself and American journalist Peter Bergen when they had interviewed bin Laden in eastern Afghanistan in 1997. "It was really strange to see myself on an al Qaeda video," Peter said.

Peter and I stopped by the Khyber political agent in Peshawar to pick up our travel permits, and to drop off some blankets for Ajman, a twenty-three-year-old British Talib from Manchester, who was being held by the Pakistanis. Of Pakistani origin, he had been captured three years earlier by United Front troops and had been filmed by Peter for the BBC. The prisoner's brother saw the story and contacted Peter for help. Peter then approached Massoud and managed to get the young Talib released, but warned him to wait in Afghanistan until his papers had come through.

Ajman, however, insisted that the Pakistanis were his friends and decided to make his way to Peshawar. After all, he told Peter, he had traveled back and forth during the Talib period without any problem, and had even carried Kalashnikovs onto Pakistan International Airways flights with the full knowledge of the ISI. With the Taliban overthrown, the Pakistanis were now playing another game. They arrested him, possibly in the hope of handing him over to the Americans as al Qaeda, which is what they often did. A substantial number of Taliban held at Guantanamo and Bagram had been palmed off to the Americans by Afghans and Pakistanis alike as al Qaeda based on little or no evidence, but in return for hard cash.

We found Ajman watching a Chuck Norris movie with his guards. Since his arrest, he recounted, he had been visited by British and American officers who wanted to know what he had been doing with the Taliban. When I asked him why he had joined the movement, Ajman shrugged. Back in Manchester he had gotten into drugs and alcohol, but then he decided to come to Pakistan to visit his family and get himself straightened out. He also met some Taliban who had convinced him to join the jihad. With almost no military training, he soon found himself in the front lines being shelled by the United Front.

"We were all really scared, trying to hide behind trees so as not to be killed," he said. The Pakistanis held Ajman for three months before allowing him to return to the UK. Unlike John Walker Lindh, the American who received twenty years' imprisonment in the United States for joining the Afghan Islamist faction and was accused without evidence of being al Qaeda, Ajman was never charged by the British. Some years later, when I asked Peter what had happened to him, he said that the ex-Talib had been tossed into jail for a barroom brawl. "Go figure that for a fundamentalist," he quipped.

Once over the border, Peter and I were met by two off-duty Afghan policemen with Kalashnikovs who had driven down from Kabul to escort us. They worked for Agha Gul, our friend from the jihad days who was now a police general; this was a way for them to earn extra money. Many never received proper salaries. Security was now relatively good along the main Jalalabad highway, but there were still problems at Sorubi, where Hezb-e-Islami and former Taliban were known to be operating. Bandits, primarily former mujahideen, were holding up or hijacking vehicles.

Driving up the Kabul gorge, we passed the point where two months earlier, on November 19, 2001, four Western journalists had been stopped at gunpoint and executed by armed men. They were Harry Burton, a Reuters cameraman; Azizullah Haidari, an Afghan-born Reuters photographer; Maria Grazia Cutuli, a reporter for the Italian daily *Corriere della Sera*; and Julio Fuentes of the Spanish daily *El Mundo*. According to their drivers, a group of turbaned individuals armed with assault rifles forced the journalists out of their cars near Tangi Abrishum bridge and accused them of being American. They responded that they were European journalists traveling to Kabul. Their assailants then tried to march them off into the mountains, but the journalists refused.

Beating their captives and pelting them with stones, the attackers then reportedly said: "Do you think the Taliban are finished? We are still in power and we will have our revenge." Moments later, they shot Cutuli and one of the others. The two remaining journalists were killed sometime afterward. The Jalalabad-to-Kabul highway was even more dilapidated than I had remembered. The asphalt had eroded away, turning the journey into a jolting ride with fine, eye-blistering dust seeping in through the windows and engine. Often, too, we were forced to veer off into the surrounding desert, much of it still mined, to avoid collapsed bridges or open craters. The hulks of burned-out or shattered tanks, APCs, and trucks still littered the roadside. Occasionally, pairs of US Chinook helicopters roared down toward Jalalabad from Bagram or Kabul following the Kabul River.

The American bombing had devastated the outskirts of Kabul along the Jalalabad road. Whole buildings—such as the military academy, which had been damaged only partially during the jihadist battle for Kabul—now lay in utter ruin with rubbled walls and collapsed roofs. Groups of Afghan de-miners wearing blue protective gear worked in the nearby fields and container lots demarcated by small piles of stones and painted red markings. Land mines were not the only problem. Rocket-propelled grenades, artillery shells, bullets, and other unexploded ordnance lay strewn like spilled beans on the ground.

For the first time, I saw US and British troops. The Americans were helmeted with full armor, while the British wore berets. The Americans were almost always in vehicles, glaring aggressively through sunglasses with their assault rifles at the ready. Their personal contact with the local population was dismal, which is one reason why so many problems later emerged. They acted like occupiers. They came across as uncommunicative and nervous. I felt desperately sorry for these young men and women, just as I had felt sorry for those young Soviets who had been thrown into their own ugly and incomprehensible occupation of the 1980s. Only near the American embassy and ISAF headquarters did I ever see regular US military foot patrols.

The UK soldiers, on the other hand, at least during the first six months when they were based in the Afghan capital, did most of their patrolling by foot. Performing what was known as the "Belfast Waltz," an experience brought with them from "the troubles" in Northern Ireland during the 1970s and '80s, they walked single-file through the streets. At least two soldiers were designated "speakers," who would chat with the kids, hand out sweets, or "*A Salaam Aleikum*" the shopkeepers. The others fixed their eyes in constant surveillance of their surroundings. Moving forward, they twirled in slow motion to ensure that every angle was covered. In this manner, they cultivated good relations but also performed their security duties with a professionalism that many Afghans came to respect.

The Norwegians, also members of the ISAF contingent, adopted a far more laid-back approach. As a convoy of vehicles drove through central Kabul, the soldiers casually looked out the windows, elbows resting on the frames. With his machine gun pointed skyward, the rear gunner was happily taking tourist snapshots of the bazaar.

Of course, in those days many thought that the Taliban had been beaten and that Kabul was now secure. For several months, this was indeed the case. But then, steadily, the security situation began to disintegrate. A car bomb, a shooting. It got worse every year with more and more attacks. The UN, the embassies, and other organizations were only allowing their personnel in the streets with permission or accompanied by security guards.

Many of the journalists who covered Kabul now stayed at Peter Jouvenal's Gandamack Lodge, which was a villa in Kabul's upmarket Shar-e-Now district. Built during the 1930s, when the Kabul bourgeoisie was gentrifying the capital, it had a large, walled garden and was already operating as a guesthouse. A slew of late-nineteenth-century Lee-Enfield rifles lined the hallway as one entered. A small British cannon from the same period, which Peter had "liberated" from a former PDPA garrison outside Jalalabad, stood vigil in the garden.

Peter had begun renovating the house in a comfortable Victorian style, strongly marked by a Harry Flashman influence in a bid to recall that cowardly character in George MacDonald-Fraser's historical novels. He ordered handmade furniture from Nuristan and Peshawar and had a team of Afghan workmen, recently returned refugees, painting the walls. His plans were to have a pub, a pizza oven, and a proper restaurant. It was a good place to relax over a cup of tea, meet new people, and sit in the garden to read. Peter, later described by one British reporter as a "soldier, combat journalist and hotelier," saw no shame in maintaining Western hotel standards.

It was astonishing to note how quickly Afghan merchants from Pakistan were already importing building materials from toilet bowls to roof tiles by the truckload. The reconstruction boom in Kabul had begun. Embassies, news agencies, NGOs: All had their own compounds. This construction industry grew rapidly as more outside groups, including the private contractors, poured in and the NATO commitment expanded. There were almost no hotels, so new guesthouses sprang up overnight.

For Afghanistan's privileged, the recovery, security, and drug economy proved a gold rush. Many were from the diaspora who had fled during the communist war. They rented out their properties at increasingly high prices. Rents quickly rose from an average one thousand US dollars a month to four or five thousand dollars, even twice or three times that. Within five years, the rental prices were higher than in Dubai. By 2011, the inflated value of some Kabul real estate was comparable to Belgravia in London and Park Lane in New York. Select sumptuous and often horrifically garish villas built by the warlords or corrupt government officials were renting for as much as fifty thousand dollars a month in the Shar-e-Now and Wazir Akbar Khan districts.

The greed of some Afghans was shameful, but many were aware that all could collapse overnight should the internationals pull out. The objective, particularly among those closely involved with the Karzai regime, was to make as much money as possible while the going was good. During

the late 1980s and early '90s, former jihadists had used their positions to
extract what they could from the war, drugs, and international aid. They
began buying houses and setting up businesses, usually "import-export,"
in the Emirates. Following the collapse of the Talib regime, the trend
spiraled into an ever-expanding avalanche of exported wealth. While
still investing in Kabul real estate, Afghans were buying properties in
Dubai and Abu Dhabi and even relocating their families there.

Returning refugees fortunate enough to own property also rented out
their houses, no matter how dilapidated. Living off the income, they
moved to crowded but cheaper accommodation elsewhere. One of my
employees, a young graduate from Peshawar University, used to come
into the office every day dressed in an Italian-style suit and patent-leather
shoes. He looked the epitome of success. His family owned a small house
a few blocks down, but they now lived in a walled compound that they
shared with relatives on the eastern outskirts of Kabul. The journey to
the office took him ninety minutes each way by bus and taxi every day.
Only by renting out their property, he explained, could they survive.

Afghan-owned land was often stolen by warlords or well-connected
government officials, who threatened the owners with beatings, kidnappings, and even murder. Illegal deals were made with ministry officials
to sell government land. One refugee returned to Kabul in 2005 only to
find that his house had disappeared and a multistory office block stood
in its place. One of the former United Front commanders, now a wealthy
warlord, had simply expropriated it. The refugee tried to fight in the
courts, but unless one was willing to bribe the judges more than one's
rival, there was no point.

Many buildings were renovated or constructed by the internationals at their own cost. They built new offices and guest rooms in the
gardens, put in modern plumbing and cisterns, and brought in comput-
ers, satellite dishes, air conditioners, power generators—plus whole fleets
of four-by-four vehicles. The offices of the World Bank, United Nations
Development Program (UNDP), and ISAF could have been in Nairobi,
Bangkok, or Los Angeles. New security walls were built, at first pleasantly low with planted bushes and trees. Later, one could gauge the worsening security situation by the steadily rising height of these perimeters.
By 2009, it was impossible to see the buildings inside.

There was little urban planning in Kabul at this time, and in the rush to build, little thought was given to dealing with traffic, pollution, sewage, and water. Environmentally friendly approaches that might benefit future generations were unheard of. As pointed out by longtime Afghan specialists such as Jolyon Leslie, it was a major lost opportunity to reconstruct Kabul using the latest affordable technologies and designs, such as solar energy. Anne Feenstra, a Dutch architect who came to Kabul to prove that cost-efficient environmental buildings could easily be integrated into any form of development construction, maintained that "there is no reason why these organizations could not create energy-efficient models that could be emulated by the private sector." But it never happened. As a result, the Afghan capital—as with the rest of Afghanistan—ended up increasingly relying on imported fuel for its energy needs. This meant constant streams of petroleum trucks driving up from the Pakistan border.

There was just as little vision among the Afghans. The entrepreneurs wished to build as quickly as possible regardless of whether the newly constructed, high-rise, Dubai-style office blocks with full-front windows needed costly energy-consuming air-conditioning in the summer or heating in the winter. They seemed to forget that a single rocket in such a war-prone country could blast out all its windows. Without hesitation, Afghan developers bribed city counselors for construction permits, including on sites of historic value. In Herat, where the Aga Khan Foundation has been trying to save what is left of the Old Town, entrepreneurs pulled down ancient wood and stone buildings with intricate latticework within hours of hearing that efforts were being made to preserve them. The presence of police did not stop them. The police had already been paid off.

The waste and lack of foresight of the recovery effort affected all areas. Suggestions were ignored for implementing a public transport system with bus and bike lanes to ease traffic for a city whose population has quadrupled since 1978. Another proposal was to construct a completely new sewage system (the old one consisted of open runoffs) and bring in fresh water from the surrounding mountains. Instead, the internationals put in their own cisterns and dug even deeper wells. The city's water level has dropped significantly, while sewage has seeped into the water table. One Japanese report maintained that Kabul would run out of fresh water by 2015.

"The problems Kabul can now expect to face in the years ahead as a livable city are mind-boggling," noted Douglas Saltmarsh, a British development researcher who has worked with Afghanistan since the mid-1980s. Obsessed by their own projects, the World Bank, Asia Development Bank, USAID, and other well-heeled donors all largely failed to explore more imaginative and coordinated possibilities for a new Afghanistan. Everyone, it seemed, wanted rapid projects with positive imagery to show that things were changing.

Another post-conflict phenomenon to emerge in Afghanistan was the brain drain of Afghans from local to international organizations. Officials in ministries gave up their civil service jobs to be hired as extremely well-paid drivers, interpreters, and office assistants. The Swedish Committee lost 30 percent of its trained professionals to the World Bank, European Union, and other well-heeled organizations. The result was that many Afghans left working in the ministries—with monthly salaries of fifty to one hundred US dollars—did not have the appropriate skills, while rural areas and the provinces were unable to hire necessary doctors. No one could afford to leave well-paying jobs in the capital. As one World Bank employee, a trained physician working as a translator at eight hundred US dollars a month, told me: "I would like to work among the villages, but I have twenty people to take care of at home. I am the only person earning money."

Such problems were clearly foreseen well before the US-led invasion. "The donors had a chance to do it right by developing according to a plan and in coordination with each other," observed Leslie, who had hoped that blueprints produced during the late 1990s for Kabul's eventual reconstruction, including protection of historic buildings, would be adopted. But this just did not happen. No one seemed interested in dealing with Afghanistan's long-term needs.

When I asked a senior UNDP official in mid-2002 why his organization was not providing a more coordinated lead, he said: "At this stage, we need to get moving with the recovery. Constructing eco-buildings or bus lanes is not what reconstruction is about. Maybe later. Right now, we need to bring better health and education to Afghans. That's the priority."

Afghanistan's civilian population during the first three or four years largely welcomed the international recovery intervention with its promise of nationwide reconstruction, jobs, and business opportunities. It was a time of trust and confidence. Once again, the streets sold music CDs and DVDs of the latest films—while the bazaars bristled with satellite dishes, construction marble, Tupperware, laser gun toys, cricket bats, and the latest cell phones. Supermarkets, previously unknown in Afghanistan, appeared overnight selling anything from peanut butter and Mars bars to breakfast cereals, spaghetti sauce, and frozen pork chops to cater to the Western expatriate crowd and diaspora Afghans.

Shopping malls, although modest by American standards, rose from the rubble, while toward the western reaches of Kabul—known as the "new Dubai"—modern office blocks, apartment buildings, and enormous wedding palaces emerged. Following the Talib ban on ostentatious marriages with dancing, singing, and music, wedding palaces—large halls with in-house catering for as many as one thousand guests—were started by former commanders and other entrepreneurs as if to catch up on the lost war years. Gyms and bodybuilding centers sporting muscle-bulging, hand-painted Rambos and Schwarzeneggers took over the second floors of new restaurants, dry cleaners, and digital photo shops.

In the countryside, people had expected major change, but soon became bitterly disappointed by the West's limited impact. Many waited patiently for the government to channel the promised aid in their direction, but then began to suspect the vaunted billions were disappearing into private coffers or being used to cover the costs of the foreigners.

However, for mainly educated urban women—such as health workers, teachers, secretaries, and entrepreneurs—the Western intervention brought a much-anticipated respite following five years of brutal Talib rule preceded by four years of jihadist chaos. Once again, they were free to hold jobs, stroll the streets, go shopping, and even attend yoga classes— although many still dressed extremely conservatively when in public. By 2005, I was counting an average of one woman in four walking through the commercial areas of downtown Kabul with only a shawl on her head.

Nevertheless, many parts of Afghanistan remained staunchly conservative. During the run-up to the 2002 Emergency Loya Jirgha, I traveled with writer Ahmed Rashid to Herat to meet with Governor Ismail

Khan. As one of the country's most effective commanders during the war against the Soviets in the 1980s, Khan was initially considered a progressive. He built a university and opened trade with Pakistan and Iran during the immediate post-Soviet period. He imposed a moderate form of Islamic law, which required women to cover their hair, but allowed them to work and attend segregated schools.

But following his capture by the Taliban, and then his dramatic escape three years later, he returned to power far more conservative. Women in Herat were prohibited from appearing in public without their all-encompassing burqas. Unlike in Kabul, there was not a single woman working at the city's state-run radio and television station.

"One of the big problems is that Ismail Khan is not focusing on our needs and our rights," said Permimah, a high school teacher and participant at a pubic meeting in western Herat province where women demanded more seats in the Loya Jirgha. Since they represented over half the country's population, they said they wanted representation and rights equal to those of men. Another woman, a health worker, added that Khan had once been good for Afghanistan. "But now he is only in power because he and his men have guns."

"Something must have happened to him during this period," Ahmed Rashid noted, referring to Khan's imprisonment by the Taliban. Having interviewed Khan repeatedly over twenty years, Rashid remembered him as someone with the interests of his people close at heart. When Rashid and I finally got to see the Herati leader at his palace offices at three in the morning, he vehemently dismissed the notion that his own people might be afraid of him. But he agreed that Afghans wanted recovery, particularly peace and security. "The people are desperate to find a way out of their poverty," he told us, pointing to a group of women, cloaked in bright blue burqas, sitting in his great hall. "Look at those women who have come to see me in the middle of the night. They are not afraid of our rule. They are afraid of poverty."

The reality, however, was that despite the ousting of the Taliban, many now in power both in Herat and elsewhere in Afghanistan were just as conservative as those they had replaced. When my wife traveled in 2002 to Herat as a WHO official to organize a women's health radio program, she met with the well-dressed regional director of Afghan

Radio and Television. He insisted that she wear a gold plastic weather map (taken from the studio decor) over her head during the discussion. This was the only way he would tolerate meeting with a woman.

In Mazar-e-Sharif, it was a different story. Women under Dostum could live as in Central Asia with only discreet shawls and could work wherever they liked. But for many of the country's highly conservative female population, including members of the urban elite, the pressure by outside groups for them to abandon the burqa did not necessarily represent a desired change. These included educated women working with international organizations. They still insisted on respecting time-honored traditions, even if seemingly backward to Westerners.

Widows were a particularly vulnerable group in Afghanistan. Tens of thousands of women had lost their husbands and other menfolk in the war. Many had children and faced extreme penury, but with no recourse for survival other than to beg. A number of international aid agencies developed programs specifically to help them and their families. This became easier with the collapse of the Taliban.

However, often ignored were the many women who did not know whether their husbands had been killed or not. They could not remarry for seven years according to Muslim tradition. Among the many bizarre projects that Peter Jouvenal undertook was a voluntary initiative that would help locate the bodies of dead Afghan soldiers and mujahideen, undertake DNA analysis, and positively identify their remains. At least this way, he explained, one could help the widows obtain closure.

Based on his reporting during the wars, Peter knew the locations of the remains of as many as five thousand Afghans. He had also tracked down at least fifteen dead Soviet soldiers. Although Peter didn't succeed in getting donor support to locate the bodies of the dead Afghans, there was a definite interest in finding out what happened to the estimated 315 Soviets missing in action in Afghanistan. Some were known to be alive, but most were presumed killed. Following the collapse of the Soviet government in Moscow, the Knights of Malta in the United States began collaborating with the Russians to find US MIAs in Vietnam and North Korea. In return, they would help locate Soviet MIAs in Afghanistan.

Peter, who had been in touch with the families of Soviet MIAs, helped with the exhuming of two Ukrainians in northern Afghanistan.

He brought them to Kabul in two metal trunks, but then the outside pledges to repatriate them evaporated. Stuck with the two trunks and their human remains, he left them for safekeeping at the German Club during the Talib period. In early 2002, he returned to collect them. Without mentioning the contents of the trunks, he asked if he could leave them at my house in Islamabad. They remained for several months under the stairwell of my house.

One day, Peter stopped by to pick them up. Admitting that they were the remains of two Ukrainians, he said: "I have to drop these off at the Russian embassy." I decided not to mention to my wife that we had been sharing the house with two dead bodies. The Russians, however, did not wish to deal with former Red Army soldiers who were no longer part of the Russian Federation and refused to accept the bodies. Peter took them back to Kabul and eventually managed to organize repatriation with the Ukrainian government.

Throughout the next few years, I made repeated trips to Afghanistan to report—but also to set up Media Action International projects. We began training novice journalists and created a Dari and Pashto youth magazine produced by young Afghan journalists. By summer 2002, my wife and I had set up our own Kabul guesthouse, Chez Ana, for the Media Action International teams (but we continued to live in Islamabad). On March 17, 2002, Lashkar-e-Jhangvi, a Pakistani militant group affiliated with al Qaeda, bombed the International Protestant Church in Islamabad—killing five people and injuring forty, most of them expatriates. This was the same group that had murdered American reporter Daniel Pearl two months earlier in Karachi and then attacked a bus—killing fifteen people, including eleven French technicians. These attacks were followed by threats against other targets, notably the French international school—where a bomb was found—and an attempted kidnapping of a boy at the American School. Finally, in early August, gunmen killed six people and wounded two at the Muree Christian School located in a former British Raj hill station some thirty-five miles north of Islamabad. Militants claimed the assaults were punishment for Pakistan's support for America's "war on terrorism" in Afghanistan. The UN quickly evacuated its non-essential staff and their families from Pakistan.

I headed back to Geneva, while my wife remained in Kabul. Our lives then became a challenging round of trading places in Kabul every few weeks. Whenever Lori or I was in Kabul, we would host an open house at Chez Ana with dinners for thirty to forty people. The idea was to bring together Afghans and expatriates—aid workers, diplomats, journalists, academics, military—so that they would have a chance to meet informally. Wine was an obvious attraction—those with commissary privileges, or who managed to smuggle in wine through Pakistan and Afghan customs, would bring a bottle or two. The customs officials were less interested in cracking down on alcohol than confiscating the bottles they could sell on the black market.

Some of my guests were former commanders Peter and I had known. They would often turn up unexpectedly at my home after traveling to Kabul from northern, eastern, or central Afghanistan. It was the least I could do to help them, particularly given all the hospitality I had received from so many Afghans.

Later, I would occasionally hold brown-bag lunches so that Afghans with interesting projects or job-creation proposals could present them to representatives from the World Bank, Asia Development Bank, UNDD, Aga Khan Foundation, and other donors or aid organizations. Many Afghans, notably from rural areas, were finding it increasingly difficult to meet internationals, who were becoming less accessible as security worsened. They felt ostracized by the foreigners, who seemed reluctant to take the time to sit down and talk with them.

One such proposal was a coordinated attempt by community leaders from the Panjshir, Badakshan, Nuristan, and Nangrahar to develop a rural-based tourism industry. Such ideas went back to the days of the Soviet-Afghan war when my colleagues and I would spend long hours talking with local commanders and villagers about the extraordinary potential of their regions for hiking, fishing, wildlife viewing, and mountain climbing—if and when peace returned. A few remembered the days from the 1970s when tourism was just beginning to become a key industry, while those living in the more isolated highland valleys would recall wealthy foreigners coming in to hunt Marco Polo sheep, markhor, and other game.

For them, the main concern was how to bring much-needed revenue from tourism to the villages. People needed something more than just subsistence farming, or even opium poppy cultivation, to survive. One idea was to set up a hotel school in Kabul to train Afghans on how to run simple but clean rural inns. Another was to have volunteer advisers from Europe, North America, or Africa to travel to mountain villages to help set up outdoor tourism facilities not unlike the alpine huts for climbers in the Swiss or French Alps. Basic models with a few bedrooms or dormitories, hot showers, and an eating area could be created and adapted according to local traditions and culture. In addition, locals could be trained as guides and work hand in hand with environmental groups to promote reforestation and wildlife conservation.

The tourism idea incited considerable interest among the donors. The Germans liked the concept of establishing an industry that would help the regions and provide significant local income. The Greeks, on the other hand, were toying with the possibility of establishing a "cultural village" for tourists in Kabul. In the end, however, there was no commitment. Already by 2005, donors were becoming wary of initiatives in hazardous rural areas. Anything that meant leaving the safety of Kabul made many of the donors nervous. The Americans, European Union donors, and others all wanted big projects, if possible with easy access. With so much talk about "empowerment" and "community involvement," it was very disappointing. In any case, by the end of 2005, even for the most intrepid traveler, most of the country was off limits because of deteriorating security.

Even if tourism wasn't widely accepted as a good investment for the future, the importance of media in the Afghan recovery was crucial from the very beginning. The Institute for War and Peace Reporting (IWPR) was setting up a network of Afghan journalists to cover the Emergency Loya Jirgha in June in Kabul, and then branched out with regular reporting from correspondents based throughout the country. A majority of the nearly two thousand Loya Jirgha members, most of them elected, eventually confirmed the nomination of Hamid Karzai as the country's interim president for the next two years. The IWPR initiative represented the first attempt to report such a major event in three languages—Pashto, Dari, and English—by a team of local print reporters trained to pursue every angle of the story. Among the stories covered was the sidelining by Zalmay Khalizad, special envoy for the United States, of the former king in favor of Karzai, and the UN decision to allow the warlords to participate in the Jirgha.

For its part, the BBC Trust was helping to reestablish Radio-Television Afghanistan, while Internews was laying the foundation for an independent network of local and regional radio stations. The training and legwork engendered by such initiatives, notably the creation of a skilled pool of production people and journalists, had eventually led to the establishment of Tolo TV—he first independent Afghan commercial station—in 2004. Most foreign journalists had gone long before—by the spring of 2002, when the principal fighting of Operation Enduring Freedom had simmered down and the Taliban were in flight. That left a hard core of reporters behind in Kabul or based elsewhere in the region. By the end of the first year of the recovery process, some two hundred Afghan newspapers, magazines, and newsletters had emerged on the local scene, although some only survived one or two editions. Nevertheless, the enthusiasm and interest were there.

But by 2005, only a small number of mainly network teams remained based out at Bagram, the former Soviet air base now occupied by the Americans, British, and other members of the Coalition forces. I rarely went to Bagram for the press briefings, the Afghan version of the "five o'clock" follies of the Vietnam days. The TV crews were camping out in tents in front of the briefing area with their own canteen. They would cover the briefings, some going out with the troops on missions. It was a highly artificial environment, and I felt completely out of touch whenever I crossed through its checkpoints. Afghanistan lay somewhere beyond the perimeter. All I could think about was how the Americans had now placed themselves in precisely the same position as the Soviets during the 1980s.

The official talk at one press briefing attended by a British and an American colonel in front of the TV cameras was about Taliban killed, twelve that day. I could not believe the military were still dealing with body counts. I thought that these had gone out with the Vietnam War. I asked how they knew the dead men had been Taliban. Well, the American colonel said, "They had guns."

Welcome to Afghanistan, I thought.

CHAPTER FIFTEEN

The Great Pretend Game

It is early 2011. The Afghan capital is in partial shutdown until the security monitors can decide whether a reported threat is real or not. "Shutdown" is when the internationals—the UN, foreign missions, aid agencies, contractors—prevent their personnel from going out. Kabul goes into full shutdown whenever there is a confirmed incident. One was the suicide attack against ISAF headquarters in early August 2009, killing seven and injuring ninety-one. Another was the assault against a United Nations guesthouse in late February 2010. At least sixteen people, mainly foreigners, died. It was up to a lone UN staffer to ward off the attackers until the police arrived, an hour late. They then shot him dead in the confusion, believing him to be a Talib.

The Taliban and their allies are after symbolic targets. ISAF and the United Nations are certainly these. The rebels are also seeking anything US-related. *ISAF*, a running joke goes, stands for "I Saw Americans Fighting." There's not much enthusiasm for combat among most NATO partners. The Swedes, Norwegians, and other Western armies, under pressure from their own electorates, have all indicated their desire to pull out.

The US surge, which came in with President Obama, has made life more difficult for the insurgents. So they are now after easy objectives that will have a strident impact on the international community. The rebels want to show that they can still operate when and where they like, regardless of American military might.

The Taliban and other anti-Western insurgents have made IEDs their most lethal—and effective—weapon: some 7,228 attacks in 2009, a 120 percent rise over the previous year. The most striking change, however, was the rise in suicide assaults. These alone had tripled. A June 2010 United Nations report cited an average of one assassination a day, with a suicide attack every two or three days. These represent the most murderous form of violence in Afghanistan today. They also account for an estimated 70 percent of civilian deaths. Furthermore, mines or bombs are hazardous for reporters and aid workers.

The expats in Afghanistan today are nervous. The guerrillas are hitting innocent civilians with IEDs or suicide attacks in Kabul, Kandahar, and other cities. One of the worst was in Jalalabad in mid-February 2011, with over thirty Afghans killed and seventy wounded outside a bank. Some of them were police waiting to pick up their paychecks. So devastating have been these assaults that some Taliban are worried that the indiscriminate killings are giving them a bad reputation among the local population; they are now trying to disclaim responsibility. Other insurgent groups—particularly those with foreign affiliations, such as the Haqqani Network—don't believe this matters. Anything to undermine the government and its outside backers.

Ordinary Afghans simply have to bear it. The traffic in the city and the jostling in the bazaars go on as usual. War becomes relative. One lives with it. And Afghans have lived with it for nearly three and a half decades.

Most expats have little idea about the real Afghanistan. Holed up in their heavily fortified compounds for weeks—even months—on end, only the chosen few are allowed out. Life in the Kabul dust bowl is too dangerous, or at least that's the impression conveyed. People are shocked when they hear that I walk through the city, but I am the first to admit I don't walk complacently. I am perpetually scanning the road for danger signals, such as idling cars. If I see a NATO convoy, I turn the other way. Foreign soldiers are the preferred targets for IEDs. Something could always happen.

Much has indeed changed in Kabul, but not the way many had hoped. The airport is the most noticeable. New beige or gray-tinged hangars and office blocks for NATO forces have been constructed, while dozens of military, civilian, and aid planes and helicopters line the runway aprons. Many helicopters are ex-Soviet Mi-8s, often with Russian or Ukrainian crews. I have to look hard to find the traces of all those aircraft wrecks from shelling of the 1980s and '90s that used to litter the ground like meteor-punctured dinosaurs. They have all been cleared away. Today there is a new marble-fronted terminal heralding the new age of "post-conflict recovery." The only problem is that Afghanistan's wars have yet to end.

On a recent trip to Afghanistan I find that my airport pickup has not arrived. I cadge a lift from Tom, a bearded American logistical coordinator wearing a *shalwar-kamiz* and a woolen *kola*. He has been here since 2005 and worked previously in Uzbekistan. He is waiting to pick up two young consultants coming in from Dubai. Tom is not optimistic and believes NATO is losing the war. There are too many contradictory interests, he maintains. The security companies simply make the expats more paranoid. Everyone is out to make money. "They need to be talking to the Taliban," Tom adds with the weary authority of an old hand.

On leaving the airport with its armored vehicles, Afghan soldiers in American-style uniforms, and police with blue bulletproof vests, one crosses into the sprawling beyond, a totally different scenario. The international obsession for security has turned Kabul into a city of siege. Whole streets have been cut off by crash barriers, concrete walls, and police checkpoints, angering numerous residents forced to make wide detours to take their children to school or get to work.

Tom drops me off at Gandamack Lodge, Peter Jouvenal's guesthouse—though it's not the same building as before. The previous landlord wanted to sell it for nine million dollars, so Peter moved. Still a cameraman-producer, Peter is also a full-fledged entrepreneur. He remains one of the best-informed foreigners on Afghanistan, always blunt with his opinions. Lack of commitment is the principal reason why the international recovery effort is failing, he explains. "They all have their own agendas. They're not here for the Afghans." The British army has embraced a far more realistic but pessimistic approach, in his opinion. They know they are fighting an impossible war. As for the UK's international aid agency, and other diplomats isolated at the British embassy, Jouvenal says, "They're living on another planet. They've no idea what's going on."

Peter and I have worked in Somalia, Liberia, and Sri Lanka, but now we're back in Afghanistan. Again. He offers to take me over in his Land Rover to Bada Bir, an agricultural research center on the outskirts of the capital, where his wife, Hassina, is training women to pick quality crops at the farm for hotels and restaurants so that they have a bit of income.

As we drive through the city, I notice that there has been even more construction since my last visit to this part of town several years earlier.

Whole sectors are now studded with garish Dubai-style villas with high walls and razor wire, armed guards sitting outside. There is a lot of money in Kabul these days, much of it in the wrong hands. The farm is a government initiative started in the Soviet era. Several fields are being cultivated as part of a USAID-funded project for sweet corn, cherry tomatoes, and peppers. They are using different types of irrigation, such as drip, flooding, and furrow, to see what can be replicated easily by the Afghan farmer.

Hassina, an energetic Afghan entrepreneur, has also set up a nonprofit NGO—the National Organization for Women (NOW)—to help women establish their own businesses. It is hard for Afghan women to earn a living. At the farm, there is resistance from the male employees, who steal the crops to make money and deeply resent the women—who remind me of Latin American migrant workers with their straw hats bending over the pepper plants in the hot late-morning sun.

We head back for lunch. Gandamack is located off a busy road near the UNHCR and Iranian embassy. There is no sign indicating a hotel and restaurant behind its walls. It's best to be discreet. But the guesthouse is a well-known watering hole and eating place for expats. It's a small world, and immediately upon entering it I am bumping into people I know from before or from other wars. One of them is a British neighbor from a nearby village in France working for the UN. We never seem to find the time to get together back home, so we arrange to have dinner in Kabul. Gandamack is not like many of the embassies and international missions, whose barriers have become so high you can no longer see the buildings. Security has defeated the whole purpose of being here. Most experienced NGOs refuse to have armed protection. Their best security, they maintain, is good relations with the communities they work in. If you lose touch, there's no point.

It is evening as I walk back to my room at the American Institute for Afghanistan Studies, a quiet place to write. Kabul may have changed with the constant traffic and well-lit shops, but I still find the same hospitality. Always a greeting coupled with a gesture beckoning me over for tea.

Nearby, just a few hundred yards from the British and German embassies, I nip into the Finest Supermarket, which caters to foreigners

and wealthy or diaspora Afghans. I purchase some batteries, the equivalent to three days' wages of an Afghan laborer, and hurry out. I am wary
about lingering. Months later, in January 2011, a suicide bomber blew
himself up at Finest Supermarket, killing five Afghans—including a
young child—and three foreign women.

Overhead, an enormous billboard flashes. A wide-screen TV the size
of two trucks relentlessly advertises new Toyota cruisers, Visa cards, and
Kam Air—now the preferred airline carrier for most expats. The weekend flights are also filled by well-heeled Afghans, including government
officials, who have made fortunes from the international recovery process
and make regular trips to Dubai and the other Gulf countries where they
have homes.

How many Afghans can afford such luxuries, particularly destitute migrants from the countryside in search of jobs? The bulk of rural
Afghans have benefited little from the billions of dollars poured in over
the past years. Ordinary Afghans may also wonder what on earth all
these foreigners are doing here. Despite the propaganda about how the
internationals have come to help promote democracy and recovery, the
Afghans are no longer buying it. Even most foreigners, if they are honest,
know that their intervention has proved largely a failure. Afghanistan
has become one great pretend game.

On November 2010, at the NATO summit in Lisbon, the United States
and its Coalition partners announced that the forty-eight-country international security force would end its combat role and withdraw the bulk
of its 150,000 troops, more than two-thirds American, by 2014. All
security operations for defending the country against the insurgency
would be handed over to the Afghan army and police. Any foreign
troops remaining after that date would operate primarily in a training or
support capacity.

For the electorates back home—and the troops—this was good news.
Militarily, and politically, it made little sense to continue a war with ever
mounting casualties that no one could win. Since 2007 or 2008, most of
the foreign governments involved with Afghanistan have been quietly
seeking an exit strategy. By the time of the Lisbon conference, official
casualty figures for NATO troops killed in Afghanistan stood at twenty-

three hundred. Of these, well over half, roughly fourteen hundred, were American. These figures did not include the mercenaries and other private military contractors also killed. According to a 2010 ProPublica analysis, more civilian contractors have died in the Iraq and Afghan wars than regular troops. Nor are Afghans part of these lists. They always seem to figure as an afterthought in Western dispatches.

The Lisbon announcement was not unexpected. Pragmatic NATO commanders have long since dropped talk of "victory," hinting NATO will instead be satisfied with reducing violence to a level that Afghan security forces can deal with largely on their own. For over 70 percent of the country, however, security remains a dominant issue—often severely hindering any real development or outside investment.

By early 2011, the United States alone was spending an average of $2.8 billion a week in Afghanistan. According to NATO, the Afghan security forces will cost an estimated $6 billion annually to run (about half the country's current GDP and more than the United States gives to Israel and Egypt), and would almost certainly have to continue relying on NATO aircraft and other support. The International Monetary Fund has calculated that Afghanistan will not be able to pay for its own military until 2023.

Despite the bleak military outlook, there have been some tangible achievements. The country's National Solidarity Program, or NSP, which was started in 2003, has proved a relative success. This consists of rural-based development and reconstruction initiatives involving local communities and supported by numerous donors and NGOs. For some observers, it is so far one of the few mechanisms that enables ordinary people to have a say in their own futures, even in hazardous zones such as Helmand.

For a country at war, the contradictions are often striking. In some parts of Afghanistan—such as Takhar or Badakshan to the north, where there are fewer security concerns—whole communities are thriving. While still only 23 percent of the population has access to safe water, the widespread construction of new pumps and wells has brought about significant improvements in the quality of life. In Nangrahar and Kunar provinces, the transformation in local agriculture and commerce has been astounding. The bazaars are crammed with new commerce ranging from tire repair shops and bodybuilding gyms to language and accountancy schools, while whole areas of once arid land have been opened up to new irrigation. Children are playing cricket, a sport brought back by the refugees from Pakistan. Afghanistan now ranks as a country with world-class players.

Even in the Pech Valley west of Kerala, where the insurgents are active, there is a massive construction boom—with new houses and shops in every town and village. The smallest villages have their own schools. Improved roads and bus services have made towns such as Jalalabad and Asadabad more accessible to once remote mountain communities. Refugees have brought back tractors and other farm appliances, radically altering the agricultural landscape. During the Soviet-Afghan war, farmers were still tilling with oxen.

Some of this new prosperity has been the result of corruption, narcotics, and timber trafficking, which has devastated most of the country's remaining forests but pumped money into the economy. Part, too, has been stimulated by aid organizations such as Madera, the Swedish Committee, and the Aga Khan Foundation. Much, however, is the result of local initiatives, such as the Nuristani villagers who pooled their funds to buy a power generator to electrify their homes.

Today enterprising Afghans have set up their own businesses, traveling from farm to farm with combine harvesters to bring in the wheat. Others have established family-run tree nurseries. Cross-border trade is vibrant. Some farmers still grow opium poppies, but the broad selection of crops, markets, and other revenue streams means that the cultivation of narcotics has become an unnecessary risk. The new wealth has enabled local residents to send their children to schools and even college, something unheard of in the 1970s except for the most privileged. One farmer told me that his eldest son was now studying business and economics in Tashkent. All his other children—including the girls, he explained proudly—were at school.

Education represents one of Afghanistan's most dramatic success stories even though improvement is still needed. Since 2002, 7 million Afghan children, 2.5 million of them girls, are now in school. Some ninety thousand graduated from twelfth grade in 2009, an astonishing feat. One drawback, however, is that many pupils—particularly at the secondary level—have no reading materials, while the Internet is only available in towns.

Nevertheless, there is an absolute hunger for books. While in Hazarajat in the mountainous areas of central Afghanistan, I encountered a small library run out of the back of a bazaar shop with three hundred books in English, Persian, French, German, and Russian. Titles included tomes by Karl Marx, *How to Cook* for bachelors, and a UNICEF annual report. One NGO that has been trying to remedy this dire situation is the Louis and Nancy Dupree Foundation, which has helped create nearly two hundred libraries throughout Afghanistan, including a major research library at Kabul University.

There is a legitimate concern that these gains will evaporate if the war in Afghanistan expands. It is hard to imagine, however, that a more secure future awaits the country if things continue the way they have. Everyone, from corrupt politicians, privileged warlords, and the insurgents who want their chance to rule the country to the Pakistanis, Iranians, Russians, and the United States still consider Afghanistan a land on which to impose their own agendas.

Ultimately, it will be up to the Afghans themselves to deal with their own problems. This is what should have been encouraged in 2001 when there was still a chance to implement a sounder and less corrupt recovery process. The international community should have placed sufficient pressure on Afghanistan's neighbors, particularly Pakistan, to halt their meddling. Without outside interference, none of Afghanistan's diverse and largely self-centered factions, including the Taliban, could have operated for as long as they have.

The United States and its partners have insisted that they will not abandon Afghanistan as they did at the end of the Soviet occupation. They consider the country vital to regional peace and stability. Ironically, the Russians, worried by the growing impact of Afghan heroin on their own population, have become players again in the Afghan game. While careful not to commit troops, except for counternarcotics operations, Moscow has declared its willingness to support NATO by allowing supplies to transit through its territory (90 percent cheaper than airlifting and less hazardous than shipping by road through Pakistan) and to provide counternarcotics training to Afghan officials. It also promised to sell the US eighteen Mi-17 helicopters, which are better adapted to the country's high altitudes and cold weather, and to lend three more to the Afghan security forces.

The NATO strategy to withdraw by 2014 was based on a few key assumptions. First, Western planners intend that the Afghan security forces will be sufficiently trained to confront the insurgents on their own. Second, NATO believes that by 2014 sufficient negotiating progress will have been made to entice the insurgents into a workable peace process. The third assumption is that the international community will have proved to the Afghan people that recovery is bringing about the improvements it promised through its "Marshall Plan for Afghanistan." And fourth, NATO assumes that the Western-backed government will become less corrupt.

In a leaked cable from Kabul's US ambassador Karl Eikenberry in 2009, he made it clear that the United States did not consider Karzai an "adequate strategic partner." The first concrete efforts by the Karzai regime in September 2010 toward more formal talks with the insurgents were reminiscent of the faltering initiatives undertaken by the communists to reach out to the mujahideen during the 1980s. Karzai's appointment of a seventy-person High Peace Council, which included nine women, but also former members of the Taliban, sounded promising enough. The only problem was that within the council were the same old factional and feuding figures of the past. Even if, as US general David Petraeus asserted, senior-level Taliban had been reaching out to NATO, the majority of those on the council seemed to oppose having anything to do with the insurgents. Nevertheless, by mid 1980, US officials claimed they were talking to some Taliban in Germany.

The immediate Talib response to the NATO Lisbon announcement was to assert that foreign troops would have to leave before they would start negotiating peace. They also welcomed the exit strategy, as all they now had to do was hold out until 2014. This did not mean that all the insurgents would categorically refuse government approaches to come to the table. The highly opportunist Hezb-e-Islami has always indicated a readiness to enter into negotiations, but only, one can assume, if they benefit Hekmatyar. On a limited basis, some rebel commanders, either tired of fighting or presented with more attractive opportunities, have been responding positively to official overtures to enter into discussions. Another factor that may help nudge some Taliban to the negotiating table is the success of drone attacks against Talib leaders. Since 2010, the CIA has been increasing its highly effective remote-controlled air assaults against Talib safe havens in Pakistan, particularly North Waziristan. At the same time, the assaults have been wiping out the very commanders crucial to future negotiation. Those rising up to replace them are younger and less willing to compromise.

Although NATO's aim is for the Afghan security forces to be in the lead by the end of 2014, Afghan troops have not been very impressive, a fact that US and NATO troops acknowledge. Nevertheless, according to Admiral James G. Stavridis, supreme Allied commander for Europe, NATO's training programs had fielded 240,000 Afghan National Security Forces by 2010 with the number expected to reach 300,000 by mid-2011. He also claimed that the Taliban are largely militarily incompetent, beyond their use of IEDs. "Their flag has come down" in areas where combined NATO-Afghan forces have made progress, Stavridis maintained.

What the commander did not mention was that barely a quarter of the army was considered "battle-ready," according to senior NATO officers. Many Afghan soldiers are quite happy to have the Coalition troops do the fighting. Furthermore, the attrition rate of the Afghan army was still over 50 percent as a result of soldiers going AWOL, desertion, or crossing over to the insurgents. Of equal concern, the Taliban, Hezb, and other opposition allies have proven far more motivated. As with the mujahideen during the 1980s, they have been infiltrating the security forces. Apart from nearly 90 percent illiteracy among ordinary soldiers, the Afghan army has suffered from severe problems of drug addiction, inadequate supplies, and logistics. Even more crucial, it is highly unrepresentative, with a striking lack of Pushtuns among the ranks. By early 2011, there was still no reliable Afghan army of significant size. It is difficult to imagine that a full standing force capable of staving off the enemy will be achieved after only four years.

Nevertheless NATO commanders have stressed that although part of a gradual process, an effective Afghan military will eventually prevail. They also readily remind one of how well the PDPA armed forces fought against the mujahideen following the Soviet pullout in 1989. There is no reason, they maintain, why the current army cannot do the same. Today's soldiers, however, are a far cry from those of the early 1990s. With their backs against the wall, the former communist forces had far fewer options. Many of their officers were considered nonbelievers and risked execution if captured. Today both the insurgents and the government security forces see themselves as true believers.

Forging a competent Afghan police force has provided a different, though equally tough, challenge. The Germans, British, and Americans have been training police since 2002, with mixed results. Poorly paid and often illiterate, the police barely command respect among ordinary Afghans. The overwhelming majority have no understanding of the rule of law and regularly abuse it. Numerous police supplement their salaries by levying "fines" or operating protection rackets. They also steal fruit and vegetables from farmers. One Kandahar peasant transporting watermelons to market complained that by the time he got through all the checkpoints, he had no fruit left. Another problem is drug addiction. Western and Afghan aid workers operating in Kandahar and Helmand provinces said that almost all the police they encountered were stoned on marijuana or opium. The end result is that police are simply not trusted.

The Ministry of Interior has been severely affected by corruption. Select factions, notably Hezb-e-Islami and the Khalq, continue to infiltrate various departments. Former ministers, such as Ali Ahmad Jalali—who headed the ministry from 2003 to 2005 and who later became a presidential candidate—said that his team was fully aware of the problems and had sought to deal with them. But they seemed helpless to prevent suspected police involvement with kidnappings, blackmail, and even murder.

In 2004, Peter Jouvenal was arrested by the Ministry of Interior because of his involvement in mediating in the release of three UN election volunteers kidnapped by unknown groups. Certain ministry officials were keen to get some of the one million dollars reportedly paid to the kidnappers by a wealthy Kosovar businessman (one of the volunteers was a Kosovar woman). In the end, no money changed hands and the captives were rescued by ISAF, but the officials still felt they had missed out. They forced Peter to sign a confession. Rather than scribbling his name, he wrote: "Your people smoke too much hash!" Various members of Peter's staff and family were later threatened and even beaten.

In early 2005, a group of eight men, several of them armed, entered my house unannounced. I was in the process of hosting an informal dinner party with diplomats, journalists, academics, aid specialists, and Afghan friends. I noticed the men and assumed they were someone's guests. The leader, a wild-haired man with a thick beard, announced in excellent English that they were from the Ministry of Interior. When I asked to see his ID, he refused. "We're Ministry of Interior," he declared. When I insisted, informing him that there was now rule of law in Afghanistan and he was obliged to show me his official ID, he physically attacked and then arrested me—ordering several of his men to force me into a waiting vehicle.

The man, it turned out, was none other than Abdul Jabar Sabet, legal adviser to the minister. He was also a former aide to Hekmatyar and Pushto editor of the Voice of America. Ironically, he had interviewed me several times during the 1980s for VOA. When he found out who I was, he angrily berated me for challenging his authority. I told him that he was obliged to identify himself to anyone, whether Afghan or foreigner. Nor was it appropriate to walk into someone's house without informing them. It simply was not Afghan.

Sabet did not take this criticism lightly, but he released me. The next morning, three uniformed police drew up in an official car. Obviously, my message about identifying themselves got through, because all three held up their ID cards and asked me to accompany them to the main Kabul police station. For the next four hours half a dozen men took turns "interrogating" me. Informing me that I faced severe charges, they demanded to know what I was doing in Kabul. Locked in a room with a large, perpetually running TV set, I found it difficult to take the proceedings seriously. My interrogators constantly glanced up at the screen, which was playing Walt Disney's *The Lion King*. Every few minutes matters came to a complete halt when, like mesmerized children, they paused to watch a particularly intriguing moment.

Eventually, an armed guard took me to the director of crime, a thuggish ex-PDPA policeman, whose gruff body language was intended to intimidate. A significant number of civil and secret police were former Khalqis or Parchami trained by the East Germans. Others were Hezb.

The chief glared at me, noting that he was fully aware of my background and that I had good contacts with the former jihadists.

"We can't touch you," he admitted, but then added that he knew the Afghans working with me. I immediately informed him that if he touched any of my staff, I would complain officially to the president of Afghanistan.

"You can do what you like," he said with a dismissive gesture. He obviously did not think much of Karzai. A few days later, Foreign Minister Abdullah invited my wife and me to dinner at his house. In typical Afghan fashion, he was concerned that Lori—who happened to be in Kabul with my five-year-old son, Alexander at the time of my arrest—would leave Afghanistan with a bad impression.

Shortly afterward, our Afghan cook—a married woman and also a journalist hosting her own family radio program—came to us in tears. The police, it appeared, had been harassing her, claiming that she was having an affair with our Pakistani house manager. This was a devastating accusation to make in such a conservative society. The police intimidated other staff by making threats. Finally, two policemen arrived with a formal-looking form saying that I had to pay them income tax. This was a common ploy to extort money from foreigners. I replied that I would be more than delighted on the condition that they worked for the Ministry of Finance and had an official bank account. Glumly, they packed their form back into a briefcase and left.

I complained to the US embassy and wrote an open letter to Karzai, which was widely published by the Afghan media. Sabet was furious. Several days later, the Ministry of Interior came out with a press release accusing me of financial crimes. The text was well drafted and in English. The Americans had contracted with the Rendon Corporation, a US firm with close relations to the Bush administration, to provide the ministry with two expatriate PR people. Obviously, this was written by them. One wondered why the US government would waste hundreds of thousands of dollars on such an unnecessary luxury.

Karzai appointed Sabet attorney general in 2006. A year later, the zealous public prosecutor launched a violent raid on Tolo TV, the country's largest independent private network, for what he maintained was "distorted" reporting. When the TV station refused to bow to his threats, Sabet's thugs destroyed equipment and took seven journalists into custody, severely beating them. Tolo responded with a formal complaint by identifying eleven potential breaches of the law and specific articles of the constitution that the attorney general had violated. Karzai fired Sabet in 2008 when it became known that the country's main public prosecutor had presidential ambitions.

Apart from corruption and abuse of the rule of law, one of the biggest problems facing Afghanistan—at least with its impact on Russia, Europe, and North America—is narcotics. To a degree, drugs are financing the insurgency, but most of the profits (nearly two hundred billion dollars a year) benefit outside traffickers. Afghan opium, which provides the basis for heroin, only accounts for three billion dollars' worth of revenue for the country. In early 2011, Afghanistan was still responsible for 90 percent of the world's opium poppy production. Although opium cultivation had dropped by one-third over the previous two years, three northern provinces—Baghlan, Faryab, and Sari Pul—have been showing the beginnings of reverting to opium poppy production, particularly in high-security areas.

Overall, however, the 2010 Afghanistan Opium Survey (Rapid Winter Assessment) by the UN Office on Drugs and Crime in Vienna was suggesting that up to twenty-five Afghan provinces could become poppy-free. Much of this, the report said, was the result of local community-inspired measures, such as *shura*-driven campaigns, governor-led eradication, and development assistance. In the more stable northern provinces, many farmers say they are not growing opium because it is "illegal." There is also a strong correlation between insurgency and cultivation. The UN survey indicated that almost 80 percent of villages with poor security conditions grew poppies. The figure was only 7 percent among those unaffected by violence.

Warlords, Afghan entrepreneurs, Taliban, and certain highly placed individuals within the Karzai regime are all known to be involved. One powerful political figure in Afghanistan often associated with the drug trade is President Karzai's half brother, Ahmed Wali Karzai. As with so many other warlords, Ahmed Wali is still held in high regard by many Americans who consider him a staunch supporter of US strategy. Furthermore, reports have been emerging of NATO military—including US soldiers, intelligence agencies, and private contractors—being directly involved with outside traffickers from Pakistan, Central Asia, and Russia. One American contractor dealing with NATO transports said that a number of foreign operators, including US and European citizens, were using military vehicles and containers to export the drugs. DEA agents are known to be investigating these channels, which have links to the Russian and Eastern European mafia.

At least four hundred drug labs were being operated in Helmand and Badakshan provinces which together accounted for 65 percent of Afghanistan's annual production. In October 2010, in an unprecedented move, Russian and US troops conducted their first joint operation in Afghanistan against the drug producers. This was the first time in over twenty years that Russian military have been deployed in Afghanistan. During the heliborne ambush, some seventy soldiers attacked four clandestine labs in eastern Afghanistan's Nangrahar province. The operation reportedly destroyed the labs and seized over two hundred million doses of heroin worth $250 million. Both the Americans and Russians have declared that "narco-trafficking" remains one of the biggest problems for both countries, particularly given the dramatic rise of heroin addiction in Russia, which now absorbs 21 percent of Afghanistan's total production.

Military-style counternarcotics operations have never succeeded in crushing opium poppy cultivation and heroin production. Destroying without compensation has only contributed to new recruits for the insurgents. An estimated 6.4 percent of the Afghan population live off opium poppy cultivation alone. Another problem is that the Americans have been propping up drug warlords in return for support. In December 2010, *The New York Times* reported that one of these, Hajii Juma Khan, who was arrested in 2008 and described by US federal prosecutors as the biggest and most dangerous drug warlord in Afghanistan, had in fact been collaborating with the CIA and the DEA.

If poppy cultivation is to be curbed, an approach consisting of a mix of rule of law measures, community collaboration, and agricultural or economic inducements is required. Afghan farmers benefit only modestly from poppy cultivation, yet still find it more lucrative to grow than other crops such as wheat (whose prices have dropped in recent years). As specialists such as veteran British agriculturalist Anthony Fitzherbert point out, no single alternative crop can replace opium. "What is needed is a basket of options such as improved access to markets, better irrigation, and an array of farm products that could eventually lure farmers away from their reliance on opium poppies," he explains. "But this also means better extension work, which is what the traffickers do. They offer fertilizers, credit, and a ready market."

Overall, it is difficult to know how much international donor funding is really being channeled toward development support in Afghanistan. More than forty billion dollars is known to have been pledged or spent in less than a decade. Yet whether it is really being dispersed for such purposes is another question. Backing for military Provincial Reconstruction Team (PRT)–led activities is often included in this figure—which, some observers maintain, obscures the lines among military, humanitarian, and development support. The United States alone has committed fifty-six billion dollars, but this covers a mix of police and military training as well as economic assistance.

Recent years have witnessed unprecedented construction of new schools, clinics, courthouses, power plants, roads, bridges, and security barracks. The wider Afghan recovery effort, however, has been faltering because of gross incompetence and corruption, with hundreds of millions wasted on misguided or shortsighted projects. One Afghan noted that his country was now run as a "mafia economy."

Financial oversight has proved how debilitated the effort has become. By 2010, an estimated $18 billion of donated American aid could not be accounted for, much of it snagged in a "labyrinth" of contract bureaucracy. The Pentagon appointed a special task force to follow the missing billions. Already one New Jersey–based US construction company, Louis Berger—which has received billions of dollars in contracts—was fined $69.3 million in November 2010 for overcharging on its operations in Iraq. Observers wonder why the US government persists in granting contracts to such corrupt companies.

Many bona fide development NGOs with solid Afghan experience, such as CARE International, Oxfam, and the International Rescue Committee, are highly critical of the manner in which many of these firms operate. Yet they themselves have been unable to absorb large contracts worth hundreds of millions of dollars, so the private contractors with the right connections grab them. But the money is poorly spent.

They also have inadequate knowledge of Afghan culture or customs. Nor do they have the long-term interests of Afghanistan at heart. It is all business. Many subcontract locally or pay off insurgents not to disrupt their operations. Relations have soured because of the unreliable reputation of certain Western contractors.

"A lot of the money going into infrastructure building is being siphoned off and never reaches the country," noted Lex Kassenberg, the highly experienced country director of CARE International in Kabul. "The US government has been pumping in phenomenal amounts, and the average Afghan is asking where the hell is all this money? A lot is going to the profit [private contractor] organizations with high salaries and to the PRTs, but huge parts of this are being spent on security, which makes no sense."

Both Kassenberg and others argue that too many private contractors are into the "numbers game," such as the building of schools—ticked off when completed, but with no concern for the future. Nor is there any effort to coordinate with other members of the aid community. While admitting that NGOs such as CARE are far from perfect, they at least have a long-term commitment. "We make mistakes, but before we implement an activity there is a lot of discussion with the local communities. What are your priorities? Where do you want it? The rule is build up a good relationship with local communities. In exchange, the community provides you with protection. You don't get protection if you're building without consultation. This is one reason why they're all forced to travel around with security details."

The end result is that numerous projects across Afghanistan have been implemented badly or not at all. Garrisons to house Afghan army and police have been shoddily built. A 2010 McClatchy Newspapers investigation found that since 2008, nearly two hundred million dollars' worth of US Army Corps of Engineers construction projects had failed or were facing serious delays. Part of this was because, in the rush to award contracts to Afghan companies, the corps accepted bids that did not properly cover costs. The survey referred to "Afghan good" projects that have failed to meet standards but can be considered complete. The vast majority of companies found doing poor work had not been banned from getting new US projects.

Since 2006, the Americans have advocated giving work to Afghan companies as part of an "Afghan First" approach. Much of what is needed by the military could easily be produced locally, such as fruit, vegetables, and bottled water. But for this to happen, there must be more local investment, which would benefit Afghanistan with desperately needed jobs and infrastructure. Afghans are capable of gearing up quickly. However, most US contracts go to the usual American companies or multinational giants, even if they are known to have performed poorly or are corrupt. According to a study by the Peace Dividend Trust (PDT), a nonprofit working with the US government, only 22 percent of American development assistance funds reach the Afghan economy. British development funding, on the other hand, delivers over 70 percent.

In early December 2009, on the day that I arrived at the British PRT compound on the outskirts of the Lashkar Gah, capital of Helmand province, there were over eighty reported IEDs throughout this largely desert region. I don't know how many people were killed or injured, but it seemed like a horrendous number. What was certain was that IEDs were accounting for over half the foreign military deaths in Afghanistan, 280 out of a total of 512 in 2009 alone. The figure was even higher in 2010. The majority were American, followed by British and Canadian troops.

The mujahideen of the 1980s never made such devastating use of roadside bombs. The only ones I saw were Chinese-made land mines to blow off the treads of tanks. It was the Soviets who calculatedly littered the countryside with butterfly mines and other anti-personnel explosives. I never heard of a single guerrilla suicide bombing, a concept only introduced in the 1990s by foreign jihadists. While willing to risk their lives, Afghans have never particularly enjoyed dying. Most of the fifteen thousand Soviet deaths were the result of rocket attacks, combat, ambushes, and (a major killer) vehicle accidents. IEDs were not a critical feature.

By 2010, the majority of IEDs were prepared by skilled outsiders, such as Chechens or Uzbeks. And the majority of those selected to die in suicide attacks were foreigners, notably Pakistanis and Arabs. Only recently has there been a cynical and rising use of mentally challenged or impoverished Afghans to do the job. Their families are paid in hard cash, two thousand dollars if they're lucky. One doesn't see the Talib or al Qaeda leaderships offering themselves up as suicide fodder.

I did not travel to Helmand as an "embed" but rather a fly-on-the-wall adviser to a World Bank team preparing the 2011 World Development Report. We traveled by plane from Kabul to Camp Bastion, the largest British military facility built since World War II. Remotely located northwest of Lashkar Gah, it is also the fifth busiest UK-operated airport in the world. We transferred to one of two newly deployed RAF Merlin helicopters to continue onto Lash, as the soldiers call it—a fifteen-minute flight. Standing at the open rear door, a helmeted gunner carefully scrutinized the ground below. Against the throbbing of engines, he strutted around in his desert-hued jumpsuit like a rock star, shifting his poses according to the slant of the chopper.

At the airstrip, two teams from ArmorGroup International (a British security company)—ex-soldiers wearing the requisite mercenary gear of dark shades, jeans, body protection, and assault rifles—stood by their four-by-four vehicles to take us to the PRT stronghold. Euphemistically referred to as "private military contractors," these hired guns do not like being called "mercenaries." It's an embarrassing term for those who hire them, but that's what they are. Somehow only the South Africans working during the apartheid era for Executive Outcomes, another UK security company, or the Africans fighting for Libyan dictator Moammar Qaddafi in early 2011 were called mercenaries.

I tried to chat with the "Group" mercs, but they were not talkative. One finally opened up when I mentioned about passing near here, a couple of miles to the east, with the mujahideen during the Soviet-Afghan war. "You were here then?" He eyed me curiously, balancing his gun between his knees. "From what I hear the Taliban are not much different. They're sly bastards." When I asked him about his job, he remained vague. "It's better than the army. More leave. Better pay. And we've a good house." He paused. "It's a job," he finally said.

Our PRT quarters consisted of rectangular containers piled on top of each other; instant rooms with bunk beds, toilet, and shower. I was curious to see the town. But the officer in charge made it clear that no one was to go wandering outside the fort gates. We had to be accompanied by the mercenaries. At dinner, we sat at long tables with the British, American, and Danish officers based here. They ate well, but unlike their French and Italian counterparts elsewhere in Afghanistan, the "Anglo-Saxons" had no wine.

There were also "civ-mil" consultants who advised on hearts-and-minds initiatives. These were part of the counterinsurgency strategy initiated by former NATO commander US general Stanley McChrystal. For McChrystal, "the shot you don't fire" is more important than the one you do. The only problem was that his approach was not working. The insurgents were gaining not only in the south, but in the northern areas, too. Six months later, Obama fired the US general for talking out of line and criticizing administration officials to *Rolling Stone* magazine.

Nevertheless, I found myself impressed by how well informed some of the officers were. One, an American colonel, recited all the books he had read on Afghanistan. He and his colleagues had done their homework. They spouted the right language regarding the country's culture and history, such as the need to mix with local Afghans. "If you're going to work here, you'd better make the effort to understand," he explained.

"We make a point of drinking tea with them whenever we come to the villages, and we leave our guns outside so that we can talk on equal terms," one female US officer added authoritatively. Of course, what she neglected to say was that the Afghans know the soldiers waiting outside have guns, and are ready to use them. The foreigners may meet with tribal officials, discuss new development projects, and pay farmers willing to embrace the NATO programs, but they have no idea what the Afghans really think.

For the most part, the Afghans in the south, where much of the fighting is, are playing both sides. They have no choice. On their patrols, the foreign soldiers quiz farmers and village elders about the insurgents, but they also promise them schools, roads, and bridges. This is easier said than done. The insurgents spread the word that anyone who collaborates with the government or the *kafirs* who back it will be punished as a traitor. So everyone is more afraid of the Taliban than the Americans. "Because during the night, maybe the Taliban will come and kill us," noted one tribal elder. It has happened many times, he ventured further. Until Kabul can ensure their security, they will certainly not embrace the government. Or at least not openly.

The more astute officers I meet in Afghanistan are perfectly aware that theirs is an impossible task, namely to combine war with development work. They acknowledge, too, that even with "field successes," the military cannot bring about peace. And to place too much emphasis on an exit strategy only plays into the hands of insurgents biding their time. The officers accept that their war is not a matter of taking and holding territory. It is far more complex than that. Afghanistan is a conflict based on perceptions and governance, or the lack thereof.

Influencing the way the United States and other Western countries have been perceived by ordinary Afghans is their use of the private military contractors, who have done more harm than good. Mercenaries first began to appear in growing numbers in 2003 and 2004 when it became clear that neither ISAF nor the Afghan security forces were able to provide sufficient protection, particularly for the internationals. As a result, American, British, and other security companies canvassed the Western embassies, UN agencies, and private companies in search of lucrative contracts. Eventually, local Afghan security companies also got into the business. As a body, they have sought to exaggerate the security threat, causing an ever-spiraling fear among foreigners living and working in Afghanistan.

Security protection has become a vicious circle. Certain organizations have corralled most of their employees into specially protected compounds. They will not even allow staff members to walk down the road to a restaurant, but insist that vehicles take them there. According to one UN official with seven years' Afghan experience, this means that the international community is dangerously cutting itself off. Nor is armed security necessarily an advantage. The UN knows full well it cannot rely on its Afghan guards to stick around if things get bad. Some have even been collaborating with the insurgents or rogue elements within the government. While the foreign mercenaries are less likely to abandon their wards, their protocols prevent aid workers from cultivating day-to-day contacts with ordinary Afghans. "So it's not really protection, but an illusion," said the official. "The end result is that we're not doing the job we should be."

With the worsening security situation in places like Jalalabad or Ghazni, many UN and other international agencies have pulled out most if not all of their expatriate field personnel. A few NGOs such as the Swedish Committee or the French agricultural group Madera have very deliberately continued operating in the eastern region, although relying mainly on Afghans to do the work. They also refuse to hire mercenaries. The ICRC, which maintains large offices with international staff, operates entirely without armed security support, sometimes to the amazement of NATO military. According to ACBAR (Agency Coordinating Body for Afghan Relief), of the 2,000 Afghan and 360 international NGOs operating across Afghanistan, no more than 6 use the services of private security companies, most commonly to provide unarmed guards at offices and homes. This is an astounding contrast with the far more costly private contracting firms obsessed by security.

The Swedish Committee believes that its best protection lies in working with local tribal leaders and communities. The organization also works with villages known to be collaborating with the insurgents. "We try to talk with everyone, explaining what we do. Many, including the Taliban, know us from the past. If we don't have the support, we don't work there," explained SCA director Anders Fange. "We had seventeen kidnappings in 2009, but all were returned within a couple of days."

Citing one incident, Fange recounted how two of his accountants traveling by bus carrying salaries for local workers in Wardak province south of Kabul were stopped by Taliban. Suspected of being government collaborators, they were taken off by armed men. They informed the SCA employees that it would be up to the commander to determine whether to shoot them or not. When the Talib chief learned that they worked for the SCA, he immediately returned their funds and had them taken back down to the main road. There the fighters stopped another bus and ordered the driver to take the aid representatives wherever they needed to go.

ICRC, MSF, and other organizations with long experience in Afghanistan all deal openly with the government, NATO, and the insurgents. "It is important to explain to everyone what you're doing," noted Emmanuel Tronc, head of MSF International's operations for Afghanistan. When MSF returned to the country in 2009 following a nearly five-year hiatus after five team members were assassinated in 2004, Tronc said that they went back to their old contacts from the Soviet-Afghan war. While some were no longer active with the government or the insurgents, they knew whom to talk with. In the long run, it is this approach that may prove the most effective for recovery to succeed in Afghanistan.

The problem with the mercenaries is that they are largely unaccountable for their actions. Their physical and verbal abuse has done more harm to the image of the internationals than anything else. Afghans deeply resent being ordered around by swaggering armed men with dark glasses and aggressive attitudes. In one incident at Kabul airport, an American mercenary hired by the US State Department to provide protection for Karzai shoved an Afghan traveler to the ground for not understanding the phrase "fuck off back," when the hapless man sought to make his way to the terminal.

The Afghans standing around were horrified. "These people think they can do whatever they want," said an Afghan teacher waiting to pick up his father. "If they are here to help us, then we prefer the Taliban." Many of the mercenaries are highly paid former US, South African, or British military. While guarding roads leading to foreign missions, they have crudely forced back residents trying to return to their homes, darkening their image among Afghan civilians.

Security companies have been involved in paying off insurgents not to attack road transport routes or construction crews. According to ISAF sources, as much as one-third of the cost of logistically supplying NATO forces in Afghanistan is spent on protection and bribery fees. "One wonders if this is the sort of standard operating procedure trade groups have in mind when they talk about private contractors making the US military the 'best supported, supplied military in any military operation in history,'" suggested David Isenberg, a specialist on mercenary companies and author of *Shadow Force: Private Security Contractors in Iraq.*

These included companies, such as Xe (formerly Blackwater and still widely known as such) which have run afoul of the law and yet continue to receive huge contracts from the US government. This firm, which is now synonymous with the widespread corruption pervading Afghan and international circles in Afghanistan, has been accused of misappropriating government weapons and hiring people with violent backgrounds. According to Spencer Ackerman of the *Washington Independent*, Xe has continued to receive contracts because of an obscure contracting rule known as the Federal Acquisition Regulation 9-406-2, which only allows a company to be banned if it has been officially "debarred" from eligibility. This has not happened to Xe although several debarment criteria appear to apply—notably, some critics say, "commission of fraud," "theft," "falsification or destruction of records," and "making false statements."

By 2010, an estimated seventy thousand registered and nonregistered contractors were believed to be working in Afghanistan. The Pentagon and NATO have been spending an average of fourteen billion dollars a year on contractors to construct and manage bases, including barracks and other facilities—but also transportation, communications, and interpreting. Other contractors have been hired specifically to provide armed security. These are the mercenaries currently protecting bases, civilian personnel, and road crews, as well as supporting counternarcotics operations. The US Department of Defense estimated that there were over 10,700 armed security contractors, popularly mercenaries, in Afghanistan by the end of 2009.

Following rising protests among ordinary Afghans regarding the behavior of mercenaries operating—often with impunity—in their country, President Karzai ordered private security firms to shut down and leave the country by the end of 2010. While temporarily postponed, the plan was welcomed by some international development agencies. Once the mercenaries are gone, some believe, there is likely to be far more successful development in Afghanistan, even if it takes longer than the "fast-track" projects currently being implemented through private contractors by the United States and other donors. Furthermore, it would encourage development organizations not only to work more closely but also to prove themselves with local communities. This would get rid of the firms that claim they cannot operate without security, and seem more interested in making money than doing a good job. In early 2011, however, US government pressure enabled Xe to continue operating in Afghanistan despite its highly negative reputation.

Given that foreign NGOs, humanitarians, contractors, and development entrepreneurs have all been lumped together under the term *aid worker*, a ban on the security companies may also help ordinary Afghans differentiate between humanitarians and those with links to the military and private corporations. "To the extent that it [the ban] helps to demilitarize the environment and to the extent that it reinforces the government's monopoly on the use of force, I think ultimately it would be a positive thing," said Nic Lee, director of the Afghanistan NGO Safety Office. He added that no type of armed action exists that is conducive to humanitarian activity. So the less armed activity there is, the more humanitarian access will improve.

Pressured by the US and British governments, plus concerned human rights groups, some sixty mercenary organizations signed a voluntary code of conduct in Switzerland in early November 2010 aimed at preventing abuse and reining in excess violence in lawless conflict zones. These include firms operating in Iraq and Afghanistan, such America's Triple Canopy and Xe, and Britain's G4 Security. The code, which is backed by thirty-five countries, incorporates a pledge that staff cannot invoke contractual obligations to justify crimes, killings, torture, kidnappings, detention, or summary executions. How this will translate to conditions in Afghanistan, where some armed mercenaries have actively pursued and hunted down suspected insurgents, is another matter.

A further issue related to the use of mercenaries is deployment of private militia by NATO and the Afghan government. In late 2010, some twenty-nine international NGOs and their partners told NATO that these poorly trained groups were doing more harm than good. Their use could lead to renewed civil war, as has happened in the past when numerous armed groups began fighting one another. In a bid to improve security, NATO has been hiring local tribesmen to provide unofficial policing against the insurgents in areas where security forces are weak or nonexistent.

Previous efforts to raise local defense units had failed for lack of government and community support. The Americans also involved the militia of local warlords—who have since become wealthy, powerful, and often criminal players in their own areas—during their initial operations against the Taliban. According to Carlotta Gall, the *New York Times*'s sterling Afghanistan reporter for nearly a decade, some NATO commanders remained cautious about using local mujahideen, or former anti-Soviet fighters. Others, however, said that village-based forces can work as part of the coordinated military and civilian strategy that began to gain traction in the south since early 2010. Under the plan, the new forces would be approved by local councils, or *shure*, to ensure that they have the support of all constituencies.

A key drawback to this approach is that many foreign military personnel come across as naive with little understanding of the often complex tribal dynamics that exist in Afghanistan. Southern Australia's *Independent Weekly* magazine reported in October 2010 that Australia had even gone as far as to fly in senior militia fighters loyal to Mattiullah Khan, a powerful warlord from Uruzgan, for training with elite special forces teams outside Sydney. The Australian military, which replaced the Dutch who pulled out of Afghanistan in 2010, maintained that Mattiullah's militia had "saved many Australian lives" and that it was important to work within "the cultural norms of Afghanistan." This astonishing approach appeared to dismiss the fact that the Dutch had refused to work with the notorious southern Afghan tribal chief, a Karzai ally, because of his links with murder and extortion.

Paramount to Afghanistan's problems remains the predicament of women. With the fall of the Talib regime, their situation improved, but only to a limited degree. Women were running for office, setting up their own businesses, establishing magazines or talk shows on radio and television, and taking on higher-profile civil service jobs. Once again, too, women were daring to speak out publicly about discrimination and violence.

Many aid agencies were able to rehire their female former employees or launch programs specifically aimed at women. For a society that suffers from the second highest maternal mortality rates in the world—with an estimated fifteen thousand women dying every year from pregnancy-related causes, where only 5 percent of women can read and write, and where over half of girls under the age of eighteen are married—it is crucial to drastically expand the role of women in Afghanistan's health services.

More often than not, male doctors and nurses are unable to treat women, except from behind a partition without physical or visual access to the patient. Only 15 percent of births are attended by trained health workers, including midwives; nine out of ten take place at home, resulting in an infant mortality rate of 165 per 1,000—one of the highest in the world. One in four children also die from preventable diseases by the age of five. For MSF's Emannuel Tronc, despite all the international aid poured into the country since 2001, basic health services remain poor.

"The training of more women should have been a priority since the very beginning, as they basically hold the key to improving access to health for women and children," he said.

The United States, Britain, World Health Organization, World Bank, and various other donors have all peddled highly favorable statistics about the progress of health in Afghanistan—with exorbitant claims that 85 percent of Afghans have access to some form of health care, compared with 9 percent in 2002. The reality, according to MSF and other health NGOs, is far different. Many see primary health services as falling "perilously short" and leaving "millions of Afghans with no or limited access to basic health care," as a December 2010 UN statement put it. "Only 52 percent of the rural population have access to a health facility within one hour walking distance." And many have no female staff.

During the first few years of Afghanistan's post-2001 recovery process, the optimism among women and girls was striking. In the weeks leading up to the Emergency Loya Jirgha in the summer of 2002, women were defiantly pushing to broaden their delegate numbers based on proportional representation rather than the token quotas imposed by the Bonn accords. When I provocatively asked one eastern Afghan tribal leader from Ghazni whether he thought it a good idea for women to express themselves, he curtly responded: "In Afghanistan, men have always protected women. That is our duty. There is no need for women to do this. These are bad habits from foreigners."

By early 2011, the precarious rights gained by women since 2001 were being unremittingly whittled away. According to a December 2010 UN report, widespread and harmful traditional practices were still causing suffering, humiliation, and marginalization for millions of Afghan women and girls. These included child marriages, the selling and buying of females for marriage, giving away girls for dispute resolution, imposed isolation in the home, denying the right to education or access to health services, and "honor" killings (whether through murder or the forced self-immolation of women to save face). In most cases, the perpetrators are never brought to justice.

Numerous Afghans, including religious leaders and even government officials, were reinforcing such customs by claiming that they were acceptable under Islamic law. Their interpretation of Islam, however, was based on ignorance and was inconsistent with not only shari'a but also Afghan and international law. The UN report noted that such practices are pervasive and occurring throughout the country regardless of tribal or ethnic group. The giving away of girls to settle disputes, known as *baad*, is broadly practiced even though the UN report found that many men and women opposed it. Women in Faryab province said that a girl married through *baad* is never respected; the family associates her with the male relative who committed the crime, and she is therefore herself a criminal. "The girl is treated like a servant as a means of revenge. Sometimes she is forced to sleep with the animals in the barn."

In August 2009, the Afghan government enacted the Elimination of Violence Against Women (EVAW) law, which (if properly implemented) could bring an end to such abuses. Yet numerous Afghans are not even aware that the law exists. Human rights advocates point out that despite the progressiveness of the new law, it fails to criminalize "honor crimes" or to clearly define rape. Nor does it distinguish it from consensual *zina*, which is sexual intercourse outside marriage and a crime under Islamic law. Many police and judges are unable or unwilling to apply the law. While a nationwide public awareness campaign to explain both the law and the rights of women may help change attitudes, it may take years to have an impact.

Growing insecurity was making it more difficult for women to operate on their own. Hundreds of girls' schools were closed because of attacks or threats by conservative hard-liners and Taliban. Both women teachers and girls were being warned, even chastised publicly, not to return to school. It was difficult for girls to walk to school, sometimes two, three, or more miles away. There has been a return to Hekmatyar-style attacks of the 1970s, with militants throwing acid in the faces of girls and women for appearing unveiled in public. In both urban and rural areas, families have been increasingly keeping their daughters at home for fear of kidnapping.

There also have been rising numbers of physical attacks against women's rights advocates. These include beatings, stabbings, and even murder. One of the most tragic was the shooting of Zakia Zaki of Peace Radio in northern Parwan province in June 2007. She was the second female journalist to be killed in a week. The first was Shokiba Sanga Amaaj, who was shot in the back by two male relatives. Apparently they did not like the fact that she was working as a newsreader for Shamshad TV, a private station.

Several years earlier, I had traveled up to Jabal Saraj north of Kabul to meet Zakia. She had been an enthusiastic advocate of the Radio Education for Afghan Children (REACH) program operated by my organization Media Action International with the BBC Trust. She was very excited because, while running a local FM radio station, which she had launched after the fall of the Taliban in October 2001, she was acquiring a new medium-wave transmitter. This meant that she would be able to cover the whole of Kabul. Radio, she felt, was the best way to reach illiterate women in their homes because, as she put it: "The men can't do anything about it. Information is gold."

The courageousness of this growing minority of women to speak out is exceptional, particularly when every critical word has its counterpart in the form of a bullet. The concern is that current efforts to resolve Afghanistan's decades of war by seeking reconciliation with the Taliban will ensure that women's rights will be the first to suffer. "Women do not want war, but none of them want the Taliban of 1996 again; no one wants to be imprisoned in the yards of their homes," Rahima Zarifi, a representative of the Ministry of Women's Affairs from Baghlan province, told the *New York Times.*

As others point out, it is convenient to blame the Taliban. There is just as much opposition within the current Karzai administration. "A lot of men working with the government are just like Taliban," noted Zukria, a female teacher from Herat. "Just because they wear suits does not mean they are open to change." Zukria's ambition is to see all four of her daughters go to university. "But I am less optimistic now. Even my own husband thinks we should send the boys first."

Organizations such as the Aga Khan Foundation have tailored projects to women, such as its Old Town reconstruction program where they receive training in carpet making, literacy, private enterprise management, and other initiatives. A small but growing number are establishing their own businesses, despite the difficulties of venturing into the bazaars. The US military has sought through the Peace Dividend Trust (PDT) to strengthen the capacity of enterprises owned by women by creating local supply chains for the Afghan security forces.

"Fifty percent of the country are women," said US Air Force major Chuck Seidel, a local procurement officer. "If we are going to make a difference, we have got to create jobs." Started in 2009 by the Pentagon's Kabul Regional Contracting Center, the PDT has set aside contracts totaling $365 million for women's companies to supply the Afghan police and army with clothes, boots, mattresses, and other equipment until 2014. By the end of 2010, the United States had committed $26 billion to train and equip Afghan security forces as part of its overall contribution toward the recovery effort.

Despite the exceptional enthusiasm and determination to establish themselves, Afghan female entrepreneurs have faced enormous obstacles from corrupt or highly traditional elements within Afghanistan's male-dominated business establishment. At a special workshop held by the World Bank in late 2009, several female entrepreneurs expressed their frustrations at not being able to operate on a level playing field. They are often denied access to both funds and contracts. A lot of deals are made over tea in the *chaikhane*, which women do not frequent. As one development specialist pointed out: "It's very much a boys' club. Some of these men are pretty incompetent, and yet they're the ones getting the government contracts."

Hassina Syed of NOW—whose nearly six hundred members consist of teachers, doctors, computer specialists, parliamentarians, and other professionals—ranks as one of Afghanistan's successful female entrepreneurs. She is also a beneficiary of the PDT. An outspoken former refugee and mother of two from Peshawar, she has confronted numerous obstacles, including threats by warlords, government officials, and rival male interests who deeply resent a female in their presence. Not only has she created her own expanding companies—including a travel agency, a bedding factory, and a house management service—but she is actively engaged with the Afghan Chamber of Commerce and Industry (ACCI). She is the only female among its three thousand members. She is also the only woman to have taken part in official trade delegations led by President Karzai to Europe and Asia.

For numerous Afghan businessmen, however, one of the main problems with the ACCI is that its management committee, which includes one of the Karzai brothers, is corrupt. Major donors, including USAID, deliberately pass their contracts on to the chamber, which in turn is supposed to inform all its members. Instead, the best contracts are kept by its directors, others are subcontracted to smaller ACCI members, and the remaining crumbs are tossed out for the rest to bid on. One US embassy official admitted that this was a severe drawback, but that the donors were trying to make the ACCI more transparent. However, as one Afghan businessman said in disgust: "The Americans always say this. We all know what's going on but no one wants to stop it. If we complain, we get threatened or have no chance at obtaining contracts."

Even with the exceptional efforts of select individuals and outspoken activists, Afghan women's push for change can expect to remain a slow and arduous one. Ironically, like Afghanistan's men, many suffer from the same historic or tribal divisions, including political bickering. This is already evident among the few female parliamentarians in the country today. And yet there is an aspiring new and educated generation of young men and women emerging who want something else other than greed and war.

Forward Operating Base Delhi is one of those defiantly named military outposts in southern Afghanistan. Consisting of camouflaged tents and sandbagged compounds bulging with soldiers, equipment, and vehicles, it sits like a road construction camp on the edge of Garmsir Bazaar. Deep in Helmand province, it lies in an area that American and British troops have dubbed "the Snake's Head"—a patchwork of irrigated fields and canals gnawing into the surrounding desert. On a map, it looks like a cobra head with its tail stretching up the Helmand River.

Normally planted with wheat or opium poppies, these well-watered farmlands are part of the massive US-backed Helmand River Valley Project dating back to the 1950s and '60s. Garmsir itself is a makeshift town, only recently "liberated" from Talib control. It boasts administrative buildings, residential compounds, workshops, and market stalls selling oranges, pomegranates, and okra, but also basic hardware ranging from shovels to TV sets.

As I walked down the main street in 2009 with a group of aid workers accompanied by US troops and the half a dozen mercenaries attached to our detail, I felt like a visiting dignitary who talked with the locals, but had no real contact. It was awkward and all a show. Some soldiers stopped to banter, holding their guns at the ready. The Afghans laughed or chatted back, while the kids defiantly asked for a dollar. None of the Westerners had any idea what these people were really thinking. I yearned to stroll the bazaar alone with shopkeepers beckoning me over for tea. Then, at least, I would be there at their welcome. Not as an imposed outsider.

Nine years had passed since the American invasion in October 2001. British forces had been fighting in Helmand for three years and, in the biggest airlift since the Vietnam War, the Second US Marine Expeditionary Force had joined them. Some four thousand infantry marines had swept in with helicopters fanning out across the desert to clear the ground and to reimpose government rule. Together they drove the Taliban out. Now they were working their way southward along the Snake's Body.

Of course, the reality was that despite all the ISAF propaganda about the Kabul government increasingly asserting itself, the insurgents would be back within hours were it not for the foreigners. Few have any confidence in the Karzai regime. Most Afghan security forces would desert the moment the wind changes. Afghans know full well that a growing swell of voters in the West want their armies out.

Not unlike the nineteenth-century British picket forts, the Americans had built heavily buttressed Fort Laramies to protect their strategic points and help the Kabul regime establish a sense of normalcy. "This is a very isolated area," said US lieutenant colonel Christian Cabaniss. "You don't just come in from the outside and start talking to people in the community. The more and more they're comfortable and they feel we're going to stay and the government is going to deliver, the more likely they are to tell us things. And when they start telling us, the Taliban have no sea to swim in. They're going to have to leave."

This is the sort of optimism senior officers are expected to exude. But did these grown men—and women—really believe it? There was a naïveté, even delusion, about this theory. As if the insurgents were really going to disappear if the government began doing what it was supposed to. One wonders whether anyone was then, or is even now, trying to learn lessons from the past—from Vietnam or the Soviet-Afghan war or Iraq.

In February 2010, the Coalition forces launched Operation Moshtarak—which means "together"—their biggest offensive so far. This target was Marjah, a sprawling district of towns and bazaars with some two hundred thousand residents just west of the Snake's Head. It was also a known center for drug traffickers and the Taliban. US forces first raided Marjah in May 2009, seizing tons of opium and bomb-making equipment. But when they pulled out, the insurgents moved back in. Their much-heralded 2010 assault, which deployed up to fifteen thousand Coalition and Afghan army troops against an estimated two thousand insurgents, was an attempt to "take and hold" new territory. Some insurgents stood and fought. Most buried their guns or faded away to other provinces. Four months later, NATO seemed surprised that the guerrillas were drifting back. The military could probably hold on to the area indefinitely, but would this really constitute success? The operation hardly empowered the local population.

Several British and Americans who have worked in the south maintain that Marjah achieved nothing except unnecessary deaths. It may have even prompted more Afghans to join the insurgency. Critics included Mathew Hoh, the former US civilian representative in Zabul province and himself an ex-marine captain. He resigned in October 2009, arguing that the war was not in America's strategic interests. Referring to the insurgency as "valleyism"—no different from the Soviet-Afghan war—Hoh argued that the United States has not understood the true nature of what is happening. "In Afghanistan everything is much more localized," he said in an interview with NPR. "Allegiance is to your family, and then to your village or your valley, and that's what they fight for."

While reporting on Marjah, some US media harped on how difficult it is to know who's a rebel. Nothing new there. Neither in Afghanistan's wars nor any guerrilla war for that matter. Even in "secure" areas, the insurgents maintain a hold, if only at night. They continue to assassinate collaborators or field their IEDs and suicide bombers. Or distribute their "night letters." There are many within the ministries who sympathize with the opposition. They even operate as Taliban when the workday ends. It was no different with the mujahideen in the 1980s.

Operation Moshtarak had clear parallels with the Red Army–Afghan offensive I witnessed twenty-seven years earlier in the spring of 1982 against the Panjshir. The push, which involved some twelve thousand Soviet-Afghan troops, was roughly the same size as Marjah's. In the Soviet-Afghan war, Western journalists reported primarily from the resistance side. In contrast with many of today's media embedded with NATO, we had constant access to ordinary Afghans. We walked through the countryside, sleeping in villages, with long evenings spent drinking tea and talking with locals. Dispatches from the British and American military fronts of today often seem to be from a different war, with assessments that have little to do with Afghanistan. Frank conversation does not happen while reporters or others are wearing body armor and sunglasses or when flanked by heavily armed soldiers. Afghans will only tell you what suits their interests. Hence, the questionable veracity of opinion polls regularly trotted out by the international community to justify its activities in Afghanistan.

Several months after the Marjah offensive, in June 2010, I found myself viewing BBC coverage of the latest repatriation of British dead to RAF Lyneham in southwest England. Seven Union Jack–draped coffins were solemnly taken off an RAF transport and driven in a slow cortege of black hearses through the neighboring Wiltshire town of Wootton Bassett. This had become an almost daily ritual, with relatives and bystanders watching the sad entourage. The seven soldiers had all been killed in Helmand. Perhaps the British are more used to having their troops killed in foreign wars. A tradition of duty from former empire days. Only recently have the Americans begun allowing the filming of US coffins. Washington, with the acquiescence of American TV networks, does everything possible to hide the harsher realities of the Afghan war. All I see is a replay of history.

EPILOGUE

When I first decided to write this book, several friends with no special knowledge of Afghanistan told me: It is important to give a sense of Afghanistan and explain what has gone wrong and why. Since the end of 2002, when it was already clear that things were beginning to go drastically wrong, I began specifically exploring ideas with both Afghans and knowledgeable expatriates to see what they thought could help put Afghanistan back on the right track.

By early 2011, however, many were positively gloomy, saying it was too late to fix Afghanistan. *Transition* had become the operative word, notably how to shape Afghanistan until the projected NATO pullout in 2014. While significant improvements have indeed been achieved, they admitted, there was still very little to show for the billions of dollars of aid spent in Afghanistan over the previous nine years. Far more could have been done, they said, had there been more commitment to Afghanistan with a more discerning allocation of resources.

Some felt that NATO's planned withdrawal of combat troops by the end of 2014 was a very positive step for Afghanistan. This would at least help detract from the West's obsession with security, PRTs, and military solutions. It was time to get back to basics. The focus should be on development, including private investment, which is what it should have been from the beginning. For once, they said, the internationals should consider what was best for ordinary Afghans.

Given the enormous complexities of the Afghan situation, many suggestions were remarkably simple and not particularly new. Effective recovery, they argued, needs to focus on what is doable, not what sounds good back in Washington, Brussels, or London. There should be an emphasis on quality rather than quantity, small rather than big, and projects that can be shown to work by example. As French agriculturalist Alain de Bures put it: Farmers always look over the wall to see how their neighbors are doing. If one is doing well with a particular new crop or method, the others will follow. Above all, nothing should be done in a hurry. The commitment has to be long-term, even if it takes years—and in some cases, decades.

Equally crucial, some stressed, is to drink tea with local communities, listen to what they have to say, and never seek to impose. Only with local ownership, whether renovating the Old Town of Kabul or establishing conservation programs in Qeshm in northern Afghanistan, can projects succeed. A beautifully constructed road is pointless if one cannot use it for security reasons—because local villagers were never brought into the process. Massive amounts of funding incite greed, corruption, and failure, so it is far better to operate with a more modest but workable budget that is transparent. Finally, the West needs to forget trying to re-create Afghanistan in its own image.

Many felt it essential that the donors immediately cease enriching corrupt Afghan elites and warlords. The West has enabled greedy Afghans to destroy their own heritage by opening a Pandora's box of inappropriate aid and military intervention. It is these Afghans whom future generations will blame for having demolished the little that remained from their cultural past.

Nor should the donors endow private foreign firms, which operate with exorbitant overheads, high-salaried consultants, and little knowledge of the country. While certain private contractors have provided value for money with sometimes innovative approaches, the majority have not. The internationals also need to reduce their dependence on security firms and mercenaries. Far more effective would be to work more closely with experienced local and international NGOs, or private firms whose commitment to the country is long-term and in the interests of Afghans.

The key to recovery is to focus more on the countryside, particularly provincial capitals and market towns, so that the bulk of Afghanistan's population can finally feel that they are benefiting from the Western intervention. This includes public and private investment aimed at better rural infrastructure, agricultural extension, health centers with full-time doctors and nurses, job creation, and public transport. It is imperative to move away from the overemphasis on Kabul.

Our distorted Western approaches toward Kabul have created an entirely new class of impoverished slum dwellers, who never existed before. Even during the height of the Soviet-Afghan war, I would never have described Afghans as "poor." For me, Afghans have always been a civilized and culturally rich people with an extraordinary sense of pride and hospitality. The "poorest" Afghan tended to be comfortable in his skin and looked you in the eye.

According to Jolyon Leslie, the whole issue of international aid has become "highly pernicious," a new form of colonialism. Struggling to save Afghanistan's cultural heritage and one of the true heroes of the foreign community, Leslie believes that the international recovery effort has failed because of the West's inability not only to provide quality but also to communicate more effectively with the local population. "The Afghans have good reason to be skeptical. This translates into quite a dangerous situation. A lot of people are doing some very good work, but there are many organizations perceived to be greedy and in it for themselves. The result is a viscerally negative attitude among Afghans."

One of the issues repeatedly raised is the urgent need for the international community to reexamine its imposition of a centralized government, an approach that has proved highly corrosive. Most Afghans seem to want a united country, but not with a powerful center that will suppress local and regional identities. A peaceful and stable environment will not move forward if Kabul remains the linchpin for everything, particularly if it's perceived as promoting its own interests. "In a country as diverse as Afghanistan, no matter what you do, the tribe—or your community—comes first," noted CARE International's Lex Kassenberg. More provincial government might also help deal with the Taliban and other insurgents in regions such as Kandahar and Helmand. It would enable local communities to have a greater say over their own affairs. "This is at the heart of the question for Afghanistan," Kassenberg added.

More responsibility placed in the hands of provincial authorities, who are better known and more accountable to their own constituents, would ensure more effective government. While visiting an agricultural project in Kunar, I encountered three ministry officials who had flown down for the day. They clearly had no understanding of local conditions, and yet sought to impose their views on a group of local specialists who regarded the visitors with total disdain. "This is the problem. Kabul sends us people who make their own deals for themselves. They are not interested in us," one of them later told me.

By and large, local rural populations, but also many in the cities, would prefer an adapted shari'a system more in line with their own needs.

While not necessarily acceptable to Western tastes and moral norms, this could lead to better security and more pragmatic relations with Kabul.

Change, including improved women's rights, is more likely to be brought about through more effective trade, investment, education, and development than anything else. The fact that communities in Kunar and other eastern areas, where opposition to female education was enormous in the late 1970s, now have girls' schools is an example of this. Access to better health care is another critical catalyst for change. According to Shaheena, a Jalalabad-based aid worker, this will happen "when men understand that only through female doctors and nurses can they help save the lives of their wives and girls."

Even if progress is slow, my interlocutors point out, the impact may prove far longer lasting. Furthermore, suggest some, international organizations such as the United Nations, World Bank, and ISAF need to stop robbing the country of qualified personnel for use as interpreters, administrative assistants, or even drivers. Afghanistan needs doctors, engineers, and teachers to work for their own people. Another critical component is to pay civil servants proper salaries with incentives for good work as a means of combating corruption and promoting efficiency.

Above all, however, the international community needs to eliminate the use of mercenaries and private armies. Donors should avoid giving contracts to organizations not willing to work without armed security. "Had the internationals bothered to train up a professional police force with good salaries from the start, they could have avoided a lot of the current problems. But the Americans tried to use retired sheriffs who understood bugger-all about Afghanistan to do a rapid turnaround. It was a complete waste of time," observed Peter Jouvenal. "And then they're surprised things don't work."

While some NGOs and private contractors fully understand the need to develop local capacity, donor contracts and funding need to reflect this. This means encouraging aid groups to reach out to all segments of Afghan society, whether the government, NATO, or the Taliban. Counterparts need to be individual leaders, not political, military, or religious groups. Such approaches, they say, are in everyone's interests and can only lead to better security. This is precisely how the ICRC, MSF, Aga Khan, SCA, and other experienced organizations operate.

Vital, too, is for donors to encourage organizations with additional funding to continue working in communities, even when the projects have supposedly ended. Too many initiatives fail because aid groups are forced to pull up stakes and leave with no local capacity in place. All in all, any organization benefiting from public funds should be more accountable in the way it undertakes projects. Promoting more effective rule of law, including making all perpetrators of crimes against humanity accountable, will respond more to Afghan needs.

This is where media can make a difference. Better reporting in the public interest has already shown itself to be a highly effective vehicle for promoting accountability. This means developing more public outreach programs—whether talk shows, soap operas, or youth magazines—aimed at informing the Afghan public about assuming responsibilities for their own country.

And finally, in a refrain echoed by so many Afghans, if their country is to become the new crossroads for peace, security, and trade for Central Asia and the Indian subcontinent—as is so often touted by the international community—then the United States, Europe, and other Western donors need to move beyond the usual hollow words and publicly confront the realities of the region. They need to actively pressure Pakistan, Iran, China, India, Saudi Arabia, and others to stop meddling in Afghan affairs. This has been, and continues to be, the principal obstacle to peace in Afghanistan.

Equally important, international vigilance needs to ensure that countries do not simply rape Afghanistan or destroy its environment by paying off the right people in order to extract what they can in the form of natural resources, whether minerals, gas, or water. This includes outside powers such as China with its three-billion-dollar investment in the Aynak copper mine in northern Afghanistan or the Central Asian republics with their overuse of water from the Oxus River (Amu Darya). As observers point out, more private investment is vital. This is where Afghanistan needs help if it is to develop what it can do best and with quality, such as the cultivation of fresh fruit, the development of eco- and cultural tourism, and the good management of its considerable natural mineral resources.

As with so many foreigners passionately involved with Afghanistan, it has been hard to see what has become of this extraordinary country and its people since war first erupted in 1978. Many of us have romanticized Afghanistan because of its harsh beauty and poetic embrace. It drew one in to confront one's own humanity. When meeting an Afghan on some lone mountain path or sitting under a mulberry tree drinking tea, it was always on equal terms, as if this is how we imagined ourselves to have once been in a past life. There was a sense of liberty we would never again find. Encountering Afghanistan was not unlike what Lewis and Clark must have felt when they first beheld the overwhelming landscapes of the Far West at the beginning of the nineteenth century. Only later did we recognize and respect the brutal realities of this high-mountain and desert land that stands so defiantly behind God's back.

For some, Afghanistan drew us too far. My friend Christophe de Ponfilly became obsessed. He produced half a dozen films and books about Afghanistan, Massoud and his wars, and the nature of clandestine existence. Then he filmed and directed his first full-length feature, *L'Étoile du Soldat* (Star of the Soldier), shot in the Hindu Kush, about the relationship between a guerrilla commander and a Soviet soldier. Shortly after the film was released in May 2006, Christophe shot himself. Although we all knew there were other reasons for his death, he had often told me he could not bear what Afghanistan had become.

Of course, as with all romantic notions, our concept of Afghanistan was a foreign one; one that most Afghans could never afford to share. They were too busy surviving. As many ordinary Afghans will themselves admit, the 1980s represented a resistance struggle of hope, which they thought would lead to a new life. Instead, they were betrayed by their own leaders and the outsiders dabbling with them. The 1990s resulted in a new period of war and violence; the Taliban did bring about enclaves of security, but only according to their own repressive terms. The new Islamists did not open the country to peace and prosperity, which is what most Afghans wanted—and still want today. When the international community entered the game toward the end of 2001, many Afghans—but also those of us who had been involved for so long—thought that, finally, all those missed opportunities of the previous two decades would now be addressed. This did not happen.

While still apprehensive, I do not share the sheer pessimism of so many of my friends and colleagues. The question now is whether we will allow all those lives lost (Afghan and foreign) and billions of dollars squandered to be for nothing. Shortly before his death in December 2010, US special envoy to Afghanistan Richard Holbrooke reportedly told his physician to "stop this war." Whether uttered in painful banter or as a serious exhortation about policy, Holbrooke clearly realized that Afghanistan's wars were unwinnable and that other options urgently needed to be pursued. The killing, or as some say, the assassination of bin Laden on May 2, 2011 is unlikely to affect the war. He was never that popular, even among the Taliban, and resentment toward Arabs remains deep. Further, al Qaeda has had an increasingly diminished impact in recent years. As one senior Afghan official reminded me, "We welcome foreigners, who come as guests but also leave when they are no longer wanted. This goes for both the Arabs and the Americans."

Personally, I still believe that a new nation at peace can emerge. Afghans have always proven themselves to be an extraordinarily resilient and dedicated people. Many share a faith in Islam, which, when not defiled by external radicalism, has given them the strength to overcome the most horrendous challenges. How many times have I watched ordinary Afghans, either alone or in groups, place their blanket, coat, or even ragged piece of cloth on the ground by the side of a river, along a mountain pass, or among some desert rocks—and then pray to their God? How could one even imagine this people could ever be vanquished?

Ultimately, Afghans need to remember that Afghanistan is their country, and they have to find their own way again. Many have sold out through greed and the willingness to rent themselves—or their country—to the highest bidder. It is now up to the Pushtuns, Tajiks, Hazaras, Uzbeks, and others to come to terms with what they have done to their homeland and to agree on whether they want a nation or not. The Afghanistan they will finally build probably won't be the romantic notion of the country that I like to imagine, but I can only hope it is a country that they can all live in peacefully together. And I still hope to see the migrating cranes again one day.

—Edward Girardet
May 2011

AFGHANISTAN: TIME LINE

1842: First Anglo-Afghan War. Destruction of 16,000-strong British expeditionary force by Afghan tribesmen.

1880: End of Second Anglo-Afghan War. Afghanistan maintains internal sovereignty, but the British control foreign affairs.

1893: British unilateral imposition of Durand Line forming current border with Pakistan (not recognized by Afghanistan).

1919: Third Anglo-Afghan War. Afghanistan regains independence.

1926: Amanullah proclaims himself king. Social reforms opposed by conservative forces.

1929: King Amanullah flees after civil unrest over reforms. Amir Habibullah Kalakani, known as Bacha-e-Saqao (son of the water carrier), becomes first Tajik to take power after 350 years of Pushtun role. He is executed after nine months.

1933: Zahir Shah becomes king. Afghanistan remains monarchy for next four decades.

1953: General Mohammed Daoud becomes prime minister. Turns to Soviet Union for economic and military assistance. Introduces social reforms, including abolition of purdah, the practice of secluding women from public view.

1963: Daoud resigns as prime minister.

1964: Constitutional monarchy introduced.

1973: Daoud seizes power and declares a republic. Tries to play off Soviet Union against the United States. Left-wing factions oppose him. Daoud cracks down on fundamentalists.

1975: First revolts in Panjshir Valley by rebels (including Ahmed Shah Massoud and Gulbuddin Hekmatyar), backed by Pakistan.

1978: Saur (April) Revolution. Daoud is overthrown and killed by communist People's Democratic Party of Afghanistan (PDPA). The communist Khalq (Masses) and Parcham (Banner) factions fall out, leading to purge of Parcham leaders.

1978 (summer): Armed revolt breaks out against radical reforms of PDPA regime. Soviet Union steps up military support. First US backing for the guerrillas.

1979: Hafizullah Amin kills Nur Mohammed Taraki in internal Khalqi coup. Revolts in countryside continue, and Afghan army faces collapse.

1979 (December 27): Soviet Red Army invades Afghanistan. Amin killed and Parcham faction leader Babrak Karmal installed at head of PDPA government.

1980: Nationwide resistance to Soviet occupation expands. United States, Pakistan, China, Iran, and Saudi Arabia supply money and arms. Osama bin Laden's first trip to Peshawar and Afghan border.

1980 (February): First Loya Jirgha (Grand Council) held in Peshawar by Afghan resistance in attempt to create a government-in-exile. The initiative fails.

1985: Mujahideen come together in Pakistan to form alliance against Soviet forces. Political infighting continues with United States and Pakistan heavily backing Islamic extremists. Half of Afghan population now displaced by war either internally or as refugees. New Soviet leader Mikhail Gorbachev says he will withdraw troops from Afghanistan.

1986: United States begins supplying mujahideen with Stinger missiles, enabling them to shoot down Soviet helicopter gunships. Mohammed Najibullah replaces Babrak Karmal as head of Soviet-backed regime.

1988: Afghanistan, USSR, United States, and Pakistan sign peace accords. Soviet Union begins pullout.

1989: Last Soviet troops leave, but civil war continues as mujahideen push to overthrow Najibullah.

1990: Bin Laden leaves Afghanistan for Saudi Arabia and Sudan.

1991: United States and USSR agree to end military aid to both sides.

1992: Resistance closes in on Kabul, and Najibullah falls from power. New civil war breaks out among rival militias.

1993: Mujahed factions agree on formation of government with Burhanuddin Rabbani, an ethnic Tajik, proclaimed president.

1994: Battle for Kabul continues. Taliban emerge as new military force.

1996: Taliban seize Kabul. Massoud and Rabbani flee. United Front (or Northern Alliance) against Taliban emerges. Return of Osama bin Laden to Afghanistan.

1997: Taliban recognized by Pakistan and Saudi Arabia. Most other countries continue to regard Rabbani as head of state. Taliban control up to two-thirds of country.

1998: Earthquakes kill thousands of people. Severe drought also affects much of country. United States launches missile strikes at suspected bases of bin Laden, accused of bombing US embassies in East Africa.

1999: UN imposes sanctions to pressure Talib regime to hand over bin Laden.

2001 (January): UN imposes further sanctions on Taliban.

2001 (March): Taliban blow up giant Buddha statues in Bamiyan.

2001 (April): Mullah Mohammad Rabbani, second most powerful Talib leader, dies of liver cancer.

2001 (May): Taliban order religious minorities to wear tags identifying themselves as non-Muslims, and Hindu women to veil themselves like other Afghan women.

2001 (September): Ahmed Shah Massoud, legendary guerrilla commander and leader of anti-Taliban opposition, killed in suicide attack by al Qaeda operatives posing as journalists, just before 9/11 attacks against the United States.

2001 (October 7): American and British warplanes launch strikes against Taliban. Start of US-led invasion.

2001 (November): Opposition forces seize Mazar-e-Sharif and within days march into Kabul and other key cities. Fall of Talib regime.

2001 (December 5). Discussions leading to Bonn accords and interim government.

2001 (December 7): Taliban flee last stronghold in Kandahar. Mullah Omar remains at large.

2001 (December 22): Hamid Karzai heads thirty-member interim power-sharing government.

2002 (January): First contingent of foreign peacekeepers. Tokyo donors' conference.

2002 (April): Former king Zahir Shah returns as Father of the Nation.

2002 (May): UN Security Council extends mandate of International Security Assistance Force (ISAF). Coalition continues campaign against remnants of al Qaeda and Taliban.

2002 (June): Emergency Loya Jirgha elects Hamid Karzai as interim president.

2003 (March): US-led invasion of Iraq, which distracts the United States from its commitment to Afghanistan.

2003 (August): NATO assumes control of Kabul security, its first operational commitment outside Europe.

2004 (January): Loya Jirgha adopts new constitution.

2004 (March): Afghanistan secures $8.2 billion in aid over three years.

2004 (October–November): Hamid Karzai elected president with 55 percent of vote.

2005 (February): Several hundred people die in harshest winter in decade.

2005 (May): Details emerge of prisoner abuse by US forces at detention centers.

2005 (September): First parliamentary and provincial elections in more than thirty years.

2005 (December): New parliament holds inaugural session.

2006 (February): Donor conference in London pledges over $10 billion in recovery aid.

2006 (October): NATO assumes responsibility for security across whole of Afghanistan.

2007 (March): Pakistan arrests Mullah Obaidullah Akhund, third most senior member of Taliban leadership council. NATO and Afghan forces launch Operation Achilles, largest offensive to date against Taliban.

2007 (May): Taliban's most senior military commander, Mullah Dadullah, killed. Afghan and Pakistani troops clash over simmering border dispute in worst violence in decades.

2007 (July): Former king Zahir Shah dies. South Korean Christian charity workers kidnapped by Taliban. Two killed, the rest freed.

2007 (August): Opium production reaches record high according to UN report.

2007 (November): Suicide attack on parliamentary delegation kills forty-one in worst such attack.

2007 (December): Two EU and UN envoys accused by Afghan officials of making contact with Taliban and expelled.

2008 (April): NATO leaders in Bucharest say Afghanistan mission remains top priority.

2008 (June): Taliban engineer massive jailbreak from Kandahar prison, freeing 350 insurgents. President Karzai warns Afghanistan will send troops into Pakistan to fight militants if Islamabad fails to take action against them.

2008 (July): Suicide bomb attack on Indian embassy in Kabul kills more than fifty. Afghan government accuses the ISI of involvement.

2008 (August): Ten French soldiers killed in an ambush by Taliban fighters in worst single NATO loss to date. Karzai accuses Afghan and US-led coalition forces of killing at least eighty-nine civilians in air strike in western province of Herat.

2008 (September): President Bush sends extra 4,500 US troops to Afghanistan as part of "quiet surge."

2008 (October): Germany extends Afghanistan mission to 2009, and boosts troop numbers by 1,000 to 4,500.

2008 (November): Talib militants reject peace talk offer by President Karzai, saying there can be no negotiations until foreign troops leave.

2008 (December): President Karzai and new Pakistani president Asif Ali Zardari agree to form joint strategy to fight militants operating in border regions.

2009 (January): US defense secretary Robert Gates says Afghanistan is President Barack Obama's "greatest test."

2009 (February): Up to twenty NATO countries pledge increase in military commitment to Afghanistan after United States announces dispatch of 17,000 extra troops.

2009 (March): President Obama unveils new US strategy for Afghanistan and Pakistan.

2009 (May): US commander General David McKiernan replaced by General Stanley McChrystal to provide "new thinking" in battle against Taliban.

2009 (July): US military launches major offensive in Helmand province.

2009 (August): Presidential and provincial elections tainted by widespread insurgent attacks, patchy turnout, and serious fraud.

2009 (September): General McChrystal says war against Taliban could be lost within twelve months without significant troop increases.

2009 (October): Karzai declared winner of fraudulent August presidential election.

2009 (November): Karzai sworn in for second term as president.

2009 (December): President Obama decides to boost US troop numbers in Afghanistan by 30,000, bringing total to 100,000. He also says United States will begin withdrawing forces by 2011. Al Qaeda double agent kills seven CIA agents in suicide attack on a US base in Khost.

2010 (January): Insurgents carry out bold attack in Kabul, leaving twelve dead, including seven militants.

2010 (February): NATO-led forces launch Operation Moshtarak in bid to secure control of southern Helmand province. Top Talib military commander Mullah Abdul Ghani Baradar is captured in Pakistan.

2010 (April): President Karzai says foreign observers responsible for fraud in disputed 2009 poll and planning of coup. White House calls his remarks "genuinely troubling."

2010 (July): Major international conference endorses Karzai's timetable for security to be transferred from foreign to Afghan forces by 2014. General David Petraeus takes command of US and ISAF forces.

2010 (August): Dutch troops leave Afghanistan. Karzai announces ban on foreign security firms.

2010 (September): Afghans brave wave of Taliban attacks to vote in parliamentary elections on September 18; turnout estimated at 40 percent.

2010 (November): NATO summit in Lisbon. Announced withdrawal of bulk of Coalition troops by 2014.

2011 (May 2): Killing of Osama bin Laden in Abottabad, Pakistan by American forces.

2011 (September 9 and 11): Tenth anniversaries respectively of the killing of Ahmed Shah Massoud and the al Qaeda attacks against the United States.

GLOSSARY

KEY PLAYERS

Abdullah Abdullah: Former aide to Ahmed Shah Massoud, born in 1960 to a Pushtun father and Tajik mother from the Panjshir Valley. Appointed foreign minister in the post-2001 government. Ran against Karzai as principal presidential candidate in 2009 but dropped out when it became apparent that the vote was rigged.

bin Laden, Osama: Saudi Islamic militant, declared a terrorist by the West. First came to Afghanistan in 1980 to support the anti-Soviet jihad. He was killed at his Pakistani hideaway by US commandoes on May 2, 2011.

Brahimi, Lakhdar: Former Algerian foreign minister and special United Nations representative to Afghanistan 2001.

Daoud, Mohammed (1909–78): Former president of Afghanistan and arch-manipulator of the two Cold War superpowers, the United States and Soviet Union. Assassinated in April 1978 during the communist putsch.

Dostum, Abdul Rashid: A ruthless Uzbek warlord and former militia chief under the Soviets. Known for changing sides as quickly as changing shirts. Responsible for numerous war crimes and crimes against humanity. He is a general and chief of staff to the commander of the Afghan army.

Fahim, Mohammed Qasim: A Tajik and former Jamiat intelligence chief, he was made head of the United Front (or Northern Alliance) following Massoud's assassination. Later made minister of defense during the post-2001 government. Appointed first vice president under Karzai's second presidency.

Gailani, Pir Sayed Ahmed: Traditional leader of the National Islamic Front of Afghanistan (NIFA), one of the seven main resistance parties during the Soviet-Afghan war. Now a respected éminence grise.

Haq, Abdul: One of the most renowned and effective Pushtun guerrilla commanders (Hezb Khales faction) during the Soviet-Afghan war. Favored by the Americans, Haq was betrayed, tortured, and killed by the Taliban in late 2001.

Haqqani Network: An independent insurgent group closely allied with the Taliban operating both inside Pakistan, notably North Waziristan, and Afghanistan. It is led by Maulawi Jalaluddin Haqqani, a former US-supported mujahed commander, and his son Sirajuddin Haqqani. The network is considered to be one of the most lethal threats to the US and NATO presence in Afghanistan.

Hekmatyar, Gulbuddin: Leader of the main Hezb-e-Islami faction. Despite having been massively supported by the Americans and Pakistanis during the Soviet-Afghan war, Hekmatyar—also known as Gulbuddin—now ranks as one of the most influential insurgent leaders against the NATO presence in Afghanistan. He has been designated an "international terrorist" by the Americans and is responsible for war crimes and crimes against humanity.

Karmal, Babrak: Former PDPA (Parcham faction) president of Afghanistan under the Soviets. Replaced by Najibullah in 1986, he went into Russian exile, where he died ten years later.

Karzai, Hamid: Afghan president since the Emergency Loya Jirgha in June 2002. An ethnic Pushtun, he was elected twice, once in 2004 and the second time in disputed elections in 2009.

Khalili, Masood: Afghan ambassador to Spain and, prior to that, India and Turkey. Former mujahed adviser to Ahmed Shah Massoud. Son of renowned twentieth-century Afghan poet Khalilullah Khalili.

Khalis, Maulawi Mohammed Younis: Pushtun US-backed resistance politician and head of the second Hezb-e-Islami faction. Provided refuge for bin Laden in 1994 and later sided with the Taliban. Former members of his faction, notably Haqqani, are now fighting with the Taliban and other insurgents against NATO forces. Died in 1996.

Khalizad, Zalmay: An Afghan-born former US ambassador to Afghanistan during the post-2001 period. Previously a special adviser to the Bush administration and a key proponent for military action in Afghanistan. He was appointed US ambassador to Iraq in April 2005.

Khalq: The "Masses" faction of the communist PDPA.

Khan, Ismail: Warlord and former key mujahed commander from Herat, and a Massoud ally with Jamiat. Captured by the Taliban and held for three years before he escaped. On retaking Herat during the post-2001 period, he became a governor and was later appointed minister of energy in a bid to weaken his hold on the western part of Afghanistan.

Massoud, Ahmed Shah (1952–2001): Renowned Tajik resistance leader from the Panjshir Valley. Considered one of the most effective guerrilla strategists of the twentieth century. He was assassinated by two al Qaeda operatives on September 9, 2001, two days prior to 9/11.

Mujaddedi, Professor Sibghatullah: Former resistance politician during the Soviet-Afghan war and first interim president following the collapse of the PDPA government. Chairman of the National Commission for Peace in Afghanistan.

Najibullah, Mohammed (1947–96): Communist president of Afghanistan under the Soviets. Was also head of the KHAD secret police under the PDPA in Afghanistan. Najibullah was tortured and killed by the Taliban in 1996.

Omar, Mullah Mohammed: Spiritual leader of the Taliban.

Parcham: The "Banner" faction of the communist PDPA.

Qadir, Hajii Abdul: Former guerrilla commander (Khalq faction of Hezb) during the Soviet-Afghan war. Brother of Abdul Haq, he was appointed minister of public works and one of Karzai's two vice presidents. Qadir was assassinated by unknown gunmen in Kabul on July 6, 2002.

Rabbani, Burhanuddin: Former resistance politician and head of Jamiat-e-Islami. President of post-1992 mujahed Islamic State of Afghanistan in Kabul. Currently head of the United National Front party in Afghanistan. Still an influential leader.

Sayyaf, Abdul Rasoul: Former resistance politician and head of the fundamentalist Ittehad-e-Islami party. He lives in Kabul as an influential lawmaker. Criticized by some for having been involved in the murder of Massoud, but also having influenced various anti-Western Islamic militants, he pushed a bill that would protect Afghans accused of war crimes during the jihad years.

Shirzai, Gul Agha: Current governor of Nangrahar province and a close ally of the Americans. He previously served as governor of Kandahar province in the early 1990s and from 2001 until 2003. He is believed to be closely linked to the illegal opium trade, becoming a millionaire in the process.

Taliban: "Islamic scholars," the name given to the insurgent spiritual movement that emerged as a military force in 1994.

Zahir Shah, Mohammed (1933–73): Former king of Afghanistan.

ACRONYMS

ACBAR: Agency Coordinating Body for Afghan Relief.

AMI: Aide Médicale Internationale.

APC: Armored personnel carrier.

IAM: International Assistance Mission.

ICRC: International Committee of the Red Cross.

IED: Improvised explosive device, or booby-trap bomb.

IRC: International Rescue Committee.

ISAF: International Security Assistance Force.

ISI: Interservices Military Intelligence agency of Pakistan.

Madera: Mission d'aide au Développement des Economies Rurales en Afghanistan (French agricultural NGO).

MSF: Médecins Sans Frontières (Doctors Without Borders).

NGO: Non-governmental organization or private voluntary agency.

NATO: North Atlantic Treaty Organization.

NWFP: Northwest Frontier Province, Pakistan.

PDPA: People's Democratic Party of Afghanistan.

PRT: Provincial Reconstruction Team (military development aid).

RPG: Rocket-propelled grenade.

SCA: Swedish Committee for Afghanistan.

UN: United Nations.

UNAMA: United Nations Assistance Mission in Afghanistan.

UNDP: United Nations Development Program.

UNESCO: United Nations Educational, Scientific, and Cultural Organization.

UNHCR: United Nations High Commissioner for Refugees.

UNICEF: United Nations Children's Emergency Fund.

USAID: United States Agency for International Development.

WFP: World Food Program of the United Nations.

WHO: World Health Organization of the United Nations.

GLOSSARY OF TERMS

al Qaeda: Arabic for "the Base" and the name given by Osama bin Laden to his guerrilla organization.

baad: Giving away a girl as compensation to settle a dispute between tribes or family.

burqa: A piece of clothing, usually blue or white, covering a woman's body from head to toe.

Coalition: The armed forces from North America, Europe, and other parts of the Western world participating in the NATO-led international security operation in Afghanistan.

Hajji: An honorific title for a Muslim who has undertaken the Hajj to Mecca.

Hezb-e-Islami (Islamic party): Led by Gulbuddin Hekmatyar, one of two Hezb factions involved in the Soviet-Afghan war, the Battle for Kabul, and now the insurgency.

jirgha: A council or gathering of tribal elders.

kola or pukul: Woolen Nuristani hat often used by northern Afghans.

Loya Jirgha: A grand council.

mujahideen: Islamic warriors who fought the Soviet-backed regime during the 1980s.

mullah: An Islamic religious leader.

nan: Bread.

Pushtunwali: Law of the Pathan, traditional Pushtun code of conduct.

shari'a law: Islamic law found in the Koran and *Sunnah.*

Shiite or Shi'a: The second largest denomination of Islam after Sunni. In Afghanistan, the Shiites are mainly Hazaras from the Central Highlands and north.

shura: A Dari term for a council of elders, commanders, and other notables.

Wahhabi: An ultraconservative form of Islam with roots in eighteenth-century Saudi Arabia. Seeking to purge Islam of "impurities," Wahhabi militants came to Afghanistan to create a new "Islamic man." The terms Wahhabi and Salafi are often used interchangeably.

zina: Act of sexual intercourse outside of marriage.

INDEX

ABOUT THE AUTHOR

Edward Girardet is a journalist, writer, and producer who has reported widely from humanitarian and conflict zones in Africa, Asia, and elsewhere since the late 1970s. As a foreign correspondent based in Paris for *The Christian Science Monitor, US News and World Report,* and *The MacNeil/Lehrer NewsHour,* he first began covering Afghanistan several months prior to the Soviet invasion in 1979. He has worked on numerous television current affairs and documentary segments on subjects ranging from the war in Angola to lost tribes in Western New Guinea and environmental issues in Africa for major European and North American broadcasters. Girardet is a founding director of the Institute for Media and Global Governance in Geneva, Switzerland. He is also editor of Crosslines Essential Media Ltd (UK).

Girardet has written widely for major publications such as *National Geographic Magazine, The Christian Science Monitor, International Herald Tribune, Financial Times,* and other media on humanitarian, media, and conflict issues. He is author or editor of *Afghanistan: The Soviet War; Somalia, Rwanda, and Beyond; Populations in Danger 1995: A Médecins Sans Frontières Report;* and *Afghanistan: CROSSLINES Essential Field Guide to Humanitarian and Conflict Zones.* Girardet lives with his family in Cessy, France, near the Swiss border with Geneva.